mySAP® HR: Technical Principles and Programming

 **PRESS**

SAP PRESS is issued by
Bernhard Hochlehnert, SAP AG

SAP PRESS is a joint initiative of SAP and Galileo Press. The know-how offered by SAP specialists combined with the expertise of the publishing house
Galileo Press offers the reader expert books in the field. SAP PRESS features
first-hand information and expert advice, and provides useful skills for professional decision-making.

SAP PRESS offers a variety of books on technical and business related topics
for the SAP user. For further information, please visit our website:
www.sap-press.com.

Sigrid Hagemann, Liane Will
SAP R/3 System Administration
2003, approx. 450 pp., ISBN 1-59229-014-4

Horst Keller, Joachim Jacobitz
ABAP Objects - The Official Reference
2 volumes and CD set
2003, 1056 pp., ISBN 1-59229-011-6

Paul Read
SAP Database Administration
with Microsoft SQL Server 2000
2002, 384 pp., ISBN 1-59229-005-1

Helmut Stefani
Archiving Your SAP Data
A comprehensive guide to plan and execute archiving projects
2003, 334 pp., ISBN 1-59229-008-6

Werner Hertleif, Christoph Wachter
SAP Smart Forms
Creating forms quickly and easily - no programming required!
2003, approx. 450 pp., ISBN 1-59229-010-8

Ewald Brochhausen, Jürgen Kielisch,
Jürgen Scherring, Jens Staeck

mySAP® HR: Technical Principles and Programming

 PRESS

Contents

Preface   **9**

Foreword   **11**

1   Introduction   **13**

1.1   Dimensions of mySAP HR 13
1.2   Adjustment Possibilities 13
1.3   The Structure of This Book.. 15

2   Data Structures in HR   **19**

2.1   Data Structures in Context 19
2.2   Personnel Administration Master Data... 19
     2.2.1   Personnel administration infotypes.. 20
     2.2.2   Subdivision of infotypes–the subtype 22
     2.2.3   Object Identification 23
     2.2.4   Time and Time Constraints in Infotypes.................................... 23
     2.2.5   Single Screen and List Screen 25
     2.2.6   Default Values for Infotypes 26
     2.2.7   An Infotype Header.. 27
     2.2.8   Features and Screen Modifiers 28
     2.2.9   Assigning Infotypes to Countries 31
     2.2.10   Technical Data Structure of Infotypes....................................... 32
     2.2.11   Data Structures and Tables: Personnel Administration Infotype . 39
     2.2.12   Infotype Views 40
2.3   Organizational Management and Personnel Planning Data 41
     2.3.1   Data Model.. 41
     2.3.2   Personnel planning infotypes... 46
     2.3.3   Technical Data Structure of Infotypes.. 47
     2.3.4   Table Infotypes 53
     2.3.5   External Object Types 54
     2.3.6   External Infotypes 55
     2.3.7   Data Structures and Tables: Personnel Planning Infotype........... 56

	2.3.8	Checking the Consistency of the Data Model	57
	2.3.9	Checking the Consistency of Infotypes	58
2.4	**Time Management Data**		**59**
	2.4.1	Time Management Master Data	59
	2.4.2	Time Events	59
	2.4.3	Time Evaluation Input	61
	2.4.4	Time Evaluation Results	63
2.5	**Payroll Data**		**65**
	2.5.1	Central Payroll Information	65
	2.5.2	Payroll Result Data	66
	2.5.3	Cluster Directory	71
	2.5.4	Payroll Data for Reporting	73

3   Reading and Processing Data   75

3.1	**Logical Databases in HR**		**75**
	3.1.1	Logical Database PNP for Personnel Master Data	77
	3.1.2	Logical Database PNPCE for Personnel Master Data	89
	3.1.3	Logical Database PCH for Personnel Planning	91
3.2	**Access Without a Logical Database**		**96**
3.3	**Using Macros**		**98**
	3.3.1	Overview	98
	3.3.2	Macros in Logical Database PNP	99
	3.3.3	Macros in Logical Database PCH	105
3.4	**Function Modules**		**106**
	3.4.1	Properties	106
	3.4.2	Using Function Modules in HR	107
	3.4.3	Using Features	110
3.5	**Accessing Clusters**		**114**
	3.5.1	Overview of Clusters	114
	3.5.2	Payroll Results	116
3.6	**Enhancements with Customer Exits and Business Add-Ins**		**120**
	3.6.1	Customer Exits	120
	3.6.2	Business Add-Ins	122

4   Roles and Authorizations   127

4.1	**The SAP Authorization Concept**		**127**
	4.1.1	Authorization Objects, Authorizations, and Profiles	127
	4.1.2	Role Concept and Profile Generator	129
	4.1.3	Functions of the Profile Generator	131
4.2	**Authorizations in the Context of SAP HR**		**133**
	4.2.1	Authorization Objects	133
	4.2.2	Authorization Level—Graded Write Authorizations	143

	4.2.3	Organizational Key	147
	4.2.4	Structural Authorization Check	150
	4.2.5	HR Authorization Main switches	157
	4.2.6	Time Dependency	159
	4.2.7	Implementation	162
	4.2.8	Enhancement Options	166
	4.2.9	Interaction Between the Application and the Authorization Check	177
	4.2.10	Searching for Errors	178

5 Adjusting the Applications 181

5.1		Personnel Administration	181
	5.1.1	Components in the Repository	181
	5.1.2	Enhancing Infotypes	183
	5.1.3	Creating Infotypes	193
	5.1.4	Enhancing Infotypes for Fast Data Entry	203
	5.1.5	Multiple-Infotype Entry with Fast Entry of Action Data	208
5.2		Organizational Management	212
	5.2.1	Enhancing infotypes	212
	5.2.2	Creating Infotypes	217
5.3		Time Recording	224
5.4		Payroll and Time Evaluation	226
	5.4.1	Controlling Payroll and Time Evaluation	226
	5.4.2	Functions	229
	5.4.3	Operations	233

6 Reporting in HR 237

6.1		Master Data	237
	6.1.1	Structuring a Report for Personnel Administration Infotypes	237
	6.1.2	Structuring a Report for Time Management Infotypes	249
6.2		Organizational Management	253
	6.2.1	Sequential Evaluation	253
	6.2.2	Structural Evaluation	255
6.3		Payroll Data	258
6.4		Time Management	262
6.5		Formatting Output with the ABAP List Viewer	265

7 Employee Self-Service 271

7.1		Functional Scope	271
	7.1.1	Business View	271
	7.1.2	Navigation	272

7.2	The "Employee" Role	273
	7.2.1	The Concept of Role	273
	7.2.2	Single Roles, Country-Specific Roles, and Composite Roles	274
7.3	Overview of the Internet Transaction Server	276
	7.3.1	Installation Variants	276
	7.3.2	The ITS Files	277
	7.3.3	Overview of the Most Important ITS Service Parameters	282
	7.3.4	The ITS Modus Operandi	284
	7.3.5	HTML Business Functions	286
7.4	Programming Models	288
	7.4.1	Internet Services Based on HTML Templates (IAC)	290
	7.4.2	FlowLogic	292
	7.4.3	SAP GUI for HTML	297
7.5	Design and Function Enhancements	298
	7.5.1	The ESS User Exits	298
	7.5.2	Design Adjustments	300
	7.5.3	Changing Fields or Flow Logic	306
	7.5.4	Creating a New Country-Dependent Service	307
	7.5.5	Creating a New Service	310
7.6	Web-enabling Reports	312
	7.6.1	ESS Report Framework	312
	7.6.2	Sample Report in ESS	315
7.7	Life and Work Events	317
	7.7.1	Concept of Life and Work Events	317
	7.7.2	Prerequisites and Functionality	319
	7.7.3	The Framework	322
	7.7.4	An Overview of L&W Tables	330
	7.7.5	Customizing	331
	7.7.6	Creating a New L&W Event	337

| A | ESS Scenarios | 339 |

| B | The Authors | 345 |

| | Index | 347 |

Preface

This book is an excellent resource for answering all your technical questions regarding SAP HR. But, since technology shouldn't be applied for its own sake, I would like to begin by discussing its importance in helping you to achieve business advantage. When companies set out to implement SAP HR, they will have as their objective maximizing the value and minimizing the associated costs. Value is obtained from improving the effectiveness of HR processes and analysis undertaken in support of decisions. It is also generated through cost reduction of HR operations. The cost of implementation is determined by the level of change to current HR practices, the scope of R/3 support to HR processes, and the degree to which SAP HR standard functionality is used. The cost of ongoing support and operations is driven by system complexity and the level of rework required, given the inevitable implementation of new releases.

Achieving an optimal solution for the cost/benefit equation requires:

▶ Deep understanding of the current company process and practice, and particularly, knowing what is fundamental to the company's HR strategy, having a view of ideal HR processes, and ascribing a dollar value to capability.

▶ Good understanding of the standard capabilities of SAP HR (that is, obtained through configuration only), and the expectations of HR processes to leverage these capabilities.

▶ Understanding of the relative cost (full life cycle) of customizing, extending, or adapting what I have called the "standard capability".

▶ Having understood the business priorities and SAP HR capability, developing a view of the target HR processes and functionality that are required to support them.

In this context, the fundamental questions to be answered are:

▶ Is each perceived need for extension or adaptation of standard capability due to:

  ▸ Lack of knowledge and understanding of standard SAP HR capability?

  ▸ An existing company practice that could be replaced by a standard process?

  ▸ A valuable customization, but one that is not worth the cost?

The implication is that avoiding extensions and adaptations is the most efficient solution.

▶ For extensions and adaptations that are worth the cost, what is the lowest full life cycle cost solution?

Which brings me back to this book. While it will not help you understand the HR-IT requirements and priorities for your company, this book serves as a unique guide for the technical reader on how to customize SAP HR for the lowest cost of implementation, and how to best withstand future releases without redevelopment. It clearly outlines the possibilities and recommends how they should be implemented.

Good luck with your implementation. It will certainly be a challenge; however, if you use this book judiciously, it will help you to achieve your goals.

The Hague, September 2003
Alan Hopwood
IT Strategy Advisor,
Shell International

Foreword

The first installation of an R/3 HR system occurred more than ten years ago. Since then, SAP HR has been greatly improved upon and many new functions have been added. Because of the constantly increasing demands made on Human Resources (HR) software packages, the standard features of the software have been enhanced with many new features and tools that allow for customization. Whereas at first, it was often necessary to modify the R/3 HR system in order to include all company-specific features, throughout its development, you no longer have to modify the system in order to accommodate customer modifications. Now, customers can customize the software without impacting the HR system. Examples of this customization capability include the ability to expand the data basis at will, enhance standard screens, or replace or add ABAP coding without the need to make modifications.

This increase in adjustment possibilities has sometimes made it more difficult to decide which is the best solution in each particular case. In an effort to help you with such issues—and at the request of many SAP HR users—the most important and basic principles of the HR system are presented in this book. With this in mind, our primary focus is with the special features of HR—not with the general cross-application fundamentals of the SAP system. Therefore, this book is intended for those of you who already have a basic knowledge of ABAP programming and SAP HR.

Now, we wish to thank the many friends and colleagues who have supported us in the realization of this project. A big thank you to all of them for their useful advice and assistance. In particular, we would like to mention Ulf Bangert, Klaus Billig, Bärbel Bohr, Udo Klein, Heiko Schultze, and Matthias Wengner. Thanks also to all at our publishers, Galileo Press, and to Florian Zimniak in particular. Their professional assistance regarding layout and other publishing issues was an important contribution to the publishing of this book. In addition, for the U.S. edition, we also want to mention Regina Brautlacht, Günter Lemoine, and Nancy Etscovitz.

Walldorf, September 2003
Ewald Brochhausen—Jürgen Kielisch—
Jürgen Schnerring—Jens Staeck

1 Introduction

Of all the applications in the core functions of mySAP, the Human Resources applications are the applications that require most adjustment possibilities. Often, the customization capabilities provided are insufficient.

1.1 Dimensions of mySAP HR

In order to use the functions of the mySAP HR solution efficiently, it is necessary to consider the implementation from different viewpoints or dimensions. These dimensions can be broken down as follows:

▶ The *process view* is central to the first analysis of the system. All the main processes regarding personnel management are supported by mySAP HR. How the standard functions are used can differ greatly, depending on the field and the context. The extent to which different functions are used is largely determined by the size of the enterprise, the sector of industry, and country-specific factors. The most important core processes are organizational management, personnel administration, time management, and payroll. In large installations, these processes are usually the first to be analyzed and implemented—this is where the most varied requirements arise, which can exceed the types of customization allowed.

Process view

▶ The second view that you need to consider is the *data view*. To understand the functions, you must be familiar with data modeling and the data structures in HR. If any adjustments need to be made, for example, you should know how the data is saved as infotypes and how the payroll results are stored in the database.

Data view

▶ The *technical view* is the third dimension of the analysis. The mySAP Basis offers an entire range of technologies that can be used to implement specific requirements. Some technical possibilities that are particularly helpful for mySAP HR will be explained here. These include the use of the Internet and Web technologies in particular.

Technical view

1.2 Adjustment Possibilities

The demands made on the supporting IT system differ from one company to another, particularly in human resources (HR) systems. To allow the use of SAP software under these very different circumstances, a wide range of customizing options is available. *Customizing* refers to the system configuration method that enables customers to adjust system settings in order to meet their company's specific needs. Customizing in the SAP system is done using the *Implementation Guide* (*IMG*), which is the tool used to adjust the SAP system to meet the requirements of an enterprise.

Enhancements to the standard If the customizing options are insufficient, more comprehensive enhancements can be made. *Enhancements* are potential customer requirements that are not defined as standard. They are anticipated in the standard system, and can be developed with customer-specific logic. Upward compatibility is ensured, which means that calling an enhancement from the standard software and the validity of the call interface are not affected by any future upgrades.

For quite some time, you could make enhancements to the standard by using *customer exits*. Within standard R/3 applications, SAP provides exits for certain programs, screens, and menus. These exits don't contain any functions; instead, they offer customers the possibility of inserting their own additional functions.

Customer exits do not affect the SAP standard source code. If customers add new functions to their SAP system using the SAP customer exits, this new functionality doesn't change the source code of the SAP standard program. Individual coding and images are merged together as customer-defined objects. These customer objects are linked with standard applications, but they exist alongside the SAP standard software package. If new functions are added using SAP customer exits, these customer-defined objects, which you developed, must follow a strict naming convention. When a new maintenance level or release upgrade occurs, these very specific names ensure that the customer objects are not affected by changes or additions to the standard software package.

Since Release 4.6, enhancements to the standard software can be implemented using a new technology–BAdIs (*Business Add-Ins*)–which is based on ABAP Objects. Just like the customer exits, BAdIs enable SAP users to add their own functions that are too specific to be included in the standard. These enhancements, however, are often required, and are therefore anticipated features or options in R/3. They exceed the scope of customizing. In contrast to customer exits, BAdIs aren't based on a two-level system landscape (SAP/customer), but rather, on a multilevel landscape (SAP/country-specific versions/, and so on). Definitions and implementations of BAdIs can be created at every level of the system landscape. In addition, BAdIs can be defined depending on a filter value, which means that the implementation of an add-in can differ according to the key mySAP HR filter value "Country" or according to other criteria. The technology is designed in such a way that it is possible to define interfaces for ABAP source codes, screens, GUIs, and tables in which customers can integrate their own enhancements.

Apart from the integration of customer-specific functions in existing SAP standard objects, you can also access and evaluate SAP HR data with your own report programs and transactions, thus greatly simplifying your work with the development tools available in the standard, such as logical databases and HR function modules.

If customizing and the possibilities for adjustment that we just mentioned are still not sufficient, you can modify the system according to customer requirements. Modifications to the standard should only be implemented if they are absolutely essential to optimize certain process flows in an enterprise. It is vital that the customer possess a comprehensive knowledge of the structure and flow structure of an application, if he or she is to determine possible modifications and ensure the coherent design of any modifications that will change the standard.

Modification

Customizing, the addition of anticipated enhancements, and the development of customer-specific programs are supported by special tools such as the IMG, transactions for customer exits, BAdIs, and the development environment. The modification wizards also enable you to modify the standard. In some older programs in mySAP HR, modification is still necessary because the functions in customer-includes, provided for this purpose, must be implemented. If possible, other more advanced modifications should not be carried out, because they would require constant maintenance.

1.3   The Structure of This Book

The individual chapters in this book deal with the subjects mentioned—each focusing on one of the dimensions of mySAP HR listed in Section 1.1.

Chapter 2 presents the data view of mySAP HR. It establishes the structuring of master data into infotypes. It discusses why master data in SAP HR is organized in the form of infotypes. Then, the infotypes used in human resources (HR) are introduced. The individual data structures and database tables that constitute an infotype are described. The enhancement possibilities for standard infotypes are also explained. Control possibilities based on the data structure are shown, which can change the appearance of the data structure on the user interface. Chapter 2 also

Data structures

highlights the data model of organizational management and personnel planning, followed by a discussion of the data structures of this area. In addition to the personnel administration data structures, the relevant information on organizational management and personnel planning is also included, of which data structures are also a main focus.

The next section in Chapter 2 deals with time management data. The underlying master data for time management is discussed briefly. Then, particular attention is paid to the tables used in time management, time events—which form the basis of what is called *positive time recording*—and time management result data.

In the last section of this chapter, you will learn more about payroll data. Regarding the nature of result data, the explanation of the data structure serves as a model or prototype for the payroll data's evaluation structure, which we explore in Chapter 3.

Reading and editing data
The technical viewpoint is described in **Chapter 3**. You will learn how HR data can be accessed, what resources are available, and what enhancement technologies can be used. The logical databases of HR master data and personnel planning are an important resource for reading and editing HR data. In addition to being able to access data via the logical database (which is generally recommended), you can also access this data without using the logical database (in special cases). Macros are provided for processing that arises frequently in the SAP standard. This chapter explains why and how the most important macros are used. Many function modules offer additional support, and the advanced functions of the features are often used in HR. Access to the payroll results requires specific procedures, which are described in greater detail here. Finally, the chapter ends with a discussion of the importance of customer exits and Business Add-Ins (BAdIs) in HR.

Roles and authorizations
Chapter 4 deals with the subject of roles and authorizations. Building on general SAP concepts, we look at roles, authorization profiles, and authorizations from the HR perspective. The most important HR authorization objects are described in detail.

Another part of the chapter deals with special constructs in the context of mySAP HR, which make it possible to have tighter control on the access possibilities of system users. This includes the structural authorization check, based on the HR organization structure, the time-based nature of the authorization check, and additional control mechanisms for controlling write accesses closely (four eye principle, test procedures).

After a detailed presentation of the general possibilities for system settings (customizing), customer-specific enhancement possibilities are discussed. The infotype authorization check can be easily enhanced to become a customer-defined authorization object and business add-ins can be implemented to redefine the flow of the authorization check in the context of HR, to consider specific requirements. The chapter concludes with notes (or tips) on a runtime analysis of the authorization check.

As a follow-up to the first chapters, **Chapter 5** discusses the adjustment possibilities in individual applications. We will show you how the data basis in personnel administration can be extended, by enhancing the standard infotypes and via the installation of customer-specific infotypes. Similar possibilities are available for the organizational management infotypes. Limitations on time management infotypes are also identified here. Payroll and time management are controlled by what are known as functions and operations. You will also learn how to set up customer-specific functions and operations in this chapter.

Despite the many standard reports and the far-reaching possibilities of queries, it is often necessary to create some customer-specific report programs using the ABAP Workbench. **Chapter 6** addresses the features of HR that pertain to these report programs. The various options are explained using example reports. First, examples from personal master data and time management master data are presented. For organizational management, the different methods of procedure for sequential and structural reporting are demonstrated in examples. Special accesses to data in payroll and time management are explained in the reports presented. The chapter concludes with tips on the possibilities for improving the layout of output lists.

Employee Self-Service (ESS) is introduced in **Chapter 7**. ESS comprises over 80 applications, in 30 different localized versions, which enables employees to change their own data via a Web browser. After a brief introduction, the Internet Transaction Server (ITS), which plays a key role in the product, is explained. If you want to make enhancements that exceed the scope of customizing, it is vital that you understand how ITS works. In addition to various files and parameters in the ITS, different programming models are also introduced.

Other primary topics discussed in this chapter include existing user-exits, the design modification options for all ESS applications, and the integration of customer-specific Web reports in the ESS Report Framework.

Adjustments

Reporting

Employee
Self-Service

At the end of Chapter 7, there is a description of *Life-and-Work-Events*. These events enable employees to react to specific events from their private or work life in a process-oriented way. Employees are lead through a menu of application and information pages. There are preconfigured life-and-work events; however, you (i.e., the employee) can also define them according to your own business processes.

2 Data Structures in HR

The data structures of mySAP HR are described in this chapter. The data in personnel administration and personnel planning form the basis for the overall HR data structure. In addition, time management data and payroll data represent the result data of the respective processes.

2.1 Data Structures in Context

The data structures of SAP HR collectively are a combination of master data, transaction data, and result data (see Figure 2.1).

The organization of data structures

The master data of personnel administration, time management, and personnel planning is arranged in the same way. In addition, there are various different data clusters that contain data from specific processing steps, such as the time events in cluster PCL1 or the payroll results in data cluster PCL2. The data in personnel administration, personnel planning, time management, and payroll is shown in the different sections of this chapter.

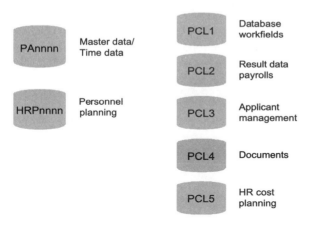

Figure 2.1 Data Structures of SAP HR

2.2 Personnel Administration Master Data

Data fields are archived as master data on entry. The master data must be organized in a practical way; however, there must be room for flexibility when arranging this data in an organization within an enterprise. We will initially explain the concept of *infotypes*; then we'll introduce selected customizing attributes of infotypes and describe the possible ways in which you can influence the behavior of infotypes.

Master data

2.2.1 Personnel administration infotypes

Infotypes refer to a grouping of fields with related content or, from a technical perspective, a grouping of attributes. When grouping according to content, business background information is of particular importance. The following example should help to illustrate this concept.

Infotype as a set of attributes

There are many different elements that are used to uniquely describe a person. First, a person usually has a first name and a surname. In addition, there may be other elements that can be included when putting a name together, such as a middle name, as is common in the U.S. In other countries, there may be other elements. For example, in accordance with name conventions in some countries, academic titles, such as Ph.D., M.B.A, or other titles, such as "Sir" may be added to a name.

Furthermore, a person also has other unique characteristics. The person's date of birth, for example. There may also be other country-specific characteristics. To cite an American example again, there is the Social Security Number (SSN). All elements in a description of this type are placed in individual data fields and then dynamically assembled again at runtime as required. For our SAP HR data structure, this means that each field has to be created individually. It certainly makes sense and is easier to comprehend if these fields are grouped together based on their content. This type of grouping, based on business requirements, is called an *infotype*. Figure 2.2 shows the example of the infotype Personal data.

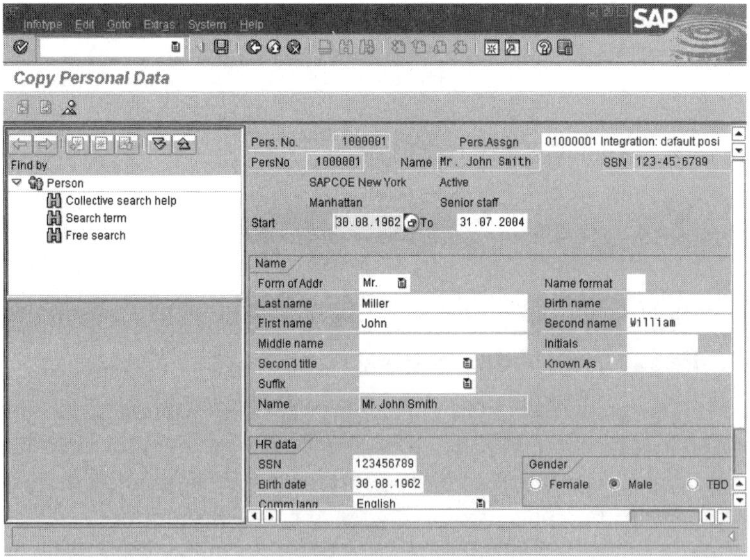

Figure 2.2 Screen of the Infotype 0002—"Personal data"

In the Implementation Guide (IMG), infotypes are managed in tables. The different infotypes are listed via the menu path **Personnel Management · Personnel Administration · Customizing procedures · Infotypes · Info-type**. Figure 2.3 shows the view **Infotype attributes**.

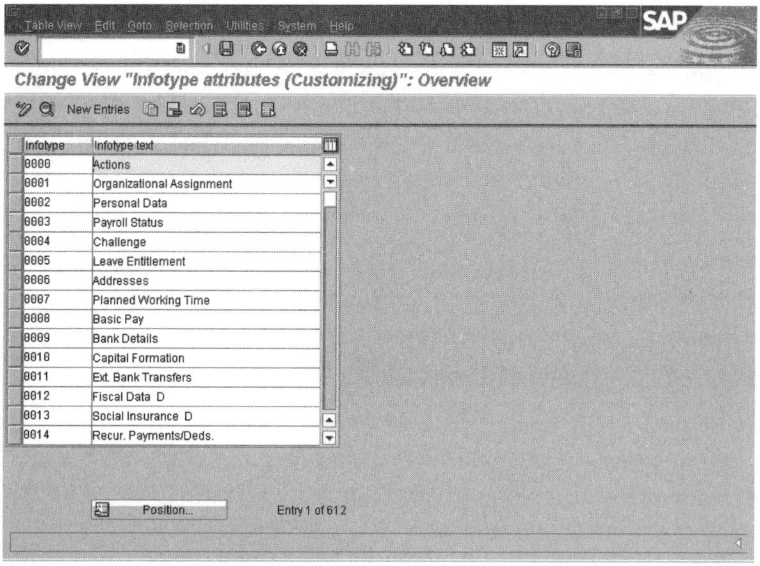

Infotypes in the Implementation Guide

Figure 2.3 Change Infotype Attributes

Not all the available infotypes will be presented here. To see a display of all infotypes, please consult the appropriate section in the IMG. The respective table in the IMG contains the entries of all available and usable infotypes. The total number of infotypes currently stands at 612.

In this context, the arrangement for infotypes is numerical. Each infotype is identified with a four-digit numerical field.

Organization of infotypes

The infotypes are grouped in different number ranges. The following table shows how the number ranges are reserved:

Number range	Reserved for
0000–0999	HR master data
1000–1999	Organizational management/personnel planning
2000–2999	Time management
4000–4999	Recruitment
9000–9999	Customer-developed enhancements

2.2.2 Subdivision of infotypes–the subtype

From subtype to
infotype

If an infotype is understood to be a logical grouping of different attributes, it can be further reasoned that there may be variants of this infotype with similar information, that is, with analogous attributes.

For example, you can imagine that the infotype Family Member/Dependents may contain information about a spouse, but it also may contain information about children (see Figure 2.4). There can also be information stored here about a person who should be contacted in case of emergency, or, depending on the employment relationship, there may be data about a legal guardian.

Within a *loan* infotype, it may be preferable to differentiate loans according to their purpose. For example, an employer will almost certainly treat a long-term, house building loan (meant to bind an employee to the company) in a different manner than a short-term salary advance.

Subtypes have been created for infotypes in order to subdivide similar information groups of this type into variants with similar information content. From a technical point of view, the subtype specification is a four-character alphanumeric data field.

Subtype as a
control feature

The subtype is not only a subdivision of an infotype. The subtype also controls the actions of the infotype. Certain attributes of the infotype are defined according to the subtype. For example, time constraints, which will be explained later, are determined on a subtype level.

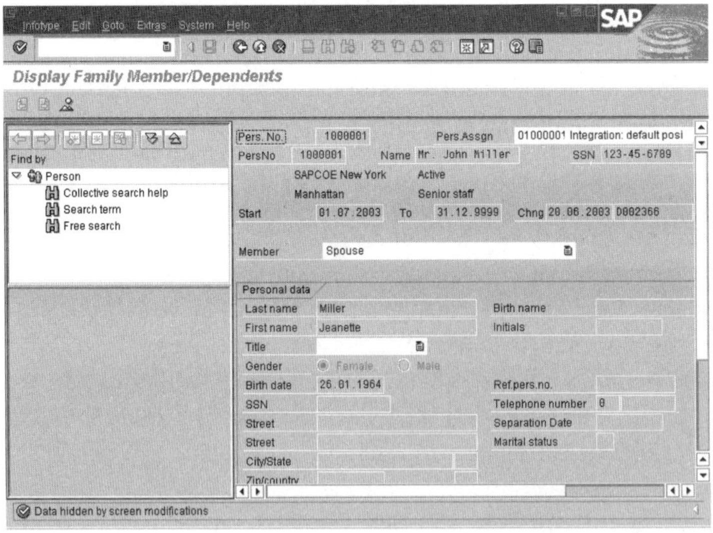

Figure 2.4 Subtype "spouse" of the Infotype "Family Member/Dependents"

2.2.3 Object Identification

The subdivision into areas of comparable yet varied information in the form of subtypes, as previously described, does not include the possibility of managing similar objects. This can only be accomplished with an *object identification* or *object ID*. But what are similar objects? We will explain this using the example of infotype Family Member/Dependents. Instead of selecting subtype 1, *spouse*, if we select subtype 2, *child,* we may find that there are several objects in this subtype, meaning that the employee has more than one child. Object identification (object ID) is used to count similar objects. The object number can be assigned by the system, as is the case, for example, in the U.S. version of the Personal data infotype. Alternatively, the object number can also be assigned by the user. The German version of the infotype Personal data is one such example. In this variant, the field "Child number" takes the object ID of the infotype.

Several similar objects in one infotype

2.2.4 Time and Time Constraints in Infotypes

In addition to information about a subtype, other data is also used to describe each infotype, namely, the start and end date of the information.

Infotype time constraints

With the start and end date of each infotype, you can provide time information. For example, a surname can change after marriage. Therefore, the data record "Family Member/Dependents" can be used once for the period from birth (as start date) up to marriage, and another instance of this infotype may be valid from the marriage date to the latest possible system date (12/31/9999). This date will always be used when precise information is not provided for a specific end date.

Infotypes can also be described according to the frequency with which they occur. Therefore, there is information that can only occur once during *a specific period*; and there is also information that can only occur once during *any period*.

Frequency of infotype occurrence

We will use the example of the infotype *personal data*—from a technical perspective infotype 0002—to illustrate this occurrence. Each person has just one name. This name may change after marriage; however, even after marriage, there will still be only one name. Technically, this infotype must also always be present. The employee "Jeanette Miller" may become "Jeanette Smith" after her marriage on July 23rd 2003. Therefore, this infotype can technically exist with one value up to July 22nd 2003 and with another value from July 23rd 2003. It is not possible, however, that this infotype would not exist from May 12th to May 30th 2004, because this would mean that the employee would have no name during this period.

Time constraint class 1

It is not always apparent that data must exist with some value. Perhaps, this can best be illustrated when viewing business data to determine one's tax bracket. In order for tax to be calculated, there must be taxation data.

Other information can be classified as information that can exist at any time. This information, however, can only exist "once" and cannot be repeated. An example of this would be infotype Family Member/Dependents, subtype 1, *spouse*. A person does not need to have a spouse, which means that this subtype can exist, but it is not obligatory. If it does exist, then, at least in western cultures, there can only be one entry (therefore, at any one time there can only be one spouse).

Other information can occur as often as necessary at any time. Again we will look at the infotype Family Member/Dependents, but this time we'll focus on the subtype *children*. The occurrence cannot be limited as it was in the other infotypes that we mentioned. It is not absolutely necessary to have children, nor is the number of occurrences limited to one.

The ways in which an infotype can occur (or on subtype level, a subtype) are broken down into *time constraint classes*:

▶ Time constraint class 1: The infotype must occur always and without exception (example: the name of an employee).

▶ Time constraint class 2: The infotype can occur, but is not necessary. It may occur only once (example: spouse).

▶ Time constraint class 3: The infotype can occur any number of times (for example, an employee's children).

The time constraint class is a necessary attribute for every infotype. The examples presented can be applied to every infotype: Travel privileges are not bound to occur (if an employee never travels); however, they can only have one value at any one given time (otherwise the information is no longer clear).

The start and end time in an infotype, however, means that an infotype can be used for historical records if this data exists.

According to the behavior of the program, information regarding the time constraint class is also significant. Therefore, the creation of a new infotype with time constraint class 1 automatically means that the old data record is now delimited by time. For an infotype of time constraint class 3, this is not automatically the case. An infotype of time constraint class 2 can be given a time limit, but it is not necessarily replaced by a new infotype. This means that there may be gaps in the creation of infotypes with time constraint class 2.

2.2.5 Single Screen and List Screen

A history can be created if infotype values have a time limit, that is to say, when infotypes have a start and end date.

There is a single screen for each infotype. In this single screen, one info- type with a time limit is displayed or edited. Technically, these single screens are assigned a screen number, ranging from screen 2000 to 2999. Figure 2.2 shows an example of such a single screen. SAP provides coun- try-specific variants for some infotypes. If this is the case, the last two characters in the screen number will usually reflect the country code (such as screen number 2001 for Germany, or screen number 2008 for the U.S.).

Single screen

In addition to the single screens, there is also a list screen for each info- type. This list screen must also be displayed when a new infotype is cre- ated. The list screen enables you to present the relevant history. The pre- sentation is prepared using the appropriate table control and it spans several infotype data records (see Figure 2.5). The list screen is assigned a screen number in the range of 3000 to 3999.

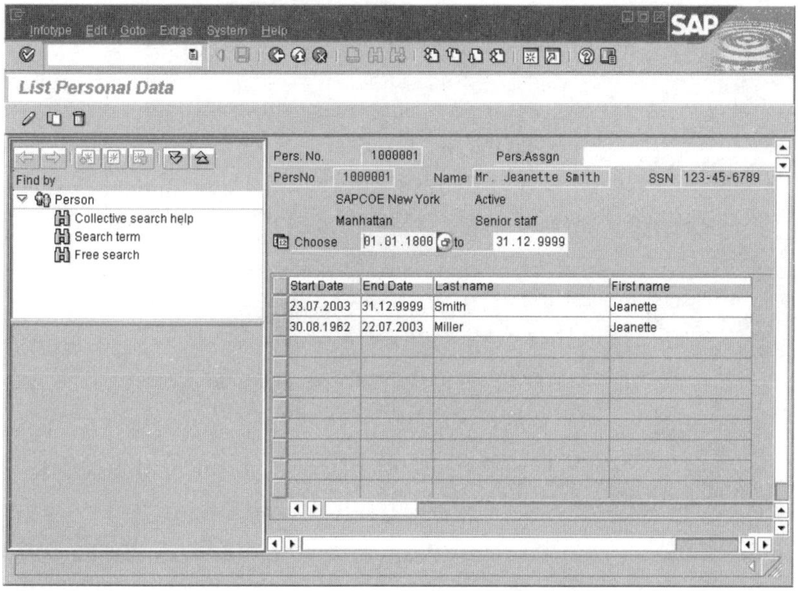

List screen

Figure 2.5 List Presentation of an Infotype

2.2.6 Default Values for Infotypes

Parameter ID as a basis for default values

Some fields of an infotype can have preallocated default values. For these default values, there must be a *parameter ID* for the fields (see Figure 2.6). You can check whether such a parameter ID is present in the standard by placing the cursor over the field in question and using the Help function. Based on the Help function, the technical information should then be displayed.

The default values in the infotypes are SET/GET parameters (SPA/GPA).

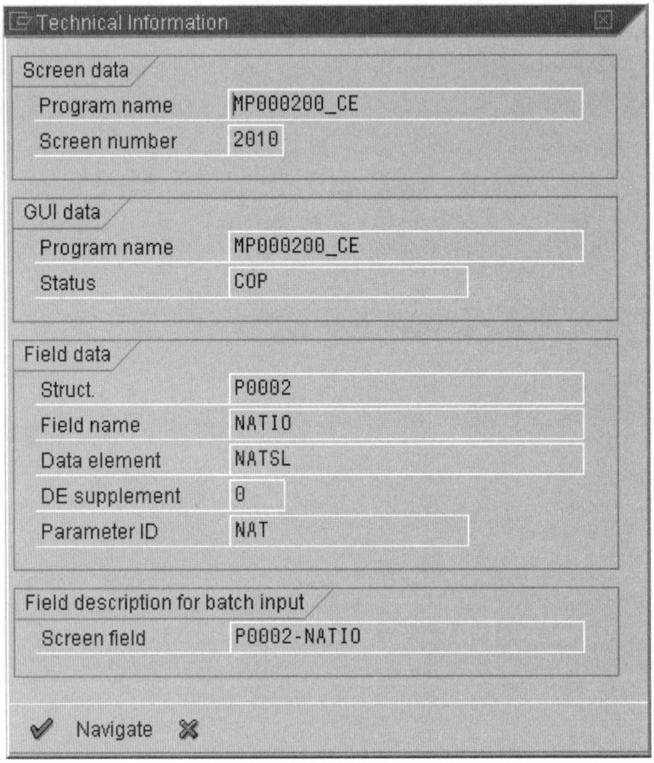

Figure 2.6 Parameter ID

In the example shown in Figure 2.6, we can see the parameter ID called "NAT". This parameter enables you to set a default nationality for an employee. In order for the parameter ID to be displayed in infotypes, you must consider it when first defining data structures. Creating your own infotypes enables you to create default values.

2.2.7 An Infotype Header

Each single screen or list screen of an infotype has a header. You can display an infotype's general information in this header, such as the name of the employee or the organizational classification. Please note that the data displayed in a header is not part of the attributes of an infotype; rather, it is read dynamically at runtime.

Control of the header structure is flexibly arranged in tables and can be executed in the IMG. When the header is generated, an appropriate source code that controls the header display at runtime is created. You can locate the header information in the IMG, using the menu path **Personnel Management · Personnel Administration · Customizing User Interfaces · Change Screen Header**. As you will see in Figure 2.7, you can set the header structure for each infotype if you want. When you combine the generation of the header with HR country modifiers and a transaction class (there are two specifications for transaction classes: "A" for HR master data and "B" for applicant data), you can also assign an infotype header.

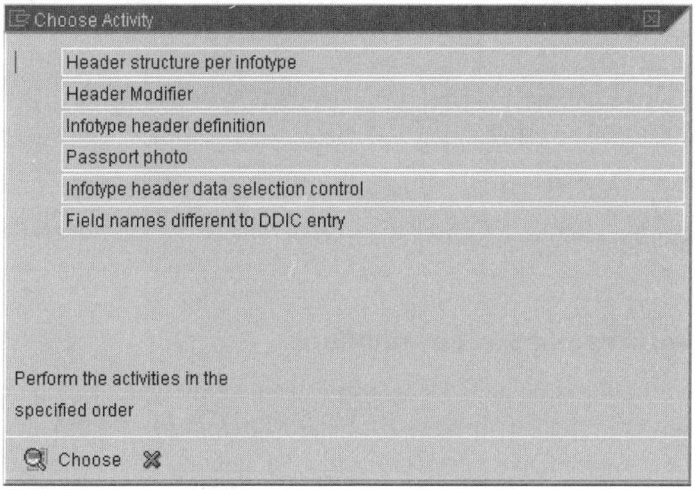

Header structure is controlled flexibly in tables

Choose Activity	☒
Header structure per infotype	
Header Modifier	
Infotype header definition	
Passport photo	
Infotype header data selection control	
Field names different to DDIC entry	

Perform the activities in the specified order

🔍 Choose ✖

Figure 2.7 Change Screen Header

Finally, when defining the infotype header, you can assign a certain header modifier to a particular display. Figure 2.8 shows the necessary steps that you must follow when defining the header. First, you must decide on the header modifier. A header contains three lines. It is therefore possible to define a field for each place within the three-line header structure, which will be displayed at a predefined position. The "field name" column sets the name of the field to be displayed, while the "field type" column sets the name of the field within the infotype header. This makes it possible not only to display a field value, but also to display text (for example, not only is the employee group "DT" displayed, but the text with the information "non-pay scale employee" is also displayed). Finally, pressing the **Check** button carries out a consistency check. This consistency check should be executed after each completed definition of a new header. Then, you create the source coding with the **Generate** button to display the header.

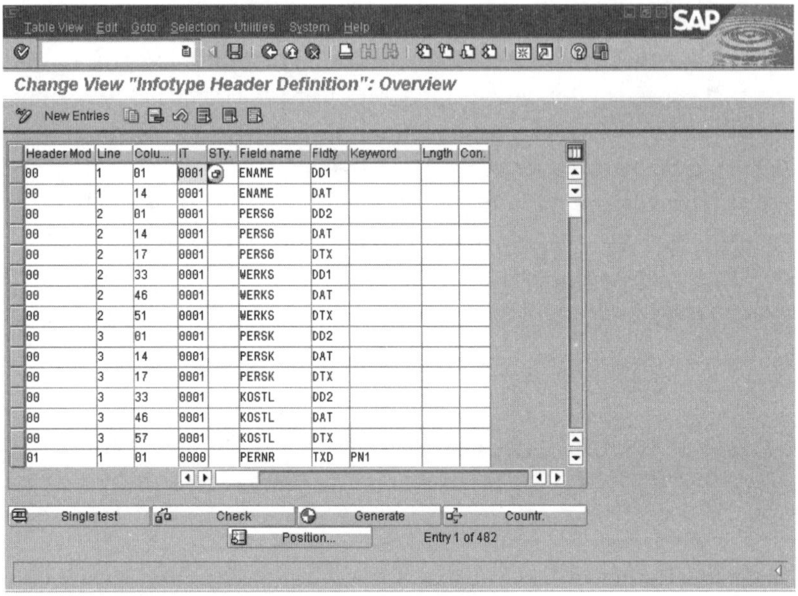

Header Mod	Line	Colu...	IT	STy.	Field name	Fldty	Keyword	Lngth	Con.
00	1	01	0001		ENAME	DD1			
00	1	14	0001		ENAME	DAT			
00	2	01	0001		PERSG	DD2			
00	2	14	0001		PERSG	DAT			
00	2	17	0001		PERSG	DTX			
00	2	33	0001		WERKS	DD1			
00	2	46	0001		WERKS	DAT			
00	2	51	0001		WERKS	DTX			
00	3	01	0001		PERSK	DD2			
00	3	14	0001		PERSK	DAT			
00	3	17	0001		PERSK	DTX			
00	3	33	0001		KOSTL	DD2			
00	3	46	0001		KOSTL	DAT			
00	3	57	0001		KOSTL	DTX			
01	1	01	0000		PERNR	TXD	PN1		

Figure 2.8 Infotype Header Definition

2.2.8 Features and Screen Modifiers

Screen modification

Screen modification is possible for an entire range of infotypes. Different entry screens are supplied for these infotypes. Different screens can also be used for these infotypes according to the HR country code. You can also change the attributes of individual fields in the screen, without having to make changes in the program. You can even use screen modification to define a field as a mandatory field, or hide fields that aren't relevant to a particular installation.

Features

First, we will present features in this context. *Features* are another form of code-generating control based on the appropriate table entries. To efficiently implement the table entries necessary for maintaining features, there is a special feature maintenance transaction (Transaction PE03). Each feature has attributes, a data structure, a decision tree, and the option of creating documentation specifically for that feature. Figure 2.9 shows the attributes that are available for each feature. Initially, someone is put in charge of a particular feature. You can also specify that maintenance of this feature must only be carried out by this designated person.

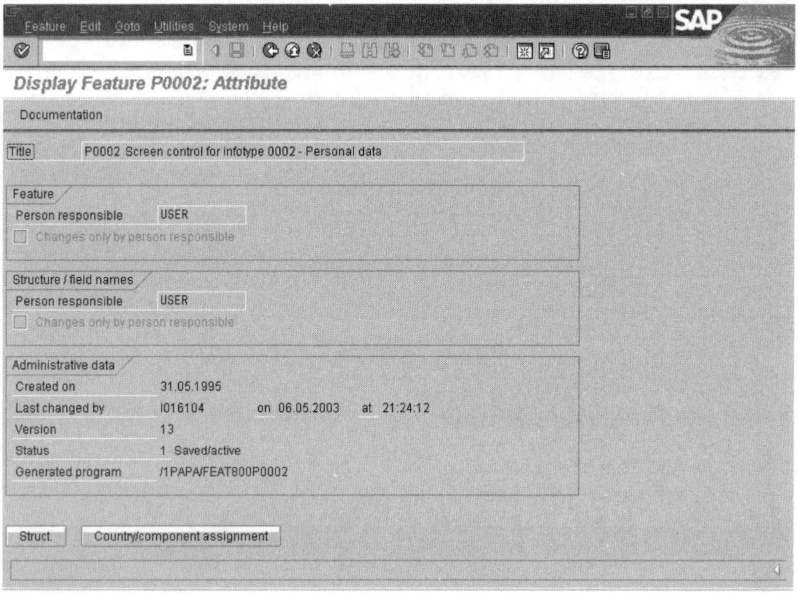

Figure 2.9 Feature P0002

Other details refer to the structure of—and certain administrative information on—the feature.

The structure of the feature is important. You can access it using the **Struct.** button. Here, *structure* refers to a definition of the data fields that is available within a feature. In feature P0002, the structure is PME04 (see Figure 2.10). This structure is stored in the Data Dictionary and can be displayed using the path **SAP menu · Tools · ABAP Workbench · Development · ABAP Dictionary**—and then, the structure name (PME04) is entered in the database table. Decision operations can then be carried out using the data fields that are available in the structure, which is accomplished via the framework of the decision tree.

Structure of a feature

Now, you can set certain values that are based on the decision tree. These values are then available as additional table arguments during screen modification. To get a better understanding, we will look at Figure 2.11 field-by-field.

Decision tree in a feature

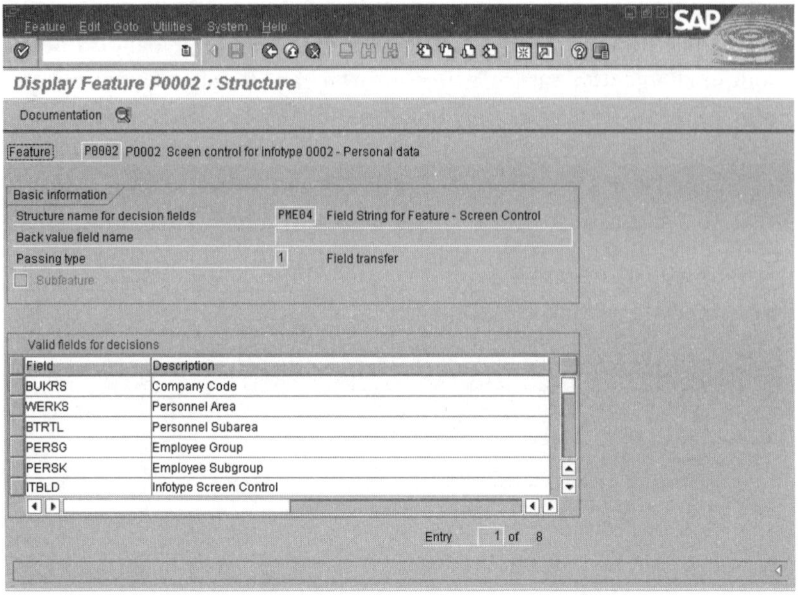

Figure 2.10 Structure of a Feature

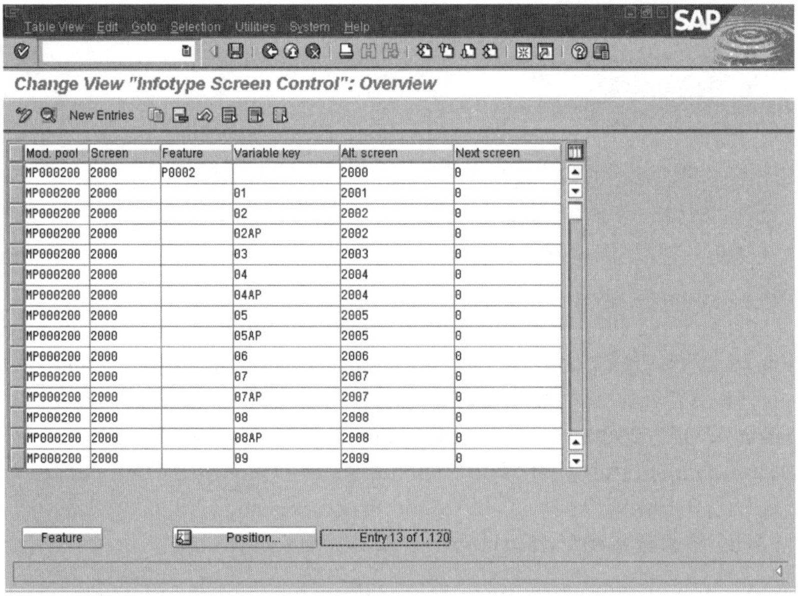

Figure 2.11 Infotype Screen Control

First, the module pool and the screen are identified. In our example, they are module pool `MP000200` and screen 2000. The next column (Feature) identifies the feature that is to be processed next. In this example, we have feature P0002, which gives a return value, based on the decision tree, for example the value "01". This return value is then used as an extended argument in the table. The screen set by the value "01" is screen number 2001, which is extracted from the "Alternative screen" column.

Module pool and screen in features

If this row is marked and you press the **Details** button, you will receive additional information on this infotype (see Figure 2.12).

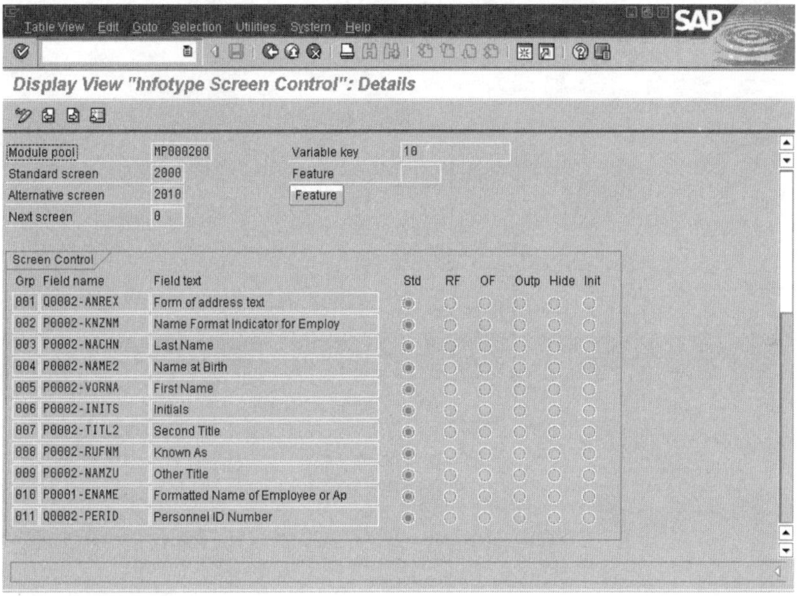

Figure 2.12 Infotype Screen Control—Individual Fields

You can change particular standard field attributes for individual field names in this table. Therefore, in column 14 of Figure 2.12, the attribute for the field name `P0002-NATIO`, nationality, has been changed and the attribute "Optional field" has been marked accordingly.

Change field action per table

2.2.9 Assigning Infotypes to Countries

It is not always practical to make all infotypes available for all countries. For example, it is logical that the infotype *German tax information* (infotype 0012) is only assigned to employees with the country grouping Germany. To ensure that certain infotypes are only visible for certain country groupings, you can effect screen control so that the infotypes can be

Infotypes for individual countries

assigned to individual countries. In the transactions *Display HR master data* (PA20) and *Maintain HR master data* (PA30), the infotypes are checked against the country grouping of the selected personnel number. Consequently, only the infotypes or subtypes that are assigned as allowed infotypes in the view **Infotypes—country specific settings,** are displayed (see Figure 2.13). In the IMG, maintenance is possible via the menu path **Personnel Management • Personnel Administration • Customizing Procedures • Infotypes • Assign Infotypes to countries.**

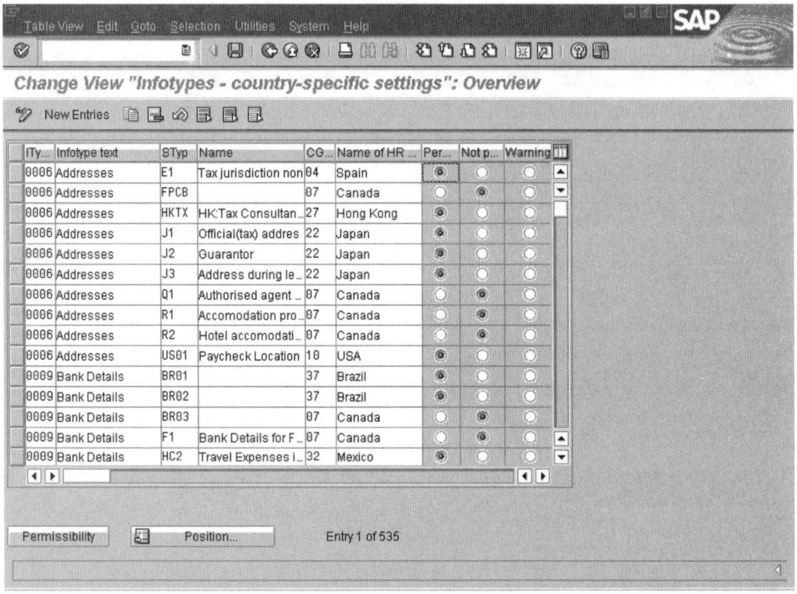

ITy...	Infotype text	STyp	Name	CG...	Name of HR ...	Per...	Not p...	Warning
0006	Addresses	E1	Tax jurisdiction non	04	Spain	●	○	○
0006	Addresses	FPCB		07	Canada	○	●	○
0006	Addresses	HKTX	HK:Tax Consultan...	27	Hong Kong	●	○	○
0006	Addresses	J1	Official(tax) addres	22	Japan	●	○	○
0006	Addresses	J2	Guarantor	22	Japan	●	○	○
0006	Addresses	J3	Address during le...	22	Japan	●	○	○
0006	Addresses	Q1	Authorised agent ...	07	Canada	○	●	○
0006	Addresses	R1	Accomodation pro...	07	Canada	○	●	○
0006	Addresses	R2	Hotel accomodati...	07	Canada	○	●	○
0006	Addresses	US01	Paycheck Location	10	USA	●	○	○
0009	Bank Details	BR01		37	Brazil	●	○	○
0009	Bank Details	BR02		37	Brazil	●	○	○
0009	Bank Details	BR03		07	Canada	○	●	○
0009	Bank Details	F1	Bank Details for F...	07	Canada	○	●	○
0009	Bank Details	HC2	Travel Expenses i...	32	Mexico	●	○	○

Figure 2.13 Infotypes—Country-specific Settings

2.2.10 Technical Data Structure of Infotypes

The infotype structure described in the previous chapter is also reflected in the data structure of an infotype. As is the case for all other data structures, this data structure can be displayed with the help of the Data Dictionary.

Structure PAKEY

It is possible to display and, if necessary, edit the data structures via the menu path **SAP menu • Tools • ABAP Workbench • Development • ABAP Dictionary**. Once you see the screen shown in Figure 2.14 (using this menu path), you can enter the data structure `PAKEY`.

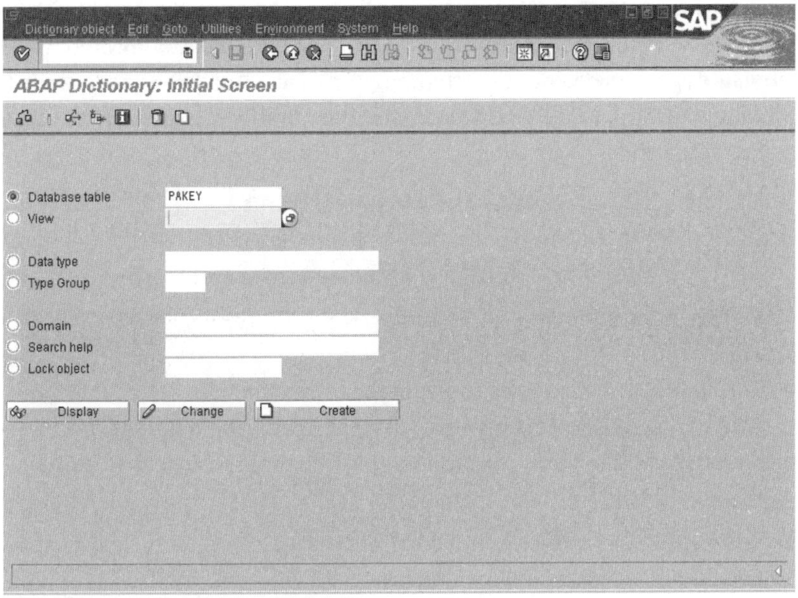

Figure 2.14 ABAP Dictionary—Initial Screen

After clicking the **Display** button, the data fields of the structure PAKEY are displayed (see Figure 2.15).

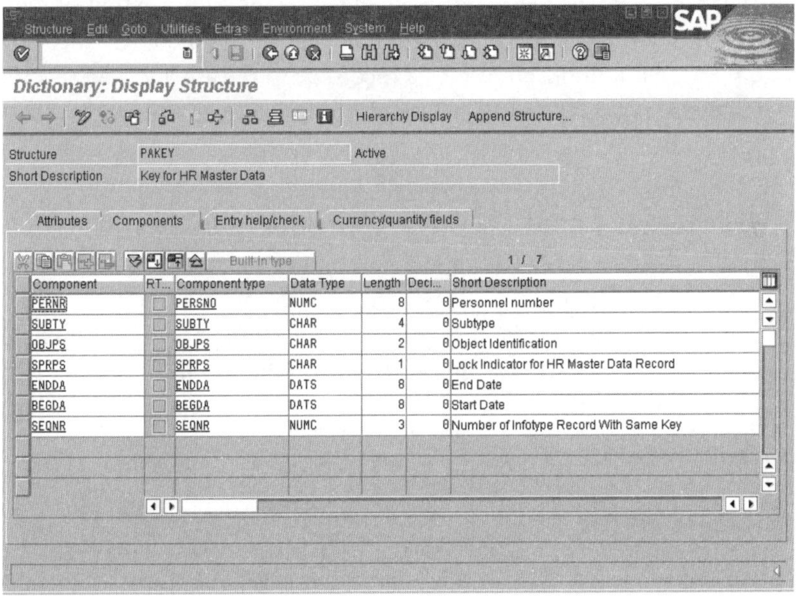

Figure 2.15 Structure PAKEY

The structure PAKEY contains the primary key of an infotype. This structure is identical for all infotypes and consists of the data fields personnel number, subtype, object identification, lock indicator for HR master record, validity end date, validity start date, and the number of an infotype record in the actual key.

▶ The field PERNR contains the personnel number, which is the only unique key in a client for identifying an employee. The personnel number is used to enter the display and maintenance of master data, and the working time data of an employee. This field is numeric and is 8 digits long.

▶ The field SUBTY contains the subtypes, the subdivisions of infotypes. One characteristic of subtypes is that they can have different time constraints and can form an independent history. This field is alphanumeric and contains four characters.

▶ The field OBJPS is the identifier of different objects. This field enables you to differentiate between records with the same infotype, subtype, lock indicator, and validity start and end dates.

▶ The field SPRPS enables you to lock and release records. This field is a prerequisite for implementing the *four eyes principle*, used with the authorization system.

The lock key of the field SPRPS is changed by the authorization system. In the authorizations for each employee, it is noted whether the employee is authorized to lock a record or to release a locked record. Please do not confuse the lock key for this field with the lock key that is set when editing a personnel number in the system lock table, if a personnel number is read in change mode. The lock key of this field is not related to the lock key that can be edited using Transaction SM12.

▶ The field ENDDA contains the end date of the validity period. The field BEGDA contains the start date of the validity period. The field SEQNR (sequence number) is for the internal administration of records of time constraint class 3. Unlike the field OBJPS, which is filled by the user, this data field is automatically assigned by the system.

Note   Structure PAKEY should never be changed.

Structure PSHD1

In addition to structure PAKEY, there is another basic structure that is identical for all infotypes in personnel administration—that is, the structure PSHD1 (see Figure 2.16). In the structure PSHD1, other basic information for each infotype is stored. This information is generally referred to as the *administrative information* on an infotype. It includes the change date, the name of the administrator who changed the infotype, an historical record flag, information on whether or not there is a text related to this infotype, and other data fields. This structure is just another of the underlying structures of an infotype.

Structure PSHD1 should never be changed. **Note**

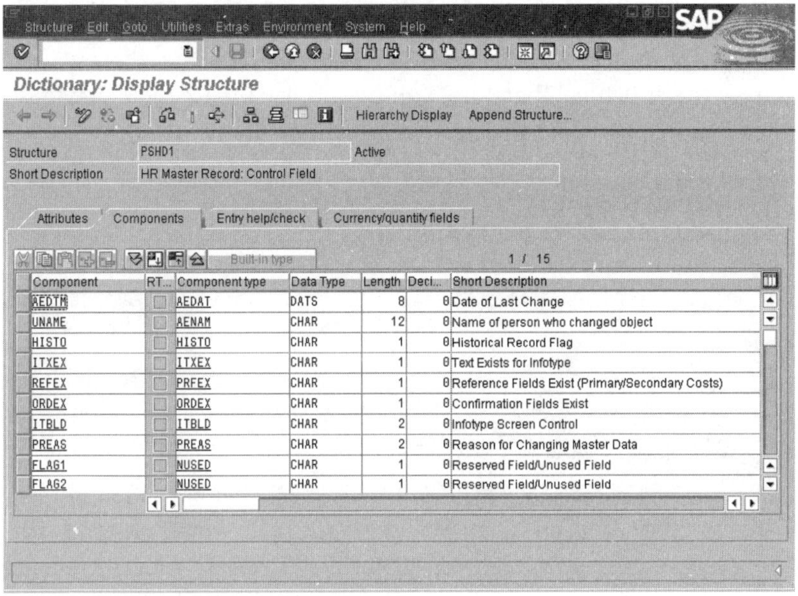

Figure 2.16 Structure PSHD1

Structure PSHDR

The structure PSHDR is a meta structure that contains the structures PSKEY and PSHD1.

Structure PSHDR should never be changed. **Note**

In addition, there are two infotype-specific data structures and a database table that must exist for every infotype. The four-digit number of the infotype is included in the names of the data structures and the database table. The following examples refer to infotype 0002, *Personal data.* Once again, you should note that the customer name range is from 9000 to 9999—that is, the customer-defined infotypes can only be created within this range. Only in this way, can you ensure that there will be no conflicts during an upgrade.

Structure PSnnnn

The structure PSnnnn is one of the necessary data structures, where "nnnn" stands for the infotype number in question; therefore, for infotype 0002, this data field structure is PS0002. All data fields of the infotype are defined in the data field structure marked PSnnnn.

This structure contains the infotype-specific data fields, that is, the data fields that contain the actual infotype-specific attributes.

It is assumed that you have the appropriate level of proficiency to take the subsequent steps and work in the Data Dictionary, which is where you can display the structure. Therefore, you can display the example previously cited, namely, structure PS0002 (see Figure 2.17).

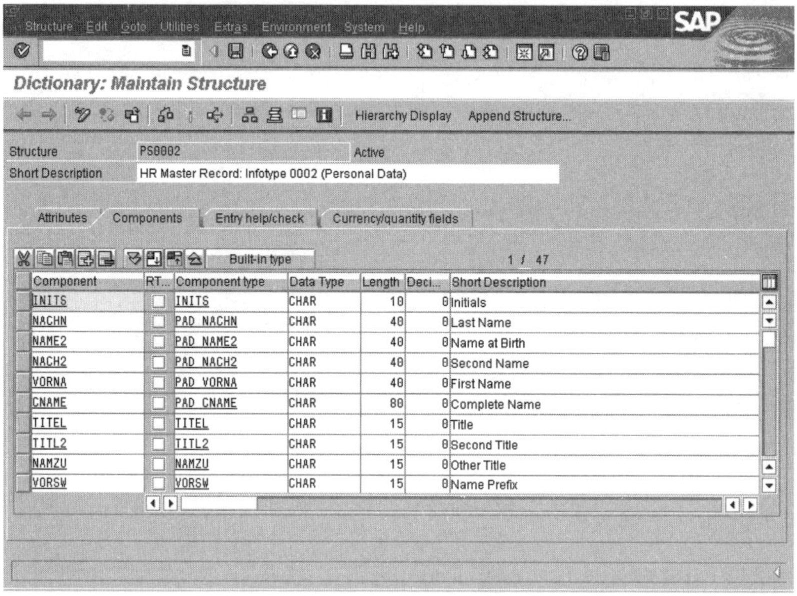

Figure 2.17 Structure PS0002

The functions of the Data Dictionary are available for defining infotypes. Direct checks against individual table fields can also be stored for specific fields in infotypes. You can access the area for defining possible values by selecting the tab **Entry help/check** (see Figure 2.18).

Subtypes It is, of course, also possible to create subtypes in customer-developed infotypes. If you want to add subtypes, in structure PSnnnn, you must incorporate a duplicate for key field Pnnnn-SUBTY in the data field structure PSnnnn. The subtype is then stored in this duplicate field, which requires its own name and data element.

This duplicate field for specifying the subtype is included in the appropriate infotype screens when the infotype is created. You can then enter data into this field.

In addition, when maintaining the characteristics of the infotype, in the field "subtype field" in table T777D, you must specify the name of the duplicate subtype field. Central infotype modules automatically write data to the key field Pnnnn-SUBTY from the entries in this field in table T777D. The key field Pnnnn-SUBTY does not appear on the infotype screens.

Therefore, you can create special check tables for the subtype assigned to the infotype. Furthermore, you can also create field-related documentation for the subtype.

The personnel administration infotypes contain an include CI_nnnn in the data field structure PSnnnn. Customer-specific enhancements to an infotype can be inserted in this include. The procedure for adding these enhancements to an infotype is described in Chapter 5. In the SAP standard package, the include CI_nnnn is delivered "empty".

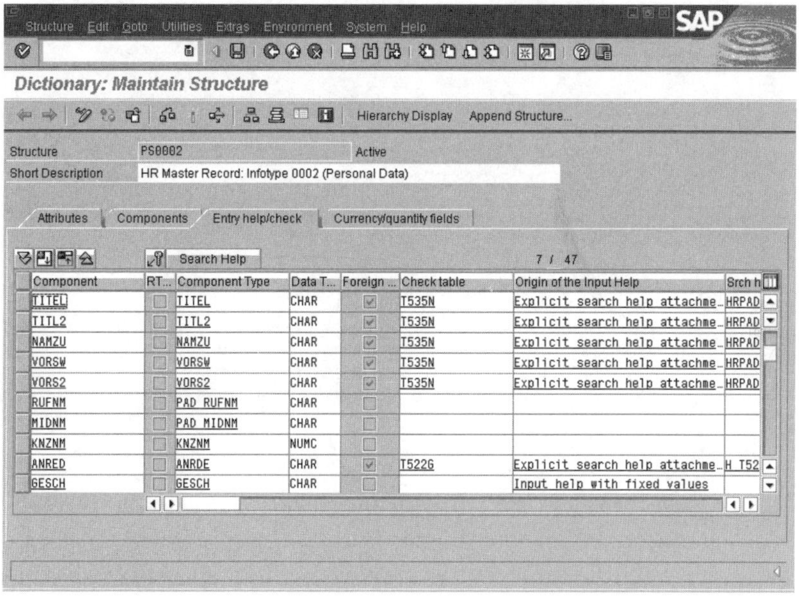

CI_nnnn—Basic rules for enhancements

Figure 2.18 PS0002, Input help/input check

Transparent table PAnnnn

The records of infotype nnnn are stored in the database table PAnnnn.

The transparent table PAnnnn—PA0002 again in this example (see Figure 2.19)—contains includes for all of the structures described above: PAKEY, PSHD1, and PSnnnn. In addition to the includes mentioned, the client is also used as part of the primary key.

Database tables are read with the help of the primary index. Therefore, it usually isn't necessary to create secondary indexes. Tables in the group PAnnnn shouldn't be buffered using the SAP database interface, because the application programs must always work with current data. For this reason, the **Buffering not allowed** check box should be marked accordingly. Infotype records are buffered in HR application programs, regardless of the settings in the Data Dictionary.

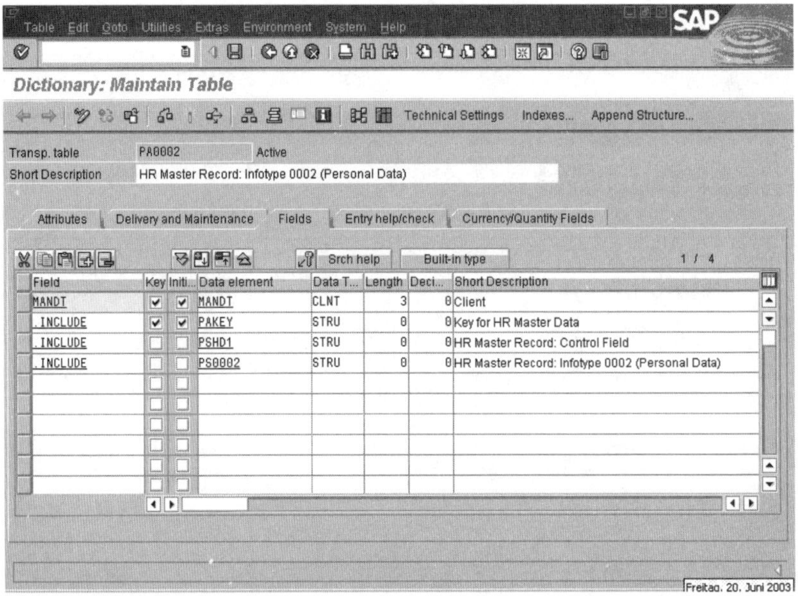

Figure 2.19 PA0002 as a Transparent Table

Structure Pnnnn

The definition of an infotype is not yet complete. There is another structure: structure Pnnnn (see Figure 2.20). This structure contains the includes PSHDR and PS0002, where PSHDR, in turn, contains the includes PSKEY and PSHD1.

This logical structure `Pnnnn` is used in the definition of interfaces between programs and interfaces between programs and screens.

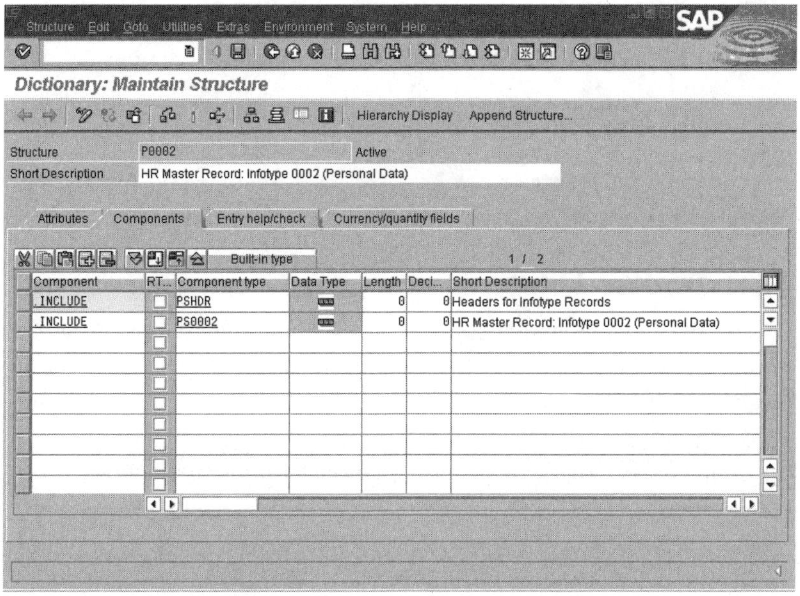

Figure 2.20 Structure P0002

2.2.11 Data Structures and Tables: Personnel Administration Infotype

The following table provides an overview of all data structures and transparent tables that constitute an infotype:

Element	Definition	Includes	Can be changed by customer
PAKEY	structure	–	no
PSHD1	structure	–	no
PSHDR	structure	PSKEY, PSHD1	no
PSnnnn	structure	(field definitions) CI_nnnn	PS9nnn: yes PS0nnn – PS8nnn: no
Pnnnn	structure	PSHDR PSnnnn	P9nnn: yes P0nnn – P8nnn: no

Table 2.1 Data Structures and Transparent Tables in an Infotype

Element	Definition	Includes	Can be changed by customer
PAnnnn	transparent table	MANDT PAKEY PSHD1 PSnnnn	PA9nnn: yes P0nnn – P9nnn: no
CI_nnnn	structure	–	yes

Table 2.1 Data Structures and Transparent Tables in an Infotype (cont.)

2.2.12 Infotype Views

View of several infotypes

Specific infotype design issues are addressed by using infotype views (see Figure 2.21). Because the Human Resource (HR) Management System is created for international use, there are, for example, international info-types that require additional country-specific fields. To avoid the balloon-ing proliferation of data fields of internationally-oriented infotypes due to the many diverse country-specific fields—and the additional fields they require—the necessary country-specific fields are stored in additional infotypes.

Primary infotype

The primary infotypes and the additional infotypes are maintained using an infotype view. When saving data, the data entered in the infotype view is split between primary infotype and secondary infotype.

The infotype view is defined in the IMG using the menu path **Personnel Management · Personnel Administration · Customizing procedures · Infotypes · Assign Infotype views · Assignment of Infotypes to Views**. These defined infotype views are captured in tables T582V and T582W.

Only the international primary infotype is contained in the infotype menu. This maintenance is not possible for additional infotypes. All attributes for the additional infotypes, such as time constraint, are defined in the same infotype as is the underlying primary infotype.

Note

SAP recommends that you do not create your own infotype views.

The feature IVWID

When creating a personnel number, you should note that when using fea-ture IVWID, an infotype view ID is assigned in the infotype *Payroll Status* (infotype 0003). Feature IVWID can be customized and modified; how-ever, the view ID should never be changed in a live system.

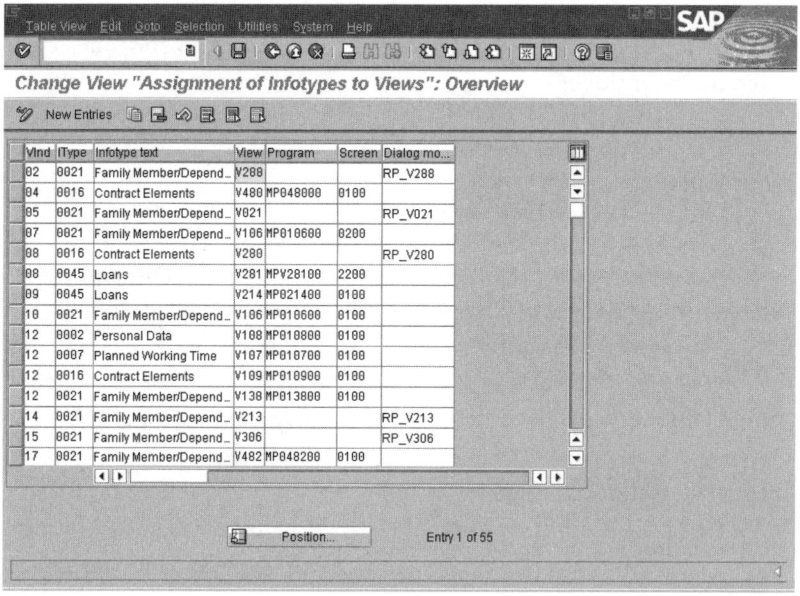

VInd	IType	Infotype text	View	Program	Screen	Dialog mo...
02	0021	Family Member/Depend...	V288			RP_V288
04	0016	Contract Elements	V480	MP048000	0100	
05	0021	Family Member/Depend...	V021			RP_V021
07	0021	Family Member/Depend...	V106	MP010600	0200	
08	0016	Contract Elements	V280			RP_V280
08	0045	Loans	V281	MPV28100	2200	
09	0045	Loans	V214	MP021400	0100	
10	0021	Family Member/Depend...	V106	MP010600	0100	
12	0002	Personal Data	V108	MP010800	0100	
12	0007	Planned Working Time	V107	MP010700	0100	
12	0016	Contract Elements	V109	MP010900	0100	
12	0021	Family Member/Depend...	V138	MP013800	0100	
14	0021	Family Member/Depend...	V213			RP_V213
15	0021	Family Member/Depend...	V306			RP_V306
17	0021	Family Member/Depend...	V482	MP048200	0100	

Figure 2.21 Assigning Infotypes to Views

2.3 Organizational Management and Personnel Planning Data

Organizational management data model

To help you to understand the data structures in organizational management and in personnel planning, we will first introduce the underlying data model. The object-based design of the data is founded on the terms of *object types, relationships,* and *infotypes.* It is important to comprehend this design if you are to efficiently execute enhancements and adjustments.

2.3.1 Data Model

Description of organizational and report structures

The organizational management data model was designed to meet a wide range of different needs. First of all, it should enable a time-related, comprehensive view of the organizational and report structures of an enterprise. It should also provide for the flexible evaluation and analysis of the data in organizational management. In addition, the data is used for planning organizational changes. Finally, Organizational Management and the underlying data model also form the basis for the inclusion and overall usage of other components. Personnel Development, Compensation Management, and the SAP workflow are just a few examples of components that use Organizational Management.

In order to meet the requirements described, an object-based design was selected for Organizational Management. Key terms in this object-oriented design include:

- ▶ Object types
- ▶ Relationships
- ▶ Infotypes

Object types A range of objects, such as organizational unit, cost center, or person, are reserved for personnel planning. The objects are classified into what are known as *object types*. Every object in personnel planning is assigned to one object type, and each object type is given an object type key. The following table contains the most important predefined object types:

Object type text	Object type
Organizational unit	O
Jobs	C
Positions	S
Cost centers	K
Persons	P
Task	T
Work center	A
Qualification	Q

Table 2.2 Predefined Object Types

Object types can be enhanced as part of Customizing. You can select this option in the IMG via the menu path **Personnel Management · Organizational Management · Basic Settings · Data Model Enhancements · Maintain Object Types.** Technically, the information is available in Table T778O (see Figure 2.22). The definition of object types in the table is alphanumeric. The name range A* to Z* is reserved for SAP. In the context of customer-developed projects, no entries can be made in this name range. The name range 0* to 9* is available for customer-specific and project-specific entries.

Note Personnel planning objects are classified by object types.

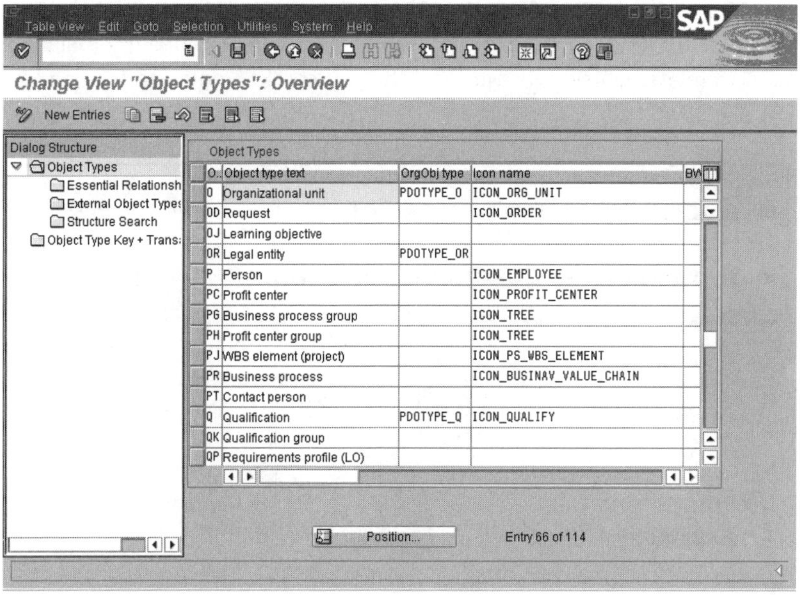

Figure 2.22 Object Types in Table T778O

Internal and external object types

Regarding the location of an object, from a technical point of view, we can differentiate between internal and external object types. The master records of objects of internal object types are located in personnel planning database tables. These objects include organizational units, positions, and jobs, among others. Objects of external object types, however, do not have their database home in personnel planning database tables; rather, they are located in other areas of the SAP system. Two examples of these objects include the cost center or person. Links from personnel planning to these external object types is done with the help of relationships. To make an external object type available in personnel planning, there must be an interface program for that object type. This program must be entered in table T77EO. You can do this by making an entry in the field "Interface name", via the previously identified menu path **Personnel Management • Organizational Management • Basic Settings • Data Model Enhancements • Maintain Object types • External Object Types**.

An example: Among the object types, there is one for *Person*, with the object type key "P". The entry in the field "Interface name" reads "RHPRELOO". This program makes it possible to access personal master data in personnel administration from personnel planning.

Relationships After the initial step of describing the object types, they must be logically associated with each other. This is done with *Relationships*. By assigning specific relationships between objects, you create a data model (see Figure 2.23).

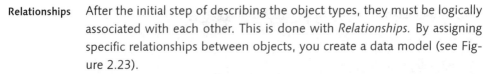

- **A job "describes" a position.**   **A 007**
- **A position "is described" by a job.**   **B 007**

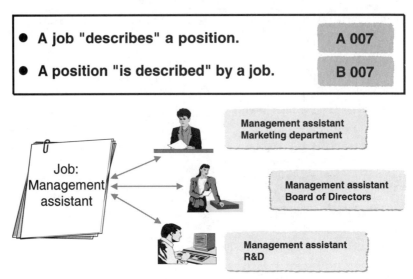

Figure 2.23 Object Relationships Between Jobs and Positions

The object type *Job* refers to a general classification for tasks and functions that an employee must carry out (for example, payroll administrator). The object type *Position* refers to the concrete position, to be occupied by a holder, in an enterprise (for example payroll administrator for the Louisburg plant, or payroll administrator for the Norfolk plant). The relationship between the object types *Position* and *Job* is shown in Figure 2.23. In this context, it is important to note that relationships are usually defined in two different directions. Therefore, "A" is used to represent the relationship in the direction bottom-up (in Figure 2.23, A007: a job "describes" a position); and "B" is used to represent the relationship in the other direction, top-down, (in Figure 2.23, B007: a position "is described" by a job).

Note Relationships describe how object types are related. Relationships between object types are defined in two directions: bottom-up (A) and top-down (B).

Technical composition of object types In this regard, the abovementioned difference between internal and external object types is important. For internal object types, every relationship is also created on the database in both directions (bottom-up and top-down). In contrast, for external object types, the relationship is not necessarily created in both directions. Sometimes, in operational systems, the relationship is only in one direction—from the internal object to the external object. This relationship is referred to as "external object types without inverse relationship".

Relationships can also be modified or adjusted in the IMG (see Figure 2.24). The path to the relationships is: **Personnel Management · Organizational Management · Basic Settings · Data Model Enhancements · Relationship Maintenance · Maintain Relationships**. The location for storing relationships is Table T778V. There is also an SAP name range and a customer name range for relationship entries. The SAP name range includes the numeric entries "000" to "999", and the customer name range includes the alphanumeric entries from "AAA" to "ZZZ".

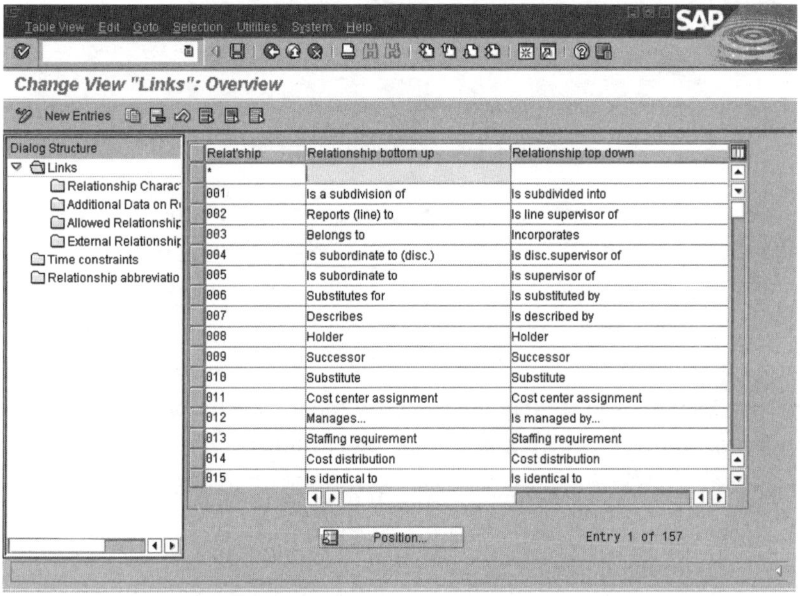

Customizing relationships

Figure 2.24 Change Relationships

Infotypes, finally, allow you to define the objects, relationships, attributes and characteristics of an object within the object-oriented structure of personnel planning. In this manner, the object itself is created as an infotype (for example, the job, the position, the organizational unit). In addition, the relationships are also recorded as infotypes. The creation of an object is shown in Figure 2.25. The object is always created in the infotype *Object* (technically, it is infotype 1000).

Infotypes in data design

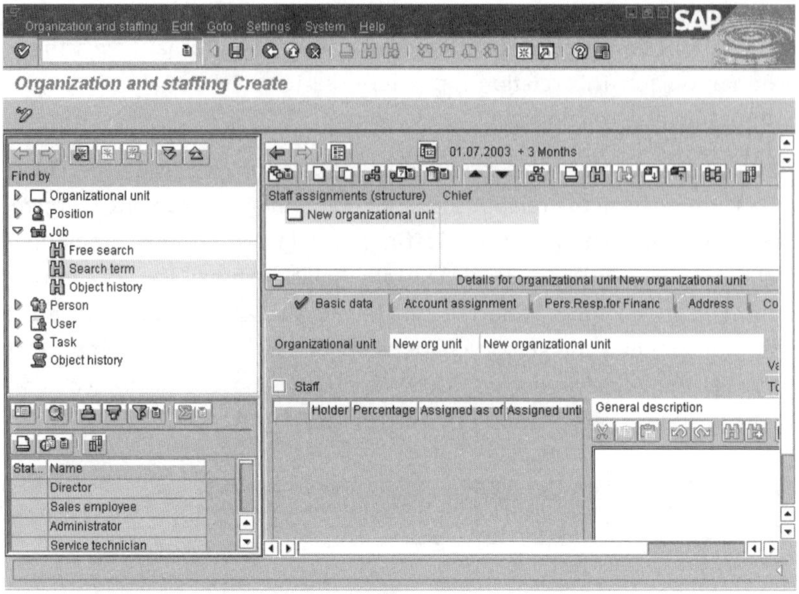

Figure 2.25 Create Organization (Infotype 1000)

Infotype "Relationships"

The inter-relations with other objects are depicted by the infotype *relationships* (infotype 1001). Only after the infotype *object* has been created, can all other infotypes in personnel planning be generated. These infotypes describe the object created under the infotype *object* (infotype 1000) in greater detail.

Note

Infotypes in personnel planning are used to create objects, to define relationships between objects, and to describe objects.

The infotype concept in personnel planning corresponds to the infotype concept in personnel administration, as shown above. In particular, just as with the infotypes in personnel administration, there is also a start and end date for each record, with which a validity date can be set for the infotype (compare Section 2.2.4).

2.3.2 Personnel planning infotypes

Control tables for infotypes

There are some control tables for the infotypes in personnel planning. You can access these tables in the IMG via the path **Personnel Management · Organizational Management · Basic Settings · Data Model Enhancements · Infotype Maintenance**.

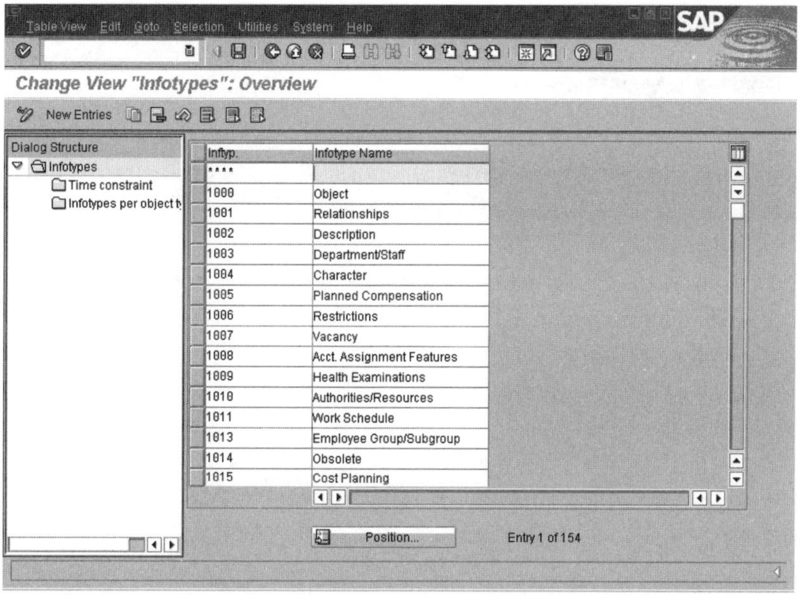

Figure 2.26 Change Infotypes

The infotypes are basically defined in these control tables (Customizing tables T778T and T777T, see Figure 2.26). You can also define the infotypes for an object (Customizing table T7771). Another way in which you can influence the performance of the infotype is to define time constraints for infotypes (table T777Z).

2.3.3 Technical Data Structure of Infotypes

The structures of infotypes as found in the area of personnel planning, are shown below.

Structure HRIKEY

The key fields of the infotypes in personnel planning are described by the structure HRIKEY (see Figure 2.27). You can display them, just like the infotypes in personnel administration, using the menu path **SAP menu · Tools · ABAP Workbench · Development · ABAP Dictionary**.

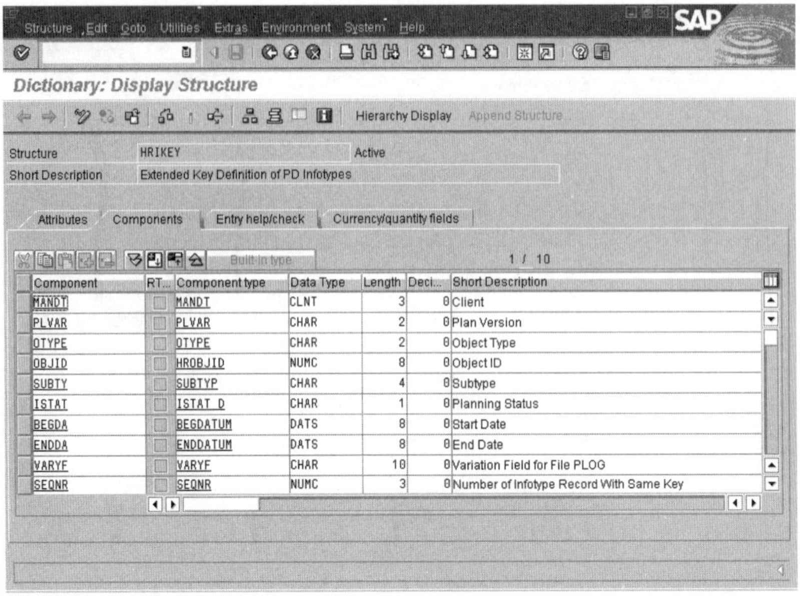

Figure 2.27 Structure HRIKEY

The structure of the key fields of infotypes in Recruitment is identical for all infotypes and consists of the following fields:

▶ The field MANDT contains the clients.

▶ The field PLVAR is a two-character alphanumeric key for the plan versions that enables you to differentiate between alternative plan versions.

▶ The field OTYPE contains the object type key, which is also a maximum of two alphanumeric characters in length.

▶ The field OBJID contains an eight-digit key that represents a single object. It is assumed that this object ID contains no descriptive key.

▶ The field SUBTY contains the specification of a subtype.

▶ The field ISTAT is a one-digit numeric key in which the planning status is indicated. There is a status for all objects and for the infotypes that describe them. By specifying the planning status, you can provide support for all objects and infotypes during a complete planning cycle (planned - submitted and so on).

▶ The field BEGDA contains the start date of the validity period.

▶ The field ENDDA contains the end date of the validity period.

▶ The field VARYF contains the target object of a relationship.

▶ The field `SEQNR` specifies a sequence number for infotypes of time constraint class 3. Because there can be any number of information records for this time constraint class during any one period, each infotype record is assigned a number by this field. The sequence number is assigned automatically by the system.

Structure HRIKEYL

The structure `HRIKEYL` is a variant of the structure `HRIKEY`, previously described. This structure supports language-dependent infotypes, which are infotypes that contain one or more text fields that can be translated into the target language (see Figure 2.28).

The structure `HRIKEYL` usually contains the same fields as the structure `HRIKEY` (see above).

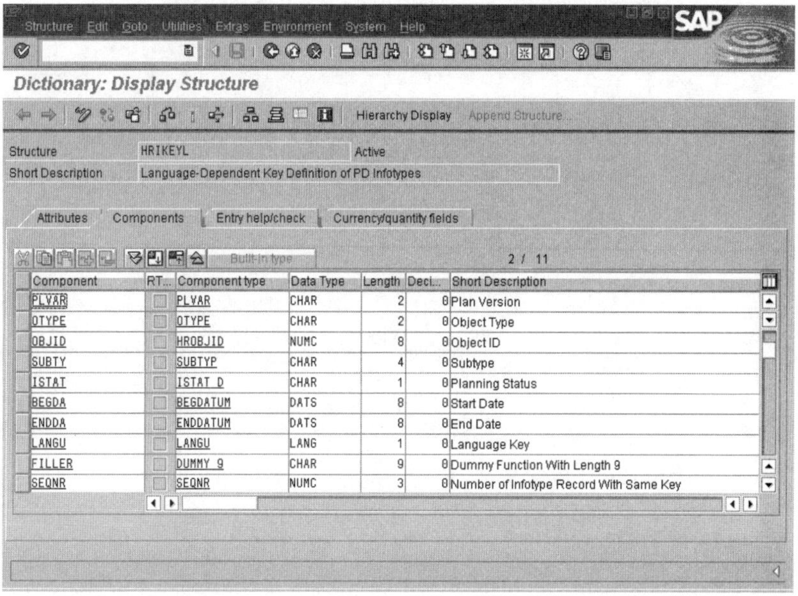

Figure 2.28 Structure HRIKEYL

There are some differences as regards field `VARYF` in the structure `HRIKEY`. The first position in this case is a one-character alphanumeric field with the name `LANGU`. The language identifier is listed in this field. This is followed by a nine-character unused field, with the field name `DUMMY`.

Structure HRIADMIN

The structure HRIADMIN is a data structure that contains administrative information on each infotype (see Figure 2.29). The technical fields are:

▶ AEDTM: date on which the infotype was last changed

▶ UNAME: name of user that made last change

▶ REASN: reason for last change (not used)

▶ HISTO: historical record flag

▶ ITXNR: text module for the infotype (not used)

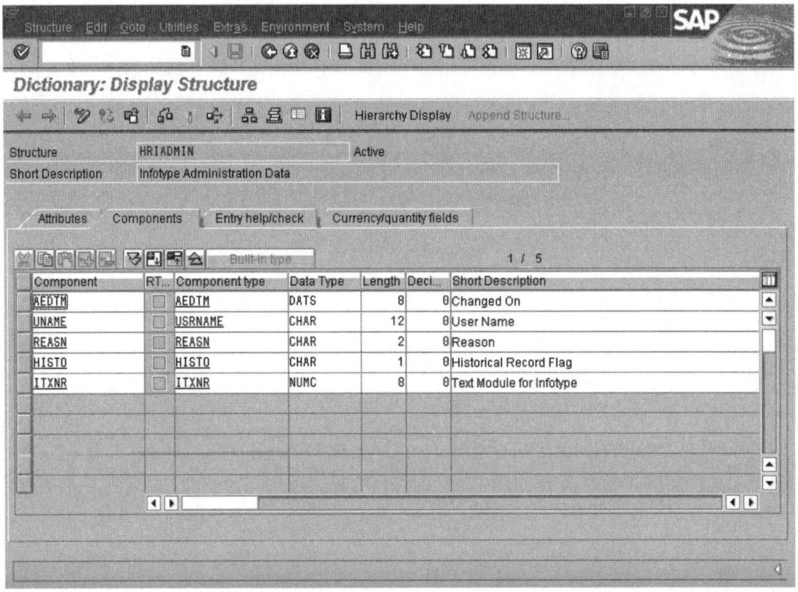

Figure 2.29 Structure HRIADMIN

Structure HRInnnn

The infotype-specific data fields for an infotype are defined in the structure HRInnnn. Here, "nnnn" stands for the four-digit infotype number, as appropriate. Thus, for infotype 1005, this would be structure HRI1005 (see Figure 2.30).

The complete functionality of the Data Dictionary is available for the definition of customer-specific infotypes. These infotypes can only be in the number range 9000 to 9999. Therefore, a customer-defined infotype could contain, for example, the structure name HRI9500. The structure itself is not saved to the database; rather, it serves as an element (include) for the subsequent definition of the transparent table.

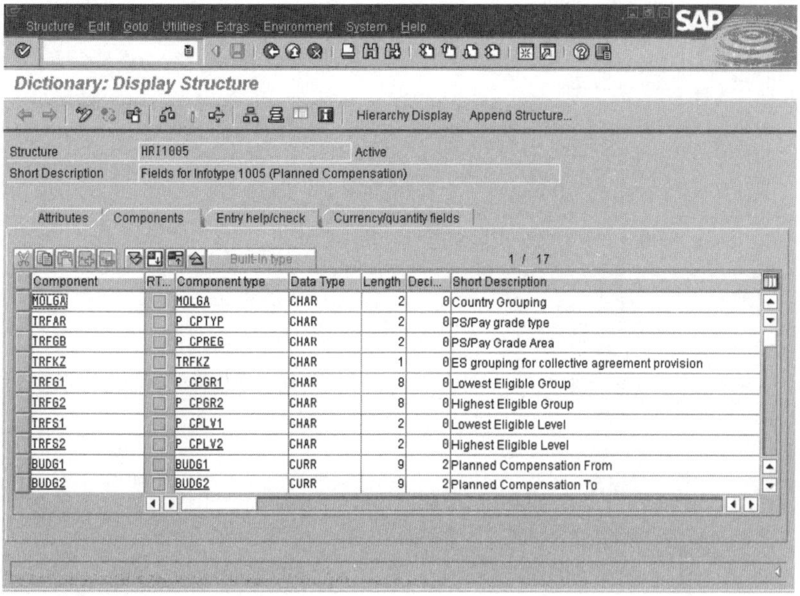

Figure 2.30 Structure: HRI1005

Transparent table HRPnnnn

The transparent table now contains the structures described above. In this way, it is guaranteed that with the following includes, the respective attributes are available:

▶ HRIKEY—the key fields of the infotype table

▶ HRIADMIN—the administrative information on the infotype record

▶ HRInnnn—the data structures of the specific infotype

To exemplify this, the transparent table is shown again as HRP1005 (see Figure 2.31).

Logical structure Pnnnn

Like the infotypes in personnel administration, the structure Pnnnn is also found in the infotypes of personnel planning (see Figure 2.32). Here too, the logical structure Pnnnn is used to define interfaces between programs and between programs and screens. It contains the includes HRIPKEY, HRIADMIN, and HRInnnn.

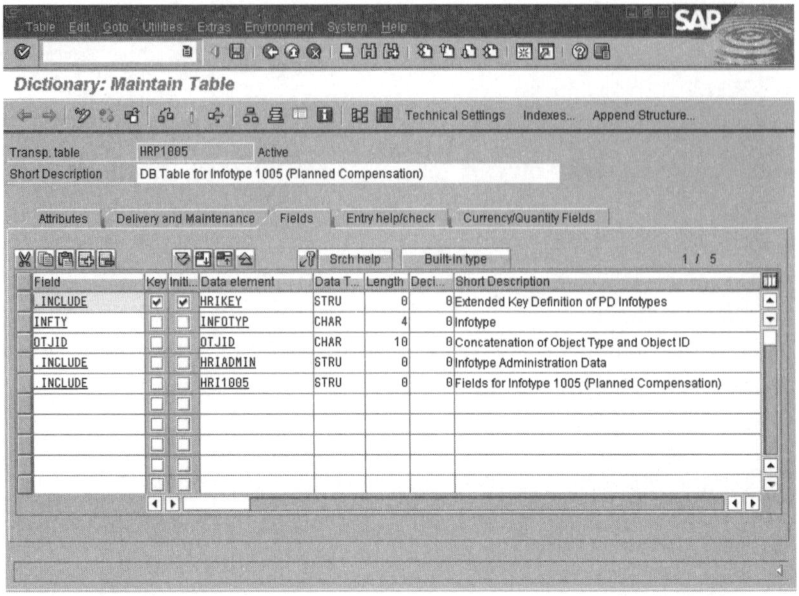

Figure 2.31 Transparent Table: HRP1005

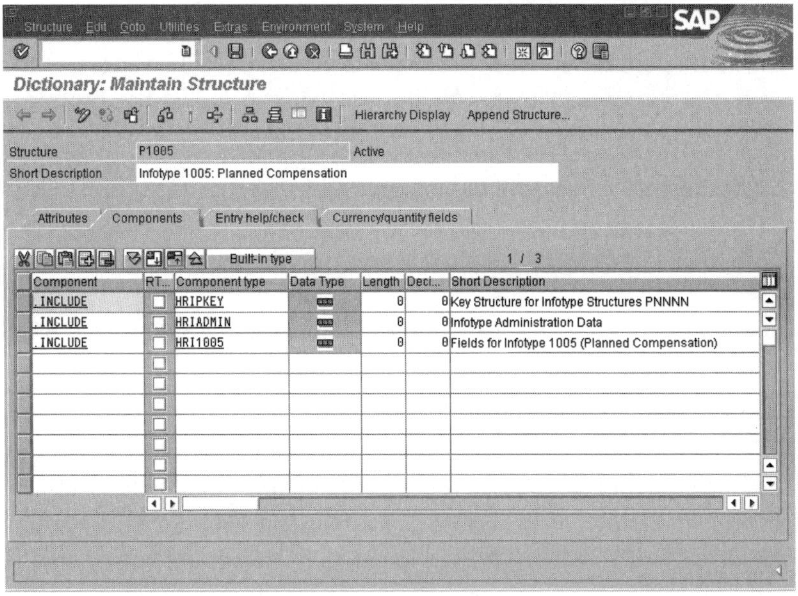

Figure 2.32 Structure P1005

2.3.4 Table Infotypes

Table infotypes are a special form of infotype used in personnel planning. *Table infotypes* are infotypes for which the data part has a repetitive structure of arbitrary length. This repetitive structure could be texts with any number of lines, or it could, for example, be a course schedule with any number of days. In order to provide the option of saving repetitions of any length, the data part must have a repetitive structure and it must be saved in a separate data table. This repetition part or table part is described in the logical structure PTnnnn and stored in the separate table HRTnnnn. This repetitive structure is illustrated with infotype 1002. Figure 2.33 shows the necessary structure definition. The transparent table necessary for a table infotype is shown in Figure 2.34.

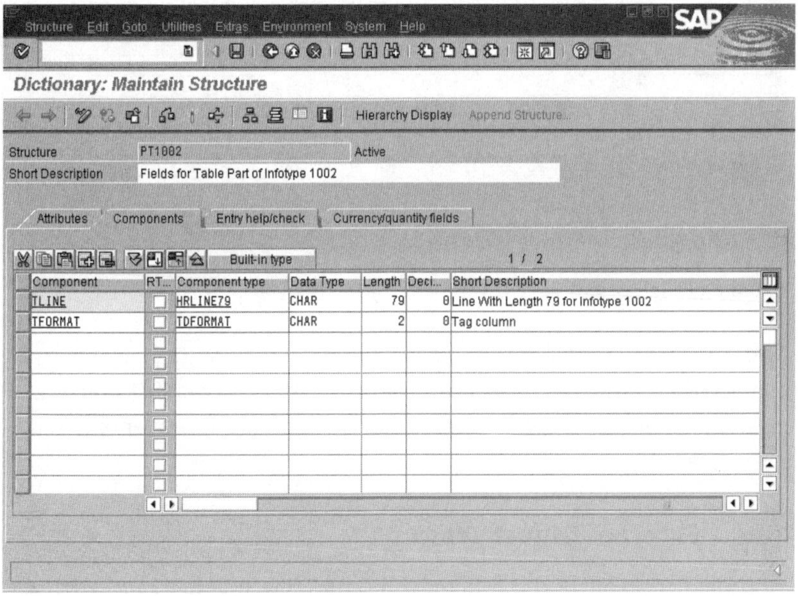

Repetitive structures in table infotypes

Figure 2.33 Structure PT1002 for Table Infotype

In addition to the definition of the logical structure and the table, for table infotypes, the name of the transparent table must also be stored in table T777D in the field "Database table for table infotype", field TBTAB (compare Section 2.3.9).

In an infotype, it is possible to create a relationship between "fix attributes" and a table part. This type of relationship between the primary record, which contains the "fix attributes" and which is described by the table HRPnnnn, and the table part of the table infotype is realized by a table pointer (field `TABNR`). The table pointer is determined internally by the system via an internal number assignment. The table pointer should not be manipulated by other programs or other procedures.

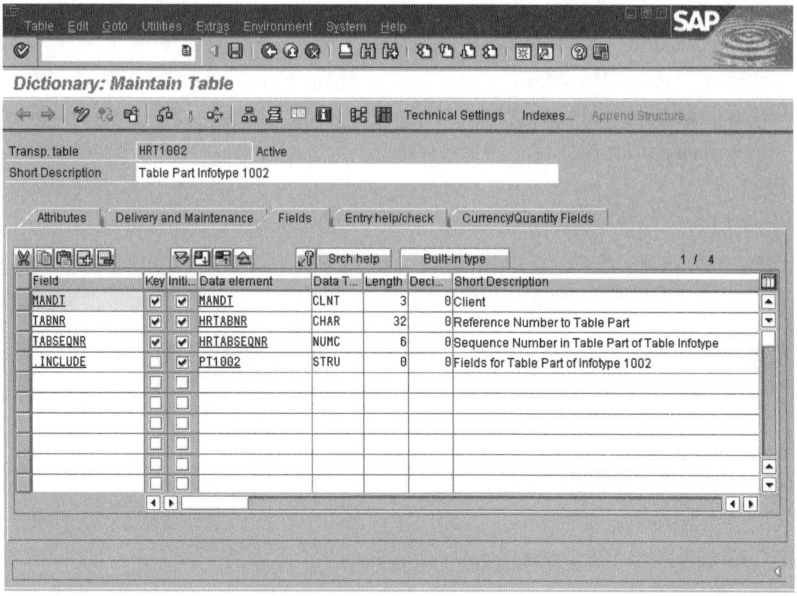

Figure 2.34 Transparent Table HRT1002 for Table Infotype

Also, for read accesses with table infotypes, the structure `PTnnnn` is available for the table part. In this way, direct database accesses to table `HRTnnnn` can be avoided. This can lead to a considerable improvement in performance.

2.3.5 External Object Types

External object types

As explained in Section 2.3.1, we can differentiate between internal and external object types. *External object types* refer to those object types that are not stored in the data structure of personnel planning. From a technical point of view, there is no record in `HRP1000` for objects of this type. External object types are only referenced in the context of a relationship record. Technically, this means that data records on the relationship are only held in `HRP1001`.

Relationship routes for object types

For *internal object types*, relationships can exist in two directions, top-down and bottom-up (see Section 2.3.1). This results in the creation of two records in infotype 1001, *Relationships.* External object types are limited in this respect. In order to create an inverse relationship for an external object type, the key structure of the external object type must be an eight-digit numeric string (type NUMC of length 8). It must, therefore, be defined with the same type as the field object ID (HRPnnnn-OBJID). In the SAP system, this is the case for the personnel number, for example, but does not apply to the cost center number.

Whether external object types have only one relationship—or if inverse relationships are also possible—is established for each object type in the Implementation Guide in table T77EO.

Where there is no physical inverse relationship for an external object type, such as, for the cost center, there may be situations in which this relationship direction can be deemed necessary. In this case, evaluations based on the objects of the external object type are necessary. In the cost center example, the question may be: Which positions are assigned to cost center ABC? The requirement is to evaluate a relationship for which there is no record in table HRP1001. A "simulated inverse relationship" can be created, as supplied by the system in structure HRI1001 (this structure should not be confused with the structure HRInnnn for the infotype). Structure HRI1001 differs from the logical structure P1001 in the relationship record only in type and in the length of the object ID field (OBJID). Instead of the format NUMC with a length of 8 characters, the field HRI1001-OBJID is an alphanumeric field and is 45 characters long. Therefore, the extended object ID can incorporate any external key with a maximum length of 45 characters, for example, the cost center key.

Inverse relationship

2.3.6   External Infotypes

Infotypes that are needed for planning purposes in personnel planning, but are not stored in transparent infotype tables of the type HRPnnnn, are referred to as *external infotypes*. This information can be physically available, for example, in the tables of personnel administration.

It can be simulated in personnel planning in the structure Pnnnn. It can also be displayed as an infotype in transactions in personnel planning such as Detail Maintenance. An evaluation is also possible in the query in the logical database. Maintenance of the external infotypes displayed in this way, however, is only possible via the corresponding primary table views.

For external tables, therefore, the structure Pnnnn exists, but not the transparent table HRPnnnn. An identifier for an external infotype appears in table T777D in the field EXT_INFTY. In addition, external tables can be controlled in table T77ID via the following fields:

▶ Primary table for external infotype, field EXT_TABNAM
The view of the corresponding customizing table for the external info-type is recorded in this field.

▶ Function modules for table name, field EXT_W_FUNC
The name of a function module can be recorded in this field, which makes it possible to define the view dynamically at runtime.

▶ Function modules for read access, field EXT_R_FUNC
The name of the function module for read access to the primary table is recorded in this field, thereby providing infotype data on an object in structure Pnnnn.

2.3.7 Data Structures and Tables: Personnel Planning Info-type

The following table shows the structures of an infotype for personnel planning:

Element	Definition	Includes	Can be changed by customer
HRIKEY	structure	–	no
HRIKEYL	structure	–	no
HRIADMIN	structure	–	no
HRInnnn	structure	(field definitions) CI_nnnn	HRI9nnn: yes HRI0nnn – HRI8nnn: no
Pnnnn	structure	HRPnnnn	P9nnn: yes P0nnn – P8nnn: no
HRPnnnn	transparent table	HRIKEY or HRIKEYL HRIADMIN	HRP9nnn: yes HRP0nnn – HRP8nnn: no
PTnnnn	structure	–	PT9nnn: yes PT0nnn – PT8nnn: no
HRTnnnn	transparent table	PTnnnn	HRT9nnn: yes HRT0nnn – HRT8nnn: no
CI_nnnn	structure	–	yes

Table 2.3 Structures of an Infotype for Personnel Planning

2.3.8 Checking the Consistency of the Data Model

For personnel planning, a separate report program is created to check the consistency of the data model that results from the customizing process. Report RHCHECK0 checks the following points (see Figure 2.35):

Check report for the consistency check

▶ Infotypes

  ▶ Object type assignment

  ▶ Time constraint

  ▶ Structures

  ▶ Database tables

▶ Relationships

  ▶ Relationships allowed

  ▶ Time constraint

▶ Integration

  ▶ Active or deactivated

  ▶ Active plan version

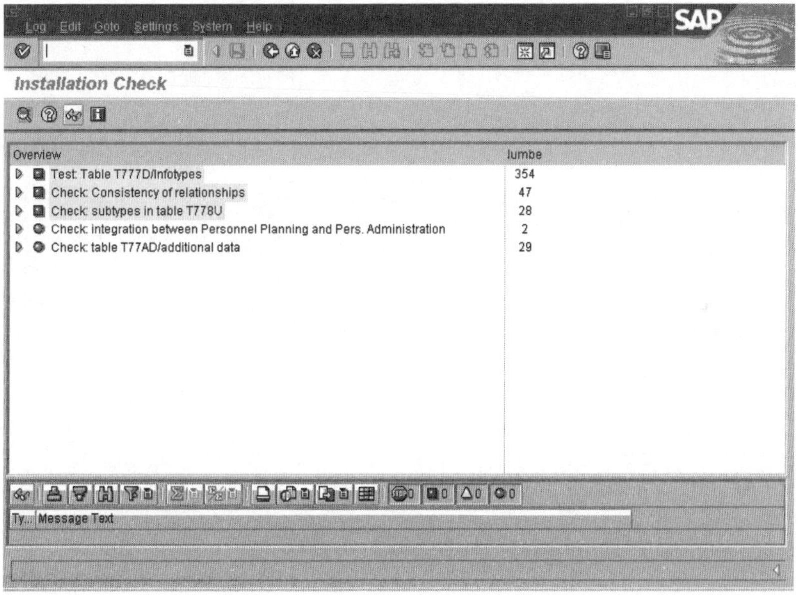

Figure 2.35 Test Result of Report RHCHECK0

2.3.9 Checking the Consistency of Infotypes

Check table for HR infotypes

Table *Infotypes—dialog/database assignment* (table T777D) is a central check table for all HR infotypes. This check applies to both the infotypes in personnel administration and personnel planning. This table contains information on all infotype-dependent repository objects, that is, tables, structures and programs.

This table is extended by the table *Infotypes—enhancements to T777D* (table T77ID). The latter table contains more information on the infotypes.

Both of the aforementioned tables are explicitly maintained with the transactions for creating an infotype.

Customer-defined settings

In addition, customer-defined settings for personnel administration infotypes are recorded in the table *Infotypes—customer-specific settings* (technical name: T582A). This table is included in the Implementation Guide.

Customer-defined settings for infotypes in personnel planning are located in the table *Infotypes—customer-specific settings* (technical name: T77CD).

The report program `RHT777DCHECK`. is provided to check the consistency of entries in the aforementioned tables (see Figure 2.36).

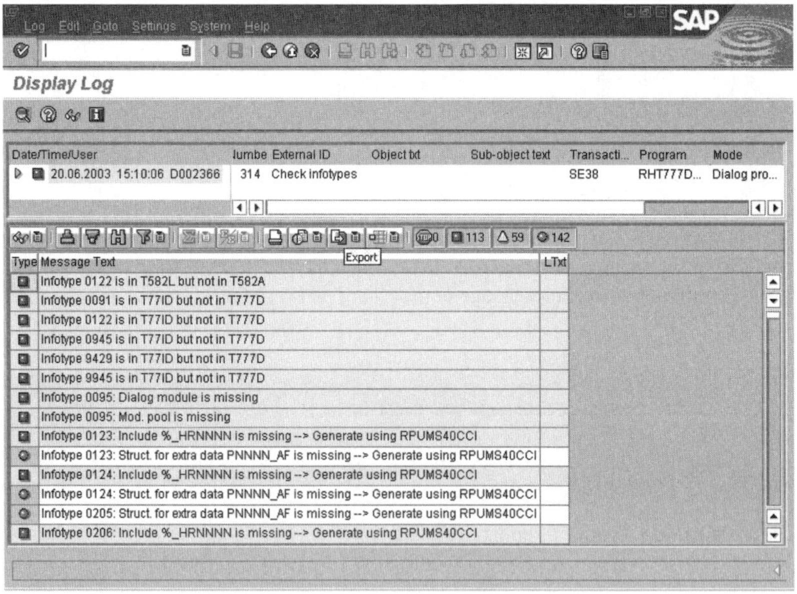

Figure 2.36 Test Results of Report RHT777DCHECK

2.4 Time Management Data

For Time Management data, the same infotype concept is used here that is used for Personnel Administration data and Personnel Planning data. A special feature of these infotypes is that they are linked to each other via the main program MP200000. Therefore, you can run what are referred to as *collision checks*.

Time management infotype concept

2.4.1 Time Management Master Data

The infotype concept also applies to the master data of Time Management. The following infotypes are used for Time Management:

Infotype name	Infotype number
Leave entitlement	0005
Leare entitlement Compensation	0083
Absences	2001
Attendances	2002
Substitutions	2003
Availability	2004
Overtime	2005
Absence Quotas	2006
Attendance Quotas	2007
Time Events	2011
Time Transfer Specifications	2012
Quota Corrections	2013

Table 2.4 Infotypes in Time Management

Time infotype records are stored in the transparent table of type PAnnnn, as previously described regarding data on personnel administration.

2.4.2 Time Events

Infotype 2011 is an exception. Where time recording devices are used, infotype 2011 displays data from table TEVEN (see Figure 2.37). These are time events from time recording. The data in table TEVEN serves as a basis for forming time pairs, that is, pairs of "coming" and "going" times which are read from the pair table PT and used for Time Evaluation.

Infotype 2011— time events

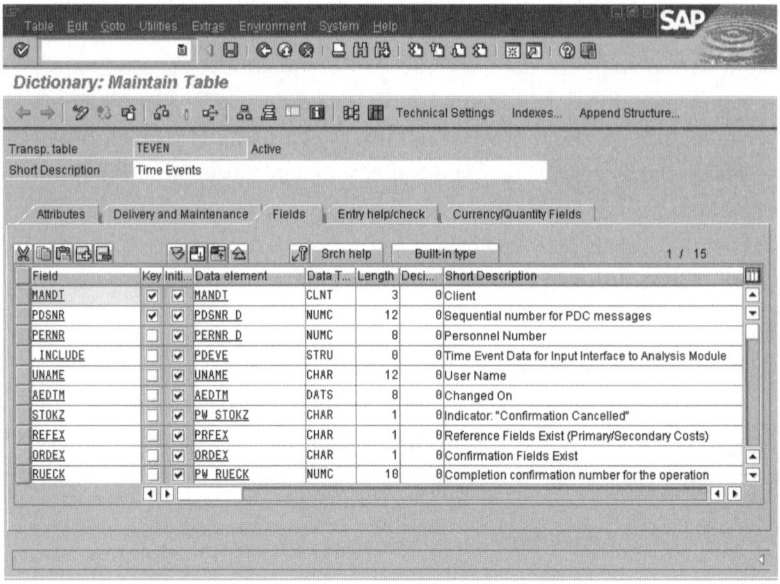

Dictionary: Maintain Table

Transp. table: TEVEN Active
Short Description: Time Events

Attributes | Delivery and Maintenance | Fields | Entry help/check | Currency/Quantity Fields

1 / 15

Field	Key	Initi...	Data element	Data T...	Length	Deci...	Short Description
MANDT	☑	☑	MANDT	CLNT	3	0	Client
PDSNR	☑	☑	PDSNR_D	NUMC	12	0	Sequential number for PDC messages
PERNR	☐	☑	PERNR_D	NUMC	8	0	Personnel Number
.INCLUDE	☐	☑	PDEVE	STRU	0	0	Time Event Data for Input Interface to Analysis Module
UNAME	☐	☑	UNAME	CHAR	12	0	User Name
AEDTM	☐	☑	AEDTM	DATS	8	0	Changed On
STOKZ	☐	☑	PW_STOKZ	CHAR	1	0	Indicator: "Confirmation Cancelled"
REFEX	☐	☑	PRFEX	CHAR	1	0	Reference Fields Exist (Primary/Secondary Costs)
ORDEX	☐	☑	ORDEX	CHAR	1	0	Confirmation Fields Exist
RUECK	☐	☑	PW_RUECK	NUMC	10	0	Completion confirmation number for the operation

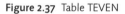

Figure 2.37 Table TEVEN

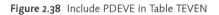

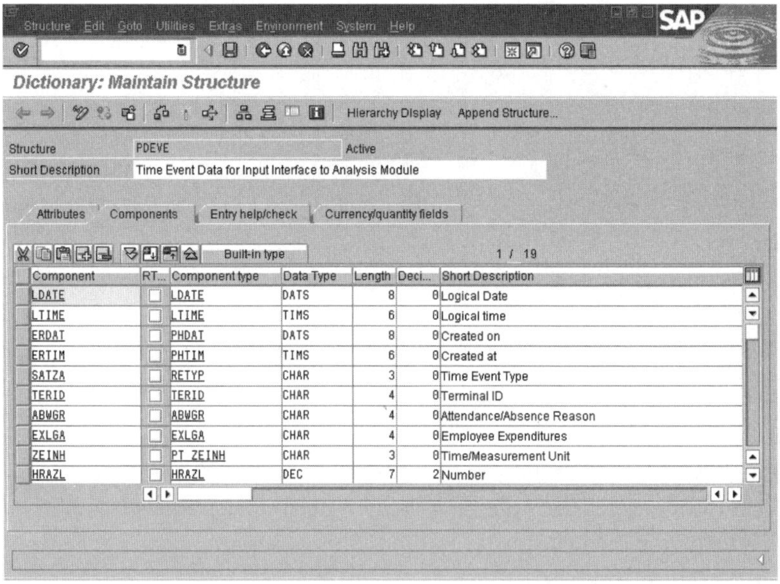

Dictionary: Maintain Structure

Structure: PDEVE Active
Short Description: Time Event Data for Input Interface to Analysis Module

Attributes | Components | Entry help/check | Currency/quantity fields

1 / 19

Component	RT...	Component type	Data Type	Length	Deci...	Short Description
LDATE	☐	LDATE	DATS	8	0	Logical Date
LTIME	☐	LTIME	TIMS	6	0	Logical time
ERDAT	☐	PHDAT	DATS	8	0	Created on
ERTIM	☐	PHTIM	TIMS	6	0	Created at
SATZA	☐	RETYP	CHAR	3	0	Time Event Type
TERID	☐	TERID	CHAR	4	0	Terminal ID
ABWGR	☐	ABWGR	CHAR	4	0	Attendance/Absence Reason
EXLGA	☐	EXLGA	CHAR	4	0	Employee Expenditures
ZEINH	☐	PT_ZEINH	CHAR	3	0	Time/Measurement Unit
HRAZL	☐	HRAZL	DEC	7	2	Number

Figure 2.38 Include PDEVE in Table TEVEN

Table TEVEN

After the time events have been uploaded from the time recording device, the new events are put into table TEVEN. Table TEVEN, therefore, includes all the entered, processed, unprocessed, and deleted time events that have ever been entered in the HR system or uploaded to it.

All time events that are new to the HR system are entered in table NT1 at the same time that they are uploaded. Therefore, table NT1 contains all unprocessed time events. Table NT1 is saved in cluster B1 in file PCL1.

Table NT1

As explained above, pairs are formed to evaluate time events. This involves linking an "in" posting for an employee with an "out" posting for the same employee. Once they have been formed, the time pairs are further processed. The time pairs formed are then located in table PT (pair table), in cluster B2. Time events that have been processed in this way can then be deleted from table NT1.

Pair formation

2.4.3 Time Evaluation Input

Time Evaluation uses data from the transparent table PCL1 as input data (see Figure 2.39).

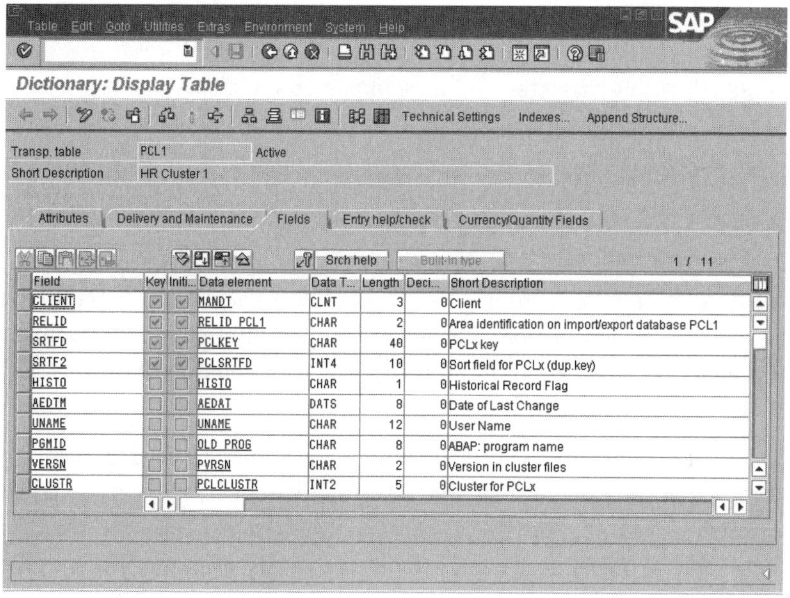

Field	Key	Initi...	Data element	Data T...	Length	Deci...	Short Description
CLIENT	✓	✓	MANDT	CLNT	3	0	Client
RELID	✓	✓	RELID_PCL1	CHAR	2	0	Area identification on import/export database PCL1
SRTFD	✓	✓	PCLKEY	CHAR	40	0	PCLx key
SRTF2	✓	✓	PCLSRTFD	INT4	10	0	Sort field for PCLx (dup.key)
HISTO			HISTO	CHAR	1	0	Historical Record Flag
AEDTM			AEDAT	DATS	8	0	Date of Last Change
UNAME			UNAME	CHAR	12	0	User Name
PGMID			OLD_PROG	CHAR	8	0	ABAP: program name
VERSN			PVRSN	CHAR	2	0	Version in cluster files
CLUSTR			PCLCLUSTR	INT2	5	0	Cluster for PCLx

Figure 2.39 Data Structure of Table PCL1

The following data clusters are stored in the transparent table PCL1:

Time management data clusters

Cluster name	Description
B1	Time events
G1	Group incentive wages

Table 2.5 Data Clusters in Table PCL1

Cluster name	Description
L1	Individual incentive wages
PC	Personal calendar
TC	Trip costs/credit card data
TX	Texts on the infotypes
ZI	PDC interface with cost accounting/materials management

Table 2.5 Data Clusters in Table PCL1 (cont.)

The key data fields in table PCL1 are:

- CLIENT: A three-character field that contains the client.
- RELID: A two-character, alphanumeric field that contains data on the cluster name.
- SRTFD: A forty-character field that contains data on the key.
- SRTF2: A ten-character field for a duplicate key field.
- HISTO: An historical record flag.
- AEDTM: A field that contains the date of the last modification.
- UNAME: A field that contains the name of the user who carried out the last modification.
- CLUSTD: This field, with a length of 3,900 characters, contains the actual data information. Details on how the information is structured cannot be obtained from this field. Only the definition of clusters provides the actual data structure.

Cluster B1   Data structures for Time Evaluation input are defined by cluster B1, which means that you can only read the data structure of CLUSTD if you are familiar with cluster B1. For this reason, attempting direct access to the data structures is futile. The clusters can only be accessed successfully with the programs supplied by SAP.

Cluster B1 contains the following information:

- Time events that have not yet been processed
- The error table ERT
- Selected monthly balances
- Information on the various different status fields for Time Evaluation in table QT

Cluster B1 contains the following tables:

Table	Description
NT1	Pointers to all as yet unprocessed time events, retroactive accounting recognition, pair formation.
NT2	Pointers to all of those time events for which errors occurred during processing.
ERT	All messages from the last evaluation run.
NCT	Date specifications for days on which pair formation must be carried out again.
IFT1	(Used internally by SAP.)
IFT2	Interface table to Incentive Wages. This table describes changes to table WST (time tickets) from cluster B2 to the time that the tickets are already posted in Incentive Wages.
ST	Selected balances that will be sent to the time-recording devices with information on employees when the next download is performed.
QT	Various items of information produced daily, for example, planned work start time, planned working time, public holiday class, and day type.
Version	Details on the version of cluster B1.

Table 2.6 Tables in Cluster B1

The display report for cluster B1 is report RPCLSTB1. It can be called using the menu path **Human Resources · Time Management · Administration · Tools · Tools Selection · Cluster · Display Temporary Time Evaluation Results**.

2.4.4 Time Evaluation Results

The results of Time Evaluation are physically recorded in the database table PCL2. Its makeup and structure are similar to database table PCL1, and the results of Time Evaluation are written to cluster B2.

Time Evaluation results in PCL2

Cluster B2 contains:

▶ Basic data and working time data
▶ Balances, wage types, and quotas
▶ Time pairs and time tickets
▶ Time data
▶ Evaluation status

The following tables are contained in cluster B2:

Table	Description
Basic data and work schedule	
WPBP	Contains information on the employee's basic pay and work center.
PSP	Daily data on the employee's personal work schedule.
Balances, wage types, and quota transactions	
ZES	Daily balances
SALDO	Cumulated balances, in month-end processing, balances from Table TES are added to SALDO.
ZKO	Quota transactions of the period.
ZL	Time wage types, this table is the interface between Time Evaluation and Payroll. The entries in Table ZL contain pointers to the following tables: ALP—alternative payment C1—cost distribution AB—Absences
ALP	Details on a different rate of payment.
C1	Details on cost distribution (account assignment).
VS	Variable balances that can be set by the user.
CVS	Contains the cumulated balances of table VS. CVS is filled automatically.
FEHLER	Messages generated in Time Evaluation are stored here.
KNTAG	Information on whether the employee does core night work. It has no function for several country versions.
Structure of absence quotas	
QTACC	Accrual entitlements, that were generated by Time Evaluation on the relevant accrual date.
QTBASE	Base entitlement that was used as the basis for calculating accrual entitlements.
QTTRANS	Indicates the transfer pool status for each day. Cumulated entitlements are indicated until transferred to the *absence quota* infotype (2006), or until the entitlement has expired.
URLAN	Information on the updating of the *leave entitlement* infotype (0005).

Table 2.7 Tables in Cluster B2

Table	Description
Time pairs and time tickets	
PT	Contains the time pairs generated in pair formation.
WST	Contains the time tickets that have been generated.
CWST	Contains the cumulated time tickets.
AT	Assignment table, which links time pairs and time tickets.

Table 2.7   Tables in Cluster B2 (cont.)

2.5   Payroll Data

Payroll data accounts for another part of the overall dataset. Just like the results of Time Management, Payroll results are presented in clusters. The clusters are, in turn, stored in the database table PCL2. The structure of the database table is broken down into different clusters. Figure 2.40 provides you with an overview of the result data of database table PCL2.

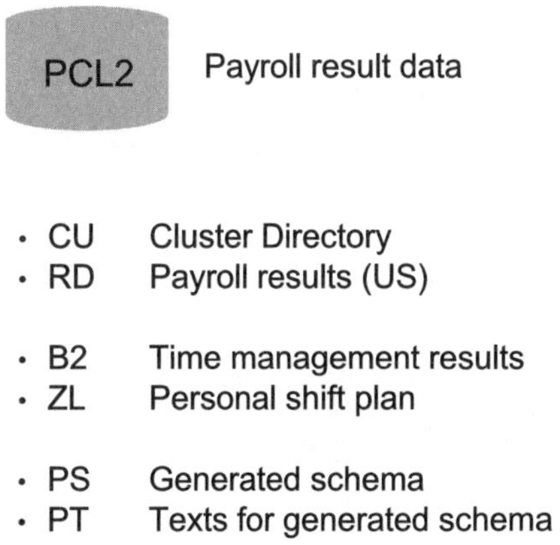

Payroll results

 PCL2   Payroll result data

- CU   Cluster Directory
- RD   Payroll results (US)

- B2   Time management results
- ZL   Personal shift plan

- PS   Generated schema
- PT   Texts for generated schema

Figure 2.40   Clusters in PCL2

2.5.1   Central Payroll Information

The calculation of payments for employees is primarily determined by the taxation and social legislation in each country. For this reason, country-specific grouping is much more significant in the area of Payroll than it is, for example, in the areas of master data, Organizational Management, or Time Management.

Table T500L

Therefore, report programs, data structures, and other elements must also be grouped according to country. Information on this country-specific grouping is stored centrally in table T500L (see Figure 2.41).

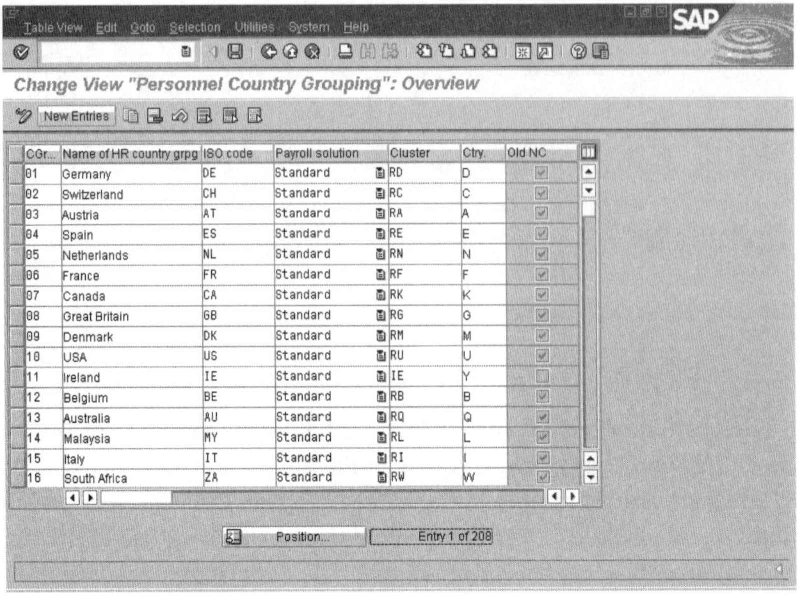

CGr...	Name of HR country grpg	ISO code	Payroll solution	Cluster	Ctry.	Old NC
01	Germany	DE	Standard	RD	D	☑
02	Switzerland	CH	Standard	RC	C	☑
03	Austria	AT	Standard	RA	A	☑
04	Spain	ES	Standard	RE	E	☑
05	Netherlands	NL	Standard	RN	N	☑
06	France	FR	Standard	RF	F	☑
07	Canada	CA	Standard	RK	K	☑
08	Great Britain	GB	Standard	RG	G	☑
09	Denmark	DK	Standard	RM	M	☑
10	USA	US	Standard	RU	U	☑
11	Ireland	IE	Standard	IE	Y	
12	Belgium	BE	Standard	RB	B	☑
13	Australia	AU	Standard	RQ	Q	☑
14	Malaysia	MY	Standard	RL	L	☑
15	Italy	IT	Standard	RI	I	☑
16	South Africa	ZA	Standard	RW	W	☑

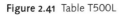

Figure 2.41 Table T500L

The country grouping contains an entry for the ISO code of the country, which is used at various places in the system; there is also information on the name used for the country-specific result cluster. The naming conventions reflected here will be referred to in the following sections.

2.5.2 Payroll Result Data

The cluster structure of database table PCL2 (see Figure 2.42) gives you a rough outline of how data is saved. The cluster structure of database table PCL2 contains the following important data fields:

- The field `CLIENT` contains information about the client.
- The field `RELID` contains the two-character cluster name, which is also known as the *Relations ID*. For the results of German Payroll, for example, the cluster name is RD, and for the results of international Payroll, the cluster name is RX.
- The field `SRTFD` is a forty-character field that contains the key structure for the database table PCL2.
- The field `SRTF2` serves as a sorting field for a duplicate key.
- The field `HISTO` serves as a flag for the historical recording of the dataset.
- The field `AEDTM` contains the date of last modification.

► The field `UNAME` contains a log of the user name in which the last update was carried out on the record.

► The field `PGMID` contains the name of the ABAP program that executed the last update on the cluster.

► The field `CLUSTD` contains the data that is stored in the record.

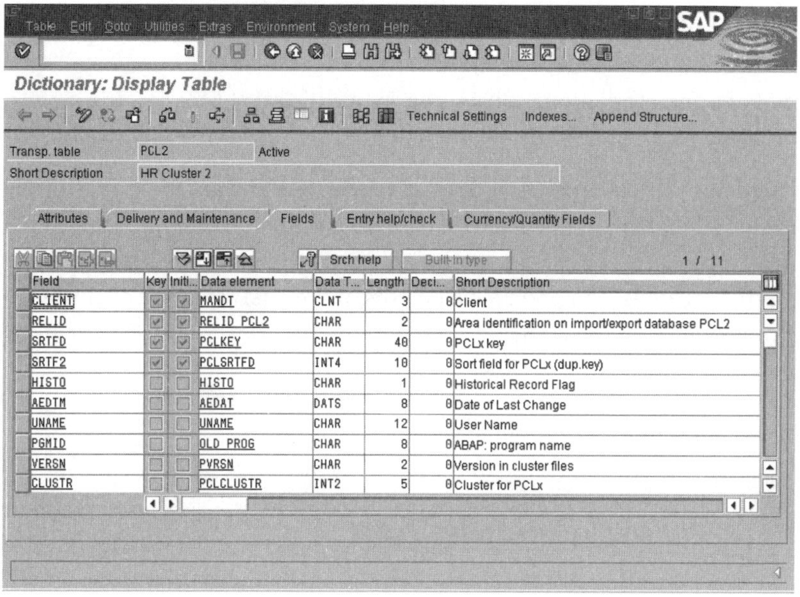

Figure 2.42 Cluster PCL2

The type of content that can be found in field `RELID` is reflected in the following table:

Result cluster

Cluster name	Description
B2	Time Evaluation results
CU	Cluster directory
PS	Personnel calculation schema generated
PT	Texts on schema generated
RX	Results of international payroll
xy	Country-specific results of payroll, where xy is the relation ID, comprised of either Rn (where n is the HR country ID) or the ISO code for the country (in accordance with Table T500L).
ZL	Personal shift schedule

Table 2.8 Contents of RELID Field

The actual data description—showing which data is stored in a cluster and how data field CLUSTR should be read—is written in an include program. The naming convention for this include program is RPCnxyz0.

Where:

▶ N is the name of the database table, which is 1 for PCL1, 2 for PCL2

▶ XY is the name of the cluster, for example, RD for Germany or RX for the international part of the payroll

▶ Z is 0 for international clusters or, for a national cluster, it is the country ID in accordance with table T500L

Therefore, in accordance with the rules cited above, the name of the include program, in the case of a data description for *international payroll,* would be RPC2RX00. Based on this include program, there can be various nested includes. The principle elements of the data structure of cluster RX are defined in program H99PAYDATA.

A first sequence contains a data structure with information about the structure of the key:

```
DATA: BEGIN OF RX-KEY.            "Cluster Key
        INCLUDE STRUCTURE PC200.
DATA: END   OF RX-KEY.
```

In the structure RX-KEY, the structure of the key for cluster RX is described.

Then, all the tables for the appropriate payroll version are defined. Currently, the program coding is as presented below. The coding shown here, therefore, mirrors the information about the structure of cluster RX. The cluster definition should not be changed by the customer. The data structure is generated automatically by SAP.

```
*************************************************************
* H99PAYDATA Data definitions for payroll cluster RX Rest
* of world
*************************************************************
* THIS INCLUDE WAS GENERATED
* BY REPORT:___H99UMACROGENERATOR
* USER:_____KIELISCH
* ON:_____28.05.2002
* DO NOT CHANGE MANUALLY!!!!!!!!!!!!!!!!!!!!
*************************************************************
```

```
*Payroll status information
DATA: BEGIN OF VERSC .
INCLUDE STRUCTURE PC202 .
DATA: END OF VERSC .
*-------------
*Cumulation of absence classes
DATA: BEGIN OF ABC OCCURS 0.
INCLUDE STRUCTURE PC206 .
DATA: END OF ABC .
*-------------
*Payroll result: result table
DATA: BEGIN OF RT OCCURS 0.
INCLUDE STRUCTURE PC207 .
DATA: END OF RT .
*-------------
*Payroll result: cumulated result table
DATA: BEGIN OF CRT OCCURS 0.
INCLUDE STRUCTURE PC208 .
DATA: END OF CRT .
*-------------
*Cost distribution
DATA: BEGIN OF CO OCCURS 0.
INCLUDE STRUCTURE PC20A .
DATA: END OF CO .
*-------------
*Variable assignment
DATA: BEGIN OF VO OCCURS 0.
INCLUDE STRUCTURE PC20C .
DATA: END OF VO .
*-------------
*Payroll result: Leave deduction
DATA: BEGIN OF VCP OCCURS 0.
INCLUDE STRUCTURE PC20D .
DATA: END OF VCP .
*-------------
*Payroll result: gross/net differences
DATA: BEGIN OF DFT OCCURS 0.
INCLUDE STRUCTURE PC20F .
DATA: END OF DFT .
*-------------
```

```
*Payroll result: result table
DATA: BEGIN OF GRT OCCURS 0.
INCLUDE STRUCTURE PC207 .
DATA: END OF GRT .
*-------------
*Payroll result: subsequent time ticket
DATA: BEGIN OF LS OCCURS 0.
INCLUDE STRUCTURE PC20G .
DATA: END OF LS .
*-------------
*Status ID
DATA: BEGIN OF STATUS .
INCLUDE STRUCTURE PC20J .
DATA: END OF STATUS .
*-------------
*Payroll result: Table Arrears
DATA: BEGIN OF ARRRS OCCURS 0.
INCLUDE STRUCTURE PC22Z .
DATA: END OF ARRRS .
*-------------
*Payroll result: Deductions not made
DATA: BEGIN OF DDNTK OCCURS 0.
INCLUDE STRUCTURE PC23E .
DATA: END OF DDNTK .
*-------------
*Payroll result: Month End Accruals
DATA: BEGIN OF ACCR OCCURS 0.
INCLUDE STRUCTURE PC23G .
DATA: END OF ACCR .
*-------------
*International Payroll Result Benefits
DATA: BEGIN OF BENTAB OCCURS 0.
INCLUDE STRUCTURE PC27S .
DATA: END OF BENTAB .
*-------------
*Payroll structure fund management
DATA: BEGIN OF FUND OCCURS 0.
INCLUDE STRUCTURE PC2FUND .
DATA: END OF FUND .
*-------------
```

```
*Frozen average value in payroll result
DATA: BEGIN OF AVERAGE OCCURS 0.
INCLUDE STRUCTURE PC2AVERA .
DATA: END OF AVERAGE .
*-------------
*HR-PAY: Modifiers
DATA: BEGIN OF MODIF OCCURS 0.
INCLUDE STRUCTURE PC214 .
DATA: END OF MODIF .
```

This include contains the various different tables that are consulted in Payroll at runtime; for example, from program coding, we have data definition for administrative information; VERSC, the result table RT; and the table for cumulated results, CRT.

This coding is used to make table and data definitions available when the clusters are accessed with the appropriate import and export modules.

Please note that the database table PCL2, just like other PCLx tables, should not be read or edited directly; rather, it must be accessed via the corresponding import and export modules. Only by using the import and export modules can error-free access to the data be ensured. A particular advantage of import and export modules is that they factor changes that are introduced when versions are updated.

Import/export modules

2.5.3 Cluster Directory

For every employee on the payroll, a payroll directory is created as a cluster directory. Specific payroll results from an individual payroll period can only be accessed later via this cluster directory (see Figure 2.43).

The cluster directory is structured as follows:

▶ The field SEQNR contains a sequence number.

▶ The field ABKRS contains details on the payroll group in which the employee's wages are calculated.

▶ The field FPPER contains information on the for-period of the payroll run, which refers to the period evaluated in the run.

▶ The field FPBEG contains information on the start date of the payroll period (field FPPER); and the field FPEND contains details of the corresponding end date of the payroll period.

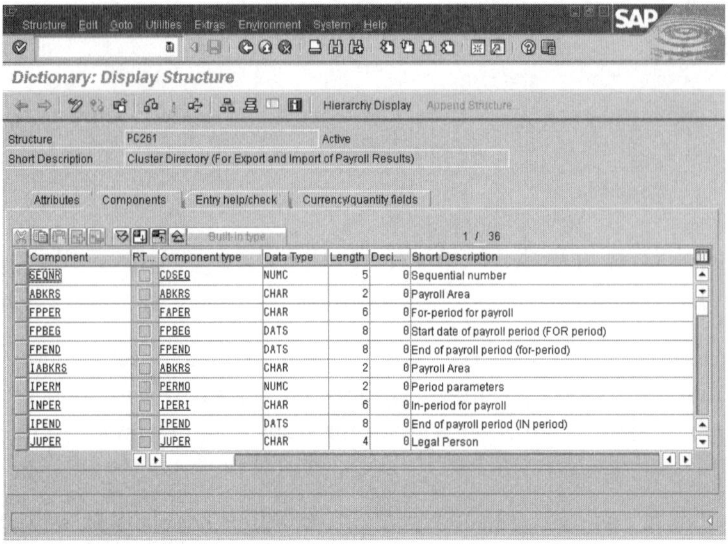

Figure 2.43 Cluster Directory

In- and for-periods In the following example, *in-period* will always refer to the period "in" which the payroll is run, and the *for-period* will always refer to the period "for" which the payroll is run.

The following example should help to explain the difference between for-period and in-period:

The payroll needs to be done for the month of January 2003. The start date for the period is January 1, 2003 and the end date is January 31, 2003. The first or "original payroll run" is done during this same month. Therefore, there would be an entry in the for-period for the month "January 2003". The entry in the in-period field would also read "January 2003".

Then, one month later, there is retroactive accounting. In the for-period field, once again, there is an entry for the month of January 2003, since the retroactive accounting refers to that month. In the in-period field, however, the entry is now for February 2003. With this simulation, you can have any number of combinations for a particular month. This means that the technical conditions will allow for any number of retroactive accounting runs in a single month.

The field IABKRS contains information on the in-period payroll group. The field INPER contains information on the in-period of the payroll run.

In addition, the structure PC261 contains yet more data fields, which will not be mentioned explicitly here.

2.5.4 Payroll Data for Reporting

To make it easier to evaluate payroll results, logical structures are set up for payroll data. These structures are different for each individual country. Figure 2.44 shows a diagram of the data structure of payroll results. The country-specific structures have the name PAYic_RESULT, where "ic" should be replaced by the ISO code for the country. The ISO codes are listed in table T500L.

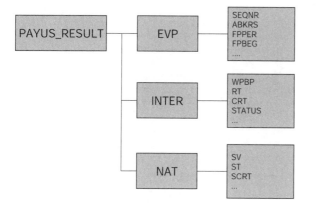

Figure 2.44 Structure of Payroll Results

The data structure for the payroll results for the U.S., for example, is structure PAYUS_RESULT (see Figure 2.45).

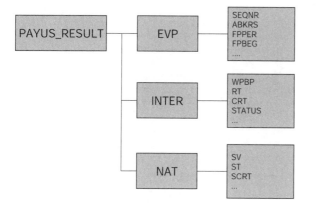

Figure 2.45 Structure PAYUS_RESULT

The structure PAYUS_RESULT contains the components EVP, with directory information, INTER for the international part, and NAT for the country-specific part.

The components INTER and NAT contain substructures with tables or field strings. An example of one such field string is VERSC; an example of a table is table RT (*Result Table*). In the international cluster RX, the country-specific part NAT is a dummy field.

3   Reading and Processing Data

Now that you have an understanding of the data structures of SAP HR, you can use the techniques introduced in this chapter to access HR data. The SAP standard provides many different options that you can use to support the reading and processing of data.

3.1   Logical Databases in HR

To reduce programming efforts, it often helps to use logical databases when creating reports. *Logical databases* are special ABAP programs that provide selection screens, additional aids, and so on. Because access to the database is programmed in the logical databases, accessing the data does not have to be explicitly executed in the actual application program. The logical database reads the data and makes it available to the application program for the evaluation of master data in HR, which occurs with the PUT PERNR statement. In the application program, this statement triggers the event GET PERNR.

Using logical databases

A logical database has yet another advantage—the option of central authorization checking. Because we know from experience that personnel information often contains very sensitive data, we highly recommend that you do not relinquish authorization checking to each application program. You can also take measures to improve performance within logical databases; these measures then take effect in all the related application programs. You define the relationship between reports (more properly called executable ABAP programs of type 1) by entering the logical database in the report attributes (see Figure 3.1).

Authorization check and performance

You can also call logical databases independently of report assignments with function module PDB_PROCESS, although doing so does not have much practical use in HR. It is more feasible to use special, easy-to-manage function modules (because the authorization checks are already included in these function modules) that can take into account the access authorization when reading data. The source text of the logical database <ldb> is stored in program SAPDB<ldb>; logical database PNP is therefore stored under the name SAPDBPNP.

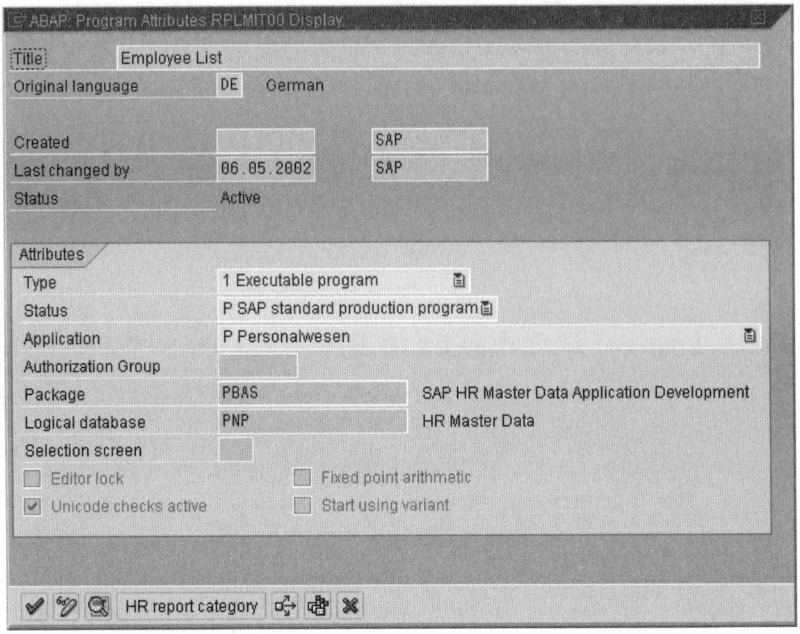

Figure 3.1 Calling a Report with Logical Database PNP

Objects of a logical database

The main objects of a logical database include the following:

▶ Structure

▶ Selection

▶ Database program

Additional functions include documentation and language-dependent texts. You can call any logical database with Transaction SE36 (see example for LDB PCH in Figure 3.2).

GET statement

The *structure* defines the data view of the logical database and determines behavior at runtime. The calling program can contain a GET statement for every node of the structure. At runtime, the event blocks are processed according to the order displayed in the hierarchical structure.

Selection screen

Every executable program can use the selections defined in the logical database and it can insert its own specific selections. The *selection screen* first displays the selections of the logical database followed by the selections of the calling program. The selections of the logical database are defined with the same statements (PARAMETERS, SELECT-OPTIONS, and SELECTION-SCREEN) as are the selections of the executable program.

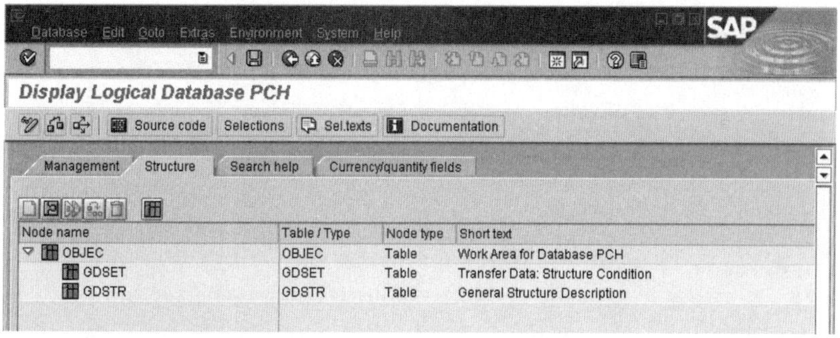

Figure 3.2 Display of the Structure of a Logical Database

The *database program* of a logical database contains all the subprograms called by the ABAP runtime environment during the processing of the logical database. The aforementioned PUT statement is the most important statement; it triggers the corresponding GET event. An access authorization check also occurs here. In HR, the following logical databases are created: PNP and PNPCE for personnel administration; PCH for organizational management; and PAB for applicant administration. The next section describes all but the last of these logical databases, that is, PNP, PNPCE, and PCH.

Database program

3.1.1 Logical Database PNP for Personnel Master Data

The logical database PNP provides the standard selection screen for personnel master data. Personnel master data is selected on the basis of the selections made. After the data is selected, it is also checked to verify if the user who started the report has the necessary authorizations required to read the data. Before you can use the logical database PNP, you must include an entry in the report properties (see Figure 3.1) and the declaration of structure PERNR as a TABLES statement.

Report Categories

You can use Customizing to tailor the selection screen of the personnel master data for each report. When you use the logical database PNP, you can assign a report category to each report. The report category determines which function keys (**Further selections**, **Search helps**, **Sort order**, and selection via the **Org. structure**) are available, which selection parameters appear, and the properties of the selection parameters. Figure 3.3 illustrates the options with the standard report *Employee list* (RPLMIT00).

Assigning report categories

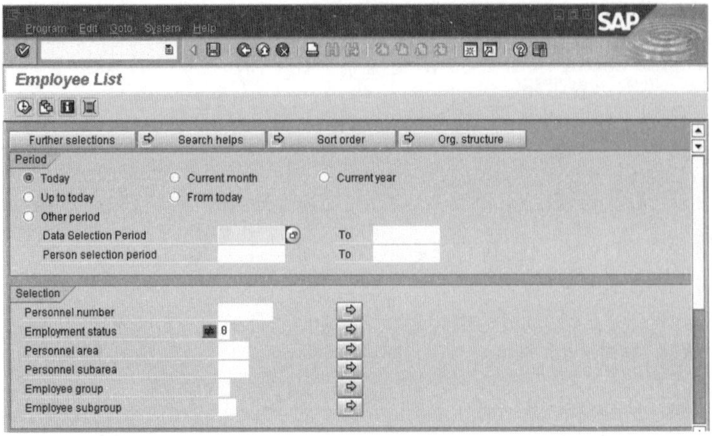

Figure 3.3 Selection Screen of Report RPLMIT00

Displaying the report category

When you call a report, a check occurs first to verify if the report is assigned to a report category. If it is, the selection screen of the assigned report category is displayed. If it isn't, the selection screen is displayed according to the standard SAP assignment of report categories. To view the assigned report category, branch out from the properties display (see Figure 3.1) to the HR report categories. Report category *X__X2201* is assigned to the report illustrated here. Reports are assigned to report categories internally in tables T599W (SAP assignments) and T599B (customer settings). Assigning a report category to a report is not required. If no report category is specified, either the SAP default class, *SPACE*, is used, or, if a customer default class, *00000000*, exists, it is used.

Parameters of the report category

The descriptions of the parameters of the report category (see Figure 3.4) are as follows:

▶ **Data selection period = Employee selection period**
This parameter means that you can make entries only during the data selection period. The entries are automatically transferred as values for the person selection period.

▶ **Matchcode allowed**
When activated, the **Search helps** button is available; this button enables you to select persons using various criteria.

▶ **Sorting allowed**
When activated, the **Sort order** button is available; this button enables you to sort the output using various criteria.

► **Org. str. allowed**

This parameter displays the **Org. structure** button; this button enables you to select by organizational structure.

► **Data select. period**

This parameter determines the corresponding option.

► **Person selection period**

This parameter determines the corresponding option.

► **Payroll area/period/year**

Select the appropriate alternative here. When evaluating payroll results, selection by payroll area, period, and year is recommended.

► **Selection view for dynamic selections**

You can use the selection view that is entered here to determine which selection view is available in **dynamic selection**. You can use the standard selection views or create your own selection views, particularly customer-specific infotypes. If **dynamic selection** does not appear on the selection screen, enter PNP_NO_FREE_SEL as the selection view.

► **Allowable selection criteria**

You maintain the displayed selection fields with the **Allowable selection criteria** folder. All fields that have been defined as selection fields in the logical database must be explicitly permitted for a report category here. When the **First page** field is checked, the selection criterion is displayed at the first call of the report. Fields without this flag can be selected by clicking on the **Further selections** button in the report.

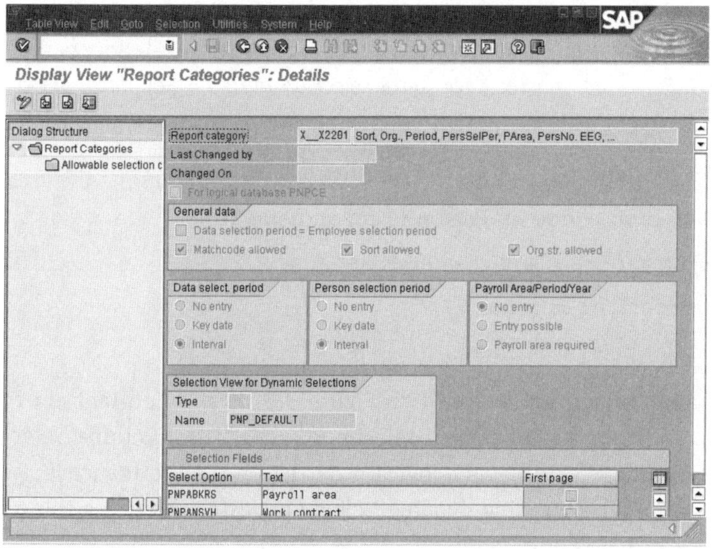

Figure 3.4 Detailed View of a Report CategoryIdentifying SAP report categories

The following naming convention is available to identify SAP report categories. Customer report categories must begin with a number.

Position	Description	Attribute	Description of the attribute
1	Sorting	blank	Do not use sorting
		X	Use sorting
2	Data selection period	Blank	<> Person selection period
		X	= Person selection period
3	Payroll area, period, and year	Blank	The row appears
		X	The row does not appear
		M	The row appears and is a mandatory field
4	Data selection period	0	No entry
		1	Key date
		2	Interval
5	Person selection period	0	No entry
		1	Key date
		2	Interval
6–8	Sequential number	001–999	Freely assigned

Table 3.1 Naming Convention for SAP Report Categories

The following attributes therefore apply to the SAP report category named *X__12001 Personnel master data (data selection period = key date, person selection period = interval)*:

1. Sorting is used
2. Data selection period <> Person selection period
3. Payroll area, period, and year: does not appear
4. Key date for data selection
5. Interval for person selection

Dynamic selection The **Dynamic selections** feature (see Figure 3.5) is an important aid to enhance reports by adding further selection criteria. The additional selections are directly affected by the logical database, and performance is significantly improved by using dynamic selections instead of doing this by coding the selection criteria directly in the report.

You create dynamic selection with Transaction SE80 (Object Navigator): **Edit Object · More · Selection View · Create**. The name of the selection view must begin with "PNP". In the **Tables** dialog window, you enter the database tables of the infotypes (such as PA0006) from which the selection fields are derived. You can use function groups to give the display an informative structure.

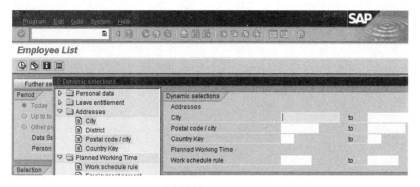

Figure 3.5 Dynamic Selection PNP_DEFAULT

Structure PERNR

During data retrieval, structure PERNR is populated with the most important information for the standard selection—the fields of infotypes 0000 and 0001. In addition, structure PN (available in the report) is supplied from the selection screen. Fields PN-BEGPS and PN-ENDPS provide the data from the beginning and ending date of the **person selection period**. This interval is also the criterion for the selection of the personnel numbers to be processed. Processing includes all personnel numbers that meet the specified selection criteria requirement at any time in the **person selection period**. Fields PN-BEGDA and PN-ENDDA accept the data from the beginning and end date of the **data selection period**.

The INFOTYPES Statement

The internal tables declared by the INFOTYPES statement are populated at the GET PERNR event. Internal table P0006 is created with the command:

```
INFOTYPES 0006.
```

The command creates an internal table in the following form:

```
DATA BEGIN OF p0006 OCCURS 10.
        INCLUDE STRUCTURE p0006.
DATA END OF p0006 VALID BETWEEN begda AND endda.
```

In addition, the INFOTYPES command populates internal table P0006 with all the entries for the selected person at the GET PERNR event. You can also use MODE N, to suppress filling the internal table at the GET PERNR event, thereby reducing used memory.

```
INFOTYPES 0006 MODE N.
```

Using this enhancement of the ABAP statement INFOTYPES, that is, the addition MODE N, can prove helpful for time management infotypes.

You can also use the NAME addition to specify alternative identifiers for the internal table. The following statement declares both internal tables (i0006_old and i0006_new) and populates both tables at the GET PERNR event.

```
INFOTYPES: 0006 NAME i0006_old,
           0006 NAME i0006_new.
```

Evaluation with PROVIDE-ENDPROVIDE

These internal tables can now be processed row-by-row with the LOOP command; however, you can also process internal tables with a specific structure, like the one in the tables of the infotype, with the PROVIDE command. The PROVIDE and ENDPROVIDE statements define a loop through a statement block. The loop can process any number of internal tables of this type, such as tables declared with INFOTYPES. However, in order for the loop to process the internal tables, the tables must have two special columns with the same data type (D, I, N, or T). Within a table, the intervals built from these special columns may not overlap and must be sorted in ascending order. This stipulation exists for fields BEGDA and ENDDA of the internal tables of the infotypes; it excludes infotypes with overlapping records, such as infotypes with the time constraint 3. The internal tables involved may not be changed in the loop.

Evaluation of individual infotypes
A PROVIDE-ENDPROVIDE loop can evaluate a single infotype table. The following statement reads from infotype table P0002 all the rows whose validity interval intersects with the interval given in the data selection period.

```
PROVIDE * FROM p0002
         BETWEEN pn-begda AND pn-endda.
* additional statements
ENDPROVIDE.
```

The beginning date of the first selected entry in the table is set to PN-BEGDA if it is less than PN-BEGDA; the end date for the last selected entry is set to PN-ENDDA if it is greater than PN-ENDDA. The following excerpt shows a sample from the processing. The first and last records are limited, according to the data selection period.

NACHN	VORNA	BEGDA	ENDDA
Meyer	Danny	01/01/2002	07/16/2002
Walsh	Susan	07/17/2002	12/31/2004

Table 3.2 Example of Infotype 0002

If you can maintain the infotype with a subtype, you are limited to one subtype. The limitation occurs with the WHERE condition for the PROVIDE statement. The following example limits the reading of the address (infotype 0006) to subtype 1 (permanent residence). Doing so avoids any overlapping of the intervals.

PROVIDE for subtypes

```
PROVIDE * FROM p0006
          BETWEEN pn-begda AND pn-endda
          WHERE p0006-subty = '1' .
* additional statements
ENDPROVIDE.
```

If 01/01/2002 and 12/31/2004 are selected for the data selection period, processing in the PROVIDE loop can appear as illustrated below.

ORT01	STRAS	BEGDA	ENDDA
Hartford	10 Pioneer Drive	01/01/2002	07/31/2002
NYC	200 W. Broadway	08/01/2002	08/31/2002
NYC	46 Madison Ave.	09/01/2002	12/31/2004

Table 3.3 Example of Infotype 0006, Subtype 1

Infotype 0006 has three valid records in the data selection period, therefore, the loop will run three times.

If you're interested in whether specific fields in the data selection period have changed, and if so, how they have changed, then, you can perform a *projection* onto the field with a simultaneous *contraction* of the validity period. To do so, you must enter the fields to be projected after the PRO-

Projection and Contraction

`VIDE` command. Infotype 0007 (*planned working time*) is present three times for the period under consideration. The table displays two fields from this infotype: SCHKZ (work schedule rule) and ZTERF (employee time management status). Only changes in field ZTERF are of interest, however.

SCHKZ	ZTERF	BEGDA	ENDDA
NORM	0	01/01/2002	07/31/2002
GLZ	2	07/01/2002	10/11/2002
FLEX	2	10/12/2002	12/31/2004

Table 3.4 Example of Infotype 0007 Before Projection

The `PROVIDE` loop now projects onto the `ZTERF` field:

```
PROVIDE zterf FROM p0007
        BETWEEN pn-begda AND pn-endda.
* additional statements
ENDPROVIDE.
```

Processing now occurs only for two part-time periods.

ZTERF	BEGDA	ENDDA
0	01/01/2002	07/31/2002
2	07/01/2002	12/31/2002

Table 3.5 Example of Infotype 0007 After Projection onto ZTERF

PROVIDE with several tables Any number of internal tables can be processed, although experience has proven that using one to five tables is optimal. If several tables are used, they are processed together with a join. Here, all the new time intervals are built when a field in the table being used changes. The following new intervals result from the fields' names in the samples for infotypes 0002 and 0006:

NACHN	VORNA	ORT01	STRAS	BEGDA	ENDDA
Meyer	Danny	Hartford	10 Pioneer Drive	01/01/2002	07/16/2002
Meyer	Danny	Hartford	10 Pioneer Drive	07/17/2002	12/31/2004

NACHN	VORNA	ORT01	STRAS	BEGDA	ENDDA
Walsh	Susan	NYC	200 W. Broadway	08/01/2002	08/31/2002
Walsh	Susan	NYC	46 Madison Ave.	09/01/2002	12/31/2004

Processing occurs with the following coding:

```
PROVIDE * FROM p0002
        * FROM p0006
            BETWEEN pn-begda AND pn-endda
            WHERE p0006-subty = '1'.
* additional statements
ENDPROVIDE.
```

If an infotype is invalid in a partial interval that is generated in a join, you can use the variable created at runtime, pnnnn_valid. If there is a valid partial interval, the variable has the value of X. The following example executes the additional statements only when the interval contains a valid permanent residence:

Query Pnnnn_VALID

```
PROVIDE * FROM p0002
        * FROM p0006
            BETWEEN pn-begda AND pn-endda
            WHERE p0006-subty = '1'.
  IF p0006_valid = 'X'.
* additional statements
  ENDIF.
ENDPROVIDE.
```

You can also combine a join and a projection onto individual fields. The following example illustrates the common processing of the cost center from infotype 0001 and the family and given names from infotype 0002.

```
PROVIDE kostl FROM p0001
        nachn vorna FROM p0002
            BETWEEN pn-begda AND pn-endda
* additional statements
ENDPROVIDE.
```

PAYROLL Event

Access to payroll results

Payroll results are stored as a cluster in cluster table PCL2. Accordingly, they cannot be declared with the `INFOTYPES` command as is master data. In addition to direct access (see Section 3.5.2), you can also evaluate payroll results with a logical database that is integrated into logical database PNP. The `GET PAYROLL` event is triggered to process payroll results. To optimize data selection, important structure information from the cluster table is stored redundantly in the following transparent tables:

- HRPY_RGDIR: Directory information (table RGDIR from cluster CU)
- HRPY_WBBP: Data on work center and basic pay (table WPBP from cluster Rx)

The tables are populated by payroll driver `RPCALCx0`. You can use report `H99U_RGDIR_WPBP` for the payroll results of earlier releases (before 4.6).

PAYROLL structure REVIEW

You can type the `PAYROLL` structure for the report under `NODES`. Enter 900 as the selection screen. Selection of the personnel number at the `GET PERNR` event occurs from the payroll results rather than the master data. You also need to declare `PYORGSCREEN` and `PYTIMESCREEN` for the selection screen in the `TABLES` statement. The selection screen has a slightly different appearance; you can vary it with the report categories just as when processing master data (see Figure 3.6).

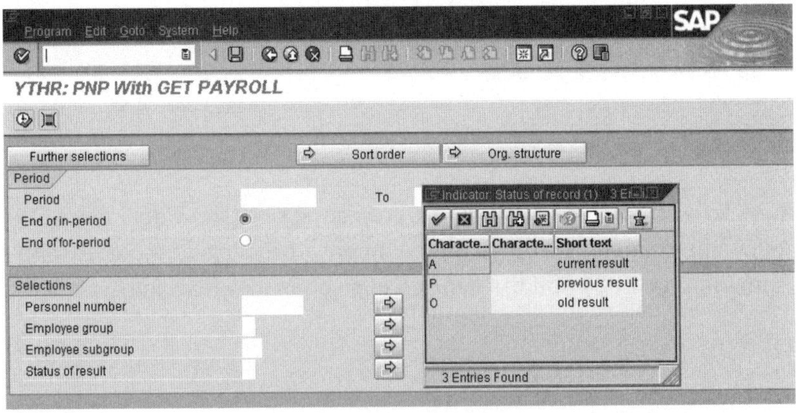

Figure 3.6 Selection Screen for Payroll Results

You can limit the selection of payroll results with the **Status of record indicator**. As indicated in Figure 3.7, the **Payroll results (Cluster)** button must be selected in order for the assignment to the HR payroll report category to occur.

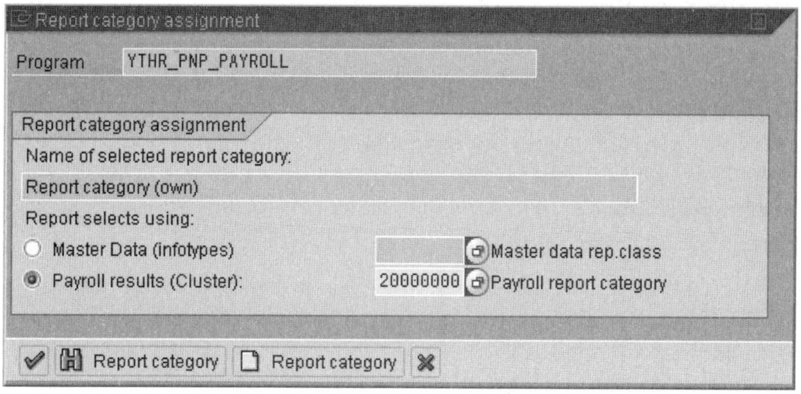

Figure 3.7 Report Category Assignment

You can then maintain the report category in the customer-naming environment that starts with a number. Figure 3.8 shows some entries that control the upper portion of the selection screen.

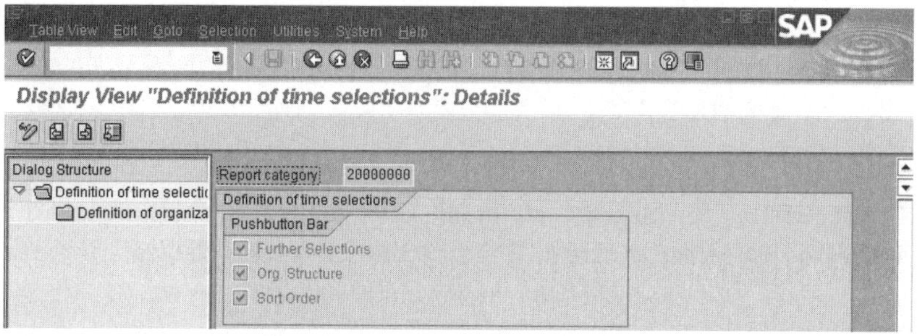

Figure 3.8 Report Category for Payroll Results

Figure 3.9 shows the definition of the criteria for the selections.

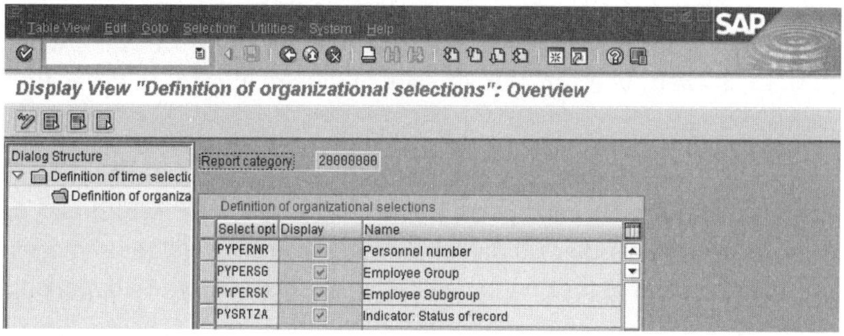

Figure 3.9 Selection Criteria for Payroll Results

A report to evaluate payroll results has the following general structure:

```
REPORT  ythr_pnp_payroll.
TABLES: pernr,
        pyorgscreen, pytimescreen.
NODES: payroll TYPE pay99_result.
INFOTYPES: 0001.
DATA: wa_rt TYPE pc207.
* alternative
* DATA: wa_rt like line of payroll-inter-rt.
GET pernr.
   PROVIDE * FROM p0001
      BETWEEN pn-begps AND pn-endps.
* additional statements
   ENDPROVIDE.
GET payroll.
   LOOP AT payroll-inter-rt
       INTO wa_rt.
* additional statements
   ENDLOOP.
GET pernr LATE.
* additional statements
```

GET PERNR   The declaration for TABLES declares PERNR for the logical database and the entries for the selection screen. The structure of the payroll results is typed under NODES; this example uses the international structure pay99_result. As is the case when evaluating master data, you can work with the INFO-TYPES command, which declares internal table P0001 with header P0001 and then fills it at the GET PERNR event. The wage type results are available in Table payroll-inter-rt. Reading the data requires a work area, which is declared here with the name wa_rt. Declaring the work area occurs with a reference from the row type: with LIKE or directly with TYPE. At the GET PERNR event, you can now process the internal infotype tables first, with PROVIDE.

GET PAYROLL   The payroll structure is filled at the GET PAYROLL event. Statement block GET PAYROLL runs for each payroll period. The runs can result in up to three records (depending on the retroactive accounting and the choices in the selection screen) for a period, which is why it's called the "for period:"

▶ A   Current result

▶ P   Previous result

▶ O   Old result

The tables of the structure can now be processed. The GET PERNR LATE event is triggered if all the payroll results have been processed. At this point, you can output summaries.

GET PERNR LATE

3.1.2   Logical Database PNPCE for Personnel Master Data

SAP R/3 Enterprise expands evaluation options to include a grouped evaluation of several personnel numbers. With one feature, an employee designated as a *concurrently employed person* can have several simultaneous personnel assignments at a company. A special personnel number is assigned for each contract. The assignment of individual personnel numbers to a **central person** (object type CP) combines the individual employment relationships. The object key for the central person is determined by the internal number assignment. An external person ID is also determined and stored in the new infotype 0709 (*person ID*). To employ the functions of concurrent employment and create reports, you must use the logical database PNPCE (CE = concurrent employment). You can also use logical database PNPCE for new developments that don't use CE functions, because it contains all the functions of logical database PNP except the function GET PAYROLL.

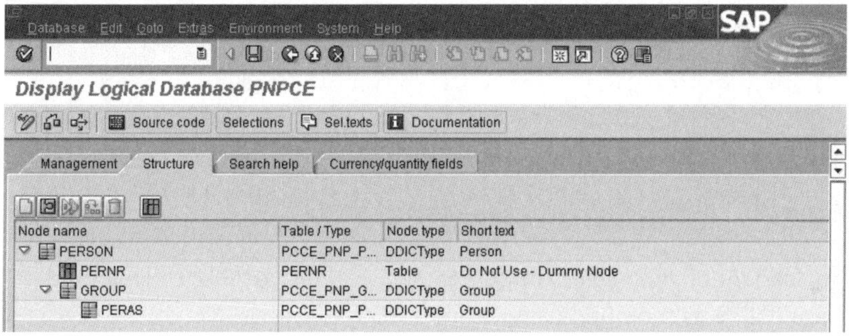

Concurrent Employment

Figure 3.10 Logical Database PNPCE

To use logical database PNPCE, it must be entered in the program attributes (as is also the case for PNP, as described above). As illustrated in Figure 3.10, the logical database contains nodes PERSON, GROUP, and PERAS. Processing at the GET PERNR event is replaced with the event GET PERAS. Additional events are also available: GET GROUP and GET PERSON. To use the events, they must all be declared with NODES. You can also add AS PERSON TABLE to the INFOTYPES statement. If you do not do this and the events GET GROUP and GET PERSON do not appear, it is assumed that the CE functions are unnecessary. In this case, the report runs in PNP mode rather than in CE mode. From here on, we will only use

CE Mode and PNP Mode

the PNP mode in our examples, because only a few companies use CE functions at present, and most reports run only in PNP mode Accordingly, a report with logical database PNPCE and PNP mode has the following structure:

```
REPORT  ythr_pnpce.
TABLES: pernr.
NODES: peras.
INFOTYPES: 0001.
GET peras.
  PROVIDE * FROM p0001
    BETWEEN pn-begda AND pn-endda.
* additional statements
  ENDPROVIDE.
```

The selection screen for this report is illustrated in Figure 3.11.

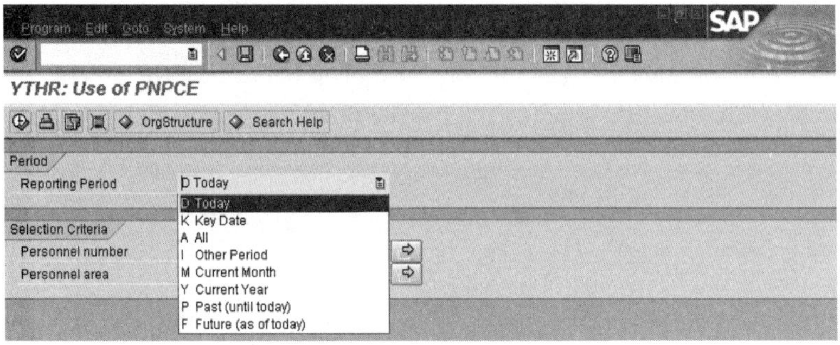

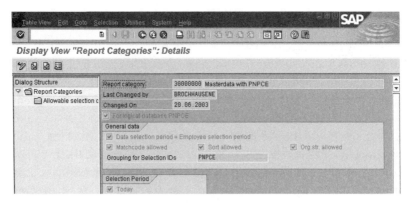

Figure 3.11 Selection Screen of Logical Database PNPCE

You can modify this selection screen, just as the screen for the logical database PNP was modified (see Figure 3.12).

Figure 3.12 Report Category for Logical Database PNPCE

3.1.3 Logical Database PCH for Personnel Planning

The logical database PCH supports the evaluation of data from organizational management and the additional areas of personnel planning, relationships, and evaluation paths. To link a report to the logical database PCH, it must be specified in the report properties (see Figure 3.13), as is also the case for other logical databases.

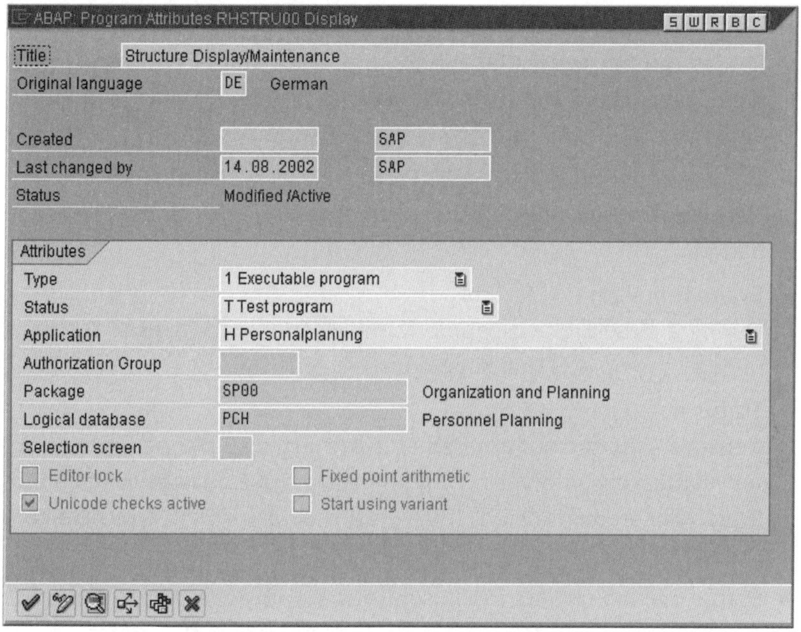

Figure 3.13 PCH Program Attributes

The selection screen for the report of this logical database can be varied as are the reports for databases PNP and PNPCE, but with the use of an alternate selection screen or the macros given below. **PCH selection screen**

As illustrated in Figure 3.14, the selection screen for report `RHSTRU00` contains the following fields: **Fields of the selection screen**

▶ **Plan version** (PCHPLVAR)
   Set to "01" — the current plan variant, for most companies.

▶ **Object type** (PCHOTYPE)
   O for organizational unit, for example.

▶ **Object ID** (PCHOBJID)
   The eight-character ID of the object.

▶ **Search Term** (PCHSEARK)
You can use the **Search Term** field to search for various objects (organizational unit, qualifications, events, and so on) if you don't know their object IDs.

▶ **Object status** (PCHOSTAT)
All **Objects** have one of the following statuses: active, planned, submitted, approved, or denied.

▶ **Data status** (PCHISTAT)
Entries can be made after pushing the **Data status** button. All infotypes have one of the following statuses: active, planned, submitted, approved, or denied.

▶ **Reporting period** (PCHOBEG, PCHOEND, PCHBEGDA, PCHENDDA)
Here you specify the object selection period and the data selection period.

▶ **Evaluation Path** (PCHWEGID)
During a structural evaluation, the evaluation path is used to determine all the objects that should be selected.

▶ **Status vector** (PCHSVECT)
Contains a list of one or more statuses (1 active, 2 planned, and so on) for relationship infotypes. Only infotypes 1001 that have the status listed here are considered. If the field is empty, all infotypes are considered.

▶ **Status overlap** (PCHACTIV)
The simulation activates all relationship infotypes with the status given under **Status vector**. Any change of the status is only temporary and does not affect the stored status of the data.

▶ **Display depth** (PCHDEPTH)
Here you indicate the hierarchy level to which the selected data is to be displayed. In general, there is no limit to the level of hierarchies and therefore, this field remains empty.

▶ **Technical depth** (TDEPTH)
This number sets how many levels of a structure are evaluated. In general, this field is empty.

▶ **Recursion check** (RECURS)
Here you can specify if the object links should be checked for recursions. A recursion is present when an evaluation does not reach an end point.

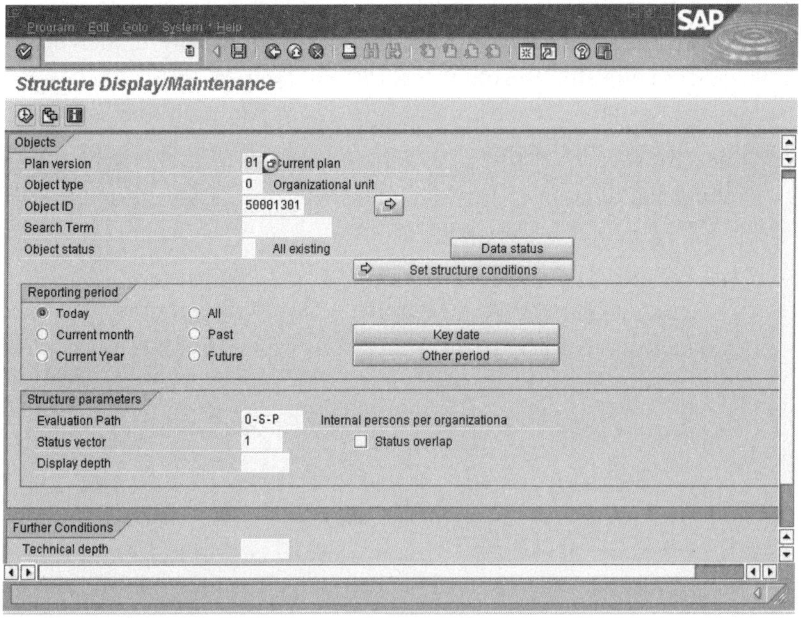

Figure 3.14 PCH Selection Screen

You can also set additional conditions for the selected object. Use the **Set structure conditions** button. For example, for report RHSTRU00, you would see an output similar to the one shown in Figure 3.15.

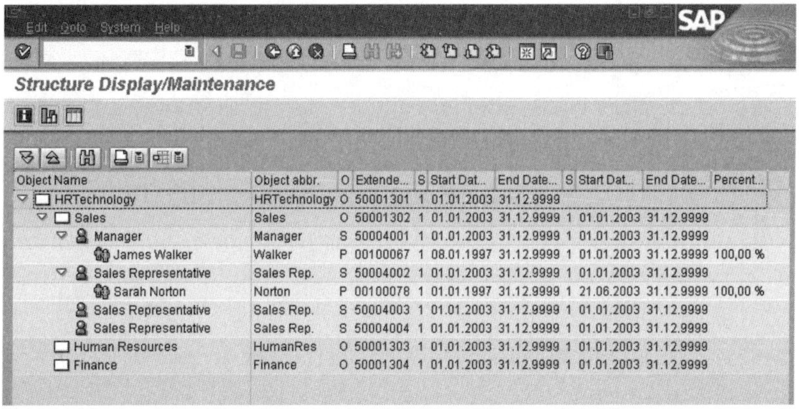

Figure 3.15 RHSTRU00 Output

You can process objects sequentially or structurally by providing an evaluation path as shown in Figure 3.15. In sequential evaluation, the objects are evaluated one after the other according to their key. In structural evaluation, the structure is set up with the evaluation path and evaluated starting from the root object.

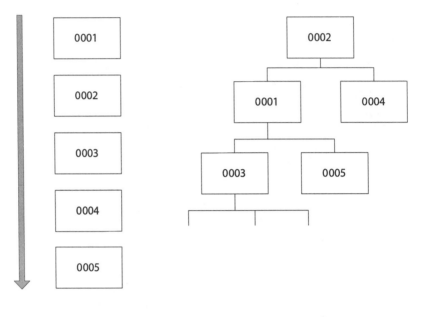

Sequential   Structural

Figure 3.16 Sequential or Structural Evaluation

You must use the TABLES statement of the report to determine if a sequential or structural evaluation occurs.

The following example generates a *sequential* evaluation:

TABLES: OBJEC.

The following example (adding GDSTR) generates a structural evaluation:

TABLES: OBJEC, GDSTR.

As is the case with logical database PNP, structure PC is populated from the selection screen. The structure contains the object selection period (PC-OBEG and PC-OEND) and the data selection period (PC-BEGDA und PC-ENDDA).

The following information is available at the GET OBJEC event:

▶ OBJEC: Structure OBJEC contains all the information from infotype 1000 at the beginning of the object selection period.

▶ GDSTR: For a structural evaluation, structure GDSTR contains the information on the current hierarchy.

▶ STRUC: For a structural evaluation, structure STRUC contains the internal structure information.

▶ Pnnnn: Internal tables Pnnnn are populated with information from organizational management and personnel master data for the infotypes declared with INFOTYPES.

The structure of a report with sequential evaluation appears as follows:

```
REPORT  ythr_pch_seq.
TABLES: objec.
INFOTYPES: 1008.
GET objec.
* additional statements
  PROVIDE * FROM p1008
    BETWEEN pc-begda AND pc-endda.
* additional statements
  ENDPROVIDE.
```

The report reads all the objects of an object type and makes the information of infotype 1008 available in internal table P1008. The table can be processed row-by-row with PROVIDE or LOOP.

When the TABLES statement contains the GDSTR argument, it is understood that a structural evaluation exists. The report parameters then indicate the quantity of objects selected by the evaluation path. Evaluation path O-S-P selects organizational units, positions, and persons, starting from a root object of type O (organizational unit). A report with an evaluation path and access to personnel data has the following rough structure:

```
REPORT  ythr_pch_stru.
TABLES: objec, gdstr.
INFOTYPES: 1008, 0002.
GET objec.
* additional statements
  CASE objec-otype.
```

```
WHEN 'O'.
   PROVIDE * FROM p1008
      BETWEEN pc-begda AND pc-endda.
* additional statements
   ENDPROVIDE.
WHEN 'P'.
   PROVIDE * FROM p0002
      BETWEEN pc-begda AND pc-endda.
* additional statements
   ENDPROVIDE.
ENDCASE.
```

When evaluating infotype tables, note that different infotypes are processed according to each object type. Under GET OBJEC, object type O (*organizational unit*) is queried first. In this example, infotype 1008 is evaluated. If object type P (*person*) is present, infotype 0002 is processed. Supplemental macros are needed to evaluate table infotypes: see Section 3.3.

3.2   Access Without a Logical Database

You can also directly access the tables of infotypes with the SELECT statement, as is true of all database tables. An evaluation of the data from infotype 0002 can appear as follows:

```
PARAMETERS: p_pernr LIKE pa0002-pernr.
TYPES: t_pa0002 TYPE TABLE OF pa0002.
DATA: ta_pa0002 TYPE t_pa0002,
      wa_pa0002 TYPE LINE OF t_pa0002.
SELECT * FROM pa0002
         INTO TABLE ta_pa0002
         WHERE pernr  = p_pernr.
LOOP AT ta_pa0002
   INTO wa_pa0002.
* additional statements
ENDLOOP.
```

Internal table ta_pa0002 now makes all the entries of infotype 0002 available for processing. Of course, you can also limit access further with SELECT, by specifying, for example, a beginning and an end date. As described in Chapter 2, this database table, PA0002, is not identical to the internal table P0002 declared with INFOTYPES. In addition, you must also ensure that no type of authorization check occurs. For less sensitive data, this stipulation is often preferable. The following list shows the reading of the ID of a position, valid on the system date, in the logon language. Plan variant 01 is set here.

```
PARAMETERS: p_plans LIKE hrp1000-objid.
TYPES: t_hrp1000 TYPE TABLE OF hrp1000.
DATA:  wa_hrp1000 TYPE LINE OF t_hrp1000.
SELECT * FROM  hrp1000
        INTO   wa_hrp1000
        WHERE  plvar = '01'
        AND    otype = 'S'
        AND    objid = p_plans
        AND    begda <= sy-datum
        AND    endda >= sy-datum
        AND    langu = sy-langu.
* additional statements
ENDSELECT.
```

You can read and change the HR table without using the logical database. In general, you change the fields of database tables with the UPDATE command. If you want to set the personnel area field to the value of 0002 for a list of objects in infotype 1008 (account assignment features), you can use the following coding:

Changes with UPDATE

```
TABLES: hrp1008.
SELECT-OPTIONS: s_objid FOR hrp1008-objid.
UPDATE hrp1008
        SET    btrtl = '0002'
        WHERE  objid IN s_objid.
IF sy-subrc = 0.
  WRITE: / sy-dbcnt, 'Records were changed.'.
ELSE.
  WRITE: / 'No change.'.
ENDIF.
```

The system field sy-subrc has the value 0 if at least one row of the database table was changed. After the UPDATE command is executed, the system field sy-dbcnt contains the number of updated rows. As was true with the SELECT statement, you must ensure that no authorization checks are performed, nor are any plausibility checks allowed. You should exercise special caution when updating data records, because you can change many data records without verifying that the data was correctly updated.

3.3 Using Macros

3.3.1 Overview

Types of Macros

In addition to subroutines and function modules, macros enable you to create modules for the source text. There are two methods for creating macros. The older method uses RMAC macros. Program code is stored in table TRMAC, and all the macros defined in table TRMAC are available in all programs. No additional declaration is required. A simple example of this kind of macro is the call of a user-dependent breakpoint.

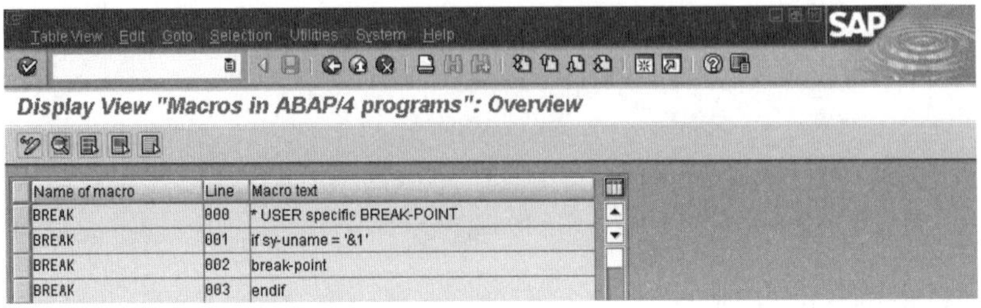

Figure 3.17 Macro Definition in Table TRMAC

The call then occurs with the following:

```
BREAK <sy-uname>.
```

Another option for creating modules for a series of frequently used statements is to define the macro in the source text of a program—usually in a special include. The statements of a macro are bounded by DEFINE and END-OF-DEFINITION.

Sample Macro

An example of this kind of macro is macro rp_provide_from_frst, which reads the first row of an internal infotype table. Parameters <p1> through <p4> are transferred to the macro, where they are available as variables &1 through &4. The parameters transferred here include infotype, subtype, beginning date, and end date. Loop processing ends at the first successful read access. When the read in the LOOP is successful, global variable pnp-sw-found receives the value of 1.

```
DEFINE rp_provide_from_frst.
*    $PNNNN$ = &1.
*    $SUBTY$ = &2.
*    $BEGDA$ = &3.
*    $ENDDA$ = &4.
   pnp-sw-found = '0'.
```

```
loop at &1.
  if &2 <> space.
    check &1-subty = &2.
  endif.
  if &1-begda <= &4 and &1-endda >= &3.
    pnp-sw-found = '1'.
    exit.
  endif.
endloop.
if pnp-sw-found = '0'.
clear &1.
endif.
END-OF-DEFINITION.
```

A call to read the first valid record of the permanent residence in the data selection period would then appear as follows:

```
rp_provide_from_frst p0006 '1' pn-begda pn-endda.
IF pnp-sw-found = '0'.
* additional statements
ENDIF.
```

3.3.2 Macros in Logical Database PNP

The macros in logical database PNP are located in include DBPNPCOM, which also contains include DBPNPMAC.

RP-LOWDATE-HIGHDATE

This RMAC macro defines the constants LOW-DATE and HIGH-DATE. The values are 01/01/1800 and 12/31/9999.

Defining Constants

RP-SEL-EIN-AUS-INIT

If separated employees are not to be considered, you can exclude them with STATUS2 (status employment) ≠ 0.

Separated Employees

Figure 3.18 Suggested Value for Status Employment

You can use RMAC macro `RP-SEL-EIN-AUS-INIT` to set this selection field at the `INITIALIZATION` event.

RP-SET-NAME-FORMAT

Name Formatting   This RMAC macro reads table T522F *(Format for HR Name Format)*. If the macro finds no entry for the report in table T522F, the format is then transferred as '01' into variable `$$FORMAT`. This value ('01') is also required as an argument for reading table T522N, which controls the name formatting.

RP-EDIT-NAME

This RMAC macro formats the name according to the entries in table T522N. The following parameters are transferred:

▶ Infotype structure 0001

▶ Infotype structure 0002 or 0021

▶ Personnel country grouping

▶ Language

```
INFOTYPES: 0001, 0002.
DATA: $edit-name(40),
      $ret-code LIKE sy-subrc.
START-OF-SELECTION.
  rp-set-name-format.
GET pernr.
...
  rp-edit-name p0001 p0002 '01' space.
...
  WRITE: / $$format, $edit-name.
```

Macro `RP-SET-NAME-FORMAT` outputs `$$FORMAT`, and macro `RP-SET-NAME-FORMAT` outputs `$EDIT-NAME` and `$RET-CODE`. If the formatting was unsuccessful, the variable `$RET-CODE` receives a value other than zero (null).

RP_SET_DATA_INTERVAL

Setting the data   You can use macro `RP_SET_DATA_INTERVAL` to change the data selection
selection period   period of individual infotypes or all infotypes at the `START-OF-SELECTION` event. Three parameters are transferred:

- ▶ Infotype
- ▶ Beginning of the data selection period
- ▶ End of the data selection period

The following example limits the selection in the internal table of infotype 0002 to the entry valid today:

```
TABLES: pernr.
INFOTYPES: 0002.
INITIALIZATION.
...
START-OF-SELECTION.
  rp_set_data_interval 'P0002' sy-datum sy-datum.
GET pernr.
...
```

If the limited selection is to be valid for all infotypes, the name of the infotype must be replaced with ALL.

```
  rp_set_data_interval 'ALL' sy-datum sy-datum.
```

RP_PROVIDE_FROM_FRST

Macro RP_PROVIDE_FROM_FRST was mentioned as an example above. It reads the first record of an internal table in the specified selection period. The following parameters are transferred:

Reading the first record

- ▶ Infotype
- ▶ Subtype, if present and wanted; otherwise, SPACE
- ▶ Beginning of the infotype interval
- ▶ End of the infotype interval

Example for a call:

```
rp_provide_from_frst p0002 SPACE sy-datum sy-datum.
```

The infotype table must be sorted in ascending order. This applies if it has not been re-sorted after GET PERNR.

RP_PROVIDE_FROM_LAST

Much like the previous macro, RP_PROVIDE_FROM_FRST, macro RP_PROVIDE_FROM_LAST reads the last valid record in the selection period. The following parameters are transferred:

Reading the last record

- ▶ Infotype
- ▶ Subtype, if present and wanted, otherwise; SPACE
- ▶ Beginning of the infotype interval
- ▶ End of the infotype interval

Example for a call:

```
rp_provide_from_last p0002 SPACE pn-begda pn-endda.
```

The last record from the selection interval is therefore available in the header of the internal table.

RP_READ_INFOTYPE

Reading without the logical database
When using the logical database PNP, an infotype is typically read at the GET PERNR event and made available in the internal infotype table. The reading of an infotype takes into account the required authorization. Outside of the logical database, you can use macro RP_READ_INFOTYPE. For example, you can use this macro if a sequential file with personnel numbers is processed without the logical database and the name is also to be read from infotype 0002. The following parameters are transferred:

- ▶ Personnel number
- ▶ Infotype number
- ▶ Name of the internal infotype table
- ▶ Beginning of the infotype interval
- ▶ End of the infotype interval

The internal infotype table is returned to the calling program. If at least one matching data record is found, the variable pnp-sw-found receives the value of 1. If at least one data record has not been selected because of a missing authorization, the value of pnp-sw-auth-skipped-record is set to 1:

```
INCLUDE dbpnpcom.
PARAMETERS: p_pernr LIKE p0002-pernr.
INFOTYPES: 0002 MODE N.
START-OF-SELECTION.
  rp_read_infotype p_pernr 0002 p0002 sy-datum
    sy-datum.
  IF pnp-sw-found = '0'.
  ...
```

```
   ENDIF.
   IF pnp-sw-auth-skipped-record = '1'.
...
   ENDIF.
```

The coding in the example above shows the reading of infotype 0002 without the logical database PNP. Because include `dbpnpcom` is not linked with the macro definition via the logical database, it must be specified explicitly here. Internal table P0002 with the header of the same name is declared with the `INFOTYPES` command and the addition of `MODE N`. The macro populates the table with an entry for today's date. If no record is found, `pnp-sw-found` has a value of 0; if no authorization exists for this record, `pnp-sw-auth-skipped-record` has the value of 1.

RP_READ_ALL_TIME_ITY

Because of the large volumes of data in time management (infotypes in areas 2000 through 2999), the data should not be read at the `GET PERNR` event. Instead, the declaration of these infotypes occurs with the `INFO-TYPES` statement and the addition of `MODE N`. If you could reduce the data selection period in the report to a meaningful period, this macro would be ideal for populating the previously declared and still empty infotype tables. Two parameters are transferred to determine the selection period:

Reading time management infotypes

▶ Beginning date of the selection

▶ End date of the selection

The internal infotype tables P2001 through P2999 listed under `INFOTYPES` are output.

```
TABLES: pernr.
INFOTYPES: 0001, 2001 MODE n.
GET pernr.
  rp_read_all_time_ity pn-begda pn-endda.
  LOOP AT p2001.
* additional statements
  ENDLOOP.
```

At the `GET PERNR` event, table P2001 is still empty. Once the macro is called, all the records of this infotype in the data selection period are present in the internal table pP2001.

RP_UPDATE

Changing infotype information

You can change infotype information directly with macro RP_UPDATE. The following parameters are used:

▶ Name of the internal infotype table before the change

▶ Name of the internal infotype table after the change

▶ Master data "A" or applicant data "B"

The key fields cannot be changed. The following listing shows the change of the retroactive accounting date in infotype 0003 (*payroll status*) to the value given in parameter rrnew.

```
TABLES: pernr.
PARAMETERS: rrnew LIKE p0003-rrdat DEFAULT '20020701'.
INFOTYPES: 0003 NAME p0003_o,
           0003 NAME p0003_n MODE N.
DATA: mess_return TYPE bapireturn1.
GET pernr.
  clear: p0003_n, p0003_n[].
  CALL FUNCTION 'BAPI_EMPLOYEET_ENQUEUE'
    EXPORTING
      number        = pernr-pernr
      validitybegin = pn-begda
    IMPORTING
      return        = mess_return.
  IF mess_return IS INITIAL.
    LOOP AT p0003_o.
      p0003_n = p0003_o.
      IF rrnew < p0003_n-rrdat
        OR p0003_n-rrdat IS INITIAL.
        p0003_n-rrdat = rrnew.
      ENDIF.
      APPEND p0003_n.
    ENDLOOP.
    rp_update p0003_o p0003_n 'A'.
  ELSE.
* additional statement
  ENDIF.
  CALL FUNCTION 'BAPI_EMPLOYEET_DEQUEUE'
    EXPORTING
      number        = pernr-pernr
      validitybegin = pn-begda.
```

First, two internal infotype tables are defined, although only the first table is populated at GET PERNR. Accordingly, the header and table p0003_n must be initialized. The personnel number must be blocked before it can be changed with the macro. The personnel number is unblocked after the change. Function modules BAPI_EMPLOYEET_ENQUEUE and BAPI_EMPLOYEET_DEQUEUE handle the consideration of the blocking logic here. The use of function modules is explored in more detail in the following section.

3.3.3 Macros in Logical Database PCH

The macros for logical database PCH are stored in include DBPCHCOM. The following three macros are the most frequently used.

RH-SEL-ONE-OBJID

This macro ensures that only one object ID and no list can be entered. This macro has the following form:

Object ID

```
INITIALIZATION.
  rh-sel-one-objid.
```

RH-SEL-KEYDATE

You can use this macro to limit the selection options to one key date:

Key date

```
INITIALIZATION.
  rh-sel-keydate.
```

Figure 3.19 shows an excerpt of a standard selection screen with selection options for several object IDs and alternatives for the evaluation period. In Figure 3.20, the options have been limited by the use of macros rh-sel-one-objid and rh-sel-keydate.

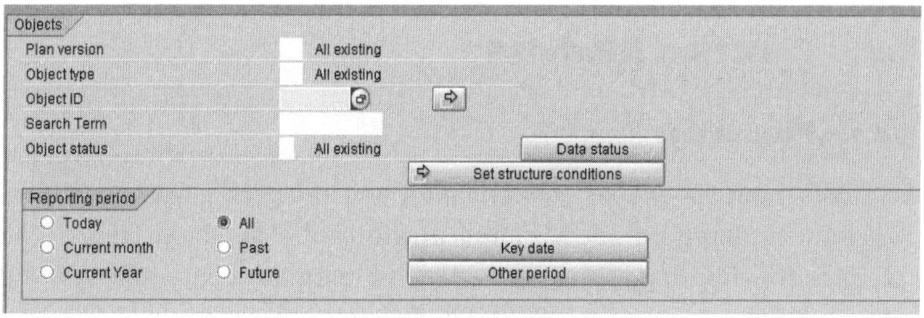

Figure 3.19 Selection Screen with an Object ID and Period

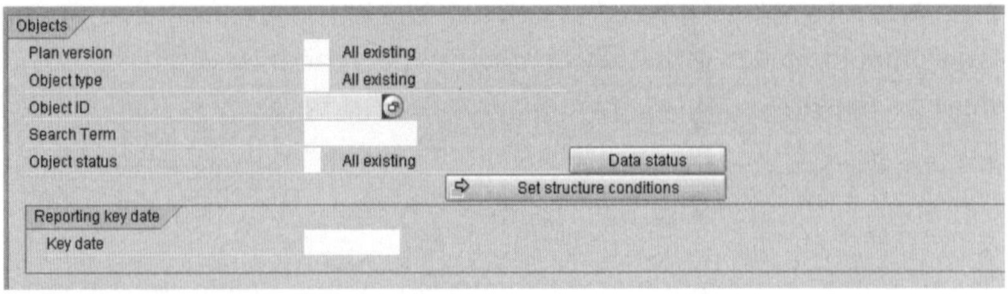

Figure 3.20 Selection Screen with an Object ID and Key Date

RH-GET-TBDAT

Table infotypes   You can use macro `RH-GET-TBDAT` to read the data of table infotypes. The following parameters are transferred:

▶ Infotype

▶ Reference field of the infotype to the table

▶ Internal table in the report to record data

The internal table must be declared with structure `PTnnnn`.

The following example shows the statements required to read table infotype 1002 in the program:

```
INFOTYPES: 1002.
DATA: i_pt1002 TYPE TABLE OF pt1002 WITH HEADER LINE.
...
PROVIDE * FROM p1002
 BETWEEN pc-begda AND pc-endda.
  rh-get-tbdat p91002-infty p1002-tabnr i_pt1002.
  LOOP AT i_pt1002.
* additional statements
  ENDLOOP.
ENDPROVIDE.
```

3.4   Function Modules

3.4.1   Properties

Function modules enable encapsulation and reuse of global functions. Function modules are administered in the central function library. The interface for subprograms is defined in the program text. However, the interface for function modules is defined with the Function Builder (Transaction SE37). *Function modules* are procedures with coding stored inside special ABAP programs, type F function groups. The function groups typically combine several topically related function modules. Function modules can be called from all ABAP programs.

When programming the call of a function module, we recommend that you use the sample function of the ABAP Editor. You only need to enter the name or use the search help. The sample function inserts both the call (with required and optional parameters) and the handling of exceptions (with a MESSAGE statement) into the calling program. Parameters are assigned by their names; the formal parameters of the function module are always listed on the left.

Export parameters are transferred by the calling program; optional parameters don't need to be itemized; and suggested values are displayed. The calling program receives import parameters. Changing parameters are both transferred and received; optional parameters don't need to be itemized; and suggested values are displayed.

Exceptions are assigned values, starting with one, according to their declaration sequence. The same value can be assigned to multiple exceptions. You can use the WHEN OTHERS statement to assign an additional value to all the non-itemized exceptions. If you specify the exceptions in the calling program, the values are placed in the system field sy-subrc if an exception occurs. The lack of a specification creates a runtime error or a message, which is dependent upon which statement in the function module triggered the exception.

Sample function

Parameters

Exceptions

3.4.2 Using Function Modules in HR

Using the function modules that are delivered with the system significantly simplifies comprehensive processing in HR and other applications. Before you set up major functions in programs or with function modules, you should check to see if the functions don't already exist (either completely or partially) in the standard function modules. A successful search can save you a lot of considerable effort.

Most function modules in HR begin with "RP" or "HR". If you're looking for a way to determine the entry date of an employee, search in the Repository Information System with "HR*" and "RP*" for the selection criterion function module and with "HR*ENTRY*" and "HR*HIRE*" (see Figure 3.21). You can access the Repository Information System with the application hierarchy (SE81); use the **Information system** button.

Searching for function modules

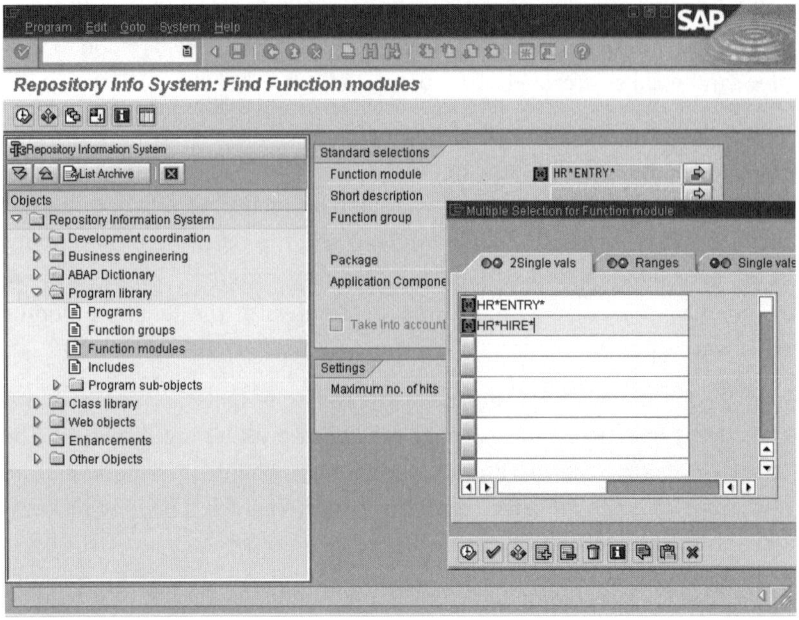

Figure 3.21 Searching for a Function Module

Figure 3.22 shows the results of the search. The three function modules of function group RPAI are suitable. Here, you must use the documentation of the function module and an analysis of the interface to decide which of the three function modules is most appropriate. In this case, function module HR_ENTRY_DATE contains the most comprehensive functions.

The function module first reads the feature ENTRY. Section 3.4.3 discusses the meaning and handling of features. This feature determines what infotypes are evaluated and the order in which to evaluate the infotypes to determine the entry date:

▶ 0000 Personnel actions

▶ 0001 Organizational assignment

▶ 0016 Contract elements

▶ 00041 Date specifications

In addition to the ENTRYDATE field, the ENTRY_DATES table can be output. This table contains all the entry dates that were determined. You can customize the table to meet your individual needs in customer exit HRRPAI01. The following example shows the call of this function module:

```
REPORT  ythr_entry.
TABLES: pernr.
INFOTYPES: 0002.
DATA: entry_date LIKE p0000-begda.
GET pernr.
  CALL FUNCTION 'HR_ENTRY_DATE'
    EXPORTING
      persnr                = pernr-pernr
    IMPORTING
      entrydate             = entry_date
*     TABLES
*       entry_dates         =
    EXCEPTIONS
      entry_date_not_found = 1
      pernr_not_assigned   = 2
      OTHERS               = 3.
  IF sy-subrc <> 0.
    CLEAR entry_date.
    MESSAGE e016(rp) WITH
'Error while determining the entry date.'.
  ENDIF.
  rp_provide_from_last p0002 space pn-begda pn-endda.
  WRITE: / p0002-nachn, entry_date DD/MM/YYYY.
```

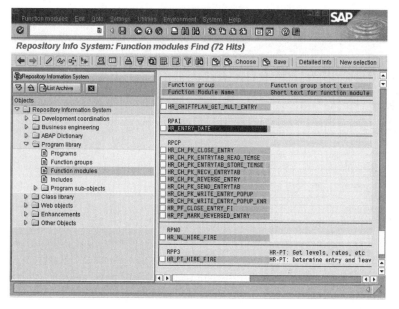

Figure 3.22 Results of the Search

The personnel number is transferred to the function module as an export parameter. The export parameter returns the entry date after evaluation, according to the rules given in the ENTRY feature. The transfer to ENTRY_ DATES does not occur here. If an error occurs while determining the entry date, processing is stopped.

3.4.3 Using Features

Two special function modules are used frequently in HR:

▶ HR_FEATURE_BACKFIELD (Reading a feature with field return)

▶ HR_FEATURE_BACKTABLE (Reading a feature with table return)

Purpose of features *Features* serve to determine certain values based upon HR structures. These return values or results can be individual values, structures, or tables. Using features enables you to do the mapping of decision trees without requiring any programming. The SAP standard supports you with its numerous features that determine suggested values and control system flows.

Maintaining features You maintain features with Transaction PE03. The three most important elements of a feature are:

▶ Attribute

▶ Structure

▶ Decision tree

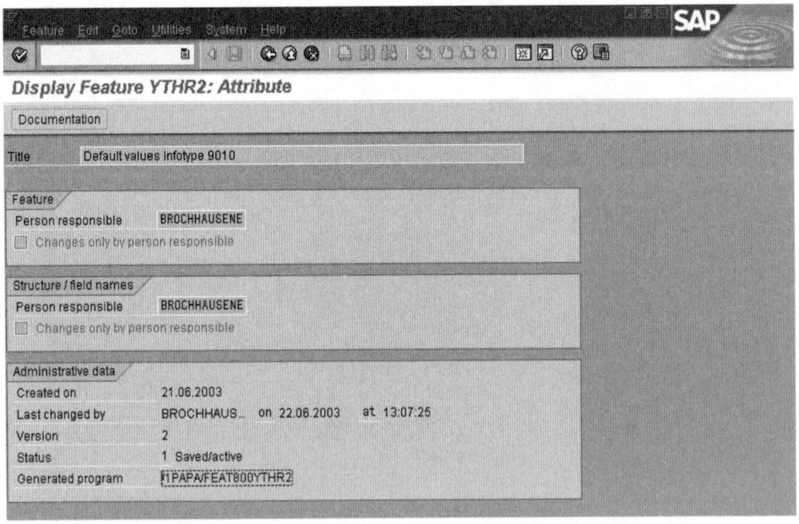

Figure 3.23 The Attribute Feature

The *attribute* (see Figure 3.23) shows the persons responsible for the entire feature and for maintenance of the structure. Using this feature element, you can regulate whether this person may be the only person responsible for maintenance of the feature and the structure. A program of type S (subroutines pool) is created from the specifications in the decision tree when the feature is activated. The feature is also assigned to countries and components.

Attribute

A *structure* for setting up the decision tree must be assigned to every feature. The specifications of the fields of the structure can be queried in the decision nodes. Structures are defined in the ABAP Dictionary. The marked fields can then be used in the decision tree. The **Employee Group** and **Employee Subgroup** fields are highlighted in Figure 3.24.

Structure

You can also enter a field name in **Back value field name** to enable more user-friendly maintenance in the decision tree. When the field specified here has a check table or refers to a domain with fixed value, these values are present in tree maintenance as entry helps and text display. The **Passing type** determines if the return occurs as a field (1) or a table (2). Accordingly, when a program calls the feature, ensure that the transfer type is compatible and that the fields required for the decision are populated.

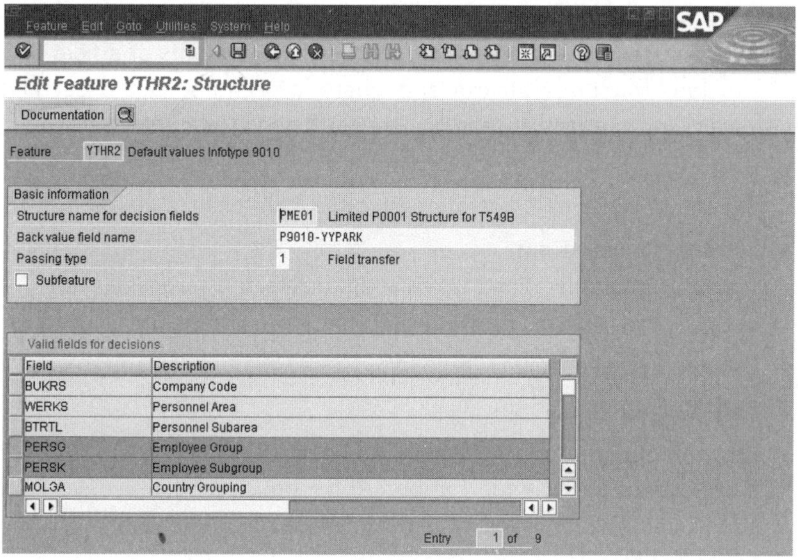

Figure 3.24 The Structure of Feature YTHR2

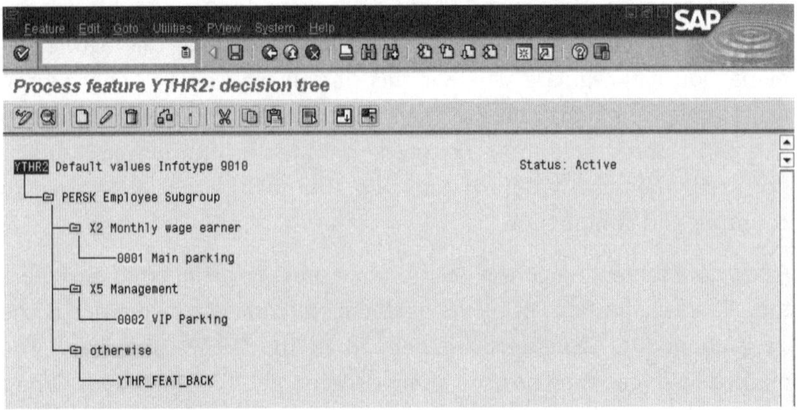

Figure 3.25 The Decision Tree

Maintaining the decision tree

You can maintain the decision tree in tree maintenance and in table maintenance. Figure 3.25 illustrates tree maintenance with various processing functions, including create, change, or delete. Maintenance of tables occurs directly. The following operations are available for tree and table maintenance:

- **Return operations**
  This operation defines the return values of the feature.
- **Decision operations**
  You can use decision operations to query the contents of a field or a decision structure. You can also query in sections with offset and length, and use smaller than (<), greater than (>), and equals to (=).
- **Next operations**
  You can only use next operations in table maintenance.
- **Subfeature operations**
  The subfeature operation calls an additional feature. Processing continues with this feature.
- **Debugging operations**
- **Error operations**
- **Program operations**
  If evaluations become too complex or if more data is needed, you can also call an ABAP routine in a customer-specific subroutine pool. The pool must contain a subprogram called `EXT_CALL_F` (for field return) or `EXT_CALL_T` (for table return). The subprograms must then populate the return value `BACK` or `BACK_TAB`. In addition, you can set `STATUS` to 2 if an error occurs.

The following code is generated at activation and saved under the name **Example** /1papa/feat800ythr2:

```
program /1papa/feat800ythr2.
* Compilation of YTHR2
form call_549b using back status struc structure pme01.
set extended check off.
case struc-persk .
when 'X2' .
back = '0001' .
when 'X5' .
back = '0002' .
when others .
perform ext_call_f(ythr_feat_back)
using 'YTHR2' back status struc .
endcase.
set extended check on.
endform.
```

Program YTHR_FEAT_BACK is called when *persk* does not have the specification "X2" or "X5". The return value is determined in routine ext_call_f.

```
PROGRAM ythr_feat_back.
FORM ext_call_f
     USING  feat back status pme01 STRUCTURE pme01.
  IF pme01-werks = '0003'.
    back = '0002'.
  ELSE.
    back = '0001'.
  ENDIF.
ENDFORM.
```

Function module HR_FEATURE_BACKFIELD calls feature YTHR2:

```
REPORT  ythr_feat_call .
TABLES: pernr.
INFOTYPES: 0001.
DATA: pme01 TYPE pme01,
      park  LIKE p9010-yypark.
GET pernr.
```

```
    rp_provide_from_last p0001 space pn-begda pn-endda.
    MOVE-CORRESPONDING p0001 TO pme01.
    CALL FUNCTION 'HR_FEATURE_BACKFIELD'
      EXPORTING
        feature                              = 'YTHR2'
        struc_content                        = pme01
*       KIND_OF_ERROR                        =
      IMPORTING
        back                                 = park
*     CHANGING
*       STATUS                               =
      EXCEPTIONS
        dummy                                = 1
        error_operation                      = 2
        No_backvalue                         = 3
        feature_not_generated                = 4
        invalid_sign_in_funid                = 5
        field_in_report_tab_in_pe03          = 6
        OTHERS                               = 7.
  IF sy-subrc <> 0.
    MESSAGE e016(rp) WITH
      'Error at feature YTHR2'.
  ENDIF.
  WRITE: / p0001-werks, p0001-persg, p0001-persk, park.
```

Structure PME01 is populated with the last valid values of infotype 0001. In
the calling program, the park field is populated from the return value of
the feature.

3.5 Accessing Clusters

Chapter 2 referred to storing data in clusters. This form of storage has great
significance in payroll and time management. In this section, we first give
you an overview of clusters and then examine clusters specifically in payroll results.

3.5.1 Overview of Clusters

Cluster TX   You can store user-defined text with infotypes. Because this use of infotypes is not very complex, it will serve you well as an introductory example. Customizing is what determines which infotypes will allow the entry
of additional text. If a user-defined text is entered while maintaining info-

types, it is stored in cluster TX of table PCL1. The descriptions of the key and the data objects are located in include RPC1TX00. Includes require the naming conventions described in Chapter 2. You can use the ABAP commands IMPORT and EXPORT to read and write clusters. You will use these elementary commands only in the rarest of cases. It is therefore preferable to use standard SAP macros and function modules.

For macros defined in table TRMAC or in includes, naming convention RP-IMP-Cn-xy applies for importing clusters and naming convention RP-EXP-Cn-xy applies for exporting clusters. For cluster table PCL1, n has the value 1; for PCL2, n has the value 2; and so on. The name of the cluster is in the last two positions, xy. Macro RP-IMP-C1-TX is used to import clusters TX from Table PCL1.

Macros

In addition to providing consistency for the importing and exporting of clusters, another advantage of using macros is the reading and writing of data with special buffering. Cluster authorization is also checked during access.

```
REPORT  ythr_read_txt.
INCLUDE rpc1tx00.
INCLUDE rpppxd00.
DATA: BEGIN OF COMMON PART buffer.
      INCLUDE rpppxd10.
DATA: END OF COMMON PART buffer.
TABLES: pernr, pcl1, pcl2.
INFOTYPES: 0016.
GET pernr.
  rp_provide_from_last p0016 space pn-begda pn-endda.
  MOVE-CORRESPONDING p0016 TO tx-key.
  rp-imp-c1-tx.
  WRITE: / pernr-pernr.
  IF sy-subrc = 0.
    LOOP AT ptext.
      WRITE: / ptext-line.
    ENDLOOP.
  ENDIF.
END-OF-SELECTION.
  INCLUDE rpppxm00.
```

The above listing reads the user-defined text of infotype 0016 (*contract elements*). Include rpc1tx00 contains the special data definition for cluster

TX. The general data definitions for buffering when using macros are found in includes `rpppxd00` and `rpppxd10`. In addition, the subroutines required here must be incorporated with include `rpppxm00`. Cluster tables PCL1 and PCL2 are recorded in the `TABLES` statement. Before the cluster can be read with macro `rp-imp-c1-tx`, the `tx-key` key defined in include `rpcltx00` must be populated. When the read is successful, `sy-subrc` receives the value of 0 and you can access the individual data objects of cluster table `ptext` in this case.

3.5.2 Payroll Results

Cluster of payroll results

The payroll programs of individual country versions (`RPCALCn0`, where n = country version) write the results into cluster table PCL2. An overview of all payroll results of the personnel number are therefore stored in cluster CU. A data object in the cluster, Table RGDIR, contains a row for each payroll. Successful retroactive accounting means that several payrolls can exist for each payroll period. The rows of Table RGDIR also contain the sequence number (SEQNR) for access to the complete payroll results. As noted in Chapter 2, the results are stored in country-specific clusters (Rn), with RU as an example for the U.S. You can use report `H99_DISPLAY_PAYRESULT` to display the payroll results. Figure 3.26 illustrates the payroll results of a personnel number with selected fields from Table RGDIR. In the example, period 03/2003 was corrected twice with retroactive accounting. Three payroll records exist. The display includes the current indicator, the for-period, the in-period, and the sequential number for access to the individual records of cluster Rn.

Current Indicator	For-Period	In-Period	Sequential number
O	01.2003	01.2003	00025
P		02.2003	00026
A		03.2003	00028
P	02.2003	02.2003	00027
A		03.2003	00029
A	03.2003	03.2003	00030

Figure 3.26 Displaying Payroll Results

Primary Procedure

The primary procedure for reading payroll results consists of three steps:

1. The cluster directory (cluster CU) is read. The read occurs best with functions module `CU_READ_RGDIR`.

2. The payroll results of interest are selected from table RGDIR. The selection can occur with various function modules.

3. The selected payroll results are read from the country-specific cluster Rn. The read occurs best with function module PYXX_READ_PAYROLL_RESULT.

The following report illustrates this procedure. The last payroll of personnel number in the data selection period is to be read. The contents of two fields from the stored data on bank transfer (direct deposit) in table BT are to be displayed.

The data definition declares the internal tables for the directory of payrolls, t_rgdir, and the complex structure of the payroll results, t_result. In addition, a work area for the bank table and a variable for the number of the payroll result are also required. **Data definition**

The cluster directory is read in the first step. If payroll results are present, they are made available in the internal table t_rgdir. This table functions as an import parameter for function module CD_READ_LAST, which determines the last current record. With this number, the payroll result (for the U.S.) is read from cluster RU and placed into a complex structure t_result for further processing. Table bt is a component of this structure: the contents of this table are output in a LOOP. **Processing steps**

```
REPORT  ythr_read_payroll.
DATA: t_rgdir TYPE pc261 OCCURS 0,
      t_result TYPE payus_result,
      w_bt TYPE LINE OF hrpay99_bt,
      out_seqnr LIKE pc261-seqnr.
TABLES: pernr.
GET pernr.
*1. ----
  CALL FUNCTION 'CU_READ_RGDIR'
    EXPORTING
      persnr          = pernr-pernr
    TABLES
      in_rgdir        = t_rgdir
    EXCEPTIONS
      no_record_found = 1
      OTHERS          = 2.
  IF sy-subrc <> 0.
    WRITE: / 'No payroll results for ',
      pernr-pernr.
  ENDIF.
```

```
*2. ----
  CALL FUNCTION 'CD_READ_LAST'
    EXPORTING
      begin_date      = pn-begda
      end_date        = pn-endda
    IMPORTING
      out_seqnr       = out_seqnr
    TABLES
      rgdir           = t_rgdir
    EXCEPTIONS
      no_record_found = 1
      OTHERS          = 2.
  IF sy-subrc <> 0.
    WRITE: / 'Error at ', pernr-pernr.
  ENDIF.
*3. ----
  CALL FUNCTION 'PYXX_READ_PAYROLL_RESULT'
    EXPORTING
      clusterid                    = 'RU'
      employeenumber               = pernr-pernr
      sequencenumber               = out_seqnr
    CHANGING
      payroll_result               = t_result
    EXCEPTIONS
      illegal_isocode_or_clusterid = 1
      error_generating_import      = 2
      import_mismatch_error        = 3
      subpool_dir_full             = 4
      no_read_authority            = 5
      no_record_found              = 6
      versions_do_not_match        = 7
      OTHERS                       = 8.
  IF sy-subrc <> 0.
    WRITE: / 'Error at ', pernr-pernr.
  ENDIF.
  LOOP AT t_result-inter-bt INTO w_bt.
    WRITE: / pernr-pernr, out_seqnr,
      w_bt-bankl, w_bt-bankn.
  ENDLOOP.
```

If the individual steps don't require any special processing, you can use function module PYXX_GET_EVALUATION_PERIODS. The output includes all the new payroll results generated in the selected period: all those with status indicator "A" and their immediate predecessors, those with status indicator "P." The data definitions are similar to those of the previous example. However, because we're dealing with an internal table with several payroll results here, processing occurs in a LOOP.

```
REPORT  ythr_read_payroll.
DATA: t_rgdir TYPE table of pc261,
      t_result TYPE table of payus_result,
      w_result TYPE payus_result,
      w_bt TYPE LINE OF hrpay99_bt,
      period(6).
TABLES: pernr.
period = pn-begda(6).
GET pernr.
  CALL FUNCTION 'PYXX_GET_EVALUATION_PERIODS'
    EXPORTING
      clusterid           = 'RD'
      employeenumber      = pernr-pernr
      inper               = period
      inper_modif         = '01'
    TABLES
      rgdir               = t_rgdir
      evaluated_periods   = t_result
    EXCEPTIONS
      No_payroll_results  = 1
      No_entry_found_on_cu = 2
      import_error        = 3
      OTHERS              = 4.
  IF sy-subrc <> 0.
    WRITE: / 'Error at ', pernr-pernr.
  ENDIF.
  LOOP AT t_result INTO w_result.
    LOOP AT w_result-inter-bt INTO w_bt.
      WRITE: / pernr-pernr, w_result-evp-seqnr,
        w_bt-bankl, w_bt-bankn.
    ENDLOOP.
  ENDLOOP.
```

3.6 Enhancements with Customer Exits and Business Add-Ins

You can use customer exits and business add-ins (BAdIs) to enhance the SAP standard without any modifications. Both techniques insert your own functions into standard SAP applications without modifying the SAP objects. The IMG refers to the existence of customer exits and BAdIs. Figure 3.27 illustrates these references to customer exits (SAP enhancements for the time sheet) and BAdIs (to change derivation values, for example).

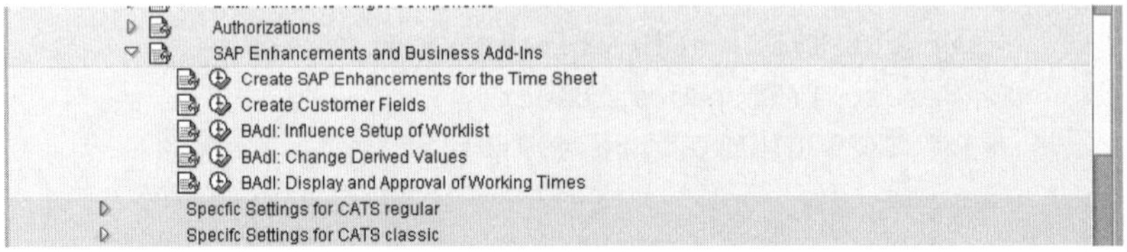

Figure 3.27 Enhancements and BAdIs in the IMG

3.6.1 Customer Exits

Within the application, SAP predefines customer exits for enhancements. *Customer exits* are customer-specific objects linked to the standard SAP system with a predefined interface. Customer objects are stored according to their own conventions. Accordingly, customer objects are not affected by a new release or an upgrade. In HR, customer exits (or *exits* for short) are usually function exits.

SAP Enhancements
Exits are summarized in groups, SAP enhancements, to structure them. The IMG references these enhancements. Another way to obtain an overview of the existing exits is to search for them in the application hierarchy. From the application hierarchy (SE81), you arrive at the Repository Information System. As Figure 3.28 shows, you can select the enhancements for application component PA.

List of enhancements
You receive a list of the enhancements for this application component (see Figure 3.29).

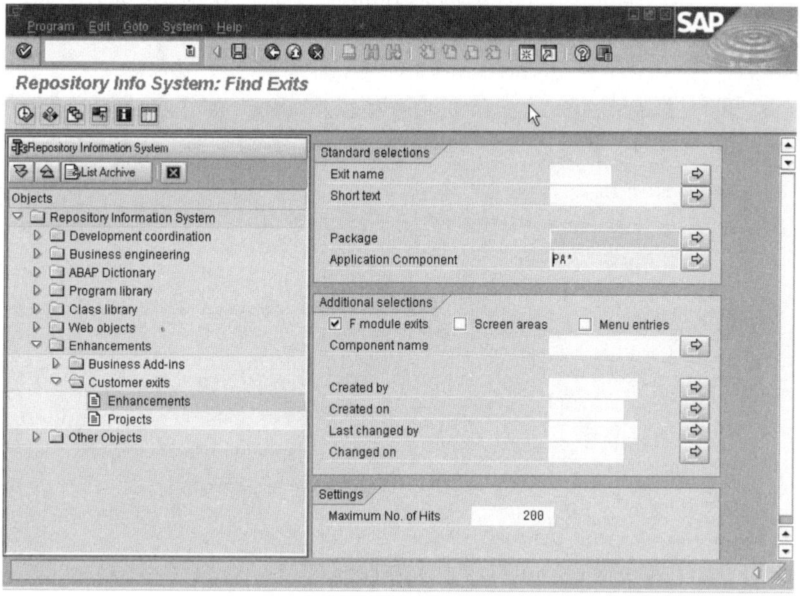

Figure 3.28 Searching for Exits with the Repository Information System

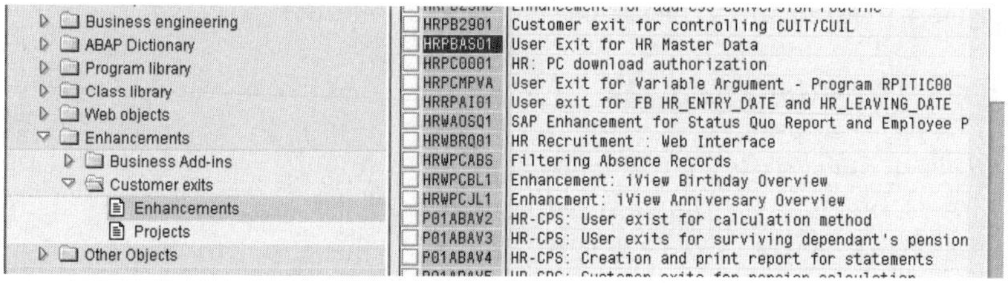

Figure 3.29 Enhancements of Application Component PA

You can double-click on the individual enhancements to display their exits. Figure 3.30 shows enhancement HRPBAS01 with function exit EXIT_SAPLRPIN_001.

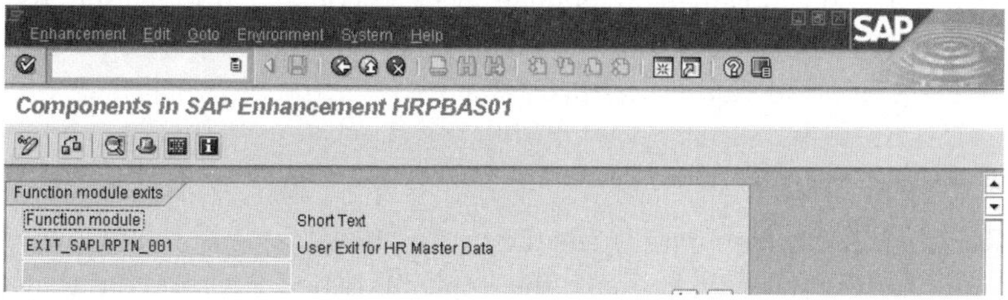

Enhancements and Exits

Figure 3.30 Function Exits of Enhancement HRPBAS01

Using the **Documentation** button provides additional information on the use of exits (see Figure 3.31).

```
The function module RP_CHECK_PERNR can be used by other applications to
check personnel numbers. Personnel numbers are checked against the HR
master record.

If you do not want the system to check personnel numbers or if personnel
numbers should be checked against your own tables, you can use the user
exit.

The example below illustrates how a personnel number is checked against
a table. You must create your own database table with the fields you
require and use the name of the table and the fields in the coding.

The input parameters are:

o    DATE: key date

o    PNR:  personnel number

The output parameters are:

o    NAME:  employee name, 40 characters maximum
```

Figure 3.31 Excerpt of Documentation on Exit EXIT_SAPLRPIN_001

3.6.2 Business Add-Ins

Business Add-Ins (*BAdIs*) provide an enhancement technique based on ABAP Objects. As is the case with customer exits, you can use BAdIs to realize customer requirements that are too specialized for the standard system or that would prove too complex for Customizing.

Layers   In the definition layer, development programmers (SAP, partners, and so on) set locations in the coding that enable you to insert additional code without having to modify the original object. BAdI users can develop the required, customer-specific functions in the implementation layer. You can define and implement at multiple levels. This feature distinguishes this design from the use of customer exits, which can only be built on a two-level system landscape.

Creating a BAdI

Procedure   Although BAdIs are typically created by SAP development, the following procedure shows how to make the implementation environment transparent to the user. It defines a BAdI that presents the postal code and location in a different order, according to the personnel country grouping.

A BAdI is created with the BAdI Builder (Transaction SE18). This example creates BAdI `YTHR_PLACE`. The BAdI Class `YCL_EX_THR_PLACE` is generated automatically. The data element MOLGA is used for filtering (see Figure 3.32).

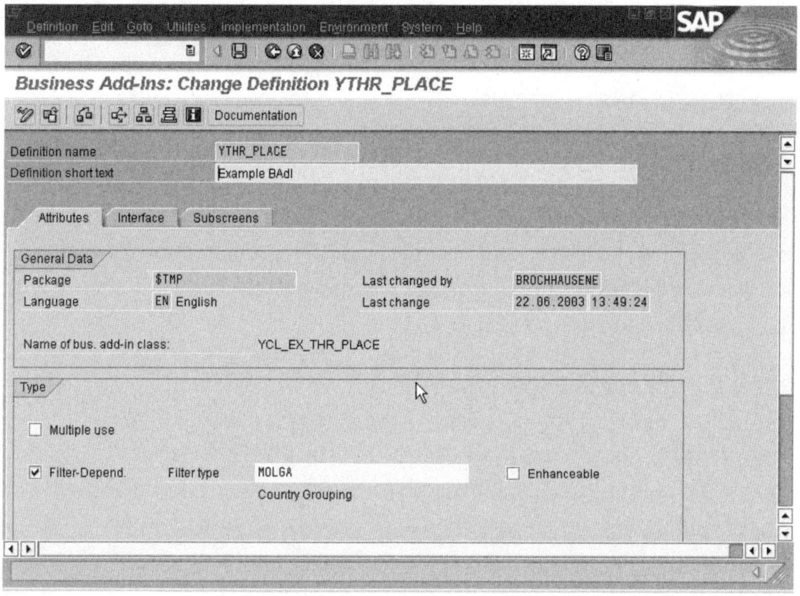

BAdI Class

Figure 3.32 Creating a BAdI

Interface `YIF_EX_THR_PLACE` is also created automatically. The PLACE method is assigned to the interface (see Figure 3.33).

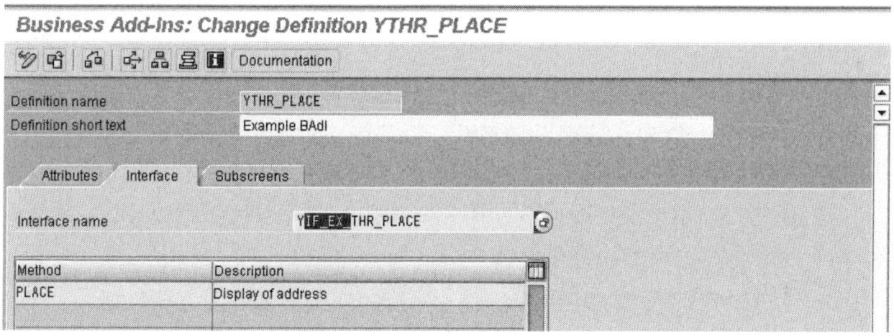

Interface and Methods

Figure 3.33 Interface with Method

Figure 3.34 illustrates the parameters of the method. The data of infotype 006 (*addresses*) is imported, and a text field with the requested information is exported. The filter is automatically inserted as an import parameter.

Parameters

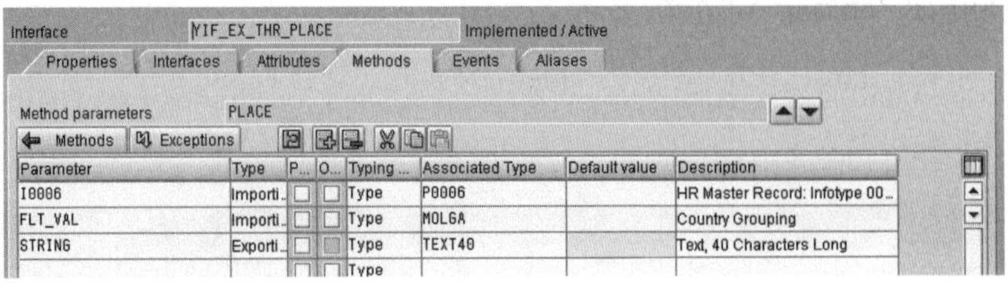

Figure 3.34 Parameters of the Method

Calling a BAdI

The following report shows the call of the PLACE method of the BAdI. To enable calling the static method get_instance, declaration of class cl_exithandler is required. The call of the method of the BAdI occurs with CALL METHOD badiexit->place.

```
REPORT  ythr_badi_example.
TABLES: pernr.
INFOTYPES: 0002, 0006.
CLASS cl_exithandler DEFINITION LOAD.
DATA  badiexit TYPE REF TO yif_ex_thr_place.
DATA  place TYPE text40.
PARAMETERS p_molga TYPE molga DEFAULT '01'.
START-OF-SELECTION.
  CALL METHOD cl_exithandler=>get_instance
    CHANGING
      instance = badiexit.
GET pernr.
  CLEAR place.
  rp_provide_from_last p0002 space sy-datum sy-datum.
  rp_provide_from_last p0006 '1' sy-datum sy-datum.
  CALL METHOD badiexit->place
    EXPORTING
      i0006   = p0006
      flt_val = p_molga
    IMPORTING
      string  = place.
  WRITE: / p0002-nachn, place.
```

Implementing a BAdI

You use Transaction SE19 to implement a BAdI (see Figure 3.35).

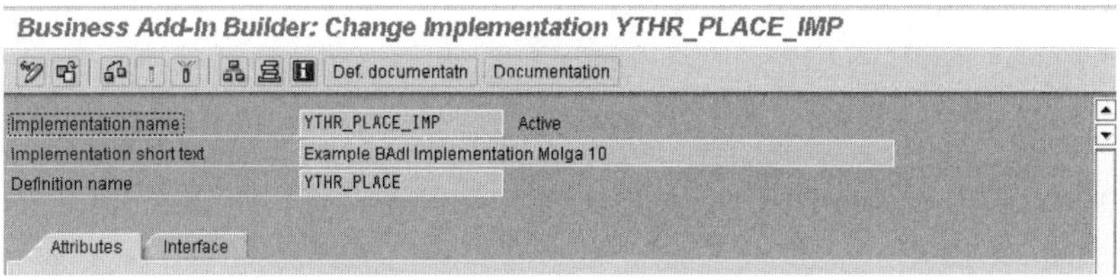

Business Add-In Builder: Change Implementation YTHR_PLACE_IMP

Implementation name	YTHR_PLACE_IMP	Active
Implementation short text	Example BAdI Implementation Molga 10
Definition name	YTHR_PLACE

Attributes   Interface

Figure 3.35 Implementation

During implementation, one or more features of the filter are specified (see Figure 3.36). In this case, the method for USA (MOLGA 10) is being implemented.

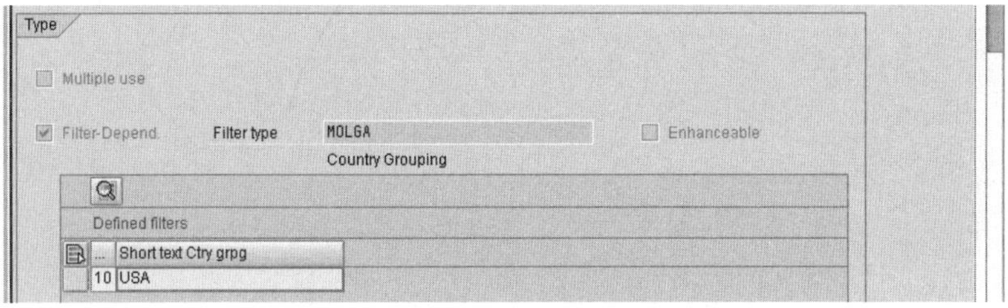

Filter

Type

☐ Multiple use

☑ Filter-Depend.   Filter type   MOLGA   ☐ Enhanceable
                                 Country Grouping

Defined filters

| | Short text Ctry grpg |
| 10 | USA |

Figure 3.36 Features of a Filter

The PLACE method is now available in the implementation of BAdIs YTHR_PLACE (see Figure 3.37).

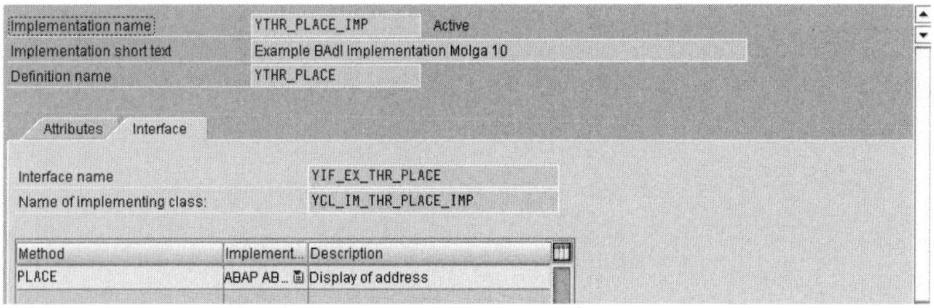

Implementation name	YTHR_PLACE_IMP	Active
Implementation short text	Example BAdI Implementation Molga 10
Definition name	YTHR_PLACE

Attributes   Interface

| Interface name | YIF_EX_THR_PLACE |
| Name of implementing class: | YCL_IM_THR_PLACE_IMP |

| Method | Implement... | Description | |
| PLACE | ABAP AB... | Display of address | |

Figure 3.37 Interface with Method

The required coding is inserted with the method (see Figure 3.38).

Coding

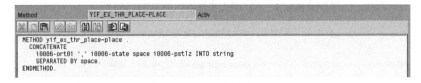

Figure 3.38 Coding of the Method

This coding is used after activation if the filter variable has the appropriate characteristic.

Chapter 5 explores the additional uses of BAdIs.

4 Roles and Authorizations

When dealing with personnel data, you must ensure that access to such highly sensitive data is restricted, in order for work to run smoothly. The role concept supports the assignment of authorizations tailored to the activity profile of system users. Users receive only the specific authorizations they need to perform their specific assigned tasks.

4.1 The SAP Authorization Concept

SAP Basis provides the applications of SAP R/3 Enterprise with a powerful authorization concept that includes the special requirements of the HR application. We'll now examine just how the HR requirements are mapped within the context of the general SAP authorization concept. A peculiarity of SAP HR is its structural authorization check: It considers the prominent significance of organizational structures and their dynamics in the HR environment.

4.1.1 Authorization Objects, Authorizations, and Profiles

The system stores all system elements that are relevant in the context of an authorization check as *authorization fields*.

Authorization fields

An *authorization object* is a selection of a maximum of ten authorization fields. An example of an authorization object that is central to Personnel Administration is P_ORGIN (HR: master data). It consists of the following authorization fields:

Authorization objects

▶ Infotype

▶ Subtype

▶ Authorization level

▶ Personnel area

▶ Employee group

▶ Employee subgroup

▶ Organizational key

At runtime, the application calls an authorization check (authority-check), providing a *specific combination of values* for a suitable authorization object—depending upon each context.

For example, let's say the user is processing personnel master data (Transaction PA30) for an employee in personnel area PSAR, employee group G, employee subgroup SG, and assigned organizational key ORG. The user wants to display an infotype record for infotype 0009 (*bank details*), subtype 0 (*main bank details*) for that employee. After reading the record from the database, the application program uses authorization object P_ORGIN to call the authorization check:

```
authority-check object 'P_ORGIN'
    id 'INFTY' field '0009'    "Infotype number
    id 'SUBTY' field '0'       "Subtype number
    id 'AUTHC' field 'R'       "Authorization level
    id 'PERSA' field 'PSAR'    "Personnel area
    id 'PERSG' field 'G'       "Employee group
    id 'PERSK' field 'SG'      "Employee subgroup
    id 'VDSK1' field 'ORG'.    "Organizational key
```

The authorization check returns a result (sy-subrc) that defines further processing in the application.

When setting up a system user, all cases in which this kind of check can yield a positive result must be described: value areas are set in relation to a single authorization object for every field. This kind of setting defines an *authorization*. The possible descriptions of value areas include:

▶ Single values

▶ Intervals

▶ Combinations of intervals

You can use an asterisk (*) as a wildcard for any character string. (Descriptions such as "from a* to x*" don't usually give you the results that you want, and therefore, should be avoided.) It's imperative that you understand that an authorization always describes a *combination of values* for individual fields.

Often, the execution of a transaction checks several authorization objects. In addition, a single transaction does not usually include in its checks all tasks performed by a given user. To simplify the assignment of authorizations to users, the authorizations are summarized in *authorization profiles*. Several authorization profiles can be assigned to a single user. The total of all authorizations assigned to a particular user, as contained in the profiles assigned to that user, determines the user's access to system data.

4.1.2 Role Concept and Profile Generator

Setting up system users is based on task descriptions: Because of the need for data protection and security requirements, user access should be restricted—users should have access only to the data required to meet their specific assigned tasks.

A group of tasks that users perform in the system is known as a *role*. Several roles make up a *composite role*. Any one user can have several roles— even those assigned by composite roles. In addition to the roles designed and delivered by SAP, new, customer-specific roles can be generated easily. The authorizations linked to roles are an integral part of a role: during role maintenance (*Profile Generator*), the appropriate authorization profile can be generated based upon the tasks defined for a role.

You can navigate to role maintenance using the menu path: **Tools ·** **Administration · User · Maintenance · Role management · Roles** (Transaction PFCG, see Figure 4.1).

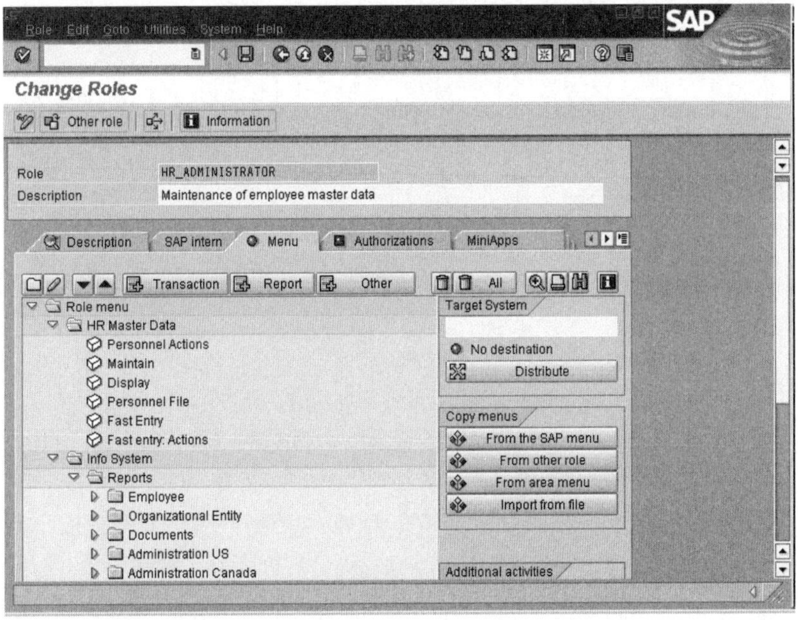

Roles

Role maintenance

Figure 4.1 Role Maintenance—Definition Menu

A role can be depicted by a menu tree. The branches are the user's tasks: transactions, reports, or other options (such as Web addresses, BSP applications, and so on). The following elements can be the basis for selecting the objects:

▶ The SAP menu

▶ An existing role

▶ An area menu

▶ A file to be imported

You can also place objects in the menu tree manually. At the end of the process, you have a *role menu*: This menu is available to a user; if the user has several roles, the menus are added to each other.

Profile Generator   Based upon a role menu, you can generate the corresponding authorizations for the tasks involved (transaction, reports, and others). To some extent, you can assign certain values automatically. A traffic light icon is displayed to indicate where manual rework is required (see Figure 4.2).

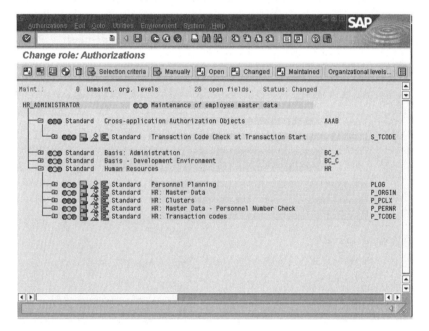

Figure 4.2 Role Maintenance After Triggering the Generation of Authorizations

The assignment of a user to one or more roles means that this user has a user menu that contains his or her limited set of functions. Therefore, the user has the authorizations to perform these functions.

You can assign a user to a role in one of two ways:

▶ Directly—by entering the user name

▶ Indirectly—with Organizational Management

4.1.3 Functions of the Profile Generator

After authorizations have been generated, traffic light icons display the status of individual authorizations. Ideally, you would now see only green traffic lights. However, many yellow traffic lights (rework required) will often be displayed. At first glance, you might feel disappointed; but, after a more detailed examination of the background and functions of the Profile Generator, you will appreciate the value of this tool.

We've learned that a role is defined by a selection of application functions. However, the assigned work—and therefore the authorizations—of a user does not depend solely on an abstract description of tasks; rather, it frequently depends on what part of the company the user is responsible for. For example: various HR administrators might well have the same task profile, but have it in different personnel areas. Obviously, the selection of application functions in such cases, by itself, means that a complete generation of authorizations cannot occur.

The concept of *organizational levels* considers this issue, but it can only partially solve the problem. SAP R/3 can characterize organizational terms— even cross-application terms—that can be used in several authorization objects as "global." When triggering the generation of profiles from the Profile Generator, the user can form the global organizational fields used in the related authorization objects (for example, plan variants). The fields of the authorization objects are then pre-populated accordingly. Of course, manual intervention is also required here, but the advantage of this approach is that it avoids repeated rework for global organizational terms.

Organizational levels

The correct *selection* of authorization objects by the Profile Generator, based upon the task descriptions, is significantly more helpful than pre-populating values in the authorizations of the respective authorization objects. Given the complexity of the system, knowing which authorization object is checked in a specific business context is no trivial matter. This knowledge is a substantial part of the Profile Generator

The core of the Profile Generator is a table containing the assignment of transactions to authorization objects, including any values that might be considered for the authorization fields. A *check indicator* is also assigned to each authorization object: it controls the Profile Generator and the runtime behavior of the authorization check. SAP delivers the complete table, but customers can modify it with Transaction SU24 if necessary.

Check indicator

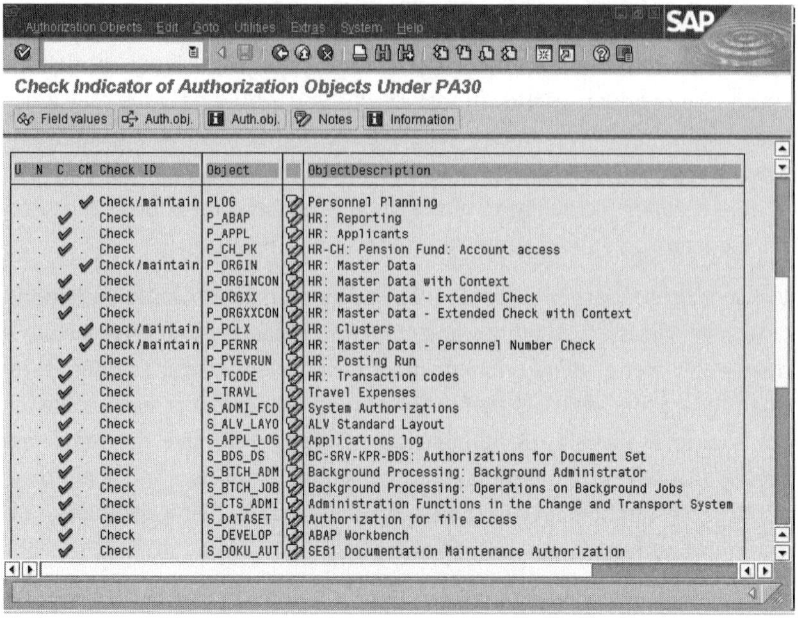

Figure 4.3 Check Indicator

Figure 4.3 shows an excerpt of the authorization objects that are included in Transaction PA30. The green checkmarks in each column ("N," "C," and "CM") refer to the runtime behavior of the authorization check (columns "N" and "C") and, if required, to the control of the Profile Generator at the point of generation (column "CM"). SAP uses column "U" internally: it should never have a checkmark.

The column headers mean the following:

▶ N: No check of the object at runtime

▶ C: Check of the object at runtime; no consideration in the Profile Generator

▶ CM: Check of the object at runtime; when generating a profile, the Profile Generator considers the field values stored with the object. Predefined *field values* can be entered on a detail screen that can be accessed via function key **Field values**.

4.2 Authorizations in the Context of SAP HR

Now that we've outlined the basics of roles and authorizations, we'll discuss these concepts in the context of SAP HR.

4.2.1 Authorization Objects

SAP HR contains a significant list of authorization objects that are all relevant—in the most varied contexts. We don't want to yield to temptation and describe all the HR authorization objects. Instead, we'll explain the basic ideas with characteristic examples.

SAP HR authorization objects

P_TCODE (HR: transaction code)

This authorization object is used to check whether a user is authorized to start specific HR transactions. It consists of a field that contains the transaction code and is similar to the cross-application object S_TCODE. However, S_TCODE is always checked at the start of a transaction; P_TCODE is relevant only in selected transactions in the context of HR. During the generation of authorizations within role maintenance, the object P_TCODE is populated with the correct check values, if necessary.

P_ORGIN (HR: master data)

This authorization object is used during the authorization check for HR infotypes. This check occurs when HR infotypes are edited or read.

To control the access of HR administrators to personnel master data, we recommend that you keep in mind the following considerations:

▶ How are the affected employees *assigned organizationally*?

▶ What *type* of master data should be processed?

▶ What *operations* contain the accesses?

Infotype 0001 describes the *organizational assignment*. The *type* of master data is derived from the infotype or subtype that maps the corresponding data, and the *operation* can be derived from the activity of the user in each situation.

Authorization object P_ORGIN (HR: master data) addresses these considerations as follows:

▶ Organizational assignment

  ▶ Personnel area

  ▶ Employee group

- ▶ Employee subgroup
- ▶ Organizational key
▶ Type of master data
  - ▶ Infotype
  - ▶ Subtype
▶ Access operation
  - ▶ Authorization level

This construction permits the mapping of cases in which dependencies between organizational assignments, type of data, and operations exist with regard to access options. Consider this example: display of all infotypes and subtypes in personnel area A and modification of a limited amount of infotypes and subtypes in personnel area B. Here, you would set up two authorizations as shown in Figure 4.4.

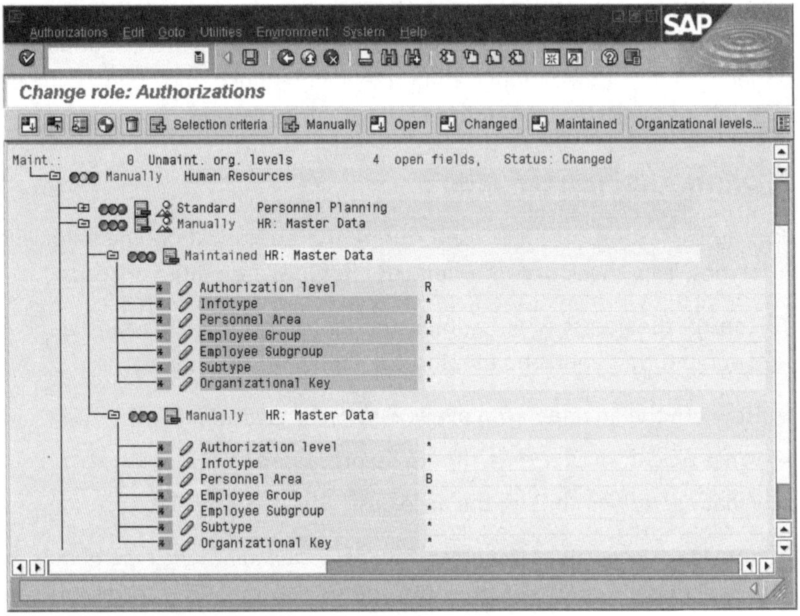

Figure 4.4 Read Personnel Area A—Write Personnel Area B

P_ORGXX (HR: master data—extended check)

This authorization object is of the same type as P_ORGIN (HR: master data): it is used to check access to employee master data and consists of the following fields:

- Administrator group
- Payroll Administrator
- Administrator for HR Master Data
- Administrator for Time Recording
- Infotype
- Subtype
- Authorization level

The difference between this object and `P_ORGIN` consists of a different selection of fields for organizational assignment. The responsibilities of an HR administrator are usually defined in the HR administrator fields in infotype 0001.

If the customer's situation generally has *no dependency* between the organizational assignment and the infotype, subtype, and authorization level (see previous section), the simultaneous use (see authorization main switch) of `P_ORGIN` and `P_ORGXX` can simplify authorization maintenance.

Combination of P_ORGIN and P_ORGXX

For example, let's assume that the organizational fields of `P_ORGIN` (particularly the personnel area) are relevant. The assumption would include the following:

- Ten personnel areas
  PA01–PA10
- The activity profiles for HR administrators. (We use the term "activity profile" to distance ourselves from the role. Within SAP terminology, a role in our context also contains the definition of organizational terms.)
  - Maintenance of basic data
    Infotypes: 0000, 0001, 0002, 0006, 0007, 0009, 0016, and 0032
  - Maintenance of payroll data
    Infotypes: 0008, 0010, 0012, 0013, 0014, 0015, and 0210
  - Maintenance of Time Management data
    Infotypes: 2001 and 2006

When mapping with `P_ORGIN` alone, thirty authorizations must be maintained: three activity profiles for each personnel area. This holds true even if there are no dependencies between the activity profile and the personnel area.

Another possibility is to use both P_ORGIN and P_ORGXX–the organizational considerations would be mapped in P_ORGIN, and the activity profile would be mapped with P_ORGXX.

For P_ORGIN, we define an authorization, Org_PAxx; for each personnel area, PAxx (xx = 01–10).

The fields of authorization Org_PAxx are defined as follows:

▶ Personnel Area: PAxx
▶ Employee Group: *
▶ Employee Subgroup: *
▶ Organizational Key: *
▶ Infotype: *
▶ Subtype: *
▶ Authorization Level: *

We map the individual activity profiles as authorizations for P_ORGXX: we mark all the fields (except infotype) with an asterisk (*) and use different definitions only for the infotype:

▶ Basic data authorization
  Infotype: 0000, 0001, 0002, 0006, 0007, 0009, 0016, and 0032
▶ Payroll authorization
  Infotype: 0008, 0010, 0012, 0013, 0014, 0015, and 0210
▶ Time Management authorization
  Infotype: 2001, 2006

Functionally, a combination of authorizations for P_ORGIN and P_ORGXX produces the same results as does using P_ORGIN by itself. However, compared to the first method, the maintenance effort for the authorizations is clearly less, even in this simplified example.

Z_NNNNN (HR: master data—customer-specific authorization object)

P_ORGIN and P_ORGXX each contain a specific selection of the fields of organizational assignment (infotype 0001). Doing so covers the current requirements. You can define *any selection desired* from the fields of infotype 0001 in the customer-specific authorization object Z_NNNNN (the name can be freely chosen within the customer-naming environment: Z_NNNNN is used for the sake of simplicity). The only limitation is that the number of fields in an authorization object is limited to a maximum of ten. Of course, the object must also contain the infotype, subtype, and authorization level fields in addition to the fields from infotype 0001. Everything that applies to objects P_ORGIN and P_ORGXX, can be applied directly to Z_NNNNN. Note that the activation of the customer-specific authorization object requires a modification to standard SAP coding. However, SAP explicitly supports this procedure; you can assume that future changes to standard SAP coding will not affect the modification.

The procedure for creating and activating a customer-specific authorization in the context of an HR infotype authorization check will be addressed later in more detail.

P_APPL (HR: applicants)

Authorization object P_APPL is the analog of P_ORGIN; it applies to access to data on applicants. It consists of the following fields:

▶ Personnel Area
▶ Applicant Group
▶ Applicant Range
▶ Organizational Key
▶ Personnel Officer Responsible
▶ Infotype
▶ Subtype
▶ Authorization Level

P_PERNR (HR: master data—personnel number check)

You cannot use P_ORGIN to control access by targeting specific personnel numbers for a given user.

Theoretically, you could mark the organization key (field VDSK1 in infotype 0001) with the personnel number for each affected employee. You could then give the user with that personnel number an authorization that allows access to employees with exactly that organizational key. However, given the effort required in assigning authorization, this method is very impractical.

Instead, what's needed here is an option to set the infotype, subtype, and authorization level and, in addition, an option to use the assignment of this system user—found in personnel master data (infotype 0105, subtype 0001)—for the authorization check.

Authorization object P_PERNR (HR: master data—personnel number check) addresses these requirements.

This authorization object consists of the following fields:

▶ Infotype
▶ Subtype
▶ Authorization Level
▶ Indicator (PSIGN) that determines the interpretation of an existing assignment in infotype 0105, subtype 0001 for each authorization.

If PSIGN has the value "I", access is guaranteed to the subtypes specified in the same authorization with the operations defined in the authorization level. If PSIGN has the value "E", access is explicitly excluded.

Typical application cases for P_PERNR include scenarios in which employees have access to their own personnel master data (ESS: Employee Self-Service). For example, to change their own address data, users receive authorization for 0006 (subtype and operation as needed); PSIGN has the value "I".

An authorization for P_PERNR with the value "I" in PSIGN can easily be combined with authorizations for other HR authorization objects. For example, an HR administrator could receive the authorizations that apply to her roles, and also have access rights to a portion of her own personnel master data, by having the appropriate authorization for P_PERNR.

An additional requirement might be the ability to remove specific write authorizations from an HR administrator, who, in the context of his work, according to his authorization for object P_ORGIN, also has access to his own data. This requirement can also be handled with an authorization for P_PERNR. In this case, PSIGN must have the value "E". The other fields are used to specify the excluded area (infotype, subtype, and authorization level). And the appropriate employee–user assignment must be stored in infotype 0105.

The semantics of PSIGN are unusual. To avoid any confusion or misunderstanding, please note the following:

For a specific combination of infotype, subtype, and authorization level, do not set PSIGN to "I" and "E" for one user. Nor does the specification of an asterisk (*) make sense in this context. Access to the given combination is *either* granted *or* prohibited. According to system implementation, if "I" and "E" are encountered at the same time, the system will regard "E" as the valid value. It will also interpret an asterisk (*) as "I". See Section 4.2.7 for more information.

P_ABAP (HR: reporting)

As a rule, access protection for personnel master data is not dependent on whether the access comes from a dialog transaction or reporting. We'll now examine the exceptions to this rule.

Authorization object P_ABAP (HR: reporting) consists of the following fields:

▶ Degree of simplification of the authorization check (COARS)
▶ ABAP Program Name (REPID)

This authorization object is used in three different ways:

The most important and perhaps most demanding method uses the object in the context of logical database PNP. Here, the authorizations for the objects work to control the semantics of authorizations for other objects (P_ORGIN, P_ORGXX, and Z_NNNNN) for specific reports. REPID contains the name of the report involved; COARS contains a "degree of simplification of the authorization check." The values "1" and "2" are supported.

Checking in PNP reports

Value "1" has the following effect. The *infotype* and *subtype* are checked on one side; the *organizational assignment* is checked on the other side; however, the checks occur *independently of each other*. Therefore, read access to master data requires read authorization for the infotype and sub-type (regardless of the organizational assignment) and authorization for the organizational assignment of the personnel number involved (without consideration of the infotype or subtype). Remember, typically, the *entire* combination is checked.

Simplified

Value "2" has the following effect: No authorization check for *access to infotypes* is performed in the reports involved. Here, it's important to understand that the basic semantics of HR-specific object P_ABAP differ from the authorization object used across applications, S_PROGRAM (*ABAP: program flow checks*). S_PROGRAM checks the authorization at the start of an ABAP program.

Turned off

An additional infotype authorization check, which is based on the authorization object for personnel master data (noted above), is performed with programs that read infotypes when using logical database PNP with GET PERNR. Authorizations for P_ABAP only affect this check.

Reporting versus dialog Note that with regard to the behavior of HR reports (reports with logical database PNP), you are not necessarily required to set up authorizations for P_ABAP. If a user doesn't have authorizations for P_ABAP, the authorization check for access to personnel master data delivers the identical results in dialog and in reporting. (However, the reaction of the application in dialog and reporting to the results of the authorization check can be different. We will address this subject later in the book.)

Sample application: PNP Reports The following sample application should clarify the affects of P_ABAP:

▶ An HR report that processes non-critical fields (first and last name) from infotype 0002 (*personal data*) should be widely available. However, only a few users have been granted read authorization for this infotype, because in addition to the non-critical data, it contains information that should be protected (date of birth, gender for example). With an authorization for P_ABAP, you can turn off the authorization check of the infotype in a targeted manner for this report: assign the COARS field the value "2". Users with this authorization can use the report without having authorization for the infotype.

▶ For users (super users) who have unrestricted access to all personnel master data, you can reduce the runtime of HR reports by avoiding unnecessary checks of infotypes. Simply use an appropriate authorization for P_ABAP: enter an asterisk (*) in both fields.

▶ Time administrator T is to use report RPTIME00 (*time evaluation*) to evaluate the employees assigned to organizational key T. To obtain the required additional information, the report also accesses infotype 0008 (*basic pay*), which means that the user also needs authorization for this infotype. Typically, time administrators do not have access to infotype 0008. With (additional) authorizations for P_ORGIN and P_ABAP, the time administrator can execute the report for the assigned employees without needing to have general read access to infotype 0008.

Figures 4.5 and 4.6 show the required authorizations for the last example.

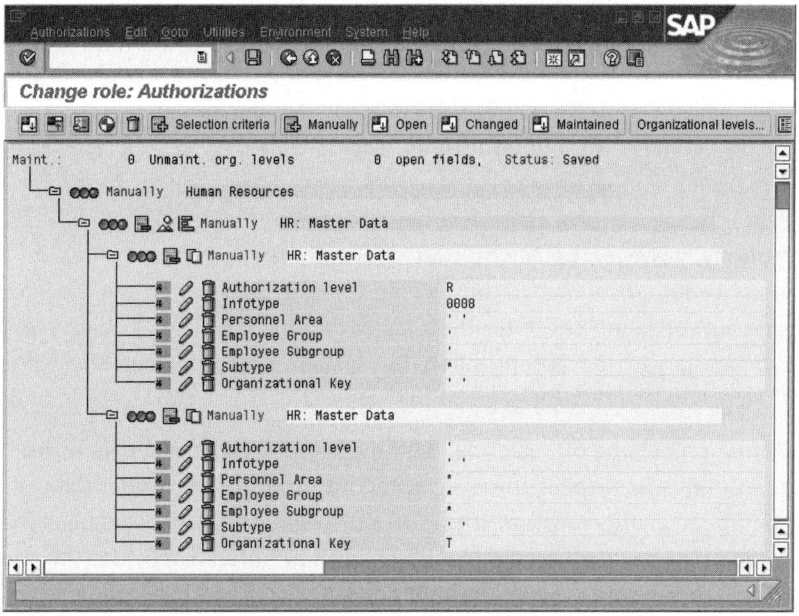

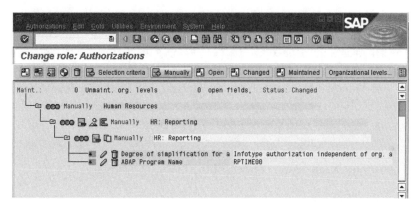

Figure 4.5 Authorizations for P_ORGIN (HR: master data)

Figure 4.6 Authorization for P_ABAP (HR: reporting)

The combination from all fields is checked in dialog; a combination with an initial personnel area or an initial infotype can never appear. In other words, no access can occur in dialog. A simplified check occurs in report RPTIME00 based upon the authorization for *HR: reporting*. Because of the first authorization for *HR: master data*, the check of infotype, subtype, and level without consideration of the organizational assignment will produce a positive result. Because of the second authorization, the same result would occur with a check of the organizational assignment without consideration of infotype, subtype, and level for all employees with organizational key T.

Now we'll address the other two uses of P_ABAP.

Document evaluation

In the context of *the evaluation Logged Changes in Infotype Data* (RPUAUD00): For security reasons, evaluations of the changes to infotype data (change documents) are subject to infotype authorization checks. Typically, however, users who start such authorizations have far-reaching infotype authorizations. In these cases, it makes sense to forego the infotype authorization check for these users in the context of RPUAUD00. You can do so with an authorization for P_ABAP: REPID is given the value "RPUAUD00" and COARS is given the value "2".

Payment medium program

During processing of personnel data by *payment medium programs* from accounting: To respect the special security level of personnel data, an additional security measure checks an authorization for object P_ABAP. The name of the payment medium program must be entered in field REPID and the value "2" must be entered in COARS.

PLOG (Personnel Planning)

The authorization object PLOG (personnel planning) controls access to personnel planning objects. Unlike P_ORGIN, this object does not consider the organizational aspect; this part of personnel planning is realized completely with a *structural authorization check*. PLOG also differs from P_ORGIN in that—in addition to the infotype, subtype, and type of access various types of objects, such as organizational unit, job, and position (which can appear in various plan statuses and plan variants)—are dealt with. For P_ORGIN, the basic object type is always the employee.

The authorization object consists of the following fields:

▶ Plan Version
▶ Planning Status
▶ Object Type
▶ Infotype
▶ Subtype
▶ Function Code

4.2.2   Authorization Level—Graded Write Authorizations

Typically, an authorization check includes the question of the *type* of processing to which the user wants to subject the data. This dimension can be handled in SAP R/3 Enterprise across applications with the ACTVT (activity) field. In the context of SAP HR, however, the "activity" has a special orientation. For that reason and for reasons of compatibility and continuity, ACTVT is not presently used in SAP HR. Instead, AUTHC (authorization level) is used.

The possible values are:

▶ "R" for read access

▶ "M" for read access in the context of input Help

▶ "W" for unrestricted write access

▶ "E" for write access to records flagged as "locked"

▶ "D" for processing the status flag

▶ "S" for restricted write access

▶ "*" for unrestricted access

Authorizations marked with an asterisk (*) encompass all other authorizations; however, there is no other hierarchy among the values. A write authorization (restricted or unrestricted) is generally assigned in combination with "R".

Combination of read and write authorization

The exclusion of access rights with authorizations for object P_PERNR (PSIGN = "E") is an exception to this rule. If a specific write authorization is to be excluded, the exclusion must be specified exactly in the authorization level field (AUTHC). In this case, an "R" (read authorization) must not be specified.

Double Verification Principle

In some application scenarios, it would be critical if only *one* user could change data without any monitoring, such that the changes would have a general effect on evaluations (for example, changes to salary data can affect payroll results). Here, we want a multilevel procedure. User A performs the changes (as a proposal); user B checks user A's input and can, if necessary, activate the modifications.

SAP HR basically supports two variations: *asymmetrical* and *symmetrical*—two users are required to write personnel master data in both cases.

Variations of the double verification principle

Asymmetrical	In the *asymmetrical* variation, each user has different roles. User A does not have complete write authorization ("W"), but only the restricted "E" (best combined with "R" and, if necessary "M"—see above). In this way, A can process records of the affected infotypes (create, change, and delete) if they have a lock indicator (date element SPRPS). The system sets the lock indicator during creation. User B has a monitoring function. B cannot change data. The task of user B is to check (display) and possibly confirm data. At a technical level, confirmation consists of removing the lock indicator. To do so, B needs "D" (combined with "R" and possibly "M") in the corresponding authorization level.
	Because the lock indicator is a component of the key for a personnel master data record, it's very simple to have parallel records, identical in the other components of the key. Only by removing the lock indicator, can the unlocked record be replaced with the record that was previously locked.
Sample ESS Scenario	Consider a change of address as an ESS scenario. Employees can perform their own change of address in the system. The employee is assigned a user with infotype 0105. This user has authorization for P_PERNR with infotype 0006 (address), subtype *, authorization levels "E" and "R," and "I" for the interpretation of the assigned personnel number. When changing the address, the employee copies the existing address and enters the new address and the correct date on which the new information will be effective. Because the user has only restricted authorization, the system assigns the new data record a lock indicator. Afterward, the new address is present (with lock indicator) in the system, valid as of the effective date. However, the old data, which does not have the lock indicator, is still operative. The new address is already available, but it has no operative affects. The personnel administrator responsible, who is informed of the address change (by workflow, for example), can verify the data and remove the lock indicator (if no concerns arise), or ask the employee to correct the data (if concerns arise). The removal of the lock indicator replaces the old address record with the new address record for the relevant period. The removal of the lock indicator also triggers the related follow-up work. As this example illustrates, various authorization objects can be relevant in a scenario with the double verification principle: P_PERNR for the user assigned to the employee and P_ORGIN/P_ORGXX for the personnel administrator.
Symmetrical	The symmetrical variation also demands the participation of two users to change data, although both users have the identical role in this case.

Both users have a restricted write authorization, "S", joined to a read authorization "R" (an "M" can be added if needed for search help). An infotype record processed by a user with these restrictions is first assigned a lock indicator. If this user is not the last person having changed the record, he/she has the authorization ("S") to remove the lock indicator.

To avoid surprises, note the semantics of the information for the "last user having changed." Implicit database changes have no affect on the "last user having changed," because of the time constraint logic (restricting a record with time constraint 2, for example). Users who explicitly change a record with "change" are entered as the "last user having changed."

The symmetrical double verification principle *does not permit deletion.* Consistent mapping of a deletion in the context of the symmetrical double verification principle would require the ability to set a delete flag. If user A with authorization "S" tried to delete an infotype record, the record would not have to be deleted immediately (similar to the procedure for a change), but instead would have to indicate that user A has flagged it for deletion. A different user could then confirm the deletion.

Note that not all infotypes support the lock indicator. The following info-type records *cannot* have a lock indicator:

► Actions (0000)
► Organizational assignment (0001)
► Personal data (0002)
► Payroll status (0003)
► Reference personnel number (0031)

Test Procedure

Test procedure offers another way to refine the authorizations for write access. Here too, a second user checks the data. However, unlike the process involving the double verification principle described above, the data becomes effective immediately—without a check. If the data up to a specified date is checked, changes that affect a period up to the specified release date can occur only with a special authorization.

The concept is similar to retroactive accounting recognition in connection with the personnel control record: Once the data has been released, info-type changes that take effect in the period released cannot occur without restrictions.

Test Procedure Infotype

A *test procedure* is a subtype of infotype 0130. You can store a test date for each test procedure (at the employee level—see Figure 4.7).

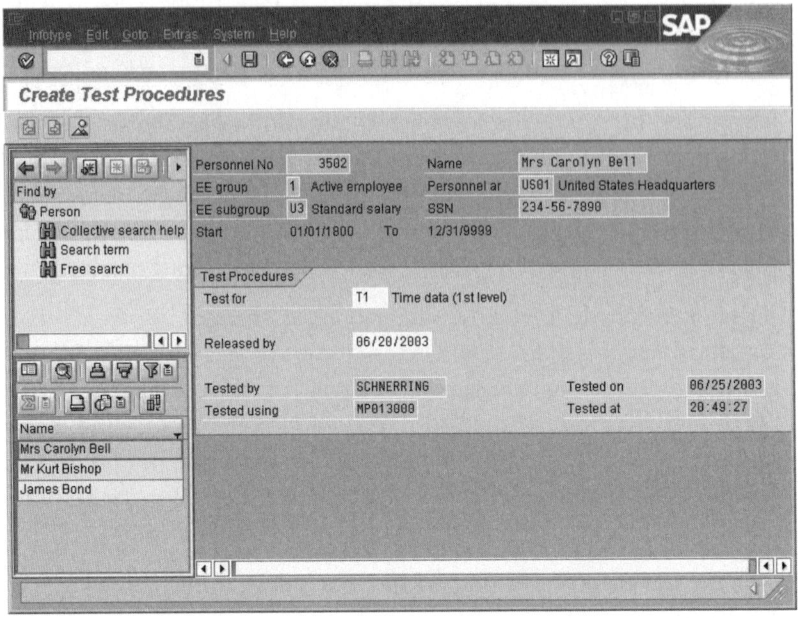

Figure 4.7 Test Procedure Infotype

Customizing test procedures

In the IMG (Customizing), follow menu path **Personnel Management · Personnel Administration · Tools · Authorization management · Test procedures · Assign infotypes to test procedures** to navigate to maintenance of assignment table T584A: the relevant infotypes and subtypes are assigned to a test procedure here. The possible test procedures must have already been set as subtype of infotype 0130.

If such an assignment exists for an infotype/subtype, you can change data in the period before the test date of the assigned test procedure, only with a special authorization. The special authorization exists in a write authorization of the test procedure.

Example: time recording

Consider decentralized time recording. Because the approach used here is decentralized, time data is entered by time administrators. The HR department checks the data up to a certain time to ensure that any later changes do not invalidate the data that it has already checked. To do so, the affected infotypes and subtypes are assigned to a test procedure (a subtype of infotype 0130) in Customizing. To adhere to testing a specific infotype or subtype up to a certain date, the date is entered in the corresponding test procedure in the employee master data (by the personnel department). After the date is entered, a change to infotypes or subtypes that are within the defined period is only possible when the user has write authorization for the testing procedure.

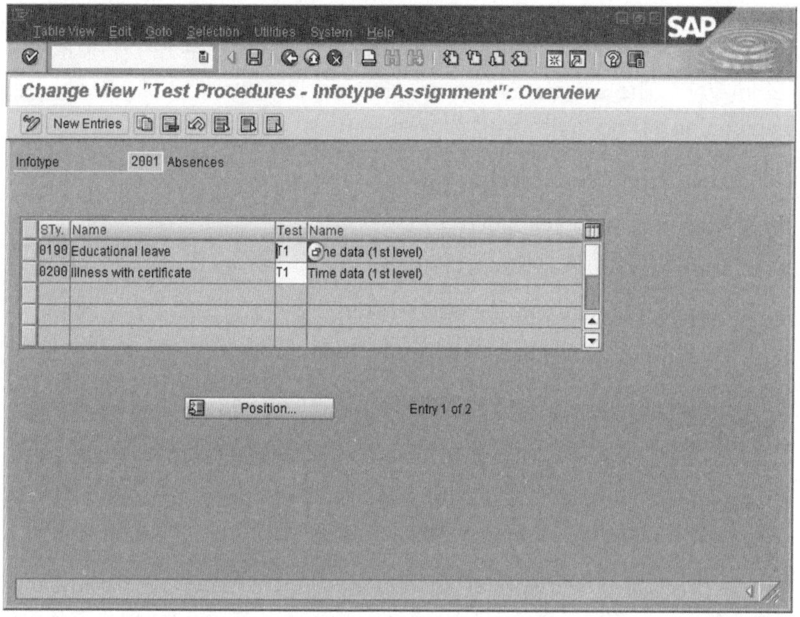

Figure 4.8 Assigning Infotypes and Subtypes to Test Procedures

4.2.3 Organizational Key

The importance of the organizational assignment of employees in controlling access authorizations to their data should now be understood (as described above): The definition of object P_ORGIN makes it clear that the personnel area, employee group, and employee subgroup are controlling values that are relevant to authorization. The same is true for the HR administrator fields in object P_ORGXX. However, the significance of the organizational key field (VDSK1) is not initially apparent.

The *organizational key* is a 14-character field that can be populated flexibly. The field is explicitly intended for authorization checks. From the SAP standard's viewpoint, you should never even consider using the organization key for any other reason.

The following keys are relevant to the control and checking of the organizational key:

Customizing the organizational key

▶ Feature organizational key (VDSK1)
▶ Table organizational key: control (T527)

- Table organizational key : creation rule (T527A)
- Table organizational key: validation (T527O)

Depending on the employee's properties, the characteristic returns a value ("variable key"). With the return value, you can determine a creation rule and the behavior of the organizational key field on the screen from table T527. The creation rules are defined in table T527A. The screen behavior is defined with the following values:

- 1: Any entry without validation
- 2: Any entry with validation
- 3: Mandatory entry with validation
- 4: Proposal that cannot be overwritten
- 5: Proposal that can be overwritten—without validation
- 6: Proposal that can be overwritten—with validation
- 7: Proposal that cannot be overwritten—with validation

Based on a creation rule, indicators 4, 5, 6, and 7 propose a value. If you use these indicators, you *must* maintain a creation rule in table T527A.

A two-character key identifies a creation rule. The description consists of a line (row) counter (SEQNO) of fields from infotype 0001 (SNAME). Entering the offset (OFFST) and length (LNGTH) can define the selection of a partial string of the field's contents.

For values 2, 3, 6, and 7, suitable entries must be maintained in the *check table* (T527O).

Permissible organizational keys are defined in column (ORGKY) in table T527O. In this context, only entries with "hierarchy" (HIRAR) 1 are relevant—organizational element (NODTY) is obsolete. "Short description" (TEXT1) and "Description" (TEXT2) might be displayed as entry helps.

Sample organizational key

Consider the following example. The organizational key is to be entered manually for employee subgroup SG: this enables differentiated authorization control for this employee subgroup. For other employee subgroups, the authorization check should reflect the employee's cost center assignment. In this case, the organizational key is automatically created from the concatenation of the controlling area and the first six characters of the cost center. The user cannot overwrite the proposal.

The requisite Customizing follows the pattern of the following three figures:

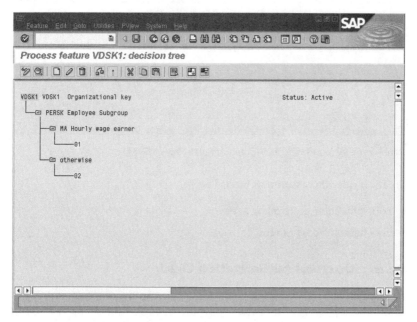

Figure 4.9 Feature VDSK1

Feature VDSK1 separates employee subgroup SG from the remaining values (variable key 01 or 02).

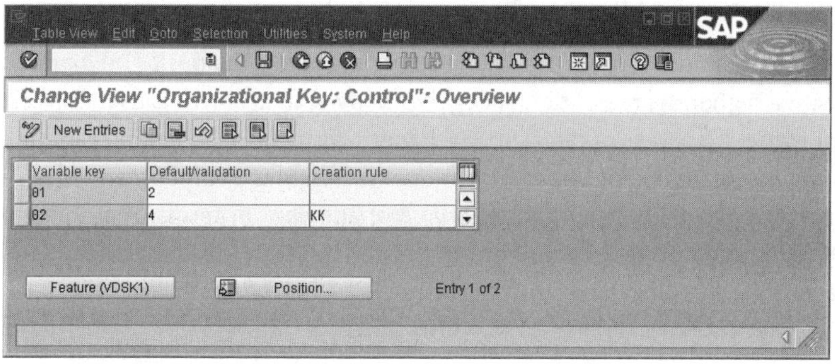

Figure 4.10 Organizational Key—Control (Table T527)

For the two values of the variable key in table T527 we set:

▶ 01: no proposal, any entry with validation (2)

▶ 02: proposal according to the creation rule, cannot be overwritten, no validation (4), creation rule KK

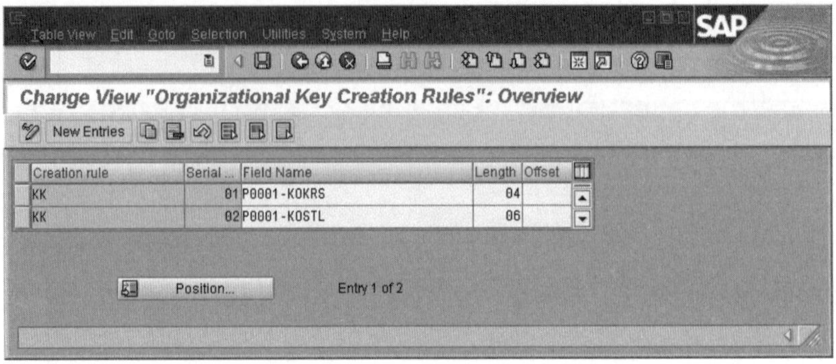

Figure 4.11 Organizational Key—Creation Rules (Table T527A)

Creation rule KK is stored in table T527A:

▶ Four-character controlling area

▶ Six-character cost center

4.2.4 Structural Authorization Check

The "organizational units" (personnel area, employee group, employee subgroup, and so on), that we have thus far discussed in the context of authorization checks, typically behave statically. Reorganizations—at the level of the personnel area, for example—or changes in users' responsibilities occur rather infrequently. Given this information, it makes sense to set subareas of the organization—for authorization purposes—by assigning certain fixed combinations.

A different situation occurs when the organizational plan is to be mapped with a higher degree of detail. *Organizational Management* is used for that purpose. It enables organizational changes with reasonable effort, and the *progression in time* of the organizational structure is alsorecorded. To support the flexibility of Organizational Management in terms of authorization, this component contains both the general authorization concept and a specific authorization concept: a *structural authorization check*.

Mapping the HR organizational plan Organizational Management can map hierarchical structures in general; however, it's not an HR application in the strict sense. Principally, we'd like to consider the employee here, as well, so we'll concentrate on the HR organizational plan. We'll assume that Organizational Management and Personnel Administration are in use and integrated. An employee is assigned to a position that is linked to an organizational unit. Using the terminology of Organizational Management, we have to deal with the following object types:

- Employee (P)
- Position (S)
- Jobs (C)
- Organizational units (O)

Various relationships are possible between the object types. The type of relationship indicates the direction of the relationship:"Bnnn", where nnn is a relationship, describes the reverse of "Annn". Relationships

Examples:

- B002: from O to O—is line manager of
- A003: from S to O—belongs to
- B008: from P to S—is owner of

An HR organizational plan is modeled by object types; permissible relationships exist between the object types. A chain of relationships defines an *evaluation path*. O-S-P is an important evaluation path. It is defined by concatenating the following relationships: Evaluation path

- O B002 O
- O B003 S
- S A008 P

A structural authorization check deals with describing cutouts (subtrees) of organizational structures as simply as possible. To do so, you define a *start object* (root object) and an *evaluation path*. All objects along the evaluation path are collected, beginning with the start object. The combination of several of these definitions provides a sufficiently general subtree.

Figure 4.12 illustrates a simple example of an organizational plan, built upon organizational units (O1–O5), positions (S1–S4), and employees (P1–P4).

Together with start object O5, evaluation path O-S-P delivers objects O5, S2, S3, P2, and P3.

Up until now, we have outlined the basics of a structural authorization. In the following section, we will explore the control options in detail.

Authorizations in the Context of SAP HR   **151**

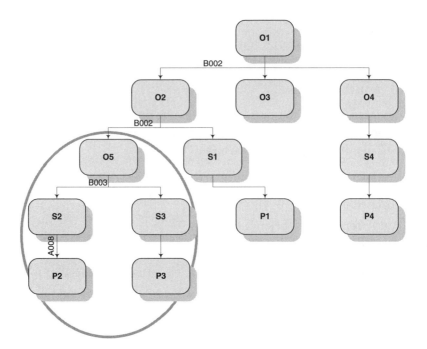

Figure 4.12 Organizational Structure

T77PR—authori-
zation profiles
Table T77PR—definition of the authorization profiles—is essential in this context. Here, the term "authorization profile" is used technically, and has a slightly different meaning than it does in the context of SAP authorizations in general. An entry in the table describes a set of objects in the organizational plan.

The table contains the following columns:

▶ **Authorization profile**
Identification of the authorization profile.

▶ **Plan version**
Only the active plan variant (usually rule 01) is relevant to the integrated operation of Personnel Administration and Organizational Management.

▶ **Object type**
In addition to the self-administered (internal) object types (such as O, C, S, et al) in Organizational Management, only the (external) objects types P (employee) and AP (applicant) are possible.

- ▶ **Object ID**

  A root object is specified in this column; the root object can also be determined at runtime (see the "function module" column).

- ▶ **Evaluation path**

  Beginning with the root object, all objects along the specified evaluation path are collected.

- ▶ **Status vector**

  You can limit the selection of evaluated relationships with this column. Only the relationships that have the status specified in the vector will be considered.

- ▶ **Depth**

  Contains the number of hierarchy levels (from the root object) that will be considered (value 0 means no limitations).

- ▶ **Processing type**

  You determine if the set of objects defined by the entry is subject to maintenance authorization ("x") or only display authorization.

- ▶ **Period**

  The period given here is used to determine the set of hits. For example, entering "D" for the current day means that only the organizational plan valid on the current day is considered. No entry in this column means that all periods will be considered.

- ▶ **Function module**

  If a root object is to be determined at runtime, the "Object ID" column is left blank. Instead, you use this column to enter a function module that determines a root object. Standard SAP contains the function modules for the two most important uses.

  - ▶ RH_GET_MANAGER_ASSIGNMENT (Determine organizational unit for the manager)

    This function module first determines the position for the current user. The result (root object) is the organizational unit, which has the position found by the function module in the first step as senior position (relationship A012).

  - ▶ RH_GET_ORG_ASSIGNMENT (Organizational assignment)

    This function module also first determines the position of the current user. It takes the organizational unit related to the position (A003) as the root object.

For structural authorization, you assign users to authorization profiles in table T77UA. At runtime, the system searches the entry for the current user, from which the profile can be determined. Note the following peculiarity. If the system does not find an entry for the current user, it will search for entry SAP* and processing will continue with the profiles entered under SAP*. If it does not find SAP*, the authorization is refused. In the standard delivery, entry SAP* has all authorizations, so that users who are not explicitly listed have all authorizations regarding structural authorization checks.

When Personnel Administration and Organizational Management are integrated, users typically have authorizations for general authorization checks (P_ORGIN, for example) and structural authorizations to process personnel master data. The general authorizations broadly determine the organizational areas (personnel area, employee group, and employee subgroup) and specify the infotypes/subtypes and the type of processing. Users' structural authorizations limit the object area along the organizational plan.

The following example shows that the concept as described thus far is still incomplete.

A user has personal responsibility for a team—the team is mapped as organizational unit A. In this role, the user has a premium budget that can be used to award team members a bonus. The user does so by creating locked records for infotype *additional payments* (0015) for a limited set of wage types. The personnel department checks and, if approved, unlocks the records created by the user. Using structural authorization checking along with authorizations for P_ORGIN, the case can be mapped as follows.

The user has a structural authorization profile:

▶ Object type O
▶ Object ID A
▶ Evaluation path O-S-P

For authorization object P_ORGIN, the user has an authorization in the following form:

▶ Infotype 0015
▶ Subtype M000–M010
▶ Authorization level R, M, E
▶ Personnel area *

- Employee group *
- Employee subgroup *
- Organizational key *

In addition, the same user appears in a different role. As a project leader, she manages an additional team (organizational unit B). She should not have access to the salary data of these team members, but she should have access to their data recorded for time absent. To grant her access to employee data in organizational unit B, she must receive an adequate structural profile. However, combined with her existing authorizations, she would also have access to infotype 0015 for the members of organizational unit B.

What's the cause of the problem? The definition of the permissible object area does not permit any kind of limitation of the affected infotypes when using a structural authorization profile. Therefore, in the object area determined by the structural authorization check, the user has access to all combinations of infotypes, subtypes, and authorization levels that result from her general authorizations.

Of course, you can circumvent the problem by creating *different user master records* for the various roles. In the case described above, the user then would have to decide which role she is operating under when she logs on to the system. Then, she can select the correct system user for the specific role.

SAP R/3 Enterprise offers a more elegant solution.

Context-Dependent Authorization Check

In addition to the authorization objects used in earlier releases, SAP R/3 Enterprise features three additional authorization objects to control access to personnel master data:

- HR: Master data with context (P_ORGINCON)
- HR: Master data—enhanced check with context (P_ORGXXCON)
- HR: Master data—customer-specific authorization object with context (Z_NNNNNCON)

The basic idea involves using appropriate authorization objects to couple the determination of permissible object areas with infotypes, subtypes, and authorization levels. In general, you can say that you're coupling the object area to the role. In this way, the new authorization object, P_ORGIN-CON, expands the familiar object P_ORGIN. In addition to the fields of P_

Additional authorization objects

ORGIN, P_ORGINCON contains yet another field for the *profile name*. The same holds true for authorization objects P_ORGXXCON and Z_NNNNNCON, which are enhancements of P_ORGXX and the customer-specific object Z_NNNNN. With these objects, you can describe a combination of the familiar fields in P_ORGIN, P_ORGXX, or Z_NNNNN with an authorization profile (according to T77PR).

The case outlined above could be handled as follows. According to structural authorization checking, two profiles are assigned to the user:

▶ **Profile A**
   ▶ Object type O
   ▶ Object ID A
   ▶ Evaluation path O-S-P

▶ **Profile B**
   ▶ Object type O
   ▶ Object ID B
   ▶ Evaluation path O-S-P

For authorization object P_ORGINCON, the user has two authorizations:

▶ **Authorization 1**
   ▶ Infotype 0015
   ▶ Subtype M000 — M010
   ▶ Authorization level R, M, E
   ▶ Personnel area *
   ▶ Employee group *
   ▶ Employee subgroup *
   ▶ Organizational key *
   ▶ Profile A

▶ **Authorization 2**
   ▶ Infotype 2001
   ▶ Subtype *
   ▶ Authorization level R, M, E
   ▶ Personnel area *
   ▶ Employee group *
   ▶ Employee subgroup *
   ▶ Organizational key *
   ▶ Profile B

In addition to the checks described earlier, the system now checks if the user's structural authorization profile permits access to employee data in the current context. In the example above, the current context could be that of someone responsible for a team or that of a project leader. The solution is therefore known as a *context-dependent structural authorization check*.

4.2.5 HR Authorization Main switches

SAP HR offers numerous options to map the most varied customer requirements. Appropriate parameterization of the system can reduce the complexity significantly. Doing so produces advantages for performance and simplifies the setup and maintenance of authorizations, profiles, and users. For example, if no dependencies exist, you can turn off context-dependent authorization checks as they occur in the example given above.

The main authorization switch to control access to employee master data, employee time data, and applicant data can be edited from the IMG under **Personnel Management Personnel Administration · Tools Authorization management · Maintain Authorization Main switches** or with transaction OOAC in system table T77S0 and group AUTSW.

Customizing

Editing deals with the following switches:

▶ **HR: Master Data** (ORGIN)
Controls whether authorization object P_ORGIN is (1) or is not (0) used for the check.

▶ **HR: Master Data—Extended check** (ORGXX)
Controls whether authorization object P_ORGXX is (1) or is not (0) used for the check.

▶ **HR: Customer-specific authorization check** (NNNNN)
Controls whether the customer-specific authorization object for checking is (1) or is not (0) used. A special section treats the customer-specific authorization object (for simplification called Z_NNNNN).

▶ **HR: tolerance time for authorization check** (ADAYS)
When an employee moves from one organization to another, the responsibility of the administrator can also change. The "new" organizational assignment might mean that the administrator loses her access rights to personnel master data. She can continue to access the data during the tolerance period, as though no reassignment had occurred. The tolerance time is specified in days with ADAYS.

► **HR: Master Data—Personnel number check** (PERNR)
Controls whether authorization object P_PERNR is (1) or is not (0) used for the check.

► **HR: Test procedure** (APPRO)
Controls whether the test procedure should (1) or should not (0) be used.

► **HR: Structural authorization check** (ORGPD)
Controls whether and how a structural authorization check is involved in access to employee master data and employee time data. If ORGPD has the value 0, the structural authorization check is not processed. You can also specify how it should be processed if it is to be processed. From the viewpoint of Organizational Management, an employee appears in an organizational plan if he is assigned to a position. In this case and according to structural authorization checks, the user has access to employees who can be reached over an evaluation path (for which he is authorized) in the organizational plan.

If an employee is *not assigned to a position*, there are varied ways for the structural authorization to behave. The following settings can be made for switch ORGPD:

► 1: If the employee is assigned to an organizational unit (infotype 0001), a user with authorization for the organizational unit can access the employee's data. If the employee is not assigned to an organizational unit, access is denied.

► 2: Access is denied.

► 3: If the employee is not assigned to an organizational unit, the user has access; otherwise this setting works like 1.

► 4: Access is granted.

► **HR: Master Data Context** (INCON)
Controls whether authorization object P_ORGINCON is (1) or is not (0) used for the check.

► **HR: Master Data—Enhanced Check Context** (XXCON)
Controls whether authorization object P_ORGXXCON is (1) or is not (0) used for the check.

► **HR: Customer-specific authorization check** (NNCON)
Controls whether the customer-specific authorization object for context-dependent structural authorization checks, Z_NNNNNCON (this is a generic name for the sake of simplicity), is (1) or is not (0) used for the check.

▶ **HR: Default Position Context (DFCON)**
This switch is the analog to ORGPD for context-dependent structural authorization checks.

4.2.6 Time Dependency

Storage of employee data in SAP HR for an exact period—especially an employee's organizational assignment—suggests consideration of temporal dependency for data that is particularly in the control of access authorizations. An employee's organizational assignment has a tremendous influence on if administrators can access that employee's data (i.e., what access options are available). An organizational change can also result in changed authorization for access to the employee's data.

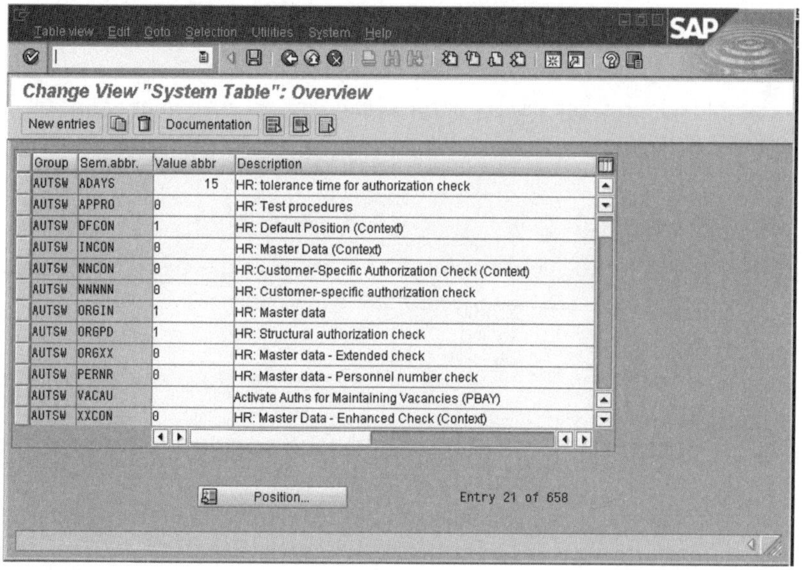

Change of organizational assignment

Figure 4.13 HR Main Authorization Switch (Table T77S0)

Three basic rules determine how the system behaves when the organizational assignment changes. To formulate the rules, we need to understand the term *period of responsibility*, which is defined as the period during which an administrator can access a specific infotype/subtype for the employee. The algorithm used to determine the period of responsibility is described as follows:

Period of responsibility

1. The employee's organizational assignments that apply to the administrator's authorizations are filtered out of all the employee's organizational assignments. If necessary, a structural authorization check is also relevant here.

2. Each of the remaining organizational assignments is checked to determine if the user is authorized for each combination of infotype/subtype that exists and the current operation. If the user is authorized, each organizational assignment returns a period.

3. The intervals determined in the previous steps are added to each other.

Example Let's say that an employee begins in personnel area A, changes to B, and then changes yet again to C. The administrator is authorized to change the main bank details in personnel area A and, in addition, to display the personal data in personnel area B.

We're interested in the period of responsibility of an administrator in regard to the following:

1. Changing the main bank details (infotype 0009, subtype 0)
2. Displaying the personal data (infotype 0002)

In simplified form, the history of the organizational assignment appears as follows:

Start	End	Personnel area
01/01/2001	06/30/2002	A
07/01/2002	09/30/2003	B
10/01/2003	12/31/9999	C

The first step examines only the organizational assignment: the infotype, subtype, and operation are not yet relevant. The user has no authorizations whatsoever for personnel area C; after filtering, the table appears as follows for further processing:

Start	End	Personnel area
01/01/2001	06/30/2002	A
07/01/2002	09/30/2003	B

The second step checks the combination of personnel area, infotype, subtype, and operation for each entry. For point 1 (above) we receive this interval [01/01/2001; 06/30/2002]; for point 2 (above), we receive the following interval [07/01/2002; 09/30/2003].

The third step (adding the periods) results in the periods of responsibility:

1. 01/01/2001—06/30/2002
2. 01/01/2001—09/30/2003

Now the aforementioned rules for time dependency (time logic) can be formulated). The determining factor is the state of the current date (`sy-datum`) in relation to the period of responsibility. If you imagine the employee data as a paper file that moves from one administrator to the next when the employee changes departments, the plausibility of the rules is easy to understand:

Rules for time-dependent access

1. The period of responsibility of the administrator for the employee *begins in the future*. If the administrator has a write authorization for the corresponding infotype/subtype, it covers all infotype records whose validity period lies within the period of responsibility. A read authorization exists for all infotype records whose validity period overlaps the period of responsibility or lies before it.

2. The period of responsibility *begins before the current date; its end date is no more than a fixed number of days (tolerance period) before the current date*. In this case, a write or read authorization covers every necessary period. No restrictions apply to the current administrator's authorizations, in terms of the validity period of the corresponding infotype records.

   The tolerance period was already addressed in the context of the main authorization switches (`ADAYS`). In this manner, the administrator retains access for a transitional period after an employee has transferred out of her department so that she can tend to any last minute details that are related to the transfer.

3. The period of responsibility *ends in the past;* even when the end date is pushed forward by the tolerance period, it still occurs before the current date.

   In this case, the administrator has no write authorization. A read authorization exists for the infotype records whose validity period overlaps with the period of responsibility.

Figure 4.14 illustrates the behavior of authorizations of the administrator responsible for personnel areas A, B, and C as the employee moves from personnel area A, to personnel area B, and finally to personnel area C. (Administrator x has an authorization that exactly covers personnel area x.)

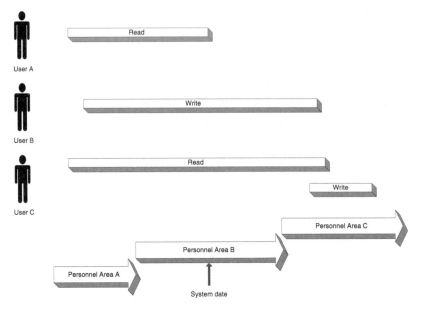

Figure 4.14 Time-Dependent Access Authorizations

In general, a time-dependent authorization check is wanted for most info-types. If it is not required in a particular instance, you can determine (for each infotype) that the period of responsibility should not depend on the progression in time of the employee's organizational assignment. If flag T582A-VALDT is *not* set for an infotype, the period of responsibility is stretched out to 01/01/1800 – 12/31/9999 as soon as the user has authorization in any (earlier, current, or future) of the employee's organizational assignments for access to the infotype/subtype with the current operation. You should be careful when setting up a system and ensure that for every infotype the flag is set if necessary. You can maintain the flag in the IMG by following the menu path **Personnel Management · Personnel Administration · Customizing Procedures · Infotypes · Infotypes**

4.2.7 Implementation

Now that we've adequately reviewed the multifaceted options for the parameters of an authorization check in the context of SAP HR, we can take a more program-oriented, technical look. We'll concentrate on employee or applicant data stored as infotype records.

During the processing of an infotype record, an application must examine the authorization check to determine if the current user has an authorization for the record. Because authorizations should check as many infotypes as possible equally, infotype-specific data is irrelevant. Input parameters for the authorization check include the transaction data and only the fields common to all infotypes.

The determinant data includes the following:

▶ Transaction data
  ▶ Transaction class (employee or applicant)
  ▶ Authorization level
▶ Application data
  ▶ Personnel or applicant number
  ▶ Infotype
  ▶ Subtype
  ▶ Beginning date
  ▶ End date

To simplify the flow of the authorization check, we have chosen to discuss this process step-by-step in the following subsections:

Flow of the authorization check

1. Check based on the personnel number
2. Time-dependent check based on organizational assignment
   ▶ Determination of the period of responsibility
   ▶ Application of time logic
3. Test procedure

Check Based on the Personnel Number

The check based on the personnel number can provide three results:

▶ No decision
▶ Authorized
▶ Not authorized

This check is not supported for applicants. In this case, the result is always "no decision." The same holds true for employees when the check is not active according to the corresponding authorization main switch (PERNR). Time-dependency does not play a role in the context of this check: The personnel or applicant number that is valid on the current date is always used.

Input parameters for a check based on the personnel number include the following:

► Transaction class (employee or applicant)

► Personnel or applicant number

► Infotype

► Subtype

► Authorization level

Flow of a check based on the personnel number The current personnel number being processed first works according to infotype 0105 to determine the system user assigned to the number (subtype 0001). If the assigned system user differs from the current user or if there is no assignment, the check ends with the result: "no decision."

If the assigned user is identical to the current user, the authorization check is called for object P_PERNR:

```
authority-check object 'P_PERNR'
    id 'AUTHC' field level  "Authorization level
    id 'PSIGN' field '*'    "Interpretation of the
                            "assignment
    id 'INFTY' field infty  "Infotype
    id 'SUBTY' field subty  "Subtype
```

In the case of sy-subrc = 0, the check ends with the result: "authorized."

Otherwise, the authorization check is called again:

```
authority-check object 'P_PERNR'
    id 'AUTHC' field level  "Authorization level
    id 'PSIGN' field 'E'    "Interpretation of the
                            "assignment
    id 'INFTY' field infty  "Infotype
    id 'SUBTY' field subty  "Subtype
```

If sy-subrc = 0, the check ends with the result: "not authorized".

If sy-subrc <> 0, the authorization check for P_PERNR is called yet again:

```
authority-check object 'P_PERNR'
    id 'AUTHC' field level  "Authorization level
    id 'PSIGN' field 'I'    "Interpretation of the
                            "assignment
    id 'INFTY' field infty  "Infotype
    id 'SUBTY' field subty  "Subtype
```

If sy-subrc = 0, the result is "authorized"; otherwise it is "no decision". In any case, the check of P_PERNR ends here.

As noted in the previous section, simultaneously populating PSIGN with the values "E" and "I" along with the same values for the remaining fields makes no sense. Doing so would equally and explicitly remove and grant the authorization. The same holds true for PSIGN = '*'.

In order to adhere the general expectation, first, PSIGN with value '*' is checked: therefore, in this procedure, an '*'authorization does not limit the user's access options.

The (inconsistent) combination of "I" and "E" will probably appear only inadvertently. In this case, the system reacts defensively. It will tend to grant the user fewer authorizations, assuming that "E" is the correct entry.

Time-Dependent Check Based on Organizational Assignment

The period of responsibility is determined based on the following parameters:

Determining the period of responsibility

▶ Transaction class (employee or applicant)

▶ Personnel or applicant number

▶ Infotype

▶ Subtype

▶ Authorization level

Depending on the setting of the authorization main switch, authorization objects P_ORGIN, P_ORGXX (or P_APPL), and possibly a *customer-specific authorization object* are involved. A structural authorization check can be called in two ways. First, it can be called for an employee directly—if the employee is assigned to a real position. Secondly, it can be called for the employee's organizational unit, in which case authorization main switches ORGPD or DFCON (with a context-dependent structural authorization) are relevant.

The result is a table of disjoint periods—the combination is the period of responsibility.

The *time logic* is processed on the basis of the period of responsibility. The input parameters for time logic include the following:

Time logic

▶ Transactions class (employee or applicant)

▶ Authorization level

▶ Infotype

- ► Beginning date
- ► End date

If the period of responsibility is empty, the user does not have authorization. In other cases, as long as the time-dependent check (T582A-VALDT) is switched on for the infotype being considered, the result is determined based on the period of responsibility according to the rules formulated in the section on *time dependency*.

Test Procedure

The following parameters are transferred to the test procedure:

- ► Transaction class (employee or applicant)
- ► Personnel or applicant number
- ► Infotype
- ► Subtype
- ► Beginning date

Infotypes 0001 and 0130 are exempt from test procedures. For all other infotypes, the assigned test procedures are determined from table T584A and the write authorization is checked (infotype 0130 with the test procedures as the subtype). If an authorization is present, further checking is unnecessary. If no authorization is present, the maximum check date from all relevant records for infotype 0130 (P0130-CKTYP) is compared with the beginning date (input parameter) of the current infotype record being checked. Only when the beginning date is greater than the maximum check date does the user have (write) authorization.

4.2.8   Enhancement Options

Customer-Specific Authorization Object

As previously noted, standard SAP checks the accesses to infotype data via the standard authorization objects in SAP HR. The main authorization switch can control which of the supported checks should be executed in the customer system.

If the supported objects cannot map the requirements, the option of including a customer-defined authorization object in the infotype authorization check is also supported. Based on the definition of the object, the applicable coding requires modifications. The coding is stored in program MPPAUTZZ–it can be generated with the utility program RPUACG00 from the requested authorization object.

The steps of the procedure include the following:

▶ Creation of a customer-specific authorization object in the customer-naming environment ("Z:ORGCC" for example)—the existing objects must not be changed.

The following can be used as authorization fields:

   ▶ Fields from structure P0001; customer-specific fields (from CI_P0001) are also possible but they must have been created previously as authorization fields: **Tools ABAP Workbench · Development · Other Tools · Authorization Objects Fields** (or Transaction SU20). At the definition of the authorization object, the field name from P0001 (without a prefix) is specified. *Exception*: If required, PERSA (not WERKS) is used as field for the personnel area.

   ▶ INFTY—Infotype

   ▶ SUBTY—Subtype

   ▶ AUTHC—Authorization level

   ▶ TCD—Transaction code

▶ Maintenance of the check indicators

   ▶ Transaction SU22

   ▶ Entry of the transaction under which checking occurs

   ▶ Insertion of the authorization object

   ▶ Marking the check indicator that you want: usually CM

This step is *not mandatory*: If the assignment of the object to the transaction does not exist, the check is executed according to the coding. However, when generating authorizations from the transaction with the Profile Generator (role maintenance), the object is not automatically considered. In this case, the object and the authorizations must be inserted manually.

▶ Creation of the corresponding authorizations and profiles

▶ Generation of the coding with utility program RPUACG00

   ▶ Starting the program (transaction SE38)

   ▶ Input of the authorization object

   ▶ Selection: is the object to be processed as part of the context authorization or not

   ▶ Entry of the user name as password: The intention of the password here is simply to block starting the program by accident. Protection from an unauthorized start is controlled by the authorization group of the program.

▶ Activation of the check with authorization main switch NNNNN (table T77S0, group AUTSW).

As an example, we'll create a customer-specific authorization object with a customer-specific field (P0001-ZZORG) from infotype "organizational assignment" and the transaction code field.

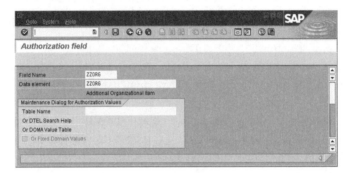

Figure 4.15 Creating an Authorization Field

Authorization Field To support entry help during the maintenance of authorizations, you can specify the check table, search help, or fixed values of the domain when defining the authorization field.

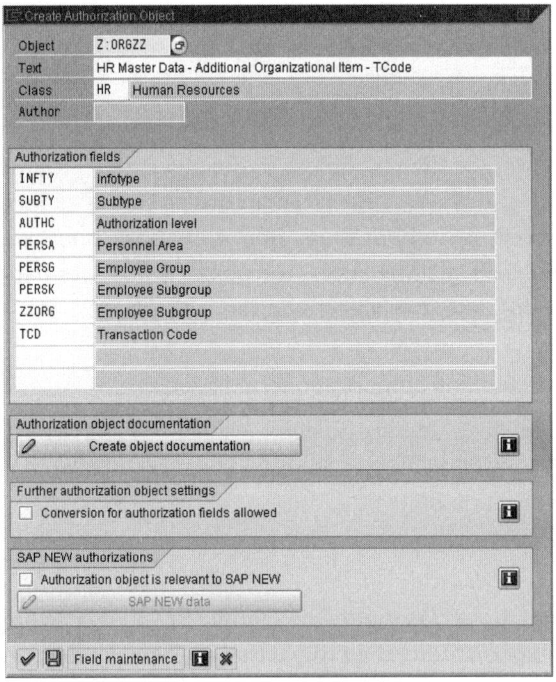

Figure 4.16 Creating an Authorization Object

We record field TCD—transaction code—in the authorization object in addition to field ZZORG, a user-defined organizational term. In this manner, the authorization can be checked for infotypes based on a transaction. For example, you can map a specific check within a customer-specific version of transaction PA30.

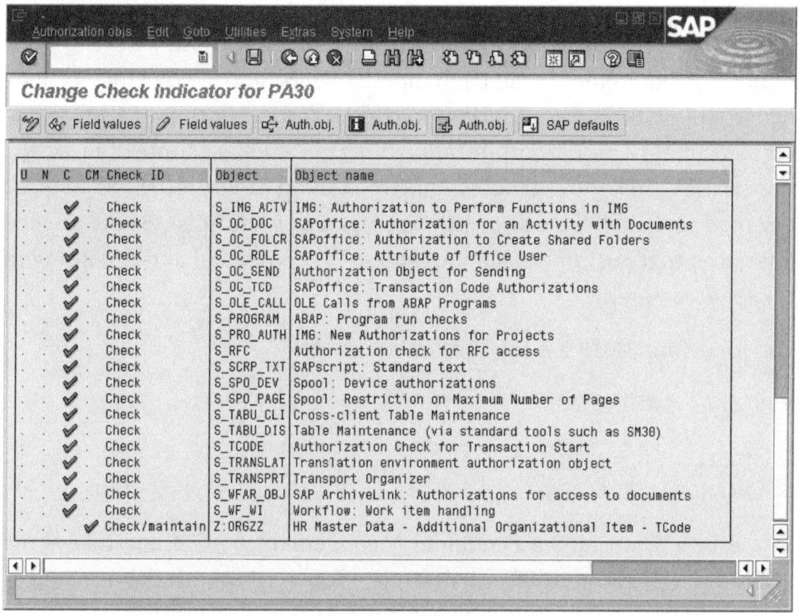

Authorization Object

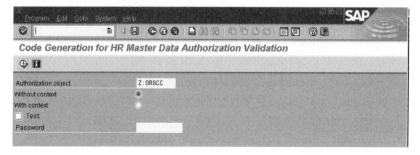

Figure 4.17 Maintaining the Check Indicator

Marking column CM has the following effects:

Check Indicator

▶ The object is considered when generating profiles for Transaction PA30 in the context of role maintenance. If field values are also maintained, they will be proposed during generation.

▶ The authorization object is checked at runtime.

Figure 4.18 Starting Report RPUACG00

Generating Code The specified parameters generate the code for the authorization check with object Z:ORGCC in SAP HR application programs. If the object is to be used within a *context-dependent structural authorization check,* mark the **With context** parameter. To prohibit an accidental change of coding, a password (current user name) must be entered.

Business Add-Ins (BAdIs)

Almost all requirements can be mapped, thanks to the wide range of configuration for infotype authorization checks and the option of also including a customer-specific authorization object in a default context. In exceptional cases, the entire standard implementation can be redefined *without any modifications*. You do so with *business add-ins* (BAdIs). BAdIs provide interfaces that customers can implement when needed and according to the logic required.

The following BAdIs are relevant in this context:

▶ HRPAD00AUTH_CHECK

▶ HRPAD00AUTH_TIME

▶ HRBAS00_STRUAUTH

In the IMG, start at the **Personnel Management** branch and follow the menu path **Personnel Administration · Tools · Authorization management · BAdI: Set Up Customer-Specific Authorization Check** to access the implementation of HRPAD00AUTH_CHECK. The methods cannot be implemented in isolation—as soon as an implementation is active for one method, the standard is inactive, and all other methods must also be implemented.

The following methods are involved:

▶ CHECK_AUTHORIZATION
This method checks the authorization for an infotype record.

Input parameters:

   ▷ TCLAS—Transaction class

   ▷ LEVEL—Authorization level (R, W, S, E, D, M)

   ▷ PERNR—Personnel or applicant number

   ▷ INFTY—Infotype

   ▷ SUBTY—Subtype

   ▷ BEGDA—Beginning date

- ENDDA—End date
- PROCESS_ONLY_PARTIAL_CHECKS—A flag that decides if the organizational assignment is ('X') or is not ('-') considered.

Parameter IS_AUTHORIZED delivers the results: 'X' is authorized or '-' is not authorized.

▶ SET_ORG_ASSIGNMENT
This method can transfer infotype 0001 data (*organizational assignment*) to the authorization check. Because the authorization check typically refers to this data, typically, only performance considerations call for an explicit transfer.

Input parameters:

- TCLAS—Transaction class
- P0001_TAB—Table with the records on the organizational assignment

▶ SET_PARTIAL_ORG_ASSIGNMENT
In certain contexts, only parts of the organizational assignment are known. For example, within a hiring action in the input screen of infotype 0000, only the personnel area, the employee group, and the employee subgroup are specified. To use this partial information of the organizational assignment as the basis for an authorization check, this method is used to transfer the known fields to the authorization check.

Input parameters:

- TCLAS—Transaction class
- P0001—Organizational assignment
- FIELDLIST—List of the fields to be considered from infotype 0001

▶ CHECK_MAX_LEVEL_AUTHORIZATION
This method determines if a user has a *maximum* authorization for a given authorization level. If this is the case, the user is authorized and no other authorization checks are executed. The primary intent of this method is performance optimization: the implementation should therefore operate efficiently.

Input parameters:

- TCLAS—Transaction class
- LEVEL—Authorization level (R, W, S, E, D, M)

Parameter IS_AUTHORIZED delivers the results: 'X' for maximum authorization or '-' for non-maximum authorization.

▶ `CHECK_MAX_INFTY_AUTHORIZATION`

Like the previous method (`CHECK_MAX_LEVEL_AUTHORIZATION`), this method determines the maximum authorization with the additional specification of the infotype.

Additional input parameter:

▶ `INFTY`—Infotype

▶ `CHECK_MAX_SUBTY_AUTHORIZATION`

Like the previous method (`CHECK_MAX_INFTY_AUTHORIZATION`), this method determines the maximum authorization with the additional specification of the subtype.

Additional input parameter:

▶ `SUBTY`—Subtype

▶ `CHECK_MIN_LEVEL_AUTHORIZATION`

This method is the opposite of `CHECK_MAX_LEVEL_AUTHORIZATION`. It determines if a user has a *minimum* authorization for a given authorization level. If this is the case, the user is not authorized and *no other authorization checks* are executed. Here too, the primary intent of the method is *performance optimization*: the implementation should therefore operate efficiently.

Input parameters:

▶ `TCLAS`—Transaction class

▶ `LEVEL`—Authorization level (R, W, S, E, D, M)

Parameter `IS_AUTHORIZED` delivers the results: `'X'` for minimum authorization or `'-'` for no minimum authorization.

▶ `CHECK_MIN_INFTY_AUTHORIZATION`

Like the previous method (`CHECK_MIN_LEVEL_AUTHORIZATION`), this method determines the minimum authorization with the additional specification of the infotype.

Additional input parameter:

▶ `INFTY`—Infotype

▶ `CHECK_MIN_SUBTY_AUTHORIZATION`

Like the previous method (`CHECK_MIN_INFTY_AUTHORIZATION`), this method determines the minimum authorization with the additional specification of the subtype.

Additional input parameter:

▶ `SUBTY`—Subtype

▶ CHECK_PERNR_AUTHORIZATION

From the viewpoint of the HR application, an infotype authorization check without specification of the infotype makes little or no sense. However, in some cases, no infotype should be checked when other applications access employee data. This method does not require specification of infotype and subtype. The standard system uses the value SPACE (infotype, subtype) for the check.

Input parameters:

  ▶ TCLAS—Transaction class

  ▶ LEVEL—Authorization level (R, W, S, E, D, M)

  ▶ PERNR—Personnel or applicant number

  ▶ BEGDA—Beginning date

  ▶ ENDDA—End date

Parameter IS_AUTHORIZED delivers the results: 'X' is authorized or '-' is not authorized.

▶ CHECK_MAX_PERNR_AUTHORIZATION

Like the CHECK_PERNR_AUTHORIZATION method; the standard checks the infotype and subtype here with an asterisk (*).

▶ CHECK_MIN_PERNR_AUTHORIZATION

Like the last two methods, the standard does not check the infotype and subtype (technically, DUMMY is used to check fields INFTY and SUBTY in authority-check.

▶ DELAYED_CONSTRUCTOR

This method is processed directly after the generation of an authorization check instance (constructor). SAP generally recommends an empty implementation.

BAdI HRPAD00AUTH_TIME (delivered within a support package of SAP R/3 4.6C and SAP R/3 Enterprise) enables a change of *only the time logic* of the authorization check. This BAdI significantly reduces the effort needed in cases that require only a modification of the time logic. You cannot navigate to the implementation of the BAdI from the IMG. Use Transaction SE19 to get to the implementation; use Transaction 'SE18' to go to the definition of the BAdI.

Details of the methods:

▶ CONSIDER_SY_DATUM_EXIT

With this method, you can use customer-specific logic to set the table of intervals in which the user is authorized.

Input parameters:

- LEVEL—Authorization level (R, W, S, E, D, M)
- INFTY—Infotype
- LOW_BEGDA—lowest beginning date for infotype 0001

Return parameter:

- EXIT_FLAG—No more processing of the standard method

Changing parameter:

- AUTHORIZATION_PERIODS_TAB—Table with time intervals in which the user is authorized

▶ BEGDA_ENDDA_COMPARE_EXIT

Using this method, you can decide if an authorization exists for a given period. This is done based on the table of intervals in which the user is authorized.

Input parameters:

- BEGDA—Beginning date
- ENDDA—End date
- AUTHORIZATION_PERIODS_TAB—Table with intervals in which the user is authorized

Return parameters:

- EXIT_FLAG—No more processing of the standard method
- IS_AUTHORIZED—'X' maximum authorization or '-' no maximum authorization

The structural authorization check can be re-implemented in BAdI HRBAS00_STRUAUTH. You can navigate to the implementation of the BAdIs in the IMG for Personnel Management by following the path **Organizational Management · Basic Settings · Authorization Management · Structural Authorization · BAdI: Structural Authorization**. If you use this BAdI, all methods (of this BAdI) must be implemented. Given the complexity of the topic, we recommend that you use the sample coding delivered by SAP as a point of orientation. You can display the definition of the BAdI with Transaction SE18. From **GoTo** you can navigate to the sample coding. The following serves as a short introduction to the methods:

▶ CHECK_AUTHORITY_VIEW

This method can change the set of objects determined for a user.

Input parameters:

- FCODE—Function code
- PLVAR—Plan version

- OTYPE—Object type
- OBJID—Object ID
- UNAME—User name
- VIEW—Set of objects for the user

Return parameters:

- EXIT_FLAG—No more processing of the standard method
- CHECK_OBJECT_OUT—changed set of objects

▶ FILL_DATE_VIEW

This method fills the table with the periods for an object. The input parameters are identical to those of the previous method.

Return parameters:

- EXIT_FLAG—No more processing of the standard method
- DATE_VIEW—periods in which authorization is present for an object

▶ FILL_HYPER_VIEW

This method fills the table of relationships for which authorization is present.

Input parameters:

- PLVAR—Plan version
- SCLAS—Type of the related object
- UNAME—User name

Return parameters:

- EXIT_FLAG—No more processing of the standard method
- HYPER_VIEW—Table of relationships for which the user is authorized

▶ CHECK_AUTH_PLAN1

This method can check the structural authorizations from the viewpoint of Personnel Administration. It returns the time periods where the user is authorized.

Input parameters:

- PLVAR—Plan version
- OTYPE—Object type
- OBJID—Object ID
- BEGDA—Beginning date
- ENDDA—End date
- MAINT—Flag: object is maintained by operation
- VIEW—Set of objects for the user

Return parameters:

- PERIODS—Periods in which authorization is present for the object
- EXIT_FLAG—No more processing of the standard method
- CHECK_OBJECT_OUT—another object that was determined and that might (EXIT_FLAG) still need to be checked

▶ CHECK_AUTHORITY_SEARCH

In the context of searching (input Help), this method can influence the execution of the structural authorization check.

Input parameters:

- PLVAR—Plan version
- OTYPES—Table with object types
- SKIP_STANDARD—Do not process the structural authorization check in the standard

Changing parameter:

- OBJECTS—Results table with the desired objects

▶ GET_PROFILES

This method determines the table of the structural profiles (including periods). A new object to be checked might be determined, which is then typically subject to the standard check.

Input parameters:

- MAINT—Flag: Operation is maintained for the object
- PLVAR—Plan version
- OTYPE—Object type
- OBJID—Object ID
- UNAME—User name
- VIEW—Set of objects for the user

Return parameters:

- EXIT_FLAG—Do not process standard coding
- CHECK_OBJECT_OUT—Another object that was determined and that might (EXIT_FLAG) be checked
- PROFL_TAB—Table with the (structural) profiles

4.2.9 Interaction Between the Application and the Authorization Check

Authorization Checks in Application Programs

Generally, the language elements available in ABAP allow unrestricted access to any data stored in the system. Accordingly, the application developer is responsible for calling an appropriate authorization check after the retrieval of critical data, and for processing the results in a manner that ensures that the application works correctly in terms of data protection and privacy. This is certainly the case with standard SAP applications. Typically, you should consider the following when processing critical personnel data:

Ideally, all applications that use infotypes access data via recommended interfaces.

Read/Write Access

Read accesses with logical databases PNP and PCH or with function module `HR_READ_INFOTYPE` automatically perform an authorization check. When `SELECT` statements (in a customer-specific program, for example) are used to read directly from the database (PAnnnn), ensure that the authorization check is called explicitly. If the user has no authorization, the application must proceed accordingly.

Both authorization and consistency considerations suggest that *write accesses* to infotypes should not go directly to the database. Calls of standard transaction with `CALL TRANSACTION` are generally non-critical. In this case, consistency and correct authorization checking is guaranteed.

Dialog vs. Reporting

Aside from authorization object `P_ABAP`, it's irrelevant to an authorization check if it is called as part of a transaction or a report. The check always occurs at the level of the individual record. The tool that is being used to read data plays no role whatsoever in determining whether a user is authorized to display data.

Nonetheless, a few peculiarities exist within system behavior processing the result of an authorization check—for example, in the behavior of dialog for standard transactions and in reporting.

In the initial screen of the maintenance transaction for employee data (PA30), the user specifies the personnel number, infotype, and (possibly) subtype and a function (display, change, delete, list, and so on). As early as this point, the system checks the available information to determine if the user is authorized. The specified subtype, in particular, is checked. If the user did not specify a subtype, SPACE is used. That leads to a problem for users with restricted subtype authorization, if they do not explicitly have authorization for subtype SPACE. However, this problem can be easily avoided by specifying subtype SPACE in the restricted authorizations.

During the processing of an individual record in the context of a dialog transaction, the system can directly quit a user's unauthorized access attempt. The user receives an error message related to the questionable record and can react accordingly.

Unauthorized access attempts during the processing of a set of employees in reporting, with logical database PNP, are handled as follows:

▶ From the start, the system checks to see if the user is authorized for all the infotypes that the report requires. If the check fails, further processing is aborted (minimum authorization).

▶ If the user has minimum authorization, and the system determines that the user does not have authorization for individual infotype records, the following variations apply:

   ▶ No data for the employee under consideration is processed

   ▶ Only that data for which the user is authorized is delivered

The first variation is the standard. For the second variant to occur, the application report must contain the statement PNP_SW_SKIP_PERNR = 'N' at the INITIALIZATION event.

Logical database PNP generally reads all the records of an infotype (all subtypes and all periods) requested by an application program. Accordingly, the following can occur. The application report is interested only in infotype records in a limited period. The logical database, however, works according to the first variant and skips over employees because the user is not authorized for data outside the period relevant to the report. This effect can be avoided with the use of macro RP_SET_DATA_INTERVAL— called in the application report at the START-OF-SELECTION event: The macro can pass a period for data selection to the logical database.

4.2.10 Searching for Errors

Transaction SU53 is a simple way of dealing with authorization problems. The transaction displays the data of the last authorization check that failed: it displays the checked object, the field values being checked, and the user's authorizations for the object. The list of user's authorizations is generally usable, but the field values are not always reliable. Buffering mechanisms and stock authorization checks mean that the last failed check is not always the cause of the failed authorization.

Debugging (processing the coding step-by-step with the possibility to display and replace the content of variables at runtime) often leads to success. SAP delivers the profile S_A.DEVELOP, which can be quickly granted to a user to authorize debugging. However, please note (especially in a productive system) that users with debugging authorization can create additional, far-reaching authorizations for themselves.

Debugging

Because of the unusual semantics of the PSIGN field in authorization object P_PERNR and the problems caused by the simultaneous appearance of values "E" and "I", incorrect authorizations for P_PERNR are frequently a source of errors.

Personnel number check

For problems relating to time dependency, you should examine the history of the organizational assignment. Often, after closer analysis of purported errors, you learn that the system actually behaves according to the rules of time-dependent authorization checks. A case of inconsistent records for the organizational assignment is a rarer occurrence, but is nonetheless problematic. The system cannot make sense out of gaps or multiple assignments on the time axis—particularly with authorization checks.

History of organizational assignment

5 Adjusting the Applications

Using Customizing, you will learn that you can make further adjustments to HR, without having to modify the system. This chapter will show you just what adjustments are possible and how best to execute them.

5.1 Personnel Administration

In personnel administration, it's often necessary to develop company-specific ways to process and save additional information—you can do this in a multitude of ways. You can implement company-specific defaults and checks for existing fields. You can include additional fields in existing infotypes. You can create customer-specific infotypes. There are even fast entry possibilities that enable you to edit the data in an infotype for many employees simultaneously. The fast entry function also allows for multiple-infotype editing on one screen. In the next section, we'll explain just how to set up these functions.

Adjustment possibilities

5.1.1 Components in the Repository

In order to create and edit infotypes, it's important that you know the specific components required in infotypes. You can have up to 10,000 infotypes in the SAP system, numbered from 0000 to 9999. We described the naming conventions in Chapter 2.

Components

The individual components can be viewed in the repository. The program `MPnnnn00` forms the basis for every infotype, where `nnnn` stands for the number of the infotype in question. In Figure 5.1, you can see the components of infotype 0007, *Planned working time*. As you can see in the Object Navigator, which is called using Transaction SE80, an infotype is consists of the following components, among others:

▶ DDIC structures (tables, table rows)
▶ Fields (local)
▶ Modules (PAI, PBO)
▶ Subprograms
▶ Screens
▶ GUI components (title, status)
▶ Dialog modules

For permanent storage in the database, the tables described in Chapter 2 are also necessary.

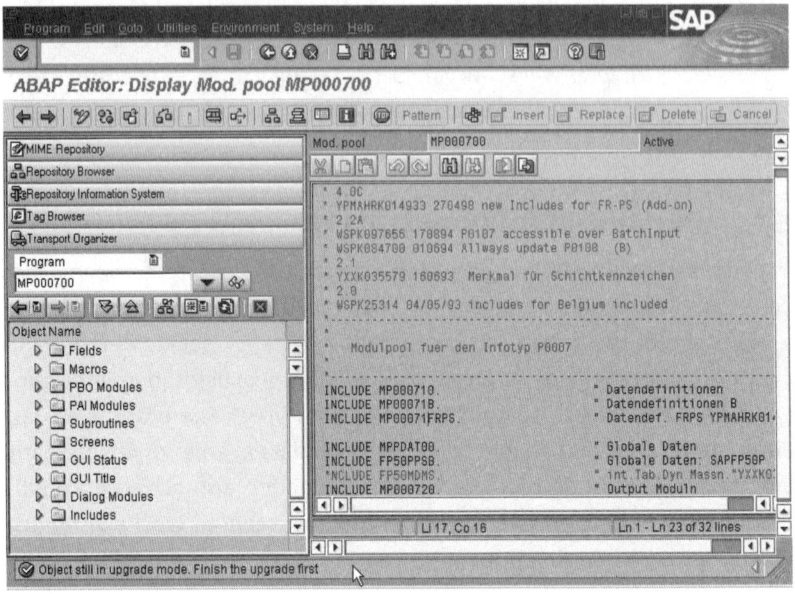

Figure 5.1 Infotype Objects in the Object Navigator

Requirements in the enterprise When SAP Personnel Administration is used in an enterprise, the following requirements are often typical:

▶ The generation of *default values,* depending on entries in the current or other infotypes. In order to create default values, customer-specific tables or features must be read.

▶ Certain *customizing checks* are required, in addition to those checks already available in the standard.

▶ *Additional fields* are required in infotypes, recorded with the same validity period as the standard fields.

▶ Customer-specific fields with little or no relation to the standard fields must be processed in a separate *customer infotype*.

▶ You may also want to maintain these fields in *fast entry for more than one person*.

▶ Fields from different infotypes need to be processed together in one screen in *fast entry for action data*.

Function module exits, enhancements using Transaction PM01, or BAdIs can be used to meet these requirements.

5.1.2 Enhancing Infotypes

Infotypes can be enhanced by adding extra default values and checks, or by adding extra fields.

Default Values

The SAP standard application offers possibilities for customizing default values for many input fields in HR master data. This is usually done by setting SET/GET parameters or by maintaining features; it is less frequently achieved with additional customizing tables. These functions can also be enhanced using function module exits and BAdIs.

Default values in the SAP standard

Furthermore, additional customer-specific checks can be implemented with the help of this functionality. Such checks can be based on information about the infotype or other infotypes; or based on data outside the realm of HR.

In Figure 5.2, you can see a diagram of the process flow when a function module exit is called.

Function module exit

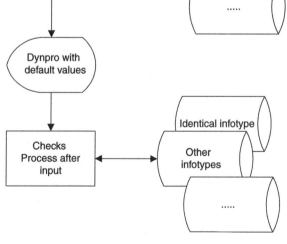

Figure 5.2 Sequence When a Function Module Exit Is Called

You call a function module exit using the module `before_output` (include `MPPERS00`) which is used by all infotypes:

```
MODULE before_output OUTPUT.
   ...
      IF psyst-iinit[1] EQ yes AND
         ...
      PERFORM customer_function_pbo(sapfp50m).
      move_cprel_to_pnnnn.
   ENDIF.
   PERFORM badi_before_output(sapfp50m).
```

The following example should help to explain the use of default values.

Example default value

Employees frequently live in the same city in which they work. Both the city and perhaps the zip code of the personnel area should be read and used as a default when the address is being created. If this infotype is copied, the default values should also be displayed, meaning that the copy template is also overwritten with the default values. The older procedure with function module exit EXIT_SAPF50M_001 from enhancement PBAS0001 is presented first. Later on, the enhancement using the BAdI HRPAD00INFTY is shown, in which the coding for implementing the method can, to a large extent, be transferred from the function module exit. The result of using default values is shown in Figure 5.3.

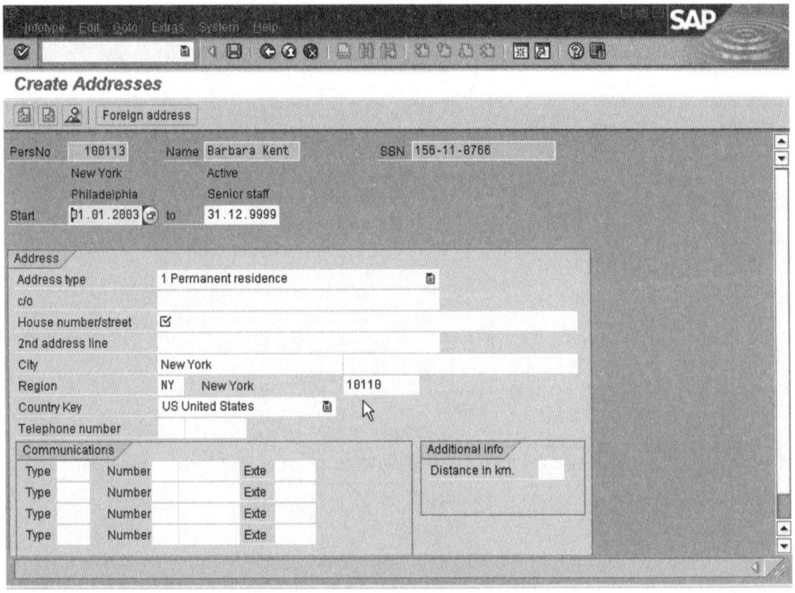

Figure 5.3 Default Values in Infotype 0006, Addresses

---

1   When the infotype is first displayed the variable has the value YES(1). The variables PSYST-IINIT will be explained below (see Section 5.1.3).

The enhancement for additional checks with the function module exit can be done by calling a *customer function* in the standard program.

Customer function

```
FORM CUSTOMER_FUNCTION_PBO.
  CALL CUSTOMER-FUNCTION '001'
      EXPORTING
            TCLAS   = PSPAR-TCLAS
            INNNN   = CPREL
            IPSYST  = PSYST
            I001P   = T001P
            I503    = T503
      IMPORTING
            INNNN   = CPREL
      CHANGING
            IPREF   = PREF
      EXCEPTIONS
            OTHERS  = 1.
ENDFORM.
```

The function module `EXIT_SAPFP50M_001`, which contains the include `ZXPADU01`, is called. The changes should not be carried out immediately. Additional structuring should be done in several includes, particularly in large projects.

```
*&---------------------------------------------------------------*
*&  Include ZXPADU01
*&---------------------------------------------------------------*
* Addresses [0006]
INCLUDE ythr_p0006_default.
```

In the actual includes, it is then necessary to use the `IF` query to check that the infotype to be edited is present. The default value is determined in the include for this infotype.

In order for the function module exit to be processed, you must perform the following steps:

1. Create an enhancement project.
2. Select the SAP enhancement.
3. Specify the functions that you want in the special coding.
4. Activate the enhancement project.

5. Test the enhancement.

6. Transport the enhancement to the production system.

The enhancement project is created using Transaction CMOD. In Figure 5.4, you can see project "YTHR0001" for SAP enhancement PBAS0001, with the two function module exits: EXIT_SAPFP50M_001 and EXIT_SAPFP50M_002.

Transfer parameter You can specify functions using the following data:

TCLAS	Transaction class (A = employee, B = applicant)
IPSYST	Work fields for dialog control and selected fields from organizational assignment (IT 0001), which is valid from the start date of the current record (INNNN-BEGDA)
INNNN	The infotype edited in structure PNNNN
PSAVE	Old value of the current infotype (only with EXIT_SAPFP50M_002)
I001P	Table T001P (personnel subareas), determined with the current organizational assignment (IPSYST-WERKS, IPSYST-BTRTL)
I503	Table T503 (employee subgroup), determined with the current organizational assignment (IPSYST-PERSG, IPSYST-PERSK)
IPREF	Assignment sizes for HR objects

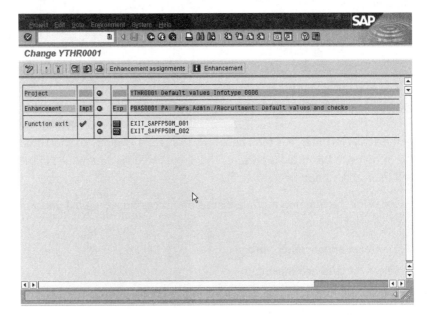

Figure 5.4 Presentation of Enhancements with Transaction CMOD

The program for determining the default values can be as follows:

```
FIELD-SYMBOLS <p0006> TYPE p0006.
DATA:  w_t500p TYPE t500p.
ASSIGN innnn TO <p0006> CASTING.
```

Zip code, city, and state are read based on the current personnel area in IPSYST-WERKS and determined from table T500P. Finally, the contents of these data fields are transferred to <p0006> and therefore, also to innnn.

```
* Fill default values for permanent residence
IF innnn-infty = '0006'.
  IF <p0006>-subty = '1'.
    SELECT SINGLE * FROM t500p
           INTO w_t500p
           WHERE  persa  = ipsyst-werks.
    IF sy-subrc = 0.
      <p0006>-pstlz = w_t500p-pstlz.
      <p0006>-ort01 = w_t500p-ort01.
      <p0006>-state = w_t500p-state.
    ENDIF.
  ENDIF.
ENDIF.
```

The effect of the coding listed above is that the fields in infotype 0006, subtype 1, are filled if an entry is found in table T500P for the current personnel area.

Validation Check

The same project is used for the validation check. The function module EXIT_SAPFP50M_002, which contains the include ZXPADU02, is called. You can now proceed in the same way as you did when implementing default values.

The following example shows how to set up a customer-defined check for the standard field ENTKM (distance in miles/kilometers) in infotype 0006. Only values between 30 and 300 miles should be permitted. If values fall short of or exceed this limit, different messages should be issued.

Example of validation check

```
FIELD-SYMBOLS: <p0006> TYPE p0006.
ASSIGN innnn TO <p0006> CASTING.
```

```
IF innnn-infty = '0006'.
  IF NOT <p0006>-entkm IS INITIAL.
    IF <p0006>-entkm LT 30.
      MESSAGE e100(ythr).
*   Distance too small.
    ELSEIF <p0006>-entkm GT 300.
      MESSAGE e101(ythr).
*   Distance too big.
    ELSE.
*   o.k.
    ENDIF.
  ENDIF.
ENDIF.
```

Realization with a BAdI

Using BAdIs   If you implement the BAdI HRPAD00INFTY, you can benefit from the same
functions for customer checks, but you have greater flexibility with these
checks. Use Transaction SE18 to display the BAdI Builder.

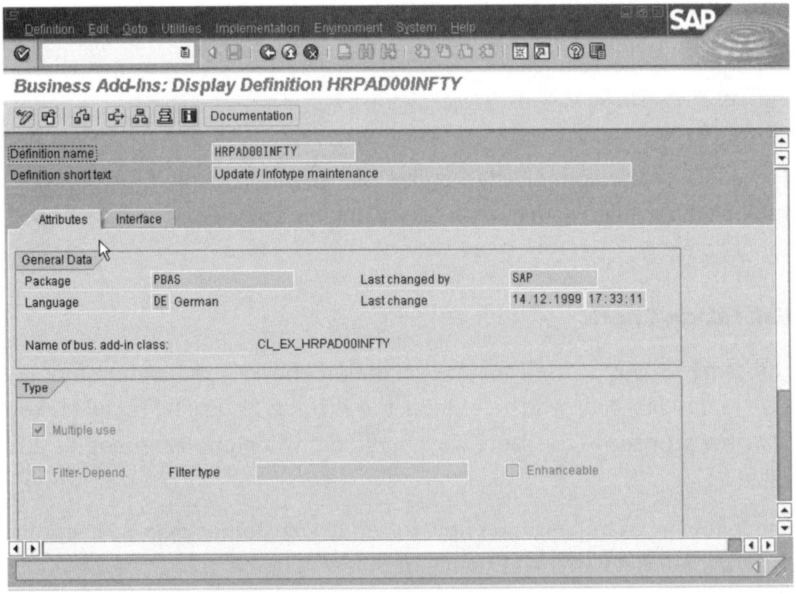

Figure 5.5 BAdI HRPAD00INFTY

Three methods are available in this BAdI. The second of these methods is
for customer checks.

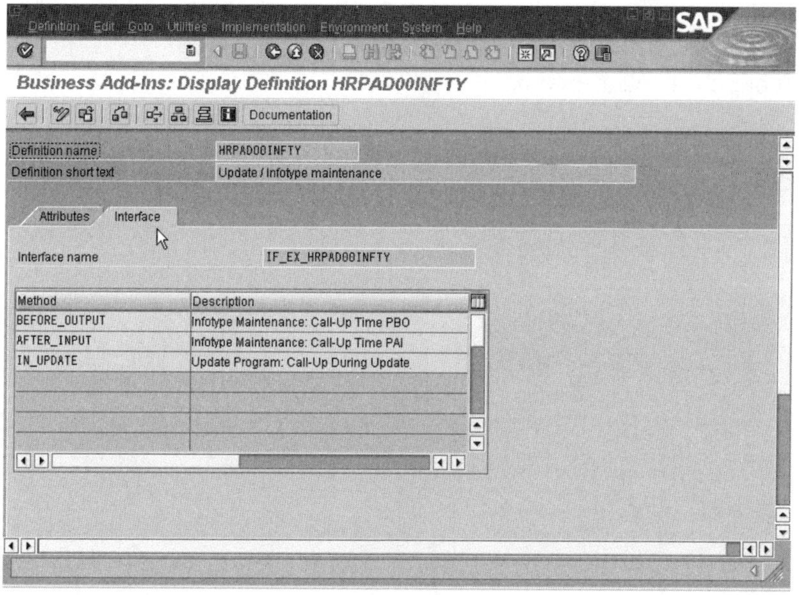

Figure 5.6 Methods in the BAdI HRPAD00INFTY

Implementation can be done with Transaction SE19, or from the **Implementation** menu in the BAdI definition.

Implementation

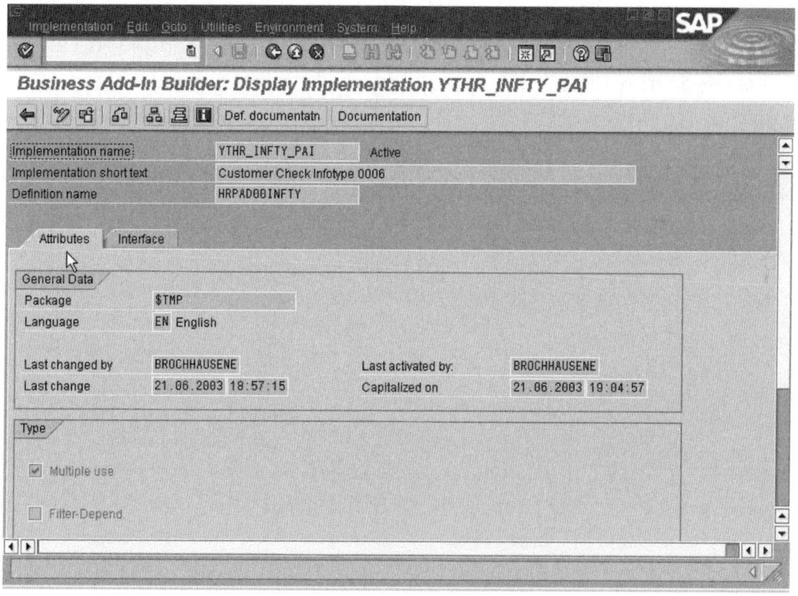

Figure 5.7 Implementing the BAdI HRPAD00INFTY

In this example, the implementation is done under the name "YTHR_INFTY_PAI" (*Customer Check*). The class YCL_IM_THR_INFTY_PAI is created during the implementation.

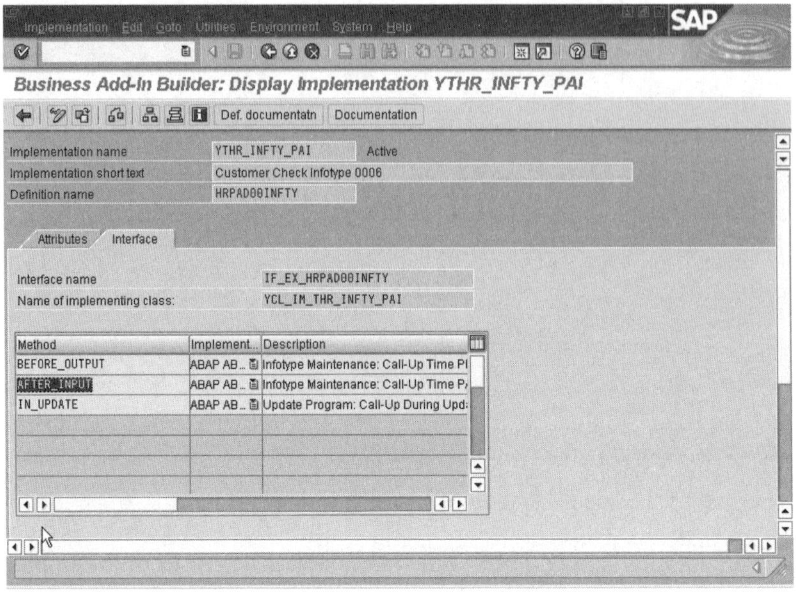

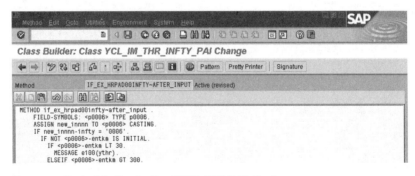

Figure 5.8 Methods of the Implementation YTHR_INFTY_PAI

Coding The coding is inserted in the method named. In this example, it can be transferred from the coding applied if function module exit EXIT_SAPFP50M_002 is used.

Figure 5.9 Start of Coding for the AFTER_INPUT Method

Enhancements with Additional Fields

In addition to the default values and validation checks for standard fields presented in the last section, there are often customer-defined fields, which, given their semantics, fit into an existing standard infotype. Transaction PM01 enables you to enhance infotypes in the SAP standard with customer-specific fields.

Customer-defined fields

These adjustments do not constitute a modification and problems don't usually arise in the event of a release upgrade. You cannot enhance the infotypes 0000 (*Actions*) and 0302 (*Additional Actions*).

The following example should help to explain how an infotype can be enhanced with additional fields.

In accordance with a special contractual agreement, some employees work at home. This adjustment should be recorded in infotype 0016 (*Contract elements*). You can add a check box for **Homeoffice** to the screen display, the result of which is shown in Figure 5.10.

Example

The enhancement functions of Transaction PM01 are used to carry out this infotype enhancement, as shown in Figure 5.11.

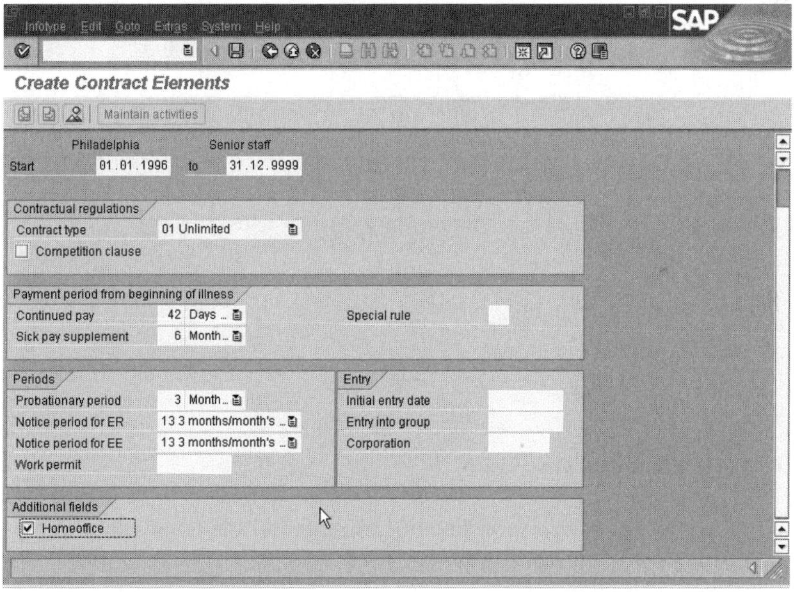

Figure 5.10 Additional Fields in Infotype 0016, Contract Elements

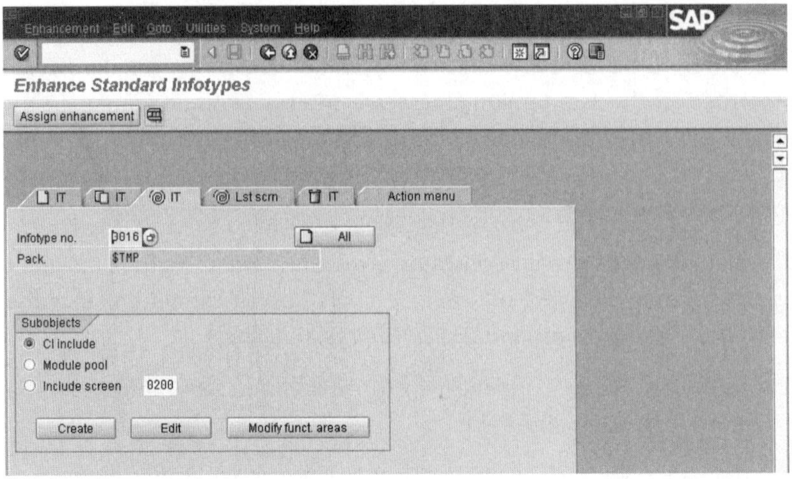

Figure 5.11 Enhancing Infotype 0016 with PM01

Method of procedure

There are four steps involved in carrying out this assignment:

1. Create the fields for enhancing infotype 0016 in the Dictionary (see Figure 5.12). You can go directly to the Dictionary from Transaction PM01. If necessary, you should create a specific component type for each CI table field. Structure CI_P0016 is activated, and along with it, the dependent structures and tables are created as well.

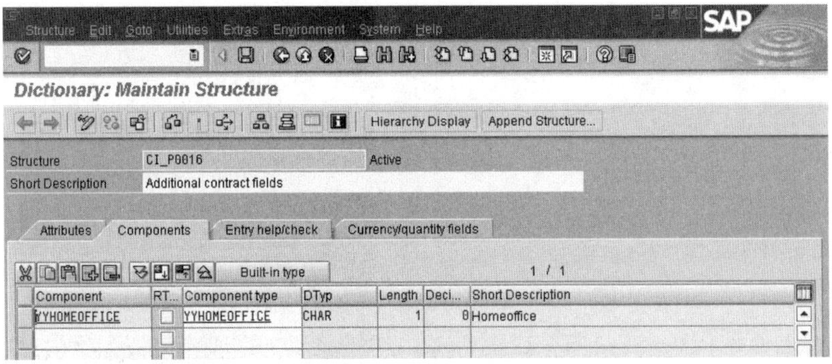

Figure 5.12 Include Structure CI_P0016

2. If you check the corresponding button, the module pool will be generated automatically and can then be enhanced to meet your specific requirements.

   It contains the following includes:

   ▶ Include ZP001610 [global data]
   ▶ Include MPPDAT00

- ▶ Include `FP50PPSB`
- ▶ Include `MPPERS00`
- ▶ Include `ZP001620` [PBO module]
- ▶ Include `ZP001630` [PAI module]
- ▶ Include `ZP001640` [form routines]

The includes `ZP0016xx` contain customer-specific coding.

3. You can customize the screen using the ScreenPainter. In the example considered, the field `YYHOMEOFFICE` is converted into a check box.

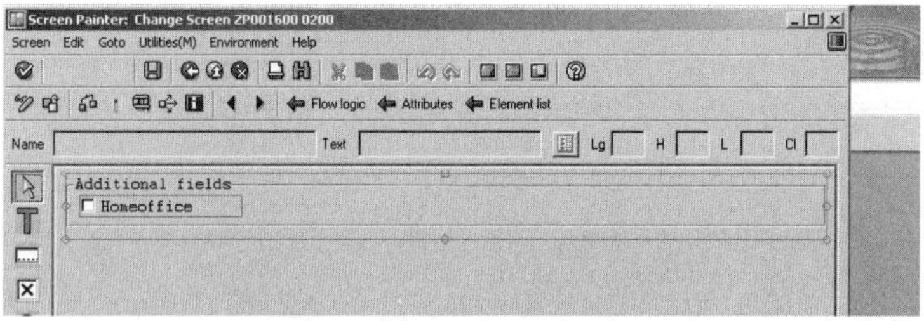

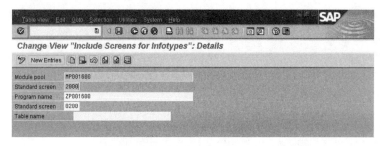

Figure 5.13 Adjusting Screen 0200 in the ScreenPainter

4. Assign the include screen to the standard screen. You do this by using the **Assign enhancement** button. This entry, which can be seen in Figure 5.14, ensures that the screen appears below the standard fields in screen 2000.

Figure 5.14 Assigning Enhancement to the Standard Screen 2000

5.1.3 Creating Infotypes

The familiar Transaction PM01 is also used for creating master data info-types. The name range 9000 to 9999 is available for customers to create infotypes for master data, personnel administration, and organizational management. It is recommended that you structure the customer name range, for example, 9000 – 9099 for master data, 9100 – 9199 for organizational management, and so on.

Customer-defined infotypes

In the following example, you'll learn how to create customer-specific infotype 9010:

▶ Parking lots are available for employees. Therefore, this infotype will be for selecting the parking lot.

▶ A default value should be determined by the employee subgroup. Parking lot "0002" should be the suggested default for employee subgroups DS and DU. For this default, you should use the specially created feature YTHR1. Enter the name of the parking lot in the screen.

▶ Enter the license plate number.

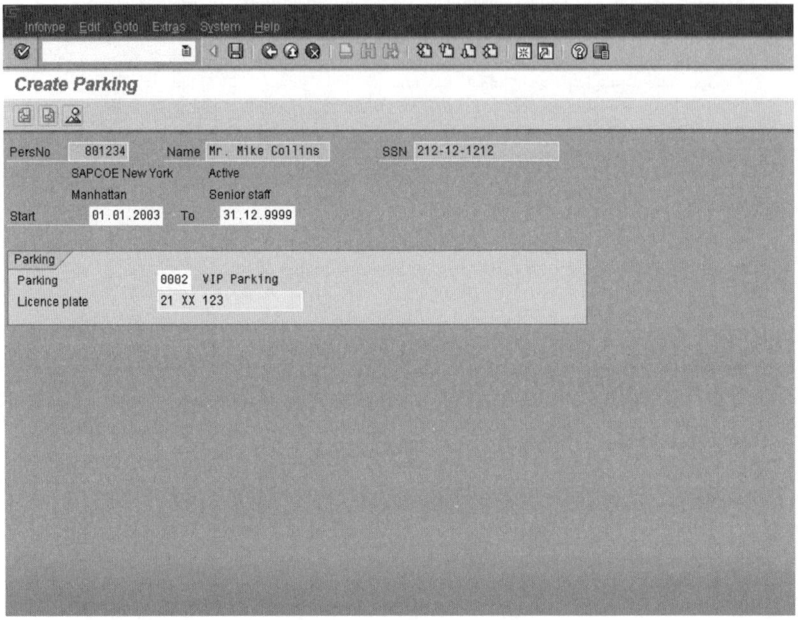

Figure 5.15 Infotype 9010, Parking Lot

The Create Parking infotype is displayed in Figure 5.15. The customer-specific infotype is displayed in Figure 5.16.

Method of procedure Two fields are created—YYPARK for the parking lot code and YYNUMBER for the license plate number. The entry YYPARK is checked using check table YTHR_PARK. The corresponding text table YTHRT_PARK is needed for input help and for displaying the text after the parking lot key. First, the structure PS9010 is created and activated for the new infotype (see Figure 5.17).

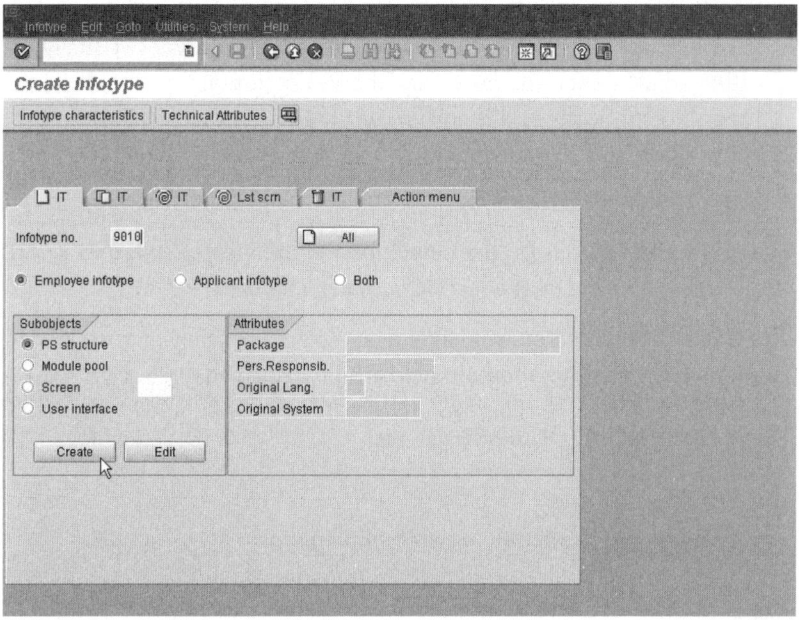

Figure 5.16 Creating Infotype 9010

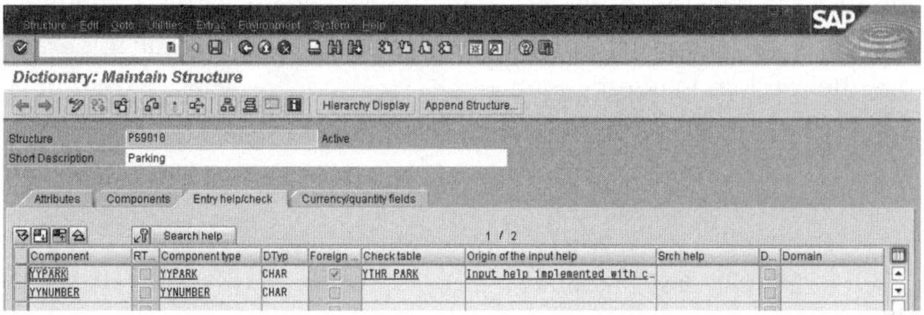

Figure 5.17 PS Structure for Infotype 9010

Using Transaction PM01, the following additional objects are created with the button **Create all**:

▶ Structure P9010: The previously created structure PS9010 is included here.

▶ Database table PA9010.

▶ Module pool MP901000 with the corresponding includes. The adjustments described below should be executed now.

▶ Screens 1000, 2000, 3000 for module pool MP901000. The components *Layout* and *Flow logic* often have to be adjusted.

▶ The GUI status with the necessary icons for standard actions, such as Create, Copy, Overview, and so on, for these infotypes. Usually, no other adjustments are necessary; however, for more complex infotypes, adding icons and menu entries may be useful, for example, to call a report.

▶ Dialog module RP_9010. No adjustments are required here.

In addition, the entries for the new infotypes are created in tables T777D (*Check table for infotypes*) and TDCT (*Dialog modules*).

Data declarations   The global data is created in include MP901010. This mainly consists of declarations for the tables and help fields to be displayed.

```
PROGRAM MP901000 MESSAGE-ID RP.
TABLES: P9010,
        ythrt_park.
FIELD-SYMBOLS: <PNNNN> STRUCTURE P9010
                       DEFAULT P9010.
DATA: PSAVE LIKE P9010.
```

PBO   The include MP901020 contains the modules that are called at PBO. To improve the structure of the program, the data editing and the additional functions are defined in form routines in include MP00901040. In this example, the routines in question are get_default and re_ythrt_park:

```
MODULE p9010 OUTPUT.
  IF psyst-nselc EQ yes.
    IF psyst-iinit = yes AND psyst-ioper = insert.
      PERFORM get_default.
    ENDIF.
  ENDIF.
  PERFORM re_ythrt_park.
ENDMODULE.                      "P9010 OUTPUT
```

PAI   The PAI modules are contained in include MP901030. Here also, as previously mentioned, we recommend that you create form routines that are used for advanced editing. As no additional checks will be carried out here, you don't need to edit this include.

Analysis of PSYST

Processing status

In order to allow for the execution of different processing steps, depending on the processing status, we suggest that you request certain values of the structure PSYST:

Switches

The switch FIRST is set at YES(1), if the first record is created for the current infotype.

The switch NSELC is set at YES(1), if a record is to be displayed on the screen for the first time. It can be queried so that in the event of repeated execution of the PBO, texts on coding are not repeatedly read over.

The switch IINIT is also set at YES(1), if a record is to be displayed on the screen for the first time. It is used to execute special processing for this record in PBO, such as default values for the Append function. In the module POST_INPUT_CHECKS, the switch is set at NO (0) at the end of the flow logic. If the infotype has a special logic, such as LEAVE SCREEN for infotypes with a loop area, the switch must be set at NO(0) in the infotype-specific module.

There is a difference between the switches IINIT and NSELC however. If you process a record and then go to the overview and to other records, when you return to the first record, IINIT is still set at NO (0). In this way, you can avoid the re-introduction of default values that have already been changed by the user. The user creates a new record. The default value is therefore overwritten. The message "This entry will delete a record" is displayed. The user calls the overview to see the existing record. If the variable IINIT is set at NO(0)—the default values will no longer be determined. The variable NSELC now has the value YES(1), because texts must be read again.

The field IOPER can have different values, the most important of which are shown in the following table.

Name constant	Value	Function
Display	DIS	Display
Display_no_list	DIS2	Display without overview
Modify	MOD	Change
Insert	INS	Append
Copy	COP	Copy
Delete	DEL	Delete

Name constant	Value	Function
List_display	LIS0	List with display function
List_modify	LIS1	List with maintenance functions
List_delim	LIS9	Delimit
Enqueue_record	EDQ	Lock

If, for example, a default value is only consulted when a new record is inserted, then, you should enhance the coding for the query in field IOPER.

The field FSTAT describes the interface status. It can therefore be used if there is no difference between Insert and Copy.

Name constant	Value	Function
FCODE_AZ	0001	Display
FCODE_AE	0002	Change
FCODE_HZ	0004	Append
FCODE_LO	0008	Delete
FCODE_SP	0010	Lock

The field INPST can have the following different values:

Name constant	Value	Function
NO_INPUT	0	No input done
INPUT_DONE	1	Input done
PUT_INPUT	2	Input confirmed
INPUT_IN_BUFFER	3	Input in buffer
INPUT_STORED	4	Input stored

In include MP901020, it is first necessary to check if the infotype is new. You can do this by using the queries of the system variables PSYST-NSECL, PSYST-IINIT, and PSYST-IOPER. If the infotype is indeed new, then the default value is determined in accordance with the feature YTHR1.

```
MODULE p9010 OUTPUT.
    IF psyst-nselc EQ yes.
```

```
      IF psyst-iinit = yes AND psyst-ioper = insert.
        PERFORM get_default.
      ENDIF.
    ENDIF.
    PERFORM re_ythrt_park.
ENDMODULE.
```

Calling a Feature

You call a feature by calling the routine get_default in include MP901040. To complete this task, you can use the fields of PSYST as a decision structure. However it is more common with features to use structures that start with "PME". When fields of these structures are to be used for the decision structure, they should be made available accordingly in advance. You can call the feature by using the function module 'HR_FEATURE_BACK-FIELD':

```
FORM get_default .
  DATA: pstatus(1).
  CALL FUNCTION 'HR_FEATURE_BACKFIELD'
    EXPORTING
      feature                      = 'YTHR1'
      struc_content                = psyst
    IMPORTING
      back                         = p9010-yypark
    CHANGING
      status                       = pstatus
    EXCEPTIONS
      dummy                        = 1
      error_operation              = 2
      no_backvalue                 = 3
      feature_not_generated        = 4
      invalid_sign_in_funid        = 5
      field_in_report_tab_in_pe03  = 6
      OTHERS                       = 7.
  IF sy-subrc <> 0.
    ...
  ENDIF.
ENDFORM.                          " GET_DEFAULT
```

In Figure 5.18, you can see the specification of the decision tree. To look at the assignment of the feature structure, see Figure 5.19.

Decision tree

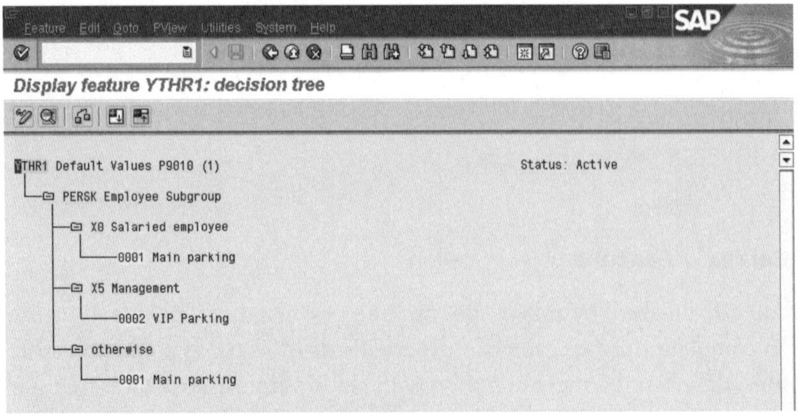

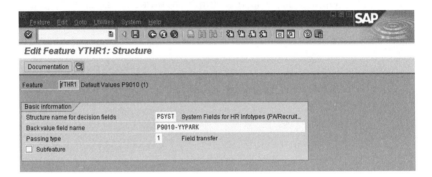

Figure 5.18 Feature for Determining the Default Value

Figure 5.19 Structure of Feature YTHR1

Table `YTHRT_PARK` must be read so that the texts will be displayed on the screen. This table is always read, even if the switch variable `PSYST-NSELC` is set at NO(0). Positioning at this point in the process offers the advantage that once the default value has been determined, the corresponding text appears on the screen.

```
FORM re_ythrt_park .
  SELECT        * FROM  ythrt_park
        WHERE  yypark  = p9010-yypark
        AND    langu   = sy-langu.
  ENDSELECT.
  IF sy-subrc <> 0.
    CLEAR ythrt_park.
  ENDIF.
ENDFORM.                        " RE_YTHRT_PARK
```

Screen 2000 now has to be enhanced with the text field `ythrt_park-text`, which is read here.

Modification Groups

When adjusting in Screen Painter, use modification groups 1 and 3 for screen control in HR.

For screen control based on the function to be performed, you can control whether you can make entries in individual screen fields, or individual screen fields need to be hidden. To establish this kind of screen control, the value of Modification group 1 in Screen Painter must be maintained for the screen fields in question. You must do this for all screen fields in which entries can be made. Screen control

The meaning of the values in Modification group 1 is defined in table T589A. The following constants are defined in the SAP standard delivery for controlling whether entries can be made in screen fields:

Entry can be made in the screen for the function	Hexadecimal constant for Modification group 1
Display	001
Change	002
Add and Copy	004
Delete	008
Lock/Unlock	010

The following constants are defined in the SAP standard for hiding screen fields:

Screen field is hidden for the function	Hexadecimal constant for Modification group 1
Delimit in list screen	200
Display in list screen and Change in list screen	400
Add and Copy	800

Modification group 1	The value in Modification group 1 is interpreted bit-by-bit. Several constants can be combined by adding their values. The value of Modification group 1 must be maintained in hexadecimal form. If you want to make entries in a screen field for the functions **Add and Copy and Change**, you must enter the value 006 in Modification group 1. If you want to make entries in a field for all functions, you must enter the value 00F in Modification group 1.

Controlling whether entries can be made or not is predefined for certain fields in single and list screens, for all infotypes. If you create the single and list screen with the Transaction **Enhance infotypes** (Transaction code PM01), the system makes the appropriate entry in Modification group 1 for these screen fields. Entries can usually be made in the fields BEGDA and ENDDA for all actions, with the exception of displaying records. The **Modification group 1** attribute for these fields is usually given the value 00E. For the fields AEDTM and UNAME, Modification group 1 has the value 800. Therefore, these fields are hidden when a record is added. In the list screen, you should be able to make entries in the fields RP50M-BEGDA, RP50M-ENDDA, RP50M-SUBTY, and RP50M-PAGEA in order to allow records to be selected. These fields are assigned the value 00F, because it must be possible to make entries for all operations. The delimitation date in field RP50M-ABGRD should only be visible on the list screen if the current function is actually **Delimit**. Modification group 1 is therefore assigned the value 400. Multiple record selection in the list screen is only possible with the functions **Display** and **Delimit**. The field RP50M-SELEC, which is contained in a loop, is assigned the value 009 for Modification group 1.

Modification group 3	An entry in Modification group 3 can also be used to control whether or not entries can be made in individual screen fields, or individual screen fields are to be hidden. Screen control is usually based on an employee's organizational data, or on the subtype of the infotype record. This is controlled in customizing in table T588M. In Modification group 3, each screen field is assigned a value between 001 and 050. The same value is used for screen fields that are to be modified in the same way. The same value is used for an input/output field as for the related keyword and any long text displayed. There is no entry in Modification group 3 for screen fields that cannot be modified using table T588M. How the individual screen fields are to be modified is determined in table T588M. An entry in table T588M overrules the entry in Modification group 1—therefore, if according to Modification group 1, entries can be made in a field, then this feature can be reversed by an entry in Table T588M.

5.1.4 Enhancing Infotypes for Fast Data Entry

Transaction PA70 offers the possibility of fast entry for multiple personnel numbers with different selection alternatives and default values. We shall build on the example that was used in the last section. Now, let's make it possible to enter and edit data in fast entry, whereby default values must be suggested for the parking lot, start date, and end date. To input default values, in addition to screen 4000, screen 5000 is also needed for data entry and editing. The result that you want is shown in Figure 5.20.

Transaction PA70

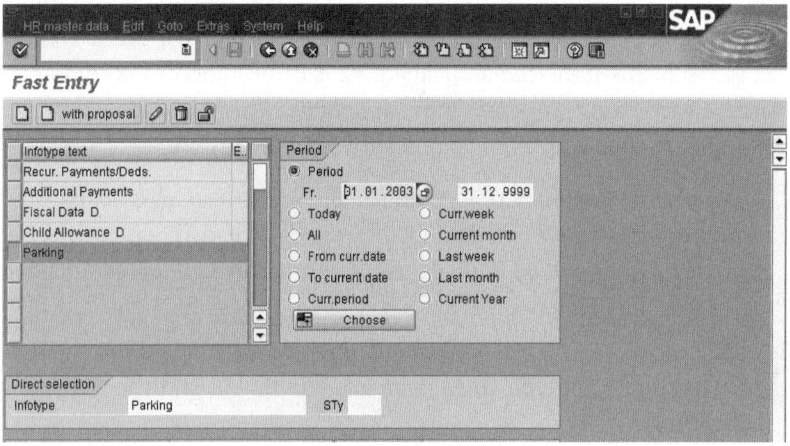

Figure 5.20 Choosing Fast Entry for Infotype 9010

Click on the **Create** [white page icon] **with proposal** button to call screen 4000.

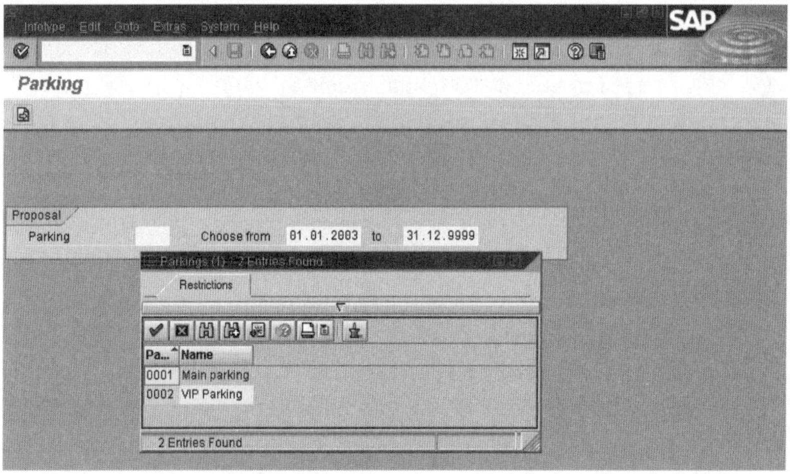

Figure 5.21 Default Values for Fast Entry

After you have entered the proposals, entries can be made in screen 5000.

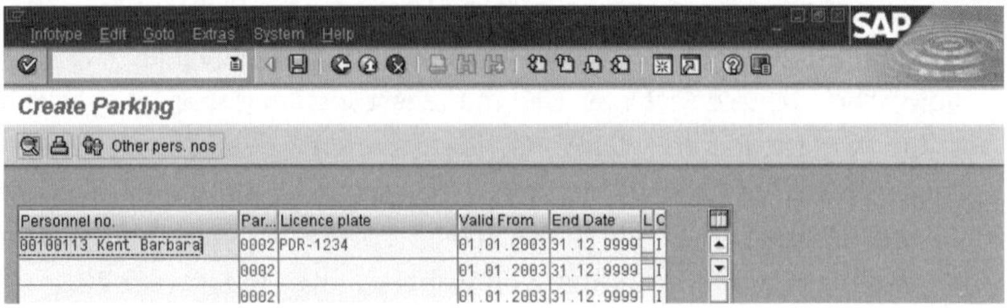

Figure 5.22 Entries with Fast Entry

Method of procedure

You can implement this functionality using existing infotypes as copy templates, if you want to use similar functions. The following steps are required:

1. First, edit module pool MP901000. The include MP901050 is deactivated because the modules contained therein are already created in other includes, which will be copied later. Insert the includes MPPERSFS and the still to be created MP9010FS.

2. Create include MP9010FS. You can use include MP0232FS, from the simply structured infotype 0232, as a copy template and then adjust it accordingly:

```
DATA: BEGIN OF proposed_values,
        yypark LIKE p9010-yypark,
      END OF proposed_values.
MODULE proposed_values INPUT.
  CHECK fcode NE back.
  MOVE: rp50m-begda TO pspar-begda,
        rp50m-endda TO pspar-endda.
  MOVE-CORRESPONDING p9010 TO proposed_values.
ENDMODULE.                       "PROPOSED_VALUES INPUT
MODULE proposed_pernr INPUT.
ENDMODULE.                       " PROPOSED_PERNR  INPUT
FORM get_proposed_values USING gpv_tabix.
  CALL METHOD cl_hr_pnnnn_type_cast=>prelp_to_pnnnn
    EXPORTING
      prelp = cprel
    IMPORTING
      pnnnn = p9010.
  MOVE-CORRESPONDING proposed_values TO p9010.
```

```
   CALL METHOD cl_hr_pnnnn_type_cast=>pnnnn_to_prelp
     EXPORTING
       pnnnn = p9010
     IMPORTING
       prelp = psfast-prelp.
   MOVE 'I' TO psfast-opera.
   IF gpv_tabix EQ 0.
     APPEND psfast.
   ELSE.
     INSERT psfast INDEX gpv_tabix.
   ENDIF.
ENDFORM.                        "GET_PROPOSED_VALUES
FORM dnnnn.
   CALL METHOD cl_hr_pnnnn_type_cast=>prelp_to_pnnnn
     EXPORTING
       prelp  = psfast-prelp
     IMPORTING
       pnnnn  = p9010.
   CLEAR bdcdata.
   bdcdata-program  = 'MP901000'.
   bdcdata-dynpro   = '2000'.
   bdcdata-dynbegin = 'X'.
   APPEND bdcdata.
   CLEAR bdcdata.
   bdcdata-fnam = 'P9010-YYPARK'.
   bdcdata-fval = p9010-yypark.
   APPEND bdcdata.
   CLEAR bdcdata.
   bdcdata-fnam = 'P9010-BEGDA'.
   WRITE p9010-begda TO bdcdata-fval(10).
   APPEND bdcdata.
   CLEAR bdcdata.
   bdcdata-fnam = 'P9010-ENDDA'.
   WRITE p9010-endda TO bdcdata-fval(10).
   APPEND bdcdata.
   CLEAR bdcdata.
   bdcdata-fnam = 'BDC_OKCODE'.
   bdcdata-fval = '=UPD'.
   APPEND bdcdata.
ENDFORM.                        "DNNNN
```

```
MODULE set_tc5000 OUTPUT.
   ASSIGN tc5000 TO <table_control>.
   DESCRIBE TABLE psfast LINES tc5000-lines.
ENDMODULE.                " SET_TC5000   OUTPUT
MODULE fill_top_line OUTPUT.
   IF sy-step1 EQ 1.
     <table_control>-top_line = rp50m-pagea.
     top_line = <table_control>-top_line.
   ENDIF.
ENDMODULE.                " FILL_TOP_LINE   OUTPUT
MODULE set_rp50m_pagea.
   IF top_line NE <table_control>-top_line.
     rp50m-pagea = <table_control>-top_line.
   ENDIF.
ENDMODULE.                " FILL_TOP_LINE   INPUT
```

3. Enhance include MP901010, which has global data definitions, with the following entries:

```
TYPE-POOLS: cxtab.
FIELD-SYMBOLS: <table_control> TYPE cxtab_control.
CONTROLS: tc5000 TYPE TABLEVIEW USING SCREEN 5000.
```

4. Create screens 4000 and 5000. The easiest way to do this is to copy the corresponding screens from infotype 0232 using Transaction SE51. You have to adjust the screen layout and the flow logic:

```
* Screen 4000
PROCESS BEFORE OUTPUT.
   MODULE pfstatus_prop.
PROCESS AFTER INPUT.
   CHAIN.
     FIELD rp50m-begda.
     FIELD rp50m-endda.
     FIELD p9010-yypark.
     MODULE proposed_values ON CHAIN-REQUEST.
   ENDCHAIN.
   MODULE fcodefast.
* Screen 5000
PROCESS BEFORE OUTPUT.
   MODULE pbo_list.
```

```
      MODULE set_tc5000.
      LOOP.
        MODULE line_fast.
        MODULE fill_top_line.
      ENDLOOP.
   PROCESS AFTER INPUT.
      MODULE exit_fast AT EXIT-COMMAND.
      MODULE cursor_selection.
      LOOP.
        MODULE get_entry.
        CHAIN.
          FIELD: rp50m-pernr,
                 p9010-begda,
                 p9010-endda.
          MODULE check_pernr ON CHAIN-REQUEST.
          MODULE proposed_pernr.
        ENDCHAIN.
        CHAIN.
          FIELD: rp50m-pernr,
                 p9010-yypark,
                 p9010-yynumber,
                 p9010-begda,
                 p9010-endda,
                 p9010-sprps.
          MODULE put_input.
        ENDCHAIN.
        FIELD rp50m-opera MODULE mark_psfast ON REQUEST.
      ENDLOOP.
      MODULE set_rp50m_pagea.
      FIELD fcode MODULE fcodefast.
```

When creating single fields, the value 006 should be entered in Modification group 1, which means that entry is possible with the functions
Add and Copy and Change.

5. You have to create the required statuses. These are FINS, FMOD, FEDQ,
   FDEL, and PROP. Infotype 0232 can once again be used as a copy template. Use Transaction SE41 to copy the interface.

6. Maintain tables T588R (selection reports for fast entry), T588Q (screen
   types for fast entry), and T588B (infotype menus). Infotype menu 07 is
   fixed for the fast entry of master data.

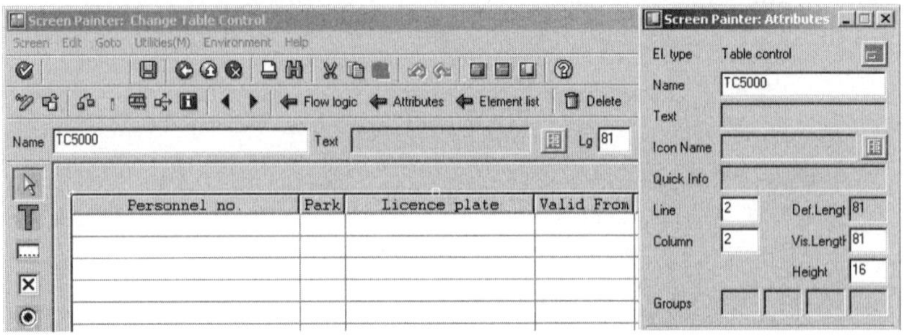

Figure 5.23 Fast Entry Layout

5.1.5 Multiple-Infotype Entry with Fast Entry of Action Data

Transaction PA42

Actions are used in Personnel Administration to enter information for several infotypes. In addition to executing a personnel action with Transaction PA40, you can also edit several infotypes on the same screen by using Transaction PA42 (fast entry of actions).

The following actions are set in the standard:

1. Hiring

2. Organizational reassignment

3. Time recording (additional)

Transaction OG42

The entry screens required for Transaction OG42 can be found in the programs SAPMP5X0 (1.) and SAPMP50F (2. and 3.). You can also use this transaction to set up customer-specific entry screens for fast entry of actions for multiple infotypes—standard infotypes and customer-defined infotypes can be used here.

The following example should help to illustrate how this works: If an employee gets a company car, only specific company-car-related fields in infotype 0032 and the fields in the customer infotype 9010 need to be maintained. You can see the result of setting up a fast entry of actions in Figure 5.24 and Figure 5.25.

After selecting the action **Company car,** you can maintain the fields required. The check box **Internal Data** allows the user to edit all fields in infotype 0032 in a single screen if necessary. After you press **ENTER**, the full name of the employee is displayed after the personnel number, and after the **Parking field**, the text for the keys is displayed.

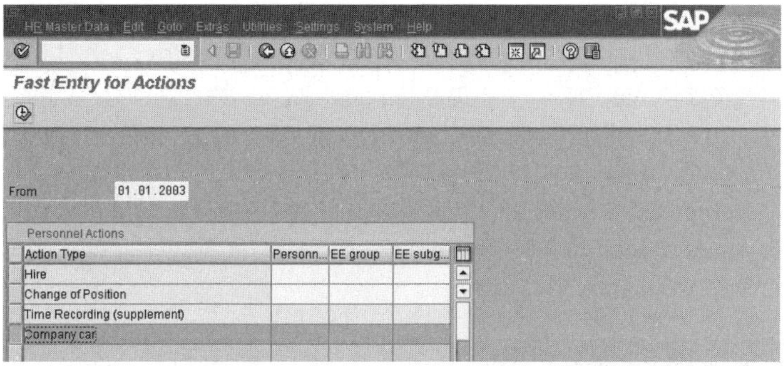

Figure 5.24 Entry Screen "Fast Entry for Action Data"

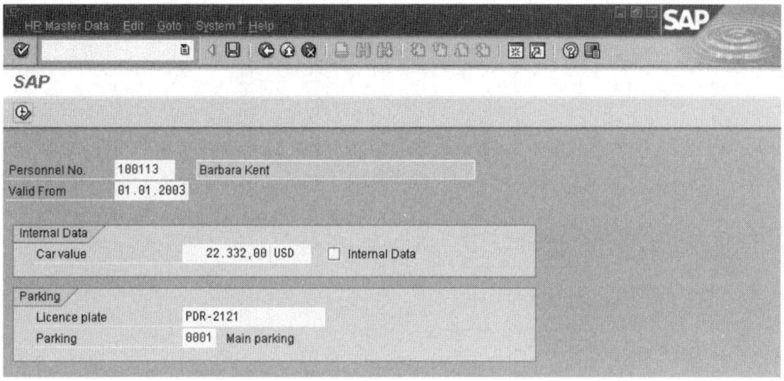

Figure 5.25 Maintaining Multiple Infotypes with PA42

First, you have to set up an action with the infotypes to be maintained and then add it to the fast entry menu. These steps are best carried out in the IMG under the menu option **Personnel management · Personnel administration · Customizing procedures · Actions**. You must edit the following activities:

▶ Define infogroups

▶ Define personnel action types

▶ Reasons for personnel action types

▶ Change action menu

Once the action has been created, the processing continues using Transaction OG42 (customizing tool for fast entry of action data). The screen of this transaction contains the following subareas:

Customizing

▶ Personnel actions for which fast entry can be used

▶ Infotypes and fields

▶ Program and preview

You can select the personnel action type that you require in the first area. Depending on the customizing settings of the actions, entries can still be made here regarding the user group and the infogroup modifier. In our example, the action **Company car** has been chosen and is selected using the **Choose action** button. In the second area, a folder list of all infotypes available in the selected personnel action type is displayed, together with a folder called **Other fields**. The fields in the latter folder are already shown in the third area, **Preview**.

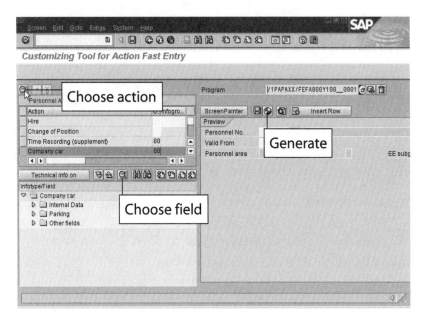

Figure 5.26 Calling Transaction OG42

You must enter a program name in the **Program** field. Analogous to the standard programs in fast entry for actions, and keeping in mind the naming conventions for customer objects, the name "SAPMYHRT" has been selected here. To show a *box* for an infotype, in the second area, position the cursor over the folder for that infotype and click on the **Choose field** button. To transfer individual *fields*, you must open the folder, position the cursor over the field, and select it using the **Choose field** button. In order to allow the user to edit the *single screen* of infotype 0032 in fast entry for action data, you must add an **Internal Data** check box. To do this, position the cursor in the field **Further information** and select it with **Choose field**. When all the necessary details have been selected, you can start generation by selecting the **Generate** button in the third area.

Screen 2000 in the program SAPMYHRT can now be further edited in the Screen Painter. The additional fields for displaying text are inserted in the layout and the texts are read from the text tables.

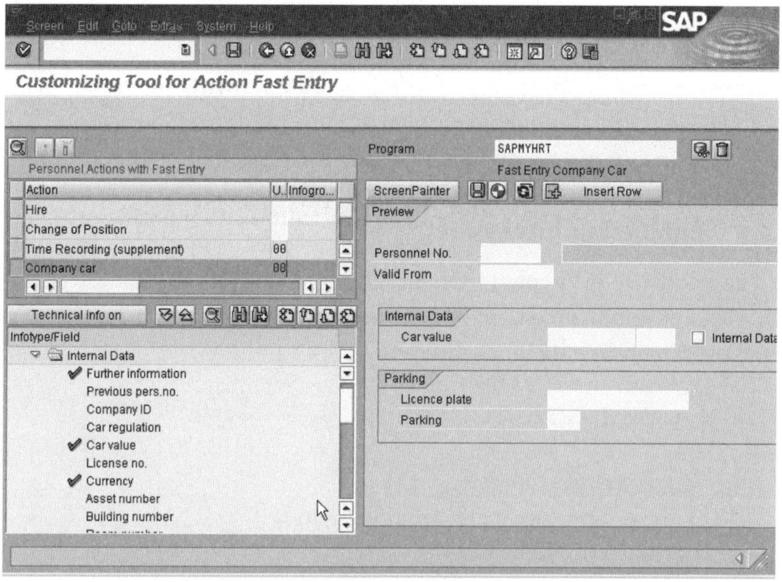

Figure 5.27 Transaction OG42 After Adapting the Screen

You can set default values and run checks in the flow logic of the screen, or you can use the BAdI that is especially provided for this purpose. The BAdI HR_FAST_ACTION_CHECK contains the method *Check fields* (CHECK_FIELDS), which you can use to set default values and to run checks. The program name of the fast entry screen generated (parameter FLT_VAL, here »SAPMYHRT«) serves as a filter value, against which the implementations of the BAdIs are controlled separately. In our example, the BAdI is used to set a default for the currency. The method CHECK_FIELDS is called in both the PBO and in the PAI of the fast entry screen. In the PBO however, only the default values are set and the entry in the parameter FIELDS_INVOLVED is ignored.

```
METHOD if_ex_hr_fast_action_check~check_fields.
  DATA:  wa_fields_to_set TYPE fast_action_fields.
  CLEAR:  wa_fields_to_set, fields_to_set.
  wa_fields_to_set-fieldname = 'P0032-WAERS'.
  wa_fields_to_set-value      = 'EUR'.
  APPEND wa_fields_to_set TO fields_to_set .
ENDMETHOD.
```

Activation is the last step in Transaction OG42. This is done in the first area of the customizing tool. The entry screen for multiple-infotype fast entry is now available.

5.2 Organizational Management

Just as was possible in Personnel Administration, in Organizational Management, you can also enhance or create new infotypes. In this case, the necessary actions are supported by a special transaction.

5.2.1 Enhancing infotypes

Transaction PPCI You can enhance infotypes in Organizational Management using Transaction PPCI. The enhancement is incorporated in the module pool of the standard screen by calling a subscreen in PBO and PAI:

```
PROCESS BEFORE OUTPUT.
. . .
   CALL SUBSCREEN SUBSCREEN_T582C
      INCLUDING SUBSCR_PROG SUBSCR_DYNNR.
. . .
PROCESS AFTER INPUT.
. . .
CALL SUBSCREEN SUBSCREEN_T582C.
```

Restrictions The following restrictions should be observed with regard to the (modification-free) enhancement of infotypes: The standard infotypes 1000 (*Object*) and 1001 (*Relationship*) cannot be enhanced. Enhancements are only possible for infotypes that can be maintained directly. You can use Transaction SE16 to determine if enhancement is allowed in infotypes for specific object types. All infotypes in table T777I, and identified as such in the field MAINT (cannot be maintained using standard transactions), are excluded from enhancements, for example, infotype 1021 (*Prices*) for the object type E (*Business event*). The infotype for calling the subscreen must also be created, which means that there must be a CALL SUBSCREEN in PBO and PAI. This is not the case for infotype 1015 (*Cost planning*), for example.

Example The following example shows a possible procedure for enhancing infotype 1003 (*Department/Staff*). Organization units should be labeled to show which hierarchical level they are assigned to. There are four possible hierarchy levels and the level should be indicated after the key. The additional field is inserted below the standard fields, as you can see in Figure 5.28.

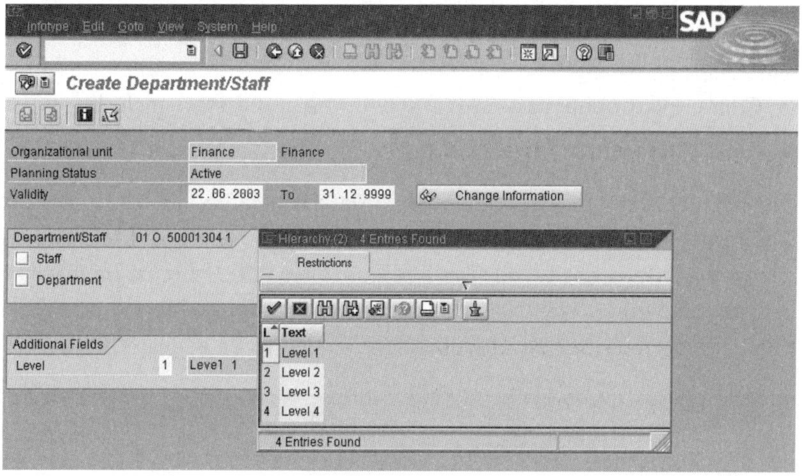

Figure 5.28 Additional Field in Infotype 1003

To enhance infotype 1003, the additional field must first be inserted into the customer include. In our example, the field YYHIER is inserted into CI_ P1003. The field is checked using table YTHR_HIER, and the name of this field is displayed using the corresponding text table YTHRT_HIER.

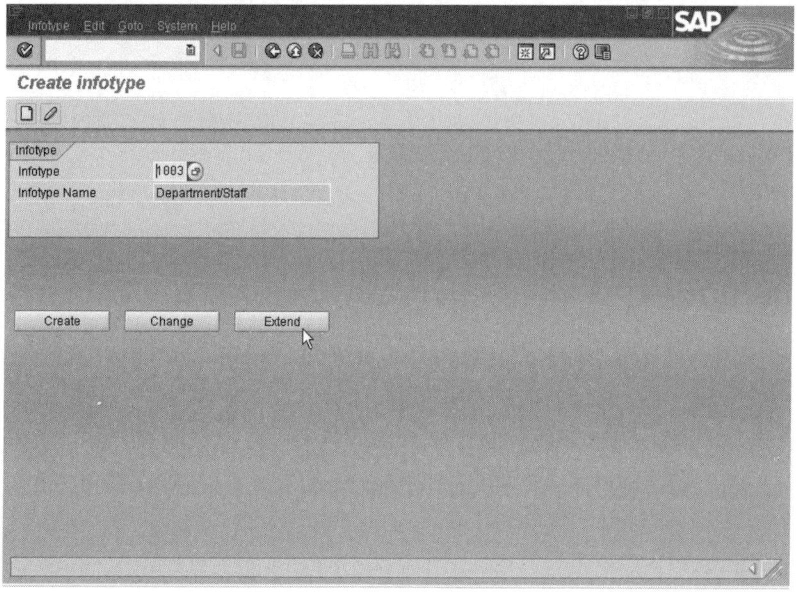

Figure 5.29 Enhancing Infotype 1003

Method of procedure

The following sequence is the best method of procedure:

- Create the CI include CI_P1003.
- Create the module pool ZP90100 with the appropriate includes.
- Create the include screen 0200.

The include CI_P1003 is contained in database table HRP1003. All the additional fields that are incorporated here are also saved to the database when this infotype is saved. The additional field YYHIER must be inserted into the include. Table YTHR_HIER is used for the foreign key check. After the field has been set up, the objects still need to be activated.

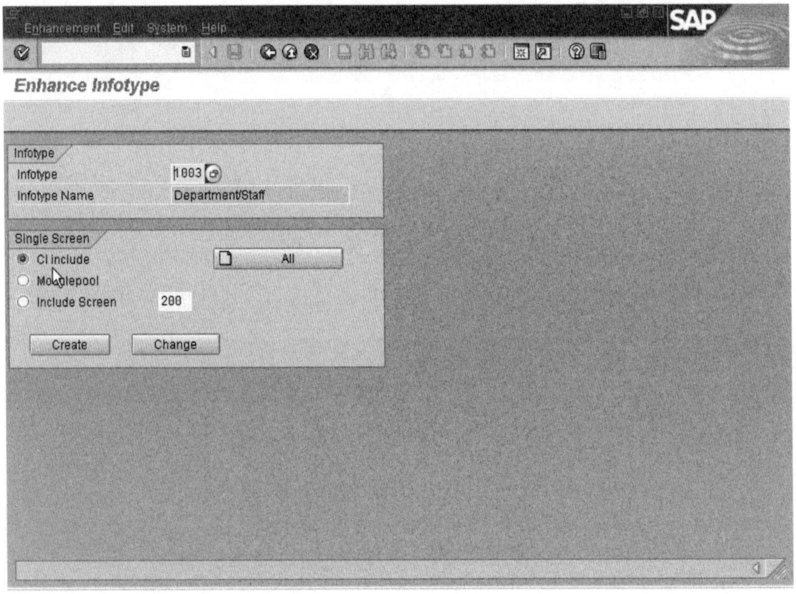

Figure 5.30 The Steps Required in Enhancing Infotype 1003

In a second step, the module pool ZP100300 is created with the necessary include:

```
*&---------------------------------------------------*
*& Module pool         ZP100300                       *
*&---------------------------------------------------*
INCLUDE ZP100310.
  INCLUDE MPH5ATOP.
  INCLUDE MPHCOM00.
  TABLES: PPPAR.
INCLUDE ZP100320.
```

```
INCLUDE ZP100330.
INCLUDE ZP100340.
```

Global data definitions are inserted into include ZP100310. Modules for the PBO event are created in include ZP100320, and for PAI in include ZP100330. The necessary forms are coded in the include ZP100340. The listings below show the coding required in the includes named.

```
*&---------------------------------------------------*
*    INCLUDE ZP100310                                 *
*&---------------------------------------------------*
PROGRAM zp100300.
TABLES: p1003.
TABLES: ythrt_hier.
FIELD-SYMBOLS: <p1003> STRUCTURE p1003 DEFAULT p1003.
DATA: call_prog LIKE sy-repid.
```

To display text, the text must be read from Table YTHRT_HIER at PBO: **Text display**

```
*&---------------------------------------------------*
*    INCLUDE ZP100320                                 *
*&---------------------------------------------------*
*&        Module  MODULE_PBO_MMMM   OUTPUT            *
*&---------------------------------------------------*
MODULE module_pbo_1003 OUTPUT.
   call_prog = 'MP100300'.
   PERFORM get_infotype_structures IN PROGRAM
     (call_prog) USING pppar.
   PERFORM dynamic_screen_variation(sapfh5am) USING
     pppar-dvary.
   PERFORM get_text.
ENDMODULE.                     " MODULE_PBO_MMMM  OUTPUT
```

Because the infotype 1003 is permitted for several object types, at the PAI, another check must be run to determine if the object type "O" is present. In the flow logic of screen 0200, the module input_status_sub-screen must be called.

```
*&---------------------------------------------------*
*    INCLUDE ZP100330                                 *
*&---------------------------------------------------*
*&        Module  MOD_PAI   INPUT                     *
```

```
*&------------------------------------------------------*
MODULE module_pai_1003 INPUT.
ENDMODULE.                        " MOD_PAI   INPUT
*&------------------------------------------------------*
*&      Module  input_status_subscreen  INPUT       *
*&------------------------------------------------------*
MODULE input_status_subscreen INPUT.
  IF p1003-otype <> '0'
    AND NOT p1003-yyhier IS INITIAL.
    MESSAGE e150(ythr).
  ENDIF.
ENDMODULE.
*&------------------------------------------------------*
*    INCLUDE ZP100340                                   *
*&------------------------------------------------------*
*&------------------------------------------------------*
*&      Form  get_text                                  *
*&------------------------------------------------------*
FORM get_text.
  SELECT SINGLE * FROM ythrt_hier
    WHERE yyhier = p1003-yyhier
      AND langu = sy-langu.
  IF sy-subrc <> 0.
    CLEAR ythrt_hier-text.
  ENDIF.
ENDFORM.
```

To ensure that the hierarchy level name is displayed on the screen, the text field has to be positioned on the screen and provided with the appropriate attributes.

Figure 5.31 Naming the Level

You cannot enhance the list screen without making some modifications. You can only enhance the table control in the standard screen 3000 if you modify the layout.

List screen enhancement

5.2.2 Creating Infotypes

If the customer-specific fields will not fit logically into existing infotypes, you should create new infotypes. You can use Transaction PPCI to create field infotypes and table infotypes. These infotypes can be defined as being language-dependent or language-independent. The infotypes can also be marked as being country-dependent or as country-independent.

Transaction PPCI

First, you must create a structure HRInnnn for field infotypes, or PTnnnn for table infotypes. All other repository objects that are required for an infotype are then created with Transaction PPCI. They include the following:

Structure

► Structure Pnnnn

► Database table HRPnnnn for field infotypes or HRTnnnn for table infotypes

► Module pool MPnnnn00 with the includes MPnnnn20 and MPnnnnBI

► Screens 1000, 2000, 3000 for this module pool

► CUA interface

► Dialog module RH_INFOTY_nnnn

► Table entries in tables T777D (*infotype check table*), T77ID (*enhancements to T777D*), T778T (*infotypes*), T777T (*texts on infotypes*), TDCT (*dialog modules*)

Once the infotype has been created, entries must still be made in the following tables:

Table entries

► T777I (infotypes per object type)

► T777Z (infotype time constraints)

► T77CD (customer-specific infotype settings)

► T77NI (country-specific infotypes)

The following example is intended to show you the creation of a field infotype: In order for data to be exchanged with other systems, an external department number must be saved with each organizational unit. Your goal is to enter this information in infotype 9110 (*External evaluation groups*).

Example

In Figure 5.32, you can see how the infotype is maintained using Transaction PP01 (*Detail maintenance*).

To carry out this function, you have to first create the structure HRI9110 with the field YYEXTABT (*External department number*) in the Dictionary, using Transaction SE11. The remaining repository objects are created in a second step with Transaction PPCI.

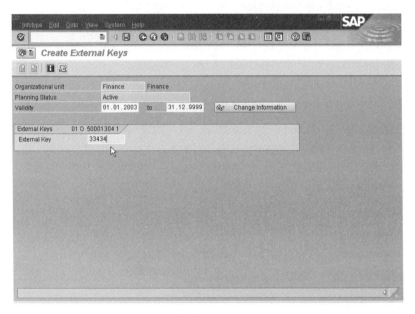

Figure 5.32 Infotype 9110 (External Evaluation Groups)

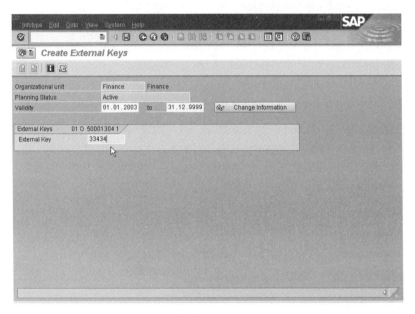

Figure 5.33 Creating an Infotype with PPCI

Use the **Change** button to get an overview of the repository objects that have been created (see Figure 5.34). From this view, you can go directly to the maintenance transactions provided for this purpose.

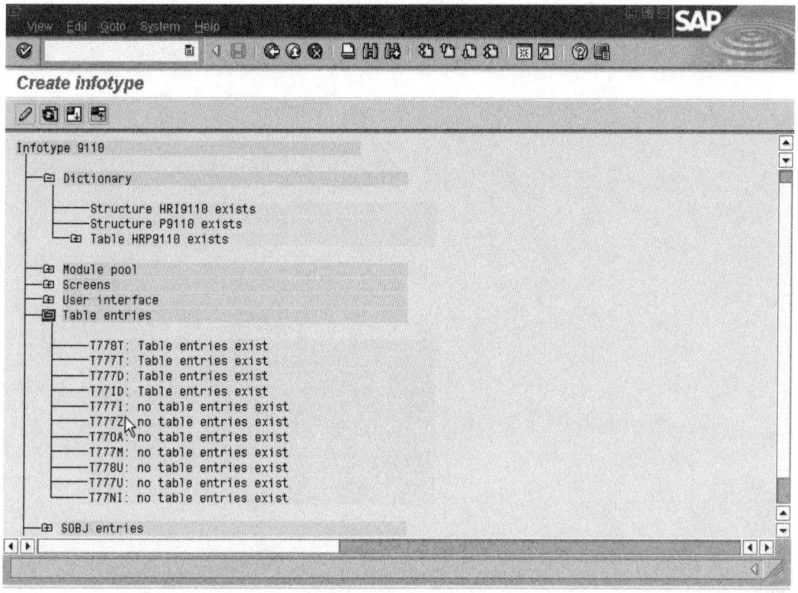

Figure 5.34 Displaying the Repository Objects Created

The entries in tables T777I and T777Z are not generated automatically. They have to be maintained manually. You can use these tables to control the time constraint shown in Figure 5.35 and the inclusion of infotype 9110 in the infotype menu of object type "O".

If the users also need to maintain the content of infotype 9110 with Transaction PPOME, as seen in Figure 5.36, then further steps are required. First, you must create screen 7000 in the module pool `MP911000`. To do this, go to the menu option **Create subscreen** in Transaction PPCI, and select the **Create** mode. In addition to creating the screen, the entry in table T771D is also enhanced.

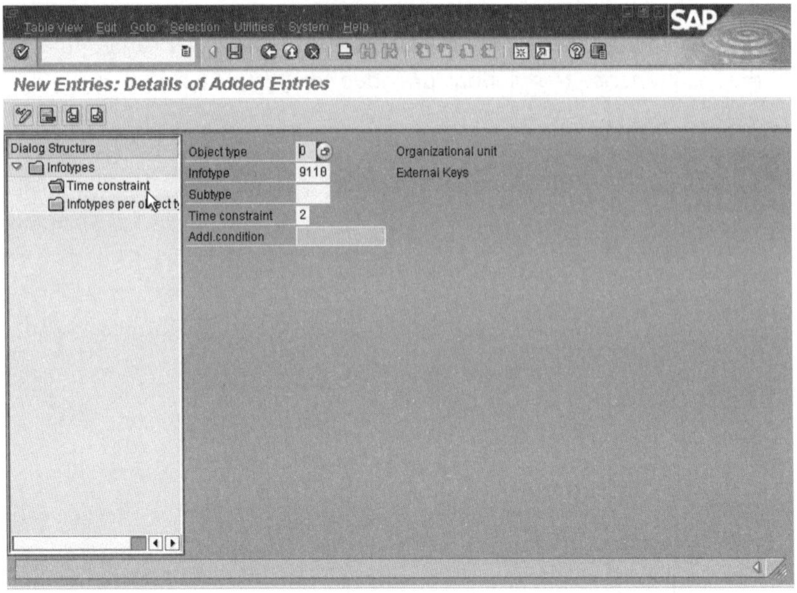

Figure 5.35 Maintaining Table T777Z

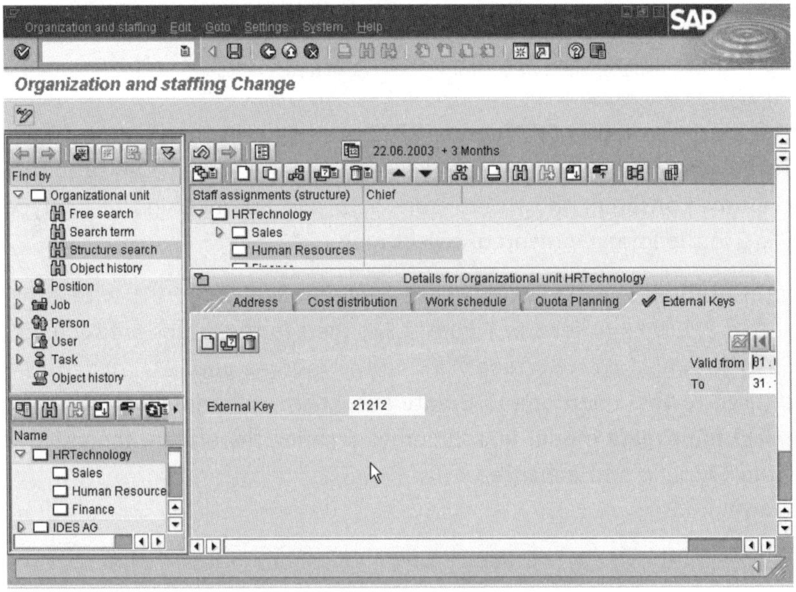

Figure 5.36 Infotype 9110 with Maintenance Transaction PPOME

To assign a tab page, it is recommended that you use the IMG (**Personnel management · Organizational management · Hierarchy framework**). The entries **Adjust tab page in detail area** and **Integrate new infotype** have to be maintained for scenario OME0.

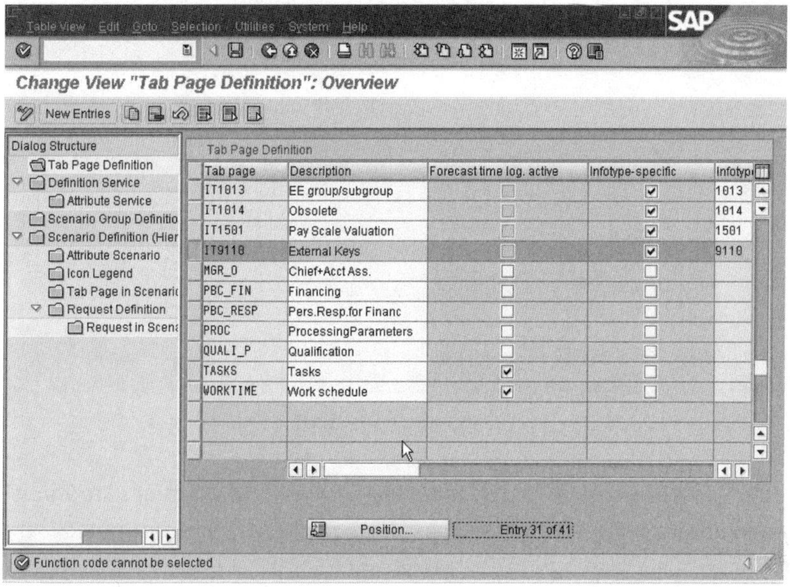

Figure 5.37 Adjusting Tab Pages for PPOME

Table Infotypes

Information that has a repetitive structure of any length is saved as a table infotype. In order to save this repetition, the table part is created in a separate table HRTnnnn. The table HRPnnnn and the table part are linked via the field TABNR. The content of this field is assigned internally and should not be changed.

The following example explains how to create a table infotype with info-type number 9111. Each organizational unit receives a different number of professional magazines. This information should be maintained in the organizational units. The list of periodicals created is shown in Figure 5.38.

Create table infotype

A table infotype can be made up only of table entries, as shown in our example, or it can have additional single fields. In the first case, you don't need to create structure HRI9111. However, you do need to create a table structure PT9111, with the components YYART (*Professional magazine*) and YYNUM (*Number of copies*). Table YTHR_INFO and the corresponding text table YTHRT_INFO are used to check and display the value help of the table field YYART.

Structure

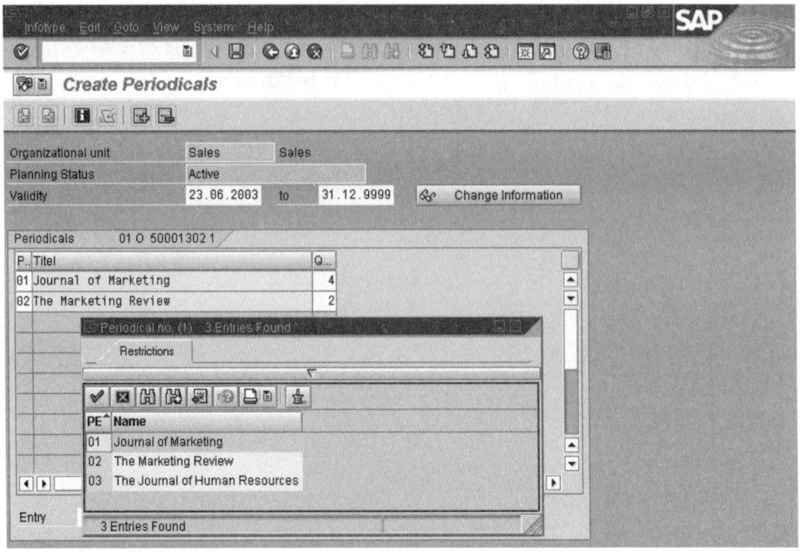

Figure 5.38 Table Infotype 9111, Professional Magazines

Table infotypes are created in the same way as field infotypes. You must assign the infotype *Table infotype*. The necessary repository objects are automatically created with Transaction PPCI.

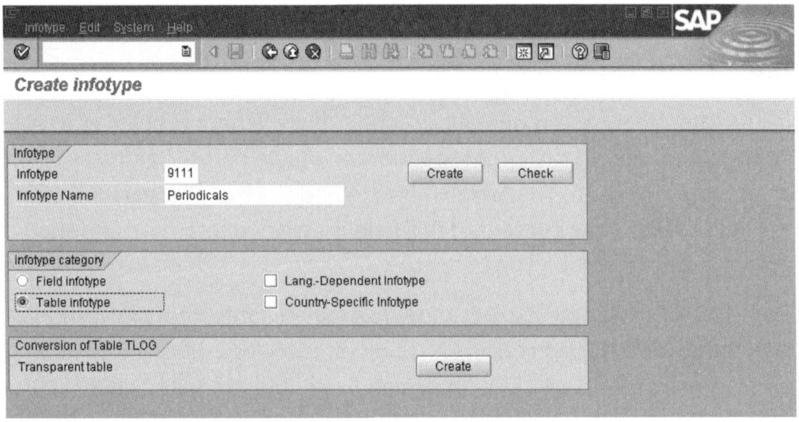

Figure 5.39 Creating a Table Infotype

Screen adjustment Some adjustment of the layout and the flow logic is still required to get the screen to look as it appears in Figure 5.38.

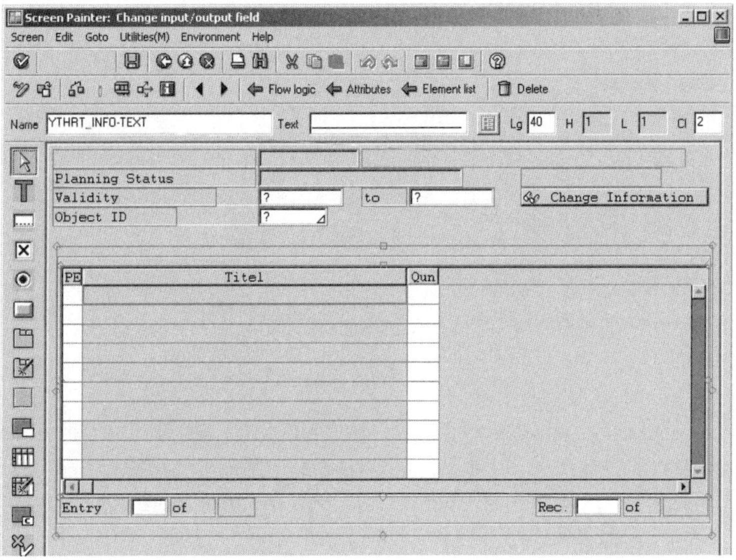

Figure 5.40 Screen 2000 of Infotype 9111

In the flow logic, text table YTHRT_INFO must be read at PBO so that the title of the magazine is displayed:

```
PROCESS BEFORE OUTPUT.
...
  LOOP AT dyn_tab WITH CONTROL tc_dyn_tab
                CURSOR dyn_tab_index.
    MODULE show_dyn_tab.
    MODULE get_text.
  ENDLOOP.
  MODULE page_numbers.
```

Table YTHRT_INFO must be declared in the module pool, so that the data is transferred to the screen:

```
PROGRAM mp911100 MESSAGE-ID 5a.
INCLUDE mph5atop.
TABLES: wplog,
        pppar, pphdr, pphdx, ppsel, ppenq,
        t777o, t777p, t777s, t777t,
        p1000, p1001.
TABLES: p9111, pt9111
TABLES: ythrt_info.
```

The text table is read in the module `get_text`, which is created in the include MP911120:

```
MODULE get_text output.
  SELECT SINGLE * FROM ythrt_info
    WHERE yyart = pt9111-yyart
      AND langu = sy-langu.
  IF sy-subrc <> 0.
    CLEAR ythrt_info-text.
  ENDIF.
ENDMODULE.
```

You must also maintain table T77CD. The field DATA_DEL should be set to "A" and TDATA_DEL should be set to "X". The entries in tables T777I and T777Z, mentioned in the last section, are also required here.

5.3 Time Recording

Restrictions

In time management, the adjustment of infotypes is limited to creating default values and checking customizing entries. Creating infotypes and adding customer-defined fields are not supported here.

In our example, we'll show you a customizing check on a specific absence type. Absence type 9000 should only be allowed for members of the works council. These absence types can only be identified by the presence of subtype 10 in infotype 0034.

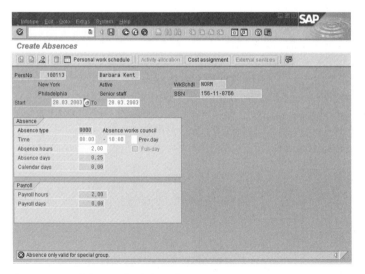

Figure 5.41 Validation Check for Infotype 2001

You can check if the absence is allowed by implementing the BAdI BAdI
HRPAD00INFTY (see Figure 5.42).

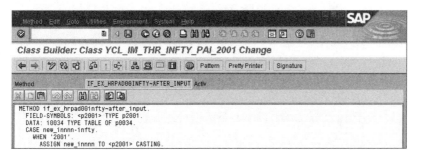

Figure 5.42 Implementing the AFTER_INPUT Method

The check is carried out using the AFTER_INPUT method in the BAdI.

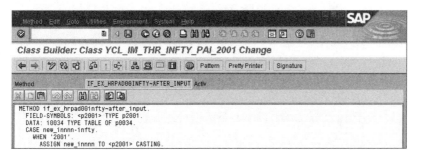

Figure 5.43 The AFTER_INPUT Method

The parameter new_innnn contains the new values for the infotype currently being edited. If the infotype 2001 is present and the subtype has the value 9000, then infotype 0034 is read with subtype 10. If the reading is not successful, a message of type E is generated, with the result that the absence entry is rejected:

```
METHOD if_ex_hrpad00infty~after_input.
  FIELD-SYMBOLS: <p2001> TYPE p2001.
  DATA: i0034 TYPE TABLE OF p0034.
  CASE new_innnn-infty.
    WHEN '2001'.
      ASSIGN new_innnn TO <p2001> CASTING.
```

```
      IF <p2001>-subty = '9000'.
        CALL FUNCTION 'HR_READ_SUBTYPE'²
          EXPORTING
            pernr           = <p2001>-pernr
            infty           = '0034'
            subty           = '10'
            begda           = <p2001>-begda
            endda           = <p2001>-begda
          TABLES
            infty_tab       = i0034
          EXCEPTIONS
            infty_not_found = 1
            invalid_input   = 2
            OTHERS          = 3.
        IF sy-subrc <> 0.
          MESSAGE e160(ythr).
        ENDIF.
        IF lines( i0034 )  = 0. ³
          MESSAGE e160(ythr).
        ENDIF.
      ENDIF.
    ENDCASE.
ENDMETHOD.
```

5.4   Payroll and Time Evaluation

Payroll and Time Evaluation do not use any rigid logic for reading, processing, and outputting data; rather you can use customizing to adapt the sequential flow of Payroll and Time Evaluation to meet the particular requirements of the company.

5.4.1   Controlling Payroll and Time Evaluation

Schemas   The Payroll and Time Evaluation programs process the logic implemented in the schemas. Program RPCALCn0 is used for Payroll, where n is the appropriate country-specific value. Program RPTIME00 is used for Time Evaluation.

---

2 In older releases, the function module HR_READ_INFOTYPE should be used, and its output should be queried in the subtype in question.
3 This function is only possible since R/3 Enterprise. For older releases, you must perform this query using the DESCRIBE statement.

The internal program flow of Payroll is depicted in Figure 5.44. The payroll Rules program reads the functions and personnel rules ('rules', for short) specified in the selected schema. The rules are in turn made up of individual operations. When the schema is processed, the individual functions are executed one after the other. This is done by calling form routines. Rules can be called to fine-tune the processing logic of specific functions. The customizing tables provided for this purpose can be read in both functions and rules.

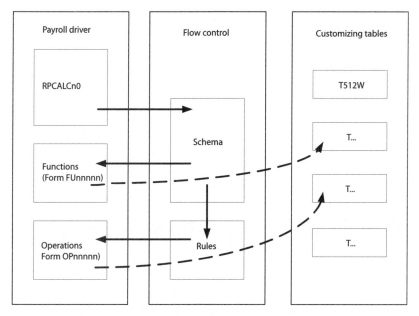

Figure 5.44 Payroll Program and Flow Control

Maintaining Schemas

The schemas are maintained using Transaction PE01. You can see an Transaction PE01 extract from the international schema X000 in Figure 5.45, which includes subschemas with the function COPY.

You can access the individual subschemas by opening the folder in the Subschema left-hand area of the screen. Subschema XLR0, which enables you to read the last payroll results, is shown in Figure 5.46. As you can see in the subschema located in the right-hand side of the screen, functions with up to four parameters are called in each row. These parameters can have different meanings, depending on the function.

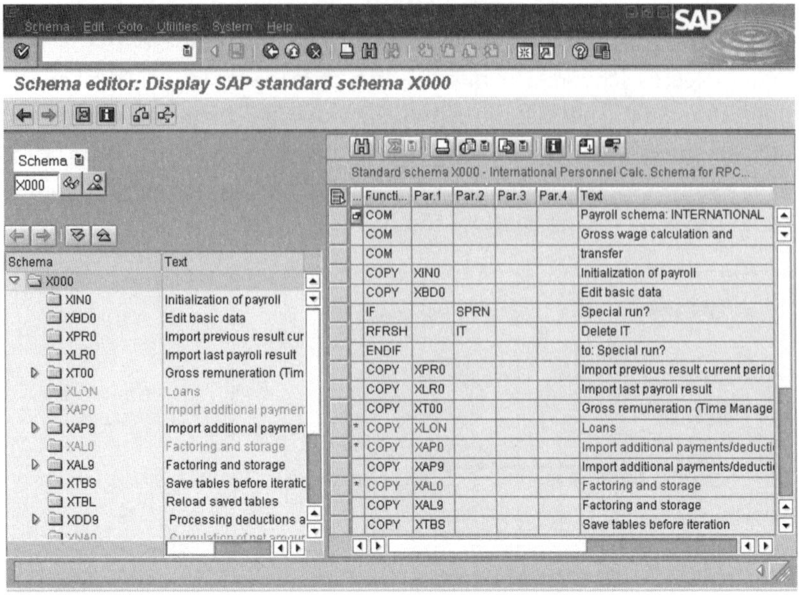

Figure 5.45 Displaying Schema X000 with Transaction PE01

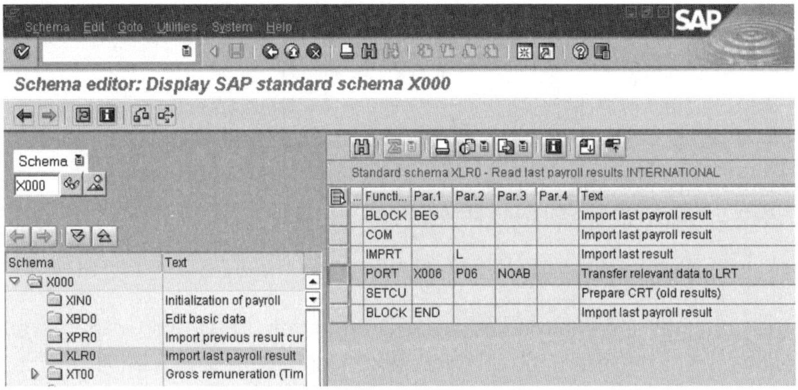

Figure 5.46 Subschema XLR0

Function
The function PORT is specified with three additional parameters. The first of these parameters refers to rule X006, which controls the processing in greater detail. The rule can be edited using Transaction PE02. Rule X006 is shown in Figure 5.47. The rule is, in turn, made up of operations (ERROR, ADDWT and so on).

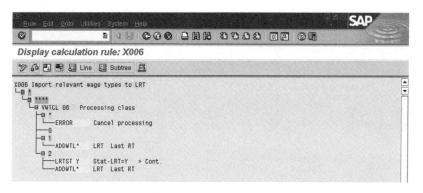

Figure 5.47 Display of Rule X006

The convention FUxxxxx pertains to the naming of functions, where "xxxxx" is the name of the function. The convention OPyyyyy pertains to operations, where "yyyyy" is the name of the operation. You can deviate from this convention by making entries in the tables associated with Transaction PE04; however, for customer-defined objects, this usually isn't necessary.

Naming conventions

You can use Transaction PE04 to display standard functions and operations, and to create user-defined functions and operations. This function and operation editor can be used to create, display, change, document, activate, delete, and transport.

5.4.2 Functions

The Payroll functions are called in Figure 5.48. You can use the **Coding** and **Documentation** icons to obtain important information about these standard functions. Usually, there is no reason to change standard functions and operations.

When you click on the **Coding** icon, the ABAP Editor is called and, in Coding, it goes to the routine used by the function or operation. If problems with standard functions arise, you can set breakpoints to carry out advanced analyses.

In the following example, we will demonstrate how to create a customer-specific function called "-F001". Data for particular employees regarding company-owned apartments is stored in a special infotype 9011 (*Rent*).

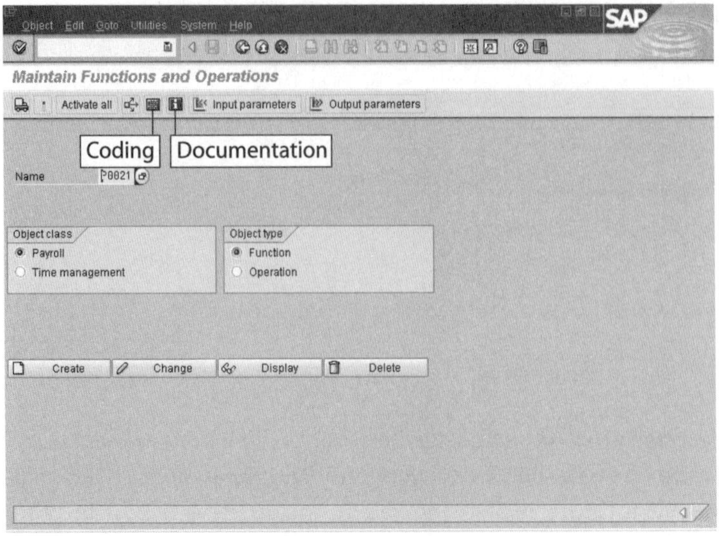

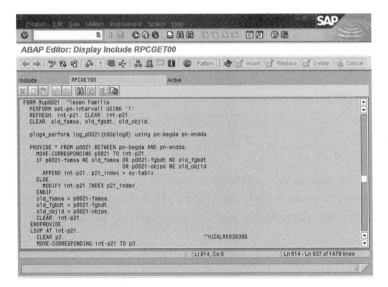

Figure 5.48 Display of the Standard Function P0021

Example In Figure 5.50, you can see the customer infotype with the fields **ObjectNo**, **Wage type** for rent deduction, **Amount** (of rent), and **Currency**. In Section 5.1.3, we learned how to create a customer-specific infotype for Personnel Administration. The information from this infotype should be read in Payroll, made available in table IT for further processing, and presented in the log, as shown in Figure 5.51.

Figure 5.49 Calling the Coding of Function P0021

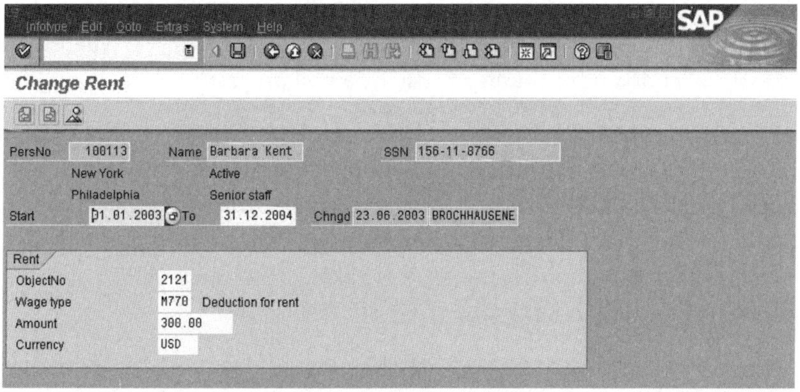

Figure 5.50 Customer Infotype 9011, Rent

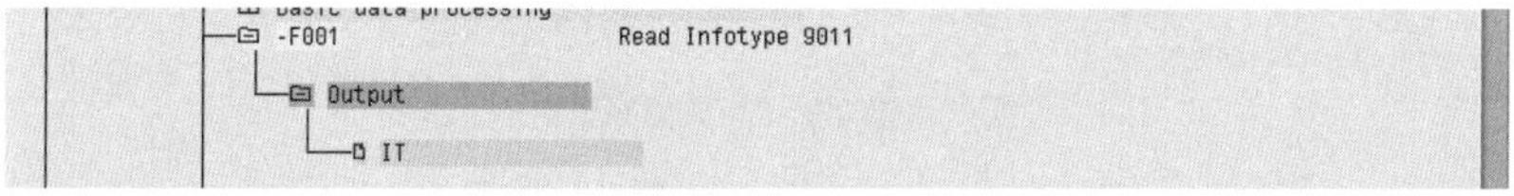

Figure 5.51 Function -F001 in the System Log

In Figure 5.52, we can also see how the amount resulting from the infotype is shown as a deduction.

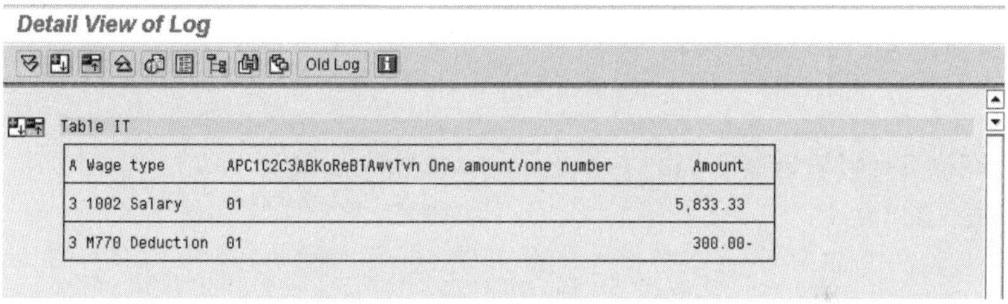

Figure 5.52 Table IT after Function -F001

The function is created using Transaction PE04. Various different conventions must be observed when naming functions (customer name range in tables, names for form routines, Unicode). Function names starting with a hyphen (-) meet all requirements. In addition to the name of the form routine, which in this case has the standard name "FU-F000", the country assignment and infotype assignment must also be specified. Table IT is specified as the output parameter, so that the output will be logged as shown above.

Transaction PE04

Coding   Coding is done in the specially provided include program RPCALCx0. The additional infotype must be declared in the include PCFDCZyy0, where "yy" is the ISO code of the country-specific payroll program.

The form routine for function -F001 must be coded in the include PCBURZyy0. The same conventions mentioned for the previous include also apply here. The last record of the payroll period is made available. The header of table IT is filled with the wage type and the negative amount. Additional information for table IT is taken from table WPBP and the record is attached to table IT.

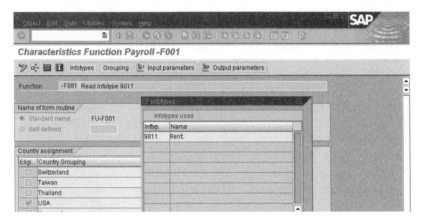

Figure 5.53 Function -F001

```
FORM fu-f001.
  PROVIDE * FROM p9011 BETWEEN pn-begda AND
pn-endda.
    it-lgart = p9011-yylgart.
    it-betrg = - p9011-yyamt.
  ENDPROVIDE.
  PERFORM pos-wpbp.
  MOVE-CORRESPONDING wpbp TO it.
  APPEND it.
ENDFORM.
```

Once you have finished customizing and coding, you must activate the function. The same procedure is used for Time Evaluation functions. The coding for these functions can be found in report SAPFP51T. Customer-specific functions and operations are stored in the include RPTM0Z00.

5.4.3 Operations

The operation should read the last record in infotype 9011 and place the contents of the **ObjectNo** field into the variable argument. An example of a rule that uses this operation is shown in Figure 5.54.

```
Rule:  ZXX1 ES grouping:      * Wage/time type: M770

VarKey  NL T Operation Operation Operation Operation Operation Operation *

             D -0001OBJ
 * * * *       ADDWT *
 2121         AMT%120   ADDWT *
```

Figure 5.54 Rule with Operation -O001

In this example, the amount of the Wage Type is multiplied by 120% if a certain object number is present.

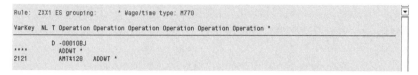

```
 ─⊟ PIT    ZXX1      NOAB      Operation -0001
     ─⊟ Input
         └─◻ IT
     ─⊟ Processing
         ─◻ 1002 Salary
         └─◻ M770 Deduction for rent
     └─⊟ Output
         └─◻ IT
```

Figure 5.55 Log of the Rule

You can access what you see in Figure 5.54 from the payroll program log for the rule shown in Figure 5.55.

Just like a function, the operation is created with Transaction PE04. Select **Operation** in the initial screen.

```
Operation    -0001  Read Attributes Rent

Name of form routine
 ⦿ Standard name    OP-OO..
 ◯ Self-defined

Country assignment
Eligi.. Country Grouping
 ☐  Thailand
 ☑  USA
 ☐  Venezuela
```

Figure 5.56 Creating Operation -O001

Additional parameter maintenance is required to check the syntax of the operations in the schemas used. In this example, the syntax check model EY has been selected. The models are stored in table T52BM. If the model you

Syntax check

need is not there, you can create one in the customer name range (Y, Z). When checking the model, note that the correct positioning of four possible character blocks and the space is checked.

Character	Description	Example -O001 (EY)
O	The name of the operation must appear in this block. The O block must be at the start and there can be up to five Os.	OOOO
F	The operation field appears in this block. The number of Fs must be five or less.	FFFFF
S	The operation ID appears in this block. The number of Ss must be two or less.	
V	The value assigned to the operation appears here.	
Space	There should be no characters here in the operation.	

The check can be further refined in the **Parameters** window. Only the value 'OBJ' should be allowed for the example operation. Enter this value under **Val. F**. Because the variable argument must be enhanced, a 'D' is entered under **Reac**. The type ALPHA and **Length** 4 are also entered for the variable argument.

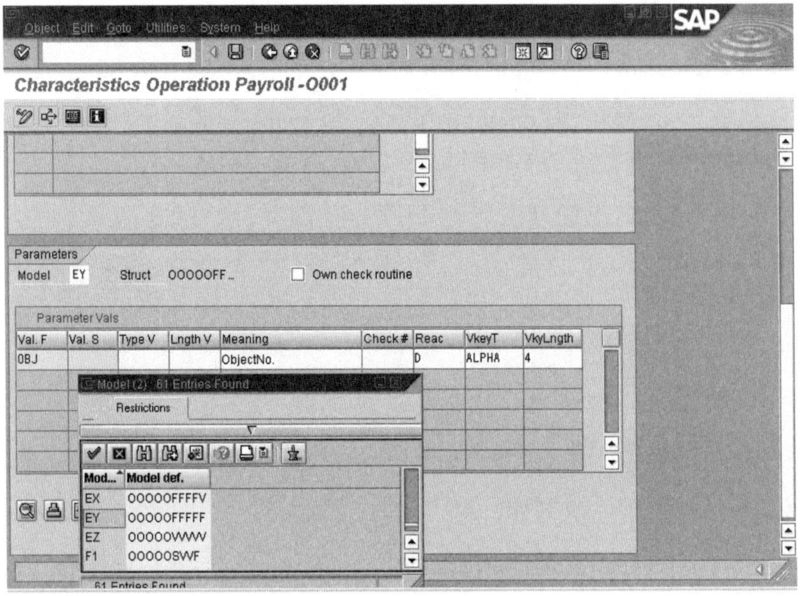

Figure 5.57 Parameters for Operation Payroll -O001

In the operation coding, it is assumed that the infotype has already been read and is available in the internal table p9011. The value of field YYMOBJ from the last record in the selection period is placed in the variable argument.

```
FORM op-o001.
  PROVIDE * FROM p9011 BETWEEN pn-begda AND
pn-endda.
  ENDPROVIDE.
  CASE op+5(5).
    WHEN 'OBJ'.
      vargt = p9011-yymobj.
  ENDCASE.
  PERFORM fillvargt.
ENDFORM.
```

The final step that you must take is to activate the operation. The same procedure applies for operations in Time Evaluation.

6 Reporting in HR

This chapter focuses on the appearance of reports in HR for various applications. Examples throughout illustrate the necessary basic elements for creating HR reports.

6.1 Master Data

Infotypes in personnel administration are numbered between 0000 and 0999; infotypes in time management are numbered between 2000 and 2999; and the numbering of customer-specific infotypes starts at 9000. The following section shows a procedure for the evaluation of master data; the next examples used show a similar approach based on the logical database PNP.

6.1.1 Structuring a Report for Personnel Administration Infotypes

Generating a Simple List

This example enhances the procedure that we used in Chapter 3, with additional notes for the creation of reports. In this example, a simple list of an employee's banking information at the end of the month is generated. It includes the account number, the bank routing number, and the name of the bank (see Figure 6.1).

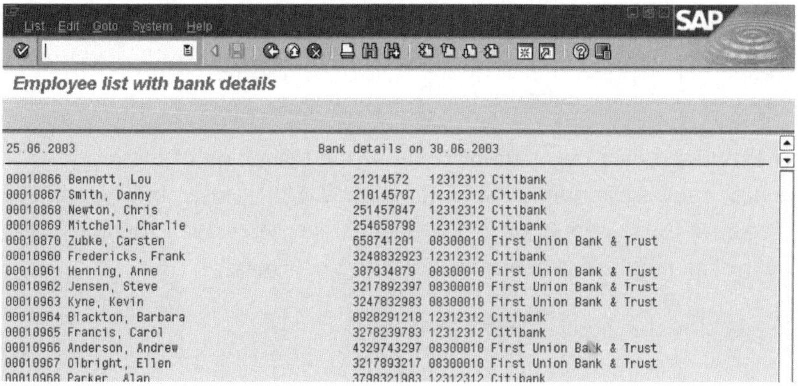

List of banking information

Figure 6.1 List of Employees with Bank Details

You must use the proper report class for the selection screen. We recommend that you use key date analysis with standard report class XX_10001.

Report class

Section 3.1 describes the structure of this report class. The logical database PNP is entered in the properties of the report (see Figure 6.2).

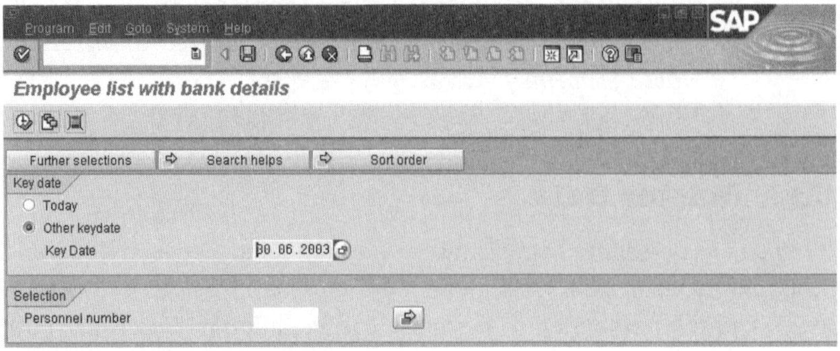

Figure 6.2 Selection Screen with Key Date

List header The key date must appear in the list header as xx.xx.xxxx. To do so, you must ensure that variable ⟨&0⟩ is recorded in the text elements, with trailing periods up to the total length (10) of the variable to be displayed in the list header (see Figure 6.3).

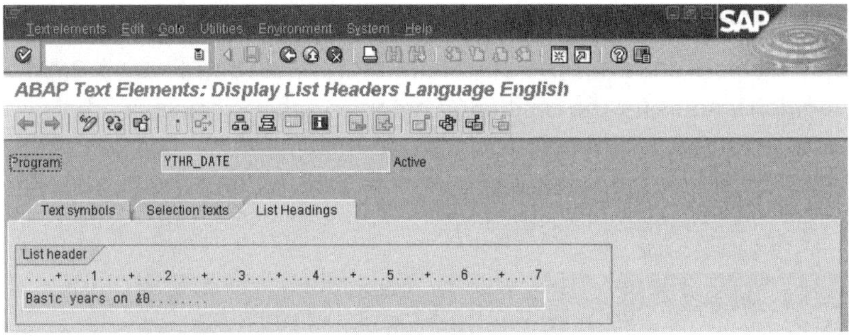

Figure 6.3 Text Elements for the "Basic Years" Report

Declarations The required data declarations occur at the beginning of the report. The logical database requires the statement: TABLES: pernr. Infotypes 0002 (Personal Data) and 0009 (*bank details*) are processed. You must also define the required variables coname and bankname.

```
REPORT  ythr_bank LINE-SIZE 132.
TABLES: pernr.
INFOTYPES: 0002, 0009.
DATA: coname(40),              "last name, first name
      bankname(40).           "Name of the bank
```

The default value is determined on the selection screen at the INITIAL- **Default values**
IZATION event. Module pool `sapfp500` contains helpful routines to calculate events, such as the addition of a number of months to the specified
data. Eternal call `last_day_in_month` determines the last day of the month
based on today's date. This default value is `pnpbegda` on the selection
screen and can be overwritten if necessary.

```
INITIALIZATION.
  PERFORM last_day_in_month(sapfp500)
    USING sy-datum prop_date.
  pnpbegda = prop_date.
```

The assignment of the date in the list header writes the (changed) date to
system variable `syst-tvar0` at the INITIALIZATION event.

```
START-OF-SELECTION.
  WRITE pn-begda TO syst-tvar0 DD/MM/YYYY.
```

Processing for each personnel number occurs at the GET PERNR event. **GET PERNR**
First, all the values calculated in the report are initialized. The current valid
values of infotypes 0002 and 0009 (with subtype 0) are placed in the
header row of internal tables P0002 and P0009. The name is concatenated
from the last name and the first name; the name of the bank is read.
Finally, the data is output to a list.

```
GET pernr.
  PERFORM clear_all.
  rp_provide_from_last p0002 space pn-begda
pn-begda.
  rp_provide_from_last p0009 '0' pn-begda
pn-begda.
  PERFORM concat_name USING coname.
  PERFORM read_bankname USING bankname.
  WRITE: / pernr-pernr,
          coname,
          p0009-bankn(10),
          p0009-bankl(8),
          bankname.
END-OF-SELECTION.
```

The tasks, which are described in the following section, are mapped to the
individual routines. The report-specific fields `coname` and `bankname` are ini-

tialized. You can use your own include to initialize report-specific fields for comprehensive reports.

```
FORM clear_all.
  CLEAR: coname, bankname.
ENDFORM.
```

Formatting the Name The name is built from the current valid fields p0002-nachn and p0002-vorna in the requested format.

```
FORM concat_name USING p_conname.
  CONCATENATE p0002-nachn p0002-vorna
    INTO p_conname SEPARATED BY ', '.
ENDFORM.
```

Interface FI The name of the bank is stored in FI tables. To read the bank name, select an appropriate function module of the HR interface. These function modules begin with "HRCA". Function module HRCA_READ_BANK_ADDRESS_2 is ideal for the purposes of this report. The function module returns a lot of information to the bankdata structure, based on input parameters bank_country (the country in which the bank is located) and bank_number (the bank routing number). Here, we need the banka field (the name of the bank).

```
FORM read_bankname USING p_bankname.
  DATA : bankdata TYPE bnka_bf.
  CALL FUNCTION 'HRCA_READ_BANK_ADDRESS_2'
    EXPORTING
      bank_country = p0009-banks
      bank_number = p0009-bankl
    IMPORTING
      bank_data    = bankdata
    EXCEPTIONS
      not_found    = 1
      OTHERS       = 2.
  IF sy-subrc = 0.
    p_bankname = bankdata-banka.
  ELSE.
    p_bankname = 'no bank details'.
  ENDIF.
ENDFORM.
```

Evaluating Repetitive Structures

In some infotypes of master data, features can be written repetitively in table form. Examples of infotypes with these characteristics include writing wage types in infotype 0008 (basic pay), infotype 0052 (wage maintenance), or infotype 0041 (date specifications) as shown in Figure 6.4.

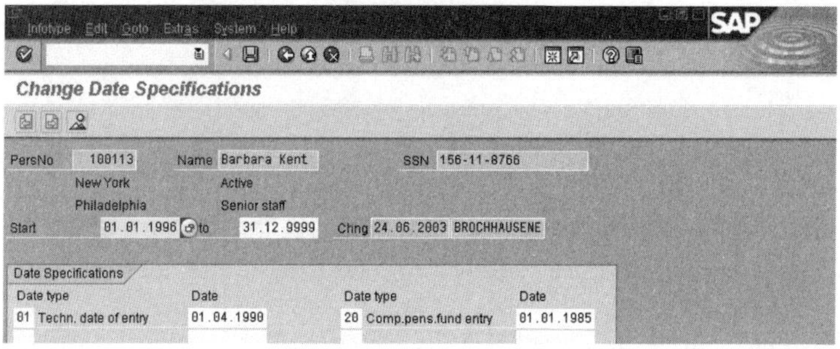

Figure 6.4 Date Specifications in Infotype 0041

A total of five types of dates are possible in this infotype. The data dictionary shows these fields as a chain of individual fields that are distinguished by the numbers in the field names. Figure 6.5 shows an excerpt of the data structure of infotype 0041.

Date specifications

The following report shows you how to access these data fields. The example determines the number of entitlement years at the beginning of the month. The entry date and the basic date (date type 20) should also appear in the list. The entitlement years are calculated from the entry date and baseline date as the difference between the selection date and the most recent date. Only the personnel numbers with date type 20 at the selection event should be processed. Figure 6.6 shows the generated list.

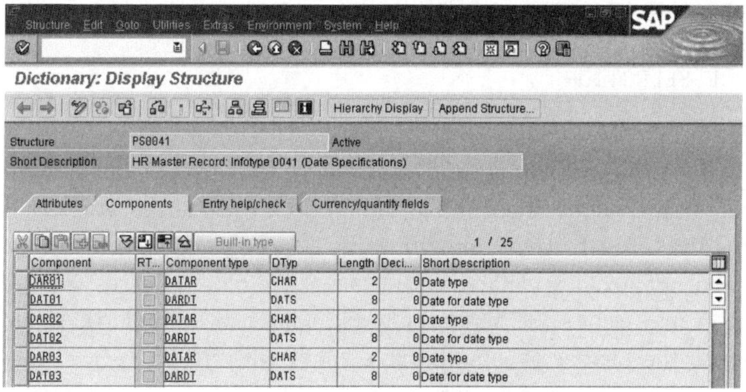

Figure 6.5 Structure for Infotype 0041 (Date Specifications)

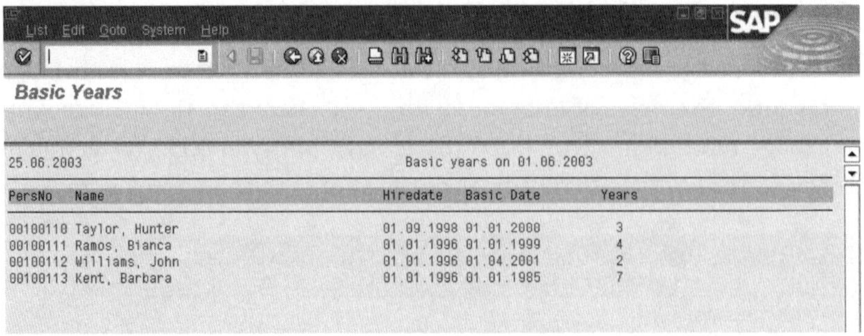

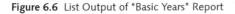

Figure 6.6 List Output of "Basic Years" Report

Data declarations   The required data declarations are first made at the beginning of the report. Fields `dar` and `dat` are required to read the repetitive structures.

```
REPORT  yrhr_date LINE-SIZE 132.
TABLES: pernr.
INFOTYPES: 0002, 0041.
DATA: hire_date LIKE sy-datum,  "Entry date
      rel_date LIKE sy-datum,   "Calculation base
      rel_years TYPE i,         "Basic years
      coname(40).               "last name, first name
DATA: dar LIKE p0041-dar01,     "Date type
      dat LIKE p0041-dat01.     "date
```

At the INITIALIZATION event, the day's date is derived from the first of the month and made available to the selection screen. System variable `syst-tvar0` is populated for the list header.

```
INITIALIZATION.
  pnpbegda = sy-datum.
  pnpbegda+6(2) = '01'.
START-OF-SELECTION.
  WRITE pn-begda TO syst-tvar0 DD/MM/YYYY.
```

GET PERNR   At the GET PERNR event, processing occurs again for each personnel number. First, all the values calculated in the report are initialized. A check is performed to verify if internal infotype table P0041 is populated. You must supply another auxiliary variable with DESCRIBE in older releases, instead of using `lines( p0041 )`. The current valid values of infotype 0041 are placed into the header of internal table P0041 with macro `rp_provide_from_last`. If a valid value is not present, field `pnp-sw-found` receives a value that is not equal to zero (null). In this case, no further processing occurs for the personnel number. Afterward, the current value of infotype 0002 is read. The name is concatenated from the last name and the first name. The date values of interest are read in routines `read_hire_date` and `read_p0041`. The entitlement years are calculated and the list is output, depending on the characteristics of these values.

```
GET pernr.
  PERFORM clear_all.
  CHECK lines( p0041 ) > 0.
  rp_provide_from_last p0041 space pn-begda
pn-begda.
  CHECK pnp-sw-found <> 0.
  rp_provide_from_last p0002 space pn-begda
pn-begda.
  PERFORM concat_name USING coname.
  PERFORM read_hire_date USING hire_date.
  PERFORM read_p0041 USING rel_date.
  IF rel_date < hire_date.
    rel_years = pn-begda+0(4) - hire_date+0(4).
    IF hire_date+4(4) >= pn-begda+4(4).
      rel_years = rel_years - 1.
    ENDIF.
  ELSE.
    rel_years = pn-begda+0(4) - rel_date+0(4).
    IF rel_date+4(4) => pn-begda+4(4).
      rel_years = rel_years - 1.
    ENDIF.
  ENDIF.
  WRITE: / pernr-pernr,
           coname,
           hire_date,
           rel_date,
           rel_years.
END-OF-SELECTION.
```

Report-specific variables are initialized in routine `clear_all`:

```
FORM clear_all.
  CLEAR: coname, rel_date, hire_date, rel_years.
ENDFORM.
```

The formatting of the name occurs in routine `concat_name`:

```
FORM concat_name USING p_conname.
  CONCATENATE p0002-nachn p0002-vorna
    INTO p_conname SEPARATED BY ', '.
ENDFORM.
```

Entry date The entry date is determined with function module `HR_ENTRY_DATE`, which was introduced in Chapter 3:

```
FORM read_hire_date USING p_hire_date.
  CALL FUNCTION 'HR_ENTRY_DATE'
    EXPORTING
      persnr                = pernr-pernr
    IMPORTING
      entrydate             = p_hire_date
    EXCEPTIONS
      entry_date_not_found = 1
      pernr_not_assigned   = 2
      OTHERS               = 3.
  IF sy-subrc <> 0.
*   ...
  ENDIF.
ENDFORM.
```

DO loop The value for date type 20 is determined with routine `read_p0041`. The following statement processes structure `p0041`:

```
DO 12 TIMES
  VARYING dar
    FROM p0041-dar01 NEXT p0041-dar02
```

Every run through the DO loop populates the field `dar`. The entry point is determined by field `p0041-dar01`; the increments are determined by the difference from the field `p0041-dar02`. The same process is applicable to the field `dat`. The loop stops if no more entries are found or date type 20 has been read:

```
FORM read_p0041 USING p_rel_date.
  DO 12 TIMES
    VARYING dar
      FROM p0041-dar01 NEXT p0041-dar02
```

```
    VARYING dat
      FROM p0041-dat01 NEXT p0041-dat02
    IF dar IS INITIAL.
      EXIT.
    ELSEIF dar = '20'.
      p_rel_date = dat.
      EXIT.
    ENDIF.
  ENDDO.
ENDFORM.
```

Evaluating Basic Pay

You often need to determine wage types and their amounts from infotype 0008 (basic pay). In the previous example, this information is stored in the repetitive groups of infotype 0008. Note that the amounts of wage types that have been calculated indirectly are not stored permanently in the tables, but are determined only at runtime. Function modules that contain the required functions can evaluate these wage types.

The sample report lists the development of basic pay for employees over the last 10 years. The standard selection screen is used. Default values for the data selection period include the end of the year and the beginning of the evaluation period (see Figure 6.7).

Development of Basic Pay

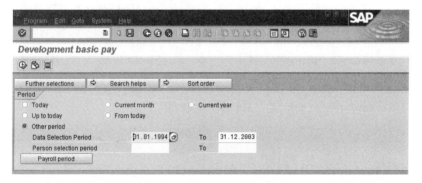

Figure 6.7 The "Development Basic Pay" Report

The list of this sample report (see Figure 6.8) should display the personnel number, the name of employee, and the valid total payments in the period. If there is a change of currency, all amounts are converted into the most recent valid currency. Also, note that the rows that contain names are highlighted in color.

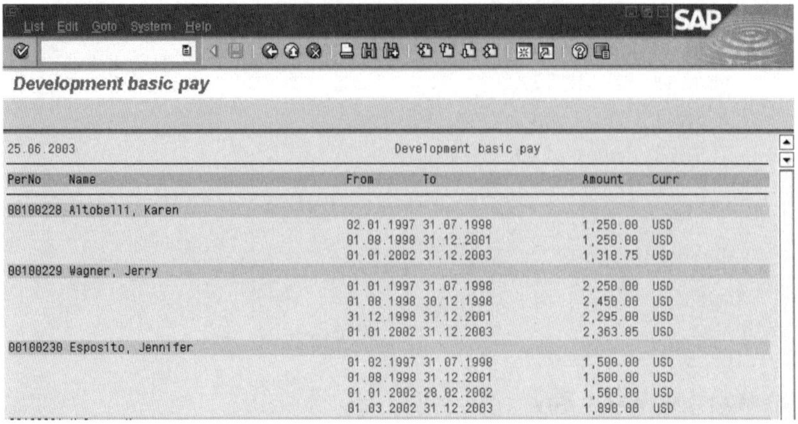

Figure 6.8 List Output of "Development Basic Pay" Report

Valuated wage types

The data declarations include the required infotypes for function module RP_FILL_WAGE_TYPE_TABLE_EXT (used later), the valuated wage types bewlart and t_bewlart, and the working area w_bewlart. A variable, last_curr, is also required for the currency used last.

```
REPORT  yrhr_p0008_list LINE-SIZE 132.
TABLES: pernr.
INFOTYPES: 0001, 0002, 0007, 0008.
DATA: bewlart TYPE TABLE OF pbwla,    "Wage types 1x
      t_bewlart TYPE TABLE OF pbwla,  "Overall wage types
      w_bewlart TYPE pbwla,           "Wage types Work
      last_curr LIKE p0008-waers,     "Last currency
      coname(40).                     "last name, first name
```

Data selection period

The default values for the data selection period, pnpbegda and pnpendda, are determined at the INITIALIZATION event.

```
INITIALIZATION.
  pnpendda = sy-datum.
  pnpendda+4(4) = '1231'.
  PERFORM day_minus_years(sapfp500)
    USING pnpendda '10' pnpbegda.
  pnpbegda = pnpbegda + 1.
START-OF-SELECTION.
```

At the beginning of processing for each personnel number, initialization occurs and the valid name is determined from infotype 0002. The wage types are read with routine read_p0008 from infotype 0008. The output of the personnel number and the name are formatted in color by the FORMAT statement. Then, the wage types for each infotype period are totaled in the subprogram and output.

```
GET pernr.
  PERFORM clear_all.
  rp_provide_from_last p0002 space pn-begda
pn-endda.
  PERFORM concat_name USING coname.
  PERFORM read_p0008.
  FORMAT COLOR COL_GROUP INTENSIFIED ON.
  WRITE: / pernr-pernr,
          coname, 132 space.
  FORMAT COLOR OFF.
  PERFORM list_sum.
END-OF-SELECTION.
```

The variables, structures, and internal tables are initialized in routine clear_all:

```
FORM clear_all.
  CLEAR: coname, bewlart, t_bewlart,
    w_bewlart, last_curr.
ENDFORM.
```

The name is built from the last name and the first name:

```
FORM concat_name USING p_conname.
  CONCATENATE p0002-nachn p0002-vorna
    INTO p_conname SEPARATED BY ', '.
ENDFORM.
```

A PROVIDE loop in subprogram read_p0008 processes infotype table p0008 for data from the data selection period. Function module RP_FILL_WAGE_ TYPE_TABLE_EXT populates the internal table of the valuated wage types, bewlart, from the current values of infotype 0008 for the period being considered. The results of all the periods for a given personnel number are collected in internal table t_bewlart. The last currency of the infotypes is stored in the variable last_curr.

```
FORM read_p0008.
  PROVIDE * FROM p0008 BETWEEN pn-begda AND
pn-endda.
    CALL FUNCTION 'RP_FILL_WAGE_TYPE_TABLE_EXT'
      EXPORTING
        begda                       = p0008-begda
        endda                       = p0008-endda
        infty                       = '0008'
        pernr                       = pernr-pernr
      TABLES
        pp0001                      = p0001
        pp0007                      = p0007
        pp0008                      = p0008
        ppbwla                      = bewlart
      EXCEPTIONS
        error_at_indirect_evaluation = 1
        OTHERS                      = 2.
    IF sy-subrc <> 0.
*   ...
    ENDIF.
    APPEND LINES OF bewlart TO t_bewlart.
  ENDPROVIDE.
  last_curr = p0008-waers.
ENDFORM.
```

Currency Conversion Internal table t_bewlart is processed further in routine list_sum. If the currency for a wage type in the table does not match the last currency, a conversion occurs with function module CONVERT_TO_LOCAL_CURRENCY and the table is modified accordingly. The values for the same period are totaled and output to the list.

```
FORM list_sum.
  LOOP AT t_bewlart INTO w_bewlart.
    IF w_bewlart-waers <> last_curr.
      CALL FUNCTION 'CONVERT_TO_LOCAL_CURRENCY'
        EXPORTING
          date             = w_bewlart-endda
          foreign_amount   = w_bewlart-betrg
          foreign_currency = w_bewlart-waers
          local_currency   = last_curr
        IMPORTING
```

```
     local_amount    = w_bewlart-betrg
   EXCEPTIONS
     no_rate_found    = 1
     overflow         = 2
     no_factors_found = 3
     no_spread_found  = 4
     derived_2_times  = 5
     OTHERS           = 6.
   IF sy-subrc <> 0.
   ELSE.
     w_bewlart-waers = last_curr.
     MODIFY t_bewlart FROM w_bewlart.
   ENDIF.
  ENDIF.
  AT END OF endda.
    SUM.
    WRITE: /50 w_bewlart-begda, w_bewlart-endda,
               w_bewlart-betrg, last_curr.
  ENDAT.
 ENDLOOP.
ENDFORM.
```

6.1.2 Structuring a Report for Time Management Infotypes

When the logical database PNP is used at the GET PERNR event, the internal tables (Pnnnn) are populated with all the infotypes (nnnn) that have been declared with INFOTYPES. However, given the large quantity of records for time management infotypes, we do not recommend that you use this procedure. A better way of proceeding is illustrated with the "Overview Absences" report for infotype 2001 (*absences*). The absence types of the current calendar year (specified in the report parameters) should be evaluated for all selected employees. Users should be able to switch the listing of individual absence records on or off. Separate summaries are provided for absences by employee group and employee subgroup. Figure 6.9 shows the list of absences in a report.

The MODE n addition should be specified along with the data declaration for infotype 2001. This addition prevents populating internal table P2001 at the GET PERNR event. Parameter s_name suppresses the individual list and selection s_abs selects only the absences that we are interested in. Internal table t_absence with working area w_absence is created for a cross-employee summary:

MODE n

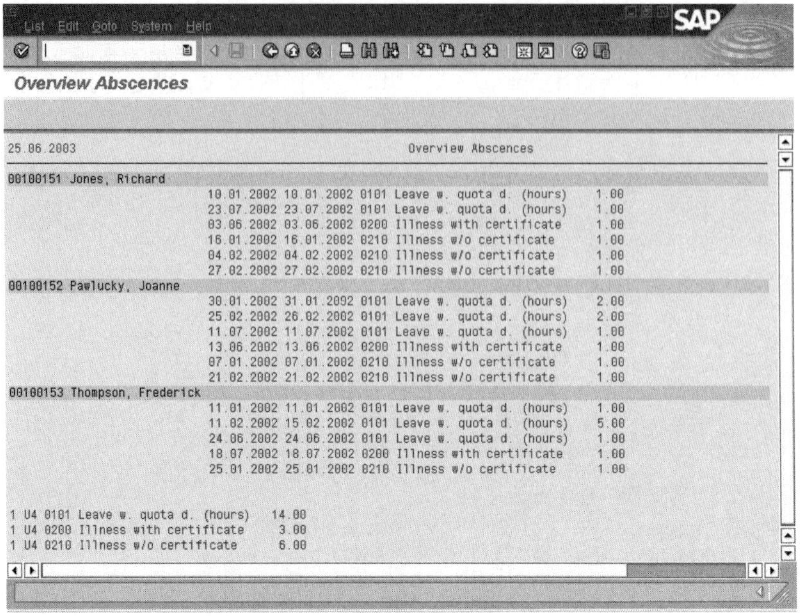

Figure 6.9 List Output of "Absences" Report

```
REPORT yrhr_p2001_list LINE-SIZE 132.
TABLES: pernr.
INFOTYPES: 0001, 0002,
           2001 MODE n.
PARAMETERS: s_name AS CHECKBOX.
SELECT-OPTIONS: s_abs FOR p2001-awart.
DATA: coname(40).   "Name, first name
TYPES: BEGIN OF absence,
          persg LIKE p0001-persg,   "Employee group
          persk LIKE p0001-persk,   "Employee subgroup
          awart LIKE p2001-awart,   "Absence type
          abwtg LIKE p2001-abwtg,   "Absence name
       END OF absence.
DATA: w_absence TYPE absence,
      t_absence TYPE TABLE OF absence.
```

The default values of the data selection period are determined at the INI-TIALIZATION event:

```
INITIALIZATION.
  pnpbegda = pnpendda = sy-datum.
```

```
   pnpbegda+4(4) = '0101'.
   pnpendda+4(4) = '1231'.
START-OF-SELECTION.
```

The processing that has been discussed so far occurs for each personnel **GET PERNR**
number and infotype 2001 is read with routine read_p2001. When parameter s_name is activated, individual processing with routine list_name is
executed. After all personnel numbers have been processed, a summary is
output with routine list_sum:

```
GET pernr.
  PERFORM clear_all.
  rp_provide_from_last p0002 space pn-begda pn-endda.
  PERFORM concat_name USING coname.
  PERFORM read_p2001.
  IF NOT s_name IS INITIAL.
    FORMAT COLOR COL_GROUP INTENSIFIED ON.
    WRITE: / pernr-pernr,
             coname, 132 space.
    FORMAT COLOR OFF.
    PERFORM list_name.
  ENDIF.
END-OF-SELECTION.
  PERFORM list_sum.
```

The processing of routines clear_all and concat_name occurs just as it
does for the other examples.

```
FORM clear_all.
  CLEAR: coname.
ENDFORM.
FORM concat_name USING p_conname.
  CONCATENATE p0002-nachn p0002-vorna
    INTO p_conname SEPARATED BY ', '.
ENDFORM.
```

At the beginning of routine read_p2001, rows of internal table p2001 are **Populating Table**
populated as determined by the data selection period. This populating of **p2001**
table p2001 occurs with function module rp_read_all_time_ity. The
entries in internal table p2001 that do not meet the specifications of the
selection options are then deleted: they do not require further processing.
If the table still contains values, the absences are processed further. The

corresponding contents of infotype p0001 are transferred to working area
w_absence. The remaining entries of internal table p2001 are also transferred.

```
FORM read_p2001.
  rp_read_all_time_ity pn-begda pn-endda.
  DELETE p2001 WHERE NOT ( awart IN s_abs ).
  IF lines( p2001 ) > 0.
    MOVE-CORRESPONDING p0001 TO w_absence.
    LOOP AT p2001.
      MOVE-CORRESPONDING p2001 TO w_absence.
      COLLECT w_absence INTO t_absence.
    ENDLOOP.
  ENDIF.
ENDFORM.
```

Absence types For a list of individual absences, subprogram list_name loops over internal table p2001 to read the text of the absence type with routine re554t.
It is assumed that the second parameter (Personnel subarea grouping for
absence and attendance types) has the constant value of "01".

```
FORM list_name.
  DATA: atext LIKE t554t-atext.
  LOOP AT p2001.
    PERFORM re554t
      USING sy-langu '01' p2001-awart atext.
    WRITE: /30 p2001-begda, p2001-endda,
      P2001-awart, atext, p2001-abwtg.
  ENDLOOP.
ENDFORM.
```

Text Table Routine re554t reads text table T554T for the absence types in the logon
language and makes the results available:

```
FORM re554t USING p_langu p_moabw p_awart p_atext.
  DATA: w_t554t LIKE t554t.
  SELECT SINGLE * FROM t554t
    INTO w_t554t
    WHERE sprsl = p_langu
      AND moabw = p_moabw
      AND awart = p_awart.
  IF sy-subrc = 0.
```

```
         p_atext = w_t554t-atext.
    ELSE.
       CLEAR p_atext.
    ENDIF.
ENDFORM.
```

The summary is output in a LOOP over table t_absence.

```
FORM list_sum.
   DATA: atext LIKE t554t-atext.
   SKIP 2.
   LOOP AT t_absence INTO w_absence.
      PERFORM re554t
         USING sy-langu '01' w_absence-awart atext.
      WRITE: / w_absence-persg, w_absence-persk,
         w_absence-awart, atext, w_absence-abwtg.
   ENDLOOP.
ENDFORM.
```

6.2   Organizational Management

As noted in Chapter 3, the use of logical database PCH enables sequential and structural evaluations.

6.2.1   Sequential Evaluation

The following report illustrates the use of sequential evaluation. The various object types in infotype 1002 can contain a description. In this example, the description of the job (object type C) on a key date is output, and the job ID and job title are highlighted in color (see Figure 6.10).

Job description

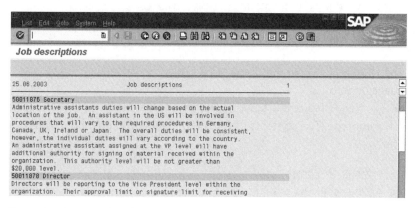

Figure 6.10 Sequential Evaluation: Job Description

In the declaration portion of the report, please do *not* specify GDSTR with the TABLES statement. By not specifying GDSTR, this ensures that a sequential evaluation, rather than a structural evaluation, will occur. Infotype 1002 (description) is declared under INFOTYPES. The table is characterized as a table infotype. Accordingly, the definition of internal table t_pt1002 is also required. A macro populates the table during further processing.

```
REPORT  ythr_org_seq LINE-SIZE 80.
TABLES: objec.
INFOTYPES: 1002.
DATA: t_pt1002 TYPE TABLE OF pt1002 WITH HEADER LINE.
```

Key date   Macro rh-sel-keydate ensures that at the INITIALIZATION event, a key date, rather than a selection period, is displayed on the selection screen. January 1 of the current year is made available as a default value ("01"). Default values for plan variant pchplvar and object type pchotype are also generated.

```
INITIALIZATION.
  rh-sel-keydate.
  pchplvar = '01'.
  pchotype = 'C'.
  pchobeg = sy-datum.
  pchobeg+4(4) = '0101'.
START-OF-SELECTION.
```

GET OBJEC   If you use GET objec, then the contents of infotype 1000 are available on the key date. The object ID and the title of the object are output.

```
GET objec.
  FORMAT COLOR COL_GROUP INTENSIFIED ON.
  WRITE: / objec-objid, objec-stext, 80 space.
  FORMAT COLOR OFF.
```

Table Infotype   The PROVIDE loop over infotype 1002 limits the values of the logon language. Macro
rh-get-tbdat reads the table entries in internal table t_pt1002 for the table infotype. The contents of the internal table can now be output in a loop.

```
PROVIDE * FROM p1002
  BETWEEN pc-begda AND pc-endda
   WHERE p1002-langu = sy-langu.
```

```
rh-get-tbdat p1002-infty p1002-tabnr t_pt1002.
LOOP AT t_pt1002.
  WRITE: / t_pt1002-tline.
ENDLOOP.
ENDPROVIDE.
```

6.2.2 Structural Evaluation

When using the logical database PCH, structural evaluations are much more common than are sequential evaluations

Create staff assignments with the following information:

Staff assignments

▶ Organizational unit and organizational title

▶ Position and title

▶ Personnel number and name (last name and first name)

Organizational (object type "O") elements are output at position 1. Line indentations occur to reflect the hierarchy. The positions (object type "S") are output from position 20, and the personnel numbers are output from position 30. Varying background colors are used for organizational unit, position, and personnel data.

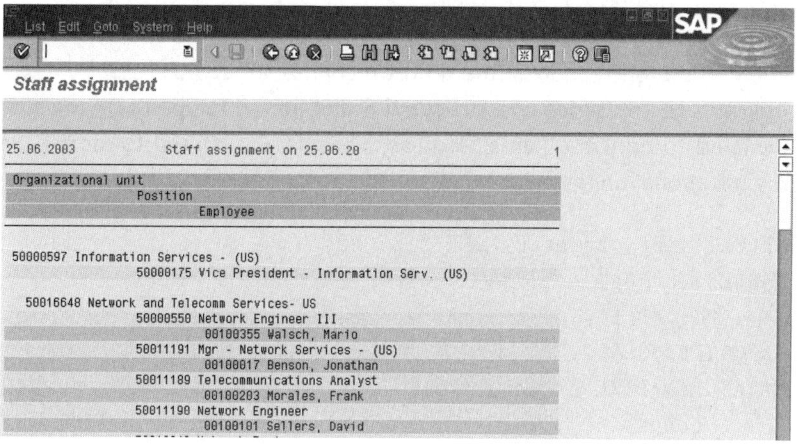

Figure 6.11 Structural Evaluation: Staff Assignment

A structural evaluation with logical database PCH reads all the objects that it can reach with the selection parameters specified in the evaluation path. Evaluation paths are set up in Customizing. In this report, the evaluation path should not appear with the selection parameters; rather, it should be fixed and unchangeable. Therefore, you must use version 900 of the selec-

Displaying the
Evaluation Path

tion screen (structural evaluation without structure parameters) with the report attributes.

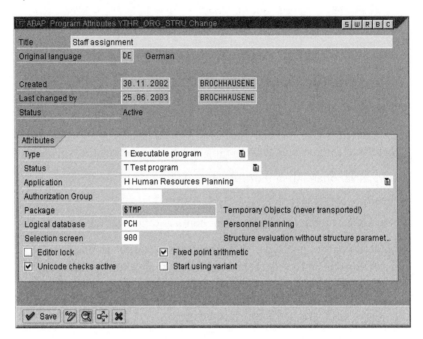

Figure 6.12 Attributes of the "Staff Assignment" Report

The declaration section of the report recognizes that TABLES entry gdstr indicates the presence of a structural evaluation. Infotype 0002 must be declared to print the name. Auxiliary variable col is used to indent the organizational units:

```
REPORT ythr_org_stru LINE-SIZE 80.
TABLES: objec,
        gdstr.
INFOTYPES: 0002.
DATA: col LIKE struc-level,
      coname(40).
```

At the INITIALIZATION event, the evaluation path is set along with the statements that should be familiar to you from the previous example. System variable syst-tvar0 is populated with the key date for the header:

```
rh-sel-keydate.
pchotype = '0'.
```

```
      pchwegid = 'O-S-P'.
START-OF-SELECTION.
   WRITE pc-begda TO syst-tvar0 DD/MM/YYYY.
```

GET objec makes available all the objects on the evaluation path along **GET OBJEC** with their infotypes. The object type is queried for object-specific formatting. The print position for object type "O" is set according to evaluation level struc-level. To output values, structure objec is used for object types "O" and "S."

```
GET objec.
  IF objec-otype = 'O'.
    col = struc-level * 2 .
    SKIP.
    FORMAT COLOR 2.
    WRITE:  AT col objec-objid, objec-stext, 80 space.
  ENDIF.
  IF objec-otype = 'S'.
    FORMAT COLOR 3.
    WRITE: /20 objec-objid, objec-stext, 80 space.
  ENDIF.
```

You can use the infotype tables declared in INFOTYPES for personnel master data. Here, infotype 0002 is evaluated, and the name is formatted with routine concat_name:

```
  IF objec-otype = 'P'.
    PROVIDE vorna nachn FROM p0002
      BETWEEN pc-begda AND pc-endda.
      PERFORM concat_name USING coname.
      FORMAT COLOR 4.
      WRITE: /30  objec-objid, coname, 80 space.
    ENDPROVIDE.
  ENDIF.
END-OF-SELECTION.
FORM concat_name USING p_conname.
  CONCATENATE p0002-nachn p0002-vorna
    INTO p_conname SEPARATED BY ', '.
ENDFORM.
```

6.3 Payroll Data

In Section 3.5, we discussed how to access and display payroll data. The following example will address additional function modules that support the evaluation of payroll data.

Evaluating NetPay

Figure 6.13 shows the results of the sample report that lists the payroll period and the net salaries paid under the name of the employee.

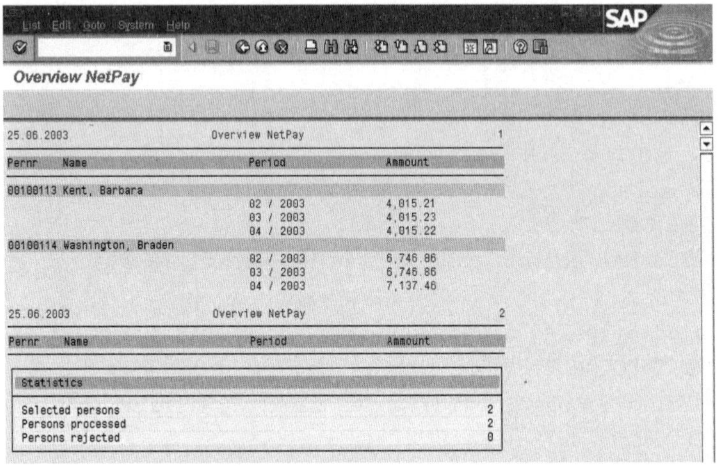

Figure 6.13 The "Overview NetPay" Report

A summary is output at the end of the list. If errors occur during processing, a list of errors is displayed (see Figure 6.14).

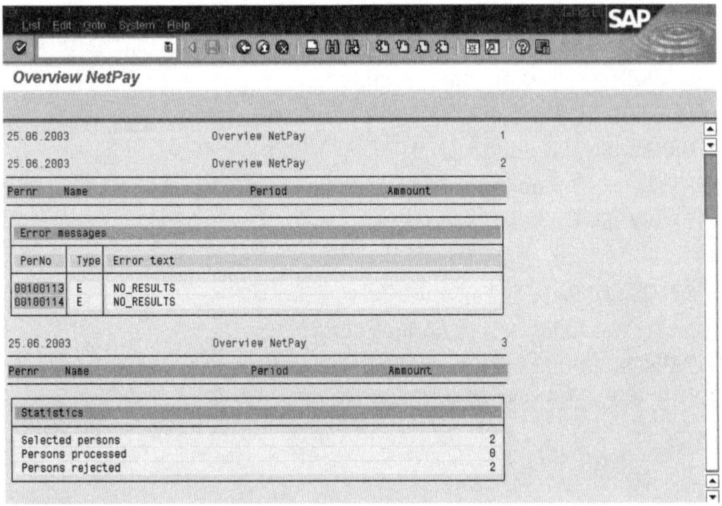

Figure 6.14 Error Messages in the "Overview NetPay" Report

Evaluating payroll results requires the definition of internal table `t_result` **Evaluating payroll results** and working area `w_result`. Processing wage types from table RT of the payroll cluster requires the definition of working area `w_rt`. Additional data definitions are required for report statistics and the output of an error table.

```
REPORT  ythr_pay_net LINE-SIZE 80.
TABLES: pernr.
INFOTYPES: 0002.
DATA: coname(40).
DATA: t_result TYPE TABLE OF payus_result,
      w_result TYPE payus_result,
      w_rt TYPE pc207.
DATA:  g_select TYPE i,
       g_proces TYPE i,
       g_reject TYPE i.
DATA: error_int TYPE TABLE OF hrerror.
```

At the beginning of processing, ABAP memory must be initialized with the two function modules given below for the error list and report statistics:

```
START-OF-SELECTION.
  CALL FUNCTION 'HR_REFRESH_ERROR_LIST'.
  CALL FUNCTION 'HR_REFRESH_STAT_LIST'.
```

At the GET PERNR event, the familiar processing occurs first. The number of **GET PERNR** selected employees is updated in variable `g_select`:

```
GET pernr.
  rp_provide_from_last p0002 space pn-begda pn-begda.
  PERFORM concat_name USING coname.
  FORMAT COLOR COL_GROUP INTENSIFIED ON.
  WRITE: / pernr-pernr,
           coname, 80 space.
  FORMAT COLOR OFF.
  g_select = g_select + 1.
```

Function module HR_GET_PAYROLL_RESULTS imports the current payroll results of the data selection period into table `t_result`:

```
  CALL FUNCTION 'HR_GET_PAYROLL_RESULTS'
    EXPORTING
      pernr                     = pernr-pernr
```

```
      pabrj                            = pn-begda(4)
      pabrp                            = pn-begda+4(2)
      pabrj_end                        = pn-endda(4)
      pabrp_end                        = pn-endda+4(2)
      actual                           = 'A'
  TABLES
      result_tab                       = t_result
  EXCEPTIONS
      no_results                       = 1
      error_in_currency_conversion     = 2
      t5001_entry_not_found            = 3
      period_mismatch_error            = 4
      t549q_entry_not_found            = 5
      internal_error                   = 6
      wrong_structure_of_result_tab    = 7.
```

Error List If an error occurs, function module HR_APPEND_ERROR_LIST is called. The function module updates error list error_int in ABAP memory with the ID "HRERRLIST". Routine list outputs the "Overview NetPay" list for every personnel number.

```
IF sy-subrc NE 0.
  CALL FUNCTION 'HR_APPEND_ERROR_LIST'
    EXPORTING
      pernr = pernr-pernr
      arbgb = sy-msgid
      msgty = 'E'
      msgno = sy-msgno
      msgv1 = sy-msgv1
      msgv2 = sy-msgv2
      msgv3 = sy-msgv3
      msgv4 = sy-msgv4.
  g_reject = g_reject + 1.
ELSE.
  g_proces = g_proces + 1.
ENDIF.
PERFORM list.
END-OF-SELECTION.
```

At the end of the selection, error table error_int is read from ABAP memory and output with function module HR_DISPLAY_ERROR_LIST.

```
NEW-PAGE.
IMPORT error_int FROM MEMORY ID 'HRERRLIST'.
CALL FUNCTION 'HR_DISPLAY_ERROR_LIST'
  EXPORTING
    no_popup          = 'X'
    no_print          = ' '
  TABLES
    error             = error_int
  EXCEPTIONS
    invalid_linesize = 1
    OTHERS           = 2.
IF sy-subrc <> 0.
  MESSAGE ID sy-msgid TYPE sy-msgty NUMBER sy-msgno
          WITH sy-msgv1 sy-msgv2 sy-msgv3 sy-msgv4.
ENDIF.
```

Function modules `HR_APPEND_STAT_LIST` and `HR_DISPLAY_STAT_` **Report Statistics** `LIST` execute the processing and output of report statistics:

```
CALL FUNCTION 'HR_APPEND_STAT_LIST'
  EXPORTING
    selected  = g_select
    processed = g_proces
    rejected  = g_reject.
CALL FUNCTION 'HR_DISPLAY_STAT_LIST'
  EXPORTING
    no_popup          = 'X'
    no_print          = ' '
  EXCEPTIONS
    invalid_linesize = 1
    OTHERS           = 2.
IF sy-subrc <> 0.
  MESSAGE ID sy-msgid TYPE sy-msgty NUMBER sy-msgno
          WITH sy-msgv1 sy-msgv2 sy-msgv3 sy-msgv4.
ENDIF.
```

Routine `concat_name` formats the name:

```
FORM concat_name USING p_conname.
  CONCATENATE p0002-nachn p0002-vorna
    INTO p_conname SEPARATED BY ', '.
ENDFORM.
```

The output of the payroll results is executed for each payroll period in a LOOP over internal table t_result. The values of wage type table RT are read at a deeper level in working area w_rt. The net remuneration is found in technical wage type "/550."

```
FORM list.
  LOOP AT t_result INTO w_result.
    WRITE : /40 w_result-evp-fpper+4(2) ,
       '/', w_result-evp-fpper(4).
    LOOP AT w_result-inter-rt INTO w_rt
       WHERE lgart = '/550'.
       WRITE: w_rt-betrg.
    ENDLOOP.
  ENDLOOP.
ENDFORM.
```

It is assumed that the same wage types are not present with several period indicators during the evaluation of results. Please consider this fact when necessary.

6.4   Time Management

Results of time evaluation

In time management, the results of time evaluation are stored in clusters, as are payroll results. This section explains how to read these clusters. Figure 6.15 shows a list of time pairs and time type "0003" (skeleton time) that have been generated. The horizontal line indicates the end of each week.

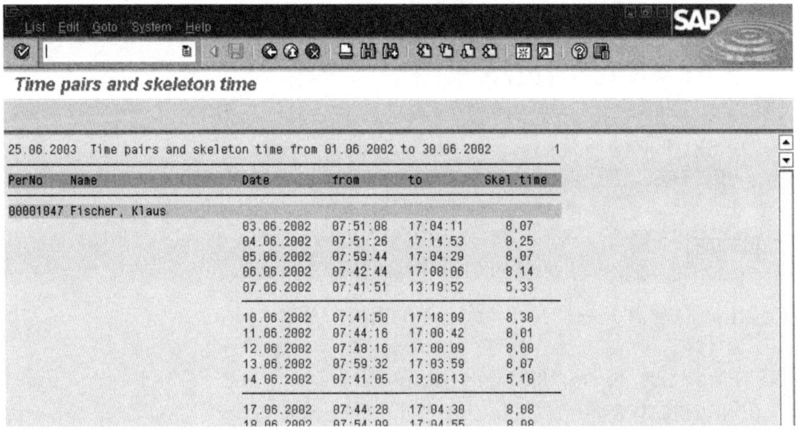

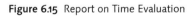

Figure 6.15 Report on Time Evaluation

The data declaration lists the includes required for buffering and the data description of the clusters. In Section 3.5, the conventions that are used here were explained.

```
REPORT  yrhr_time LINE-SIZE 80.
TABLES: pernr,
        pcl1,
        pcl2.
INFOTYPES: 0002.
INCLUDE rpppxd00.        "Data for PCL1/2-Puffer
DATA:   BEGIN OF COMMON PART buffer.
INCLUDE rpppxd10.
DATA:   END OF COMMON PART.
INCLUDE: rpc2b200.
DATA: coname(40),               "last name, first name
      odate LIKE pt-ldate,      "first of the week
      odate_old LIKE pt-ldate.  "old first of the week
```

The month-end and first-of-the-month of the previous month are default values for the data selection period. System variables syst-tvar0 and syst-tvar1 are populated for the header.

```
INITIALIZATION.
  pnpbegda = sy-datum.
  pnpbegda+6(2) = '01'.
  PERFORM day_minus_months(sapfp500)
    USING pnpbegda '1' pnpbegda.
  PERFORM last_day_in_month(sapfp500)
    USING pnpbegda pnpendda.
START-OF-SELECTION.
  WRITE pn-begda TO syst-tvar0 DD/MM/YYYY.
  WRITE pn-endda TO syst-tvar1 DD/MM/YYYY.
```

Unlike the previous examples, here at the GET PERNR event, a new routine, read_time, lists and outputs the time evaluation data:

```
GET pernr.
  PERFORM clear_all.
  rp_provide_from_last p0002 space pn-begda pn-begda.
  PERFORM concat_name USING coname.
  FORMAT COLOR COL_GROUP INTENSIFIED ON.
  WRITE: / pernr-pernr,
```

```
                coname, 80 space.
    FORMAT COLOR OFF.
    PERFORM read_time.
END-OF-SELECTION.
```

Include rpppxm00 contains the standard routines for buffering the data when using macros:

```
INCLUDE rpppxm00.
```

Routine concat_name formats the name:

```
FORM concat_name USING p_conname.
  CONCATENATE p0002-nachn p0002-vorna INTO p_
conname SEPARATED BY ', '.
ENDFORM.
```

Cluster B2 The routine read_time populates the key for reading cluster B2 of cluster table PCL2. Macro rp-imp-c2-b2 reads the cluster. If the import was successful, the time pairs from imported table PT are read and output. When the week changes (which is recognized by routine get_first_day_in_week), a horizontal line is output. Time type "0003" (skeleton time) from imported table ZES is listed for each day.

```
FORM read_time.
  b2-key-pernr = pernr-pernr .    "Personnel number
  b2-key-pabrp = pnpbegda+4(2).   "Payroll period
  b2-key-pabrj = pnpbegda(4).     "Payroll year
  b2-key-cltyp = '1'.             "original
  rp-imp-c2-b2.
  IF sy-subrc EQ 0.
    LOOP AT pt.
      PERFORM get_first_day_in_week(sapfp500)
        USING pt-ldate '01' odate.
      IF ( NOT odate_old IS INITIAL )
        AND ( odate_old <> odate ).
        NEW-LINE.
        ULINE AT 35.
      ENDIF.
      odate_old = odate.
      WRITE: /35(12) pt-ldate,
        (10) pt-begtm USING EDIT MASK '__:__:__',
        (10) pt-endtm USING EDIT MASK '__:__:__'.
```

```
      LOOP AT zes WHERE reday = pt-ldate+6(2)
        AND ztart = '0003'.
        WRITE: zes-anzhl.
        EXIT.
      ENDLOOP.
    ENDLOOP.
  ELSE.
* ...
  ENDIF.
ENDFORM.
```

6.5 Formatting Output with the ABAP List Viewer

The formatting used in this chapter can be enhanced with additional features by employing the ABAP List Viewer (ALV). For example, you can sort the list displayed or download it to Excel. You can configure the display to individual preferences and save the settings as a display variant. Figure 6.16 shows the list from Section 6.1 as formatted with function module REUSE_ALV_LIST_DISPLAY.

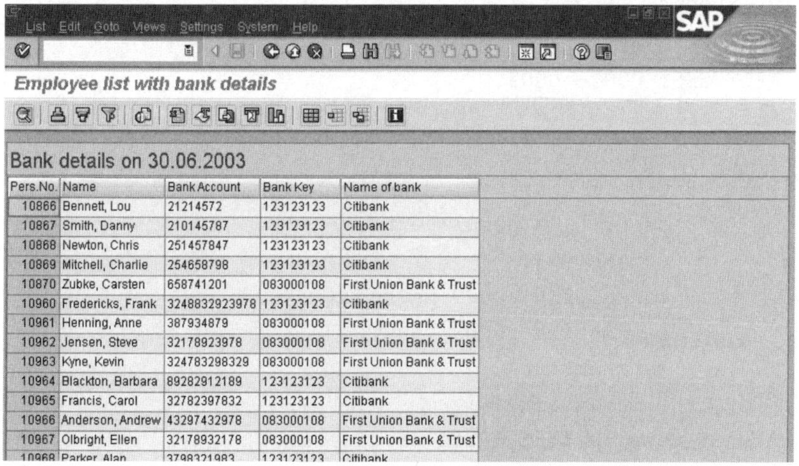

Figure 6.16 Output of a List with REUSE_ALV_LIST_DISPLAY

Function module REUSE_ALV_GRID_DISPLAY offers another option (see Figure 6.17).

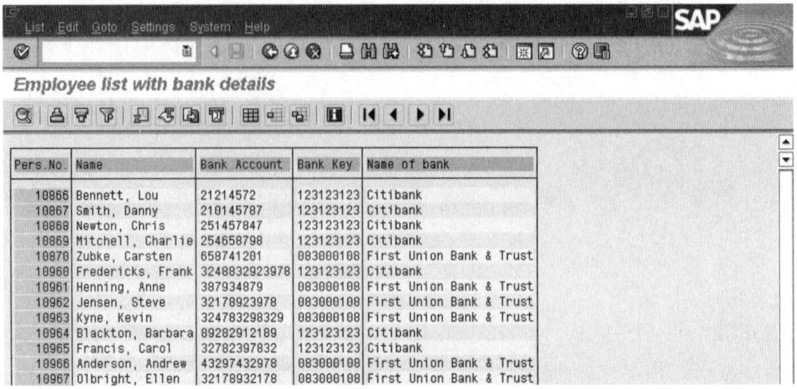

Pers.No.	Name	Bank Account	Bank Key	Name of bank
10866	Bennett, Lou	21214572	123123123	Citibank
10867	Smith, Danny	210145787	123123123	Citibank
10868	Newton, Chris	251457847	123123123	Citibank
10869	Mitchell, Charlie	254658798	123123123	Citibank
10870	Zubke, Carsten	658741201	083000108	First Union Bank & Trust
10960	Fredericks, Frank	3248832923978	123123123	Citibank
10961	Henning, Anne	387934879	083000108	First Union Bank & Trust
10962	Jensen, Steve	32178923978	083000108	First Union Bank & Trust
10963	Kyne, Kevin	324783298329	083000108	First Union Bank & Trust
10964	Blackton, Barbara	89282912189	123123123	Citibank
10965	Francis, Carol	32782397832	123123123	Citibank
10966	Anderson, Andrew	43297432978	083000108	First Union Bank & Trust
10967	Olbright, Ellen	32178932178	083000108	First Union Bank & Trust

Figure 6.17 Output of a List with REUSE_ALV_GRID_DISPLAY

TYPE-POOLS

Declaration of `TYPE-POOLS: slis` is required to use ALV. The structure defined in the report for outputting `display` is used to define internal table `t_display` and working area `w_display`. Additional definitions apply to field catalog `alv_fieldcat`, specifications for the layout, and storing variants:

```
REPORT  yrhr_bank_alv.
TYPE-POOLS: slis.
TABLES: pernr.
INFOTYPES: 0002, 0009.
DATA: coname(40),        "Name, first name
      bankname(40).      "Bank name
TYPES: BEGIN OF display,
         pernr LIKE pernr-pernr,
         coname(40),
         bankn LIKE p0009-bankn,
         bankl LIKE p0009-bankl,
         bankname(40),
       END OF display.
DATA: t_display TYPE TABLE OF display,
      w_display TYPE display.
DATA: alv_fieldcat TYPE slis_t_fieldcat_alv,
      w_alv_fieldcat TYPE LINE OF slis_t_fieldcat_alv,
      alv_layout TYPE slis_layout_alv,
      alv_variant TYPE disvariant.
INITIALIZATION.
  PERFORM last_day_in_month(sapfp500)
```

```
    USING sy-datum pnpbegda.
START-OF-SELECTION.
```

The familiar processing is executed at the GET PERNR event. Unlike the sit‐ **GET PERNR**
uation with a simple list, here the output is performed in internal table t_
display with the use of working area w_display. To clarify this method,
assignment occurs here for each individual field instead of using MOVE-
CORRESPONDING:

```
GET pernr.
  PERFORM clear_all.
  rp_provide_from_last p0002 space pn-begda pn-begda.
  rp_provide_from_last p0009 '0' pn-begda pn-begda.
  PERFORM concat_name USING coname.
  PERFORM read_bankname USING bankname.
  MOVE: pernr-pernr TO w_display-pernr,
        coname TO w_display-coname,
        p0009-bankn TO w_display-bankn,
        p0009-bankl TO w_display-bankl,
        bankname TO w_display-bankname.
  APPEND w_display TO t_display.
END-OF-SELECTION.
```

At the end of processing, table t_display is populated and can be output   **Output**
with routine show_list:

```
  PERFORM show_list.
```

You should already be familiar with the routines listed below:

```
FORM clear_all.
  CLEAR: coname, bankname.
ENDFORM.
FORM concat_name USING p_coname.
  CONCATENATE p0002-nachn p0002-vorna
    INTO p_coname SEPARATED BY ', '.
ENDFORM.
FORM read_bankname USING p_bankname.
  DATA : bankdata TYPE bnka_bf.
  CALL FUNCTION 'HRCA_READ_BANK_ADDRESS_2'
    EXPORTING
      bank_country = p0009-banks
      bank_number  = p0009-bankl
```

```
        IMPORTING
          bank_data     = bankdata
        EXCEPTIONS
          not_found     = 1
          OTHERS        = 2.
    IF sy-subrc = 0.
      p_bankname = bankdata-banka.
    ELSE.
      CLEAR p_bankname.
    ENDIF.
ENDFORM.
```

The processing of routine `show_list` is new. To display the title, variables `grid_titel` and `list_begda` are defined and populated:

```
FORM show_list.
  DATA: grid_title TYPE lvc_title,
        list_begda(10).
  WRITE pn-begda TO list_begda DD/MM/YYYY.
  CONCATENATE 'Employees' bank details on'
    list_begda INTO grid_title SEPARATED BY space.
```

Layout   For the layout that you want, the appropriate transfer parameters of structure `alv_layout` are specified.

```
    alv_layout-colwidth_optimize = 'X'.
    alv_layout-zebra = 'X'.
```

Field Catalog   Special characteristics are defined for individual columns of the output and recorded in the field catalog. To get a description of each of the fields, see the documentation for the function modules called below.

```
    CLEAR w_alv_fieldcat.
    w_alv_fieldcat-fieldname = 'PERNR'.
    w_alv_fieldcat-ref_tabname = 'PERNR'.
    w_alv_fieldcat-key = 'X'.
    APPEND w_alv_fieldcat TO alv_fieldcat.
    CLEAR w_alv_fieldcat.
    w_alv_fieldcat-fieldname = 'CONAME'.
    w_alv_fieldcat-reptext_ddic = 'Name'.
    APPEND w_alv_fieldcat TO alv_fieldcat.
    CLEAR w_alv_fieldcat.
```

```
w_alv_fieldcat-fieldname = 'BANKN'.
w_alv_fieldcat-ref_tabname = 'P0009'.
APPEND w_alv_fieldcat TO alv_fieldcat.
CLEAR w_alv_fieldcat.
w_alv_fieldcat-fieldname = 'BANKL'.
w_alv_fieldcat-ref_tabname = 'P0009'.
APPEND w_alv_fieldcat TO alv_fieldcat.
CLEAR w_alv_fieldcat.
w_alv_fieldcat-fieldname = 'BANKNAME'.
w_alv_fieldcat-ref_tabname = 'BNKA_BF'.
w_alv_fieldcat-ref_fieldname = 'BANKA'.
APPEND w_alv_fieldcat TO alv_fieldcat.
```

Once the field catalog has been completely populated, function module REUSE_ALV_GRID_DISPLAY can be called and the output transferred. The parameter list includes parameters i_save and is_variant, both of which are required to store list variants.

```
CALL FUNCTION 'REUSE_ALV_GRID_DISPLAY'
  EXPORTING
    I_callback_program = 'YTHR_BANK_ALV'
    I_grid_title       = grid_title
    is_layout          = alv_layout
    it_fieldcat        = alv_fieldcat
    i_save             = 'A'
    is_variant         = alv_variant
  TABLES
    t_outtab           = t_display
  EXCEPTIONS
    program_error      = 1
    OTHERS             = 2.
IF sy-subrc <> 0.
  WRITE: / 'Formatting error'.
ENDIF.
ENDFORM.                    "show_list
```

Function module HR_ALV_LIST_DISPLAY offers similar formatting options. This function module encapsulates the call of function module REUSE_ALV_LIST_DISPLAY for applications in HR.

7 Employee Self-Service

Since Release 4.5, SAP offers many Internet-based scenarios for employees in the framework of Employee Self-Service (ESS). These scenarios allow you to improve the efficiency and quality of processes that are integral to HR.

7.1 Functional Scope

Before delving into the technical aspects of Employee Self-Service (ESS), we'll give you a brief outline of the product—from a business-management point of view.

7.1.1 Business View

Employee Self-Service is a package of easy-to-use applications that allow individual employees to execute certain business processes that affect them directly.

All ESS scenarios are grouped together in the R/3 composite role *SAP_Employee* and they include the following areas, which are listed in alphabetical order (you can find a list of all ESS scenarios in the table in Appendix A):

▶ Appraisals
My appraisals, and so on

▶ Benefits
Enrollment, Savings, pension funds, and so on

▶ Business trips
Travel management, travel expenses, and so on

▶ Office
Workflow inbox, Who's who, and so on

▶ Payroll
Paycheck inquiry, employment and salary verification, and so on

▶ Personal information
Addresses, bank details, and so on

▶ Purchase orders
Office supplies, and so on

▶ Qualifications profile
Profile match up with own position, edit skills profile, and so on

- Recruitment
  Application status, employment opportunities, and so on
- Time management
  Recording working time, leave request, and so on
- Training
  Training center, my bookings, and so on
- Life and work events (*My first days at work, Change of job,* and so on)
  Process support of events in the employee's working or private life. The employee is shown all the steps in a process and can edit them in the predefined sequence–or any sequence–and mark them as complete.
- MiniApps/iViews (*Web search, currency converter,* and so on)
  MiniApps are small applications that can be used quickly and directly in a part of the user interface, for information on particular themes, or to allow the execution of simple processes. *iViews* are the counterpart of MiniApps in the SAP Enterprise Portal. They are realized as Java Servlets and are the containers for all applications in the SAP Enterprise Portal.

The main advantages offered by ESS are:

Access at any time

- **Reduces work for the HR department**
  The HR department does not have to spend so much time on the administration of forms; instead, it can concentrate on personnel development and other strategic areas.
- **The data in the backend system will be current and correct**
  Data is entered by the owner of that data, thereby avoiding the scenario of employees sending forms to HR, which must then be entered into the system by personnel administrators.
- **24/7 entry**
  Employees can access ESS from any Internet connection and at any time.

7.1.2   Navigation

The ESS scenarios are grouped together in different areas, to make it easier for users to find the services they require. In release R/3 Enterprise, the ESS menu is dependent on the Portal installation. In Workplace (WP) 2.11, the menu is defined by the composite role *SAP_WP_EMPLOYEE.* As an alternative to WP, there is the ESS menu transaction PZM3, whereby the menu is defined by the ESS tables T77WWW_* (see OSS Note 0321439 for details). In Enterprise Portal 5.0 and 6.0, ESS forms part of the Portal User Package. The menu is defined by what are known as *worksets*, which are service catalogs containing the individual ESS scenarios.

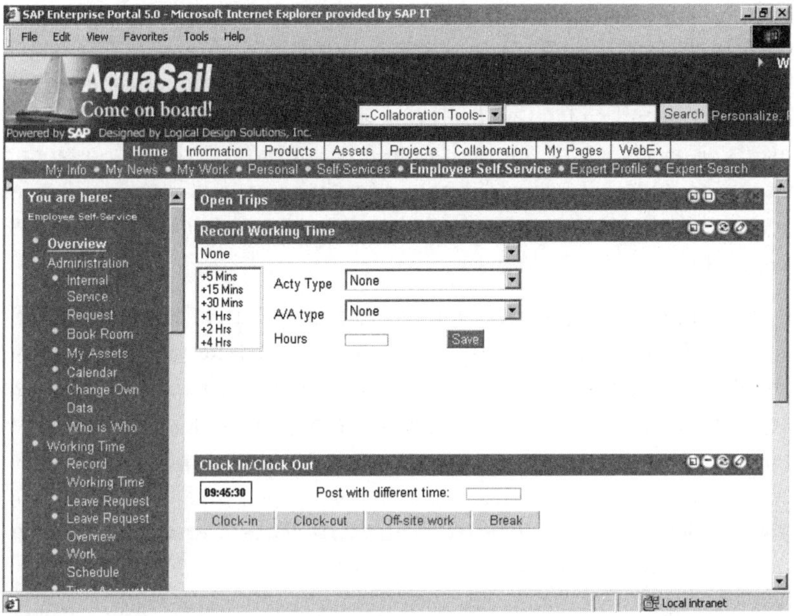

Figure 7.1 ESS in Enterprise Portal 5.0

7.2 The "Employee" Role

The term *Role* is used in two areas in the SAP environment—in SAP R/3 and in the SAP Enterprise Portal. With the enhancement of ESS and other components made available to the user via the SAP Enterprise Portal, both kinds of roles—R/3 and portal roles—are used. Because the Enterprise Portal is the successor to SAP Workplace 2.11, the term *Enterprise Portal* in the following text also refers to Workplace.

R/3 and portal roles

7.2.1 The Concept of Role

As just noted, we can differentiate between portal roles and R/3 roles. *Portal roles* define a user's menu; they determine what navigation nodes are available; and they decide what R/3 services, URLs, and MiniApps are displayed in the portal for a user. The URLs generated by the *PCD* (*Portal Content Directory*) and which lie behind each link, are also included. The *PCD* is a file system in which all objects that are required for a role and its creation are stored.

The *R/3 roles*, on the other hand, are "authorization roles," as they determine which R/3 statements (transactions, MiniApps, reports and so on) the user is allowed to execute.

Therefore, if a particular menu entry should not be displayed for a user, it must be removed from the portal role. However, if you want to exclude the execution of a menu entry, then the R/3 role must be restricted in this respect. The "role migration tool" or the "transfer of role data and assignments" is available for transferring role data from R/3 to the portal and vice versa. In WP 2.11, no distinction has been made between R/3 roles and portal roles. Nevertheless, most statements made here apply to WP 2.11, also.

One or more R/3 roles can be assigned to each R/3 user. The roles supplied are intended as a sample for customers. The role that best suits a particular employee group in the enterprise is copied and can then be adjusted accordingly using Transaction PFCG. In the next section, the term *role* refers to R/3 roles, which determine user authorizations.

7.2.2 Single Roles, Country-Specific Roles, and Composite Roles

In R/3, authorizations for individual transactions are grouped in a single role. These transactions must all be in the same R/3 component. For example, the role *SAP_ESSUSER* contains authorizations related to the HR functions in ESS and another *SAP_FI_EMPLOYEE* contains authorizations related to FI functions in ESS. The authorizations for country-specific services can also be grouped in single roles. All services that are only relevant to a particular country are grouped together in roles such as *SAP_HR_EMPLOYEE_AU* for Australia. Figure 7.2 shows an excerpt of all single roles in the composite role *SAP_EMPLOYEE*.

In order to create menus for portal users from roles, you can group them together in composite roles (see Figure 7.3). Therefore, on the one hand, you have small, flexible single roles for individual adjustment, and on the other hand, there are composite roles from which menus can be derived directly when they are migrated to portal roles.

R/3 roles are managed in the R/3 system using Transaction PFCG. You can get detailed documentation on the role concept under **http://help.sap.com/ · SAP NetWeaver SAP Enterprise Portal · <Choose release, e.g. "EP 6.0 SP0> · English · Administration Guide · Portal Platform · Content Administration · Roles, Worksets and Navigation.**

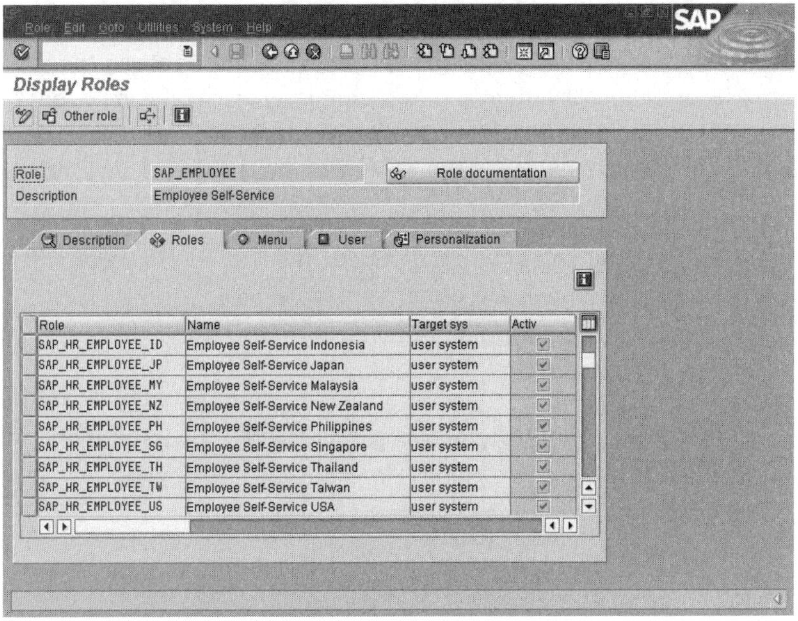

Figure 7.2 Single Roles in the Composite Role SAP_EMPLOYEE

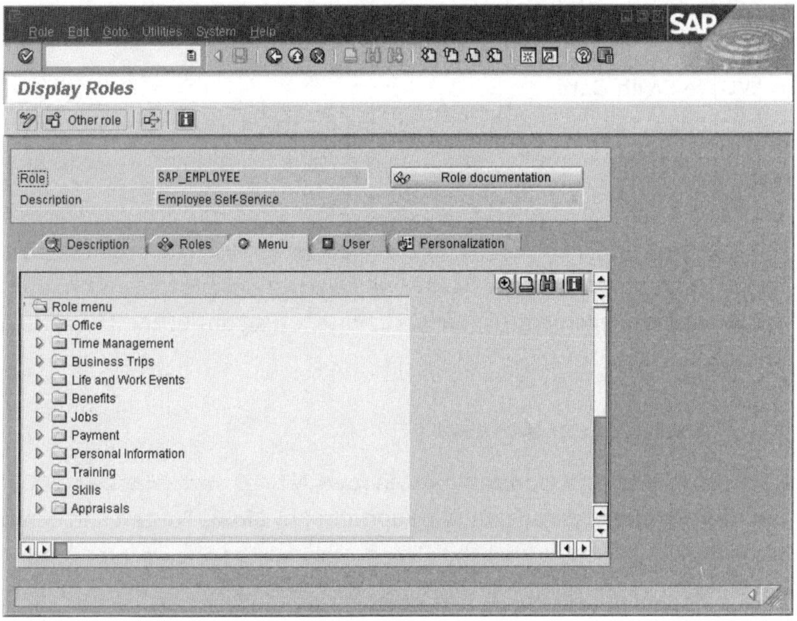

Figure 7.3 Menu of the Role SAP_EMPLOYEE

7.3　Overview of the Internet Transaction Server

R/3 on the Web The *Internet Transaction Server (ITS)* provides the link between the Web browser and the R/3 system and as such it is an essential component of the ESS. The following section describes the tasks and functions carried out by the ITS, to help enable you to implement changes of any kind.

The basic principle of the ITS is that R/3 transactions are no longer viewed in the SAP GUI, but in all current browsers. The ITS and its various different programming models are also presented below.

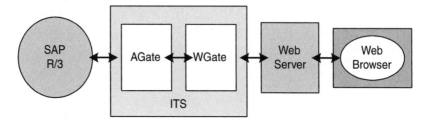

Figure 7.4　Diagram of the ITS System Landscape

The ITS is made up of two components:

▶ **AGate (Application Gate)**
ensures communication with the R/3.

▶ **WGate (Web Gate)**
is installed together with the Web server (such as Apache, Microsoft Internet Information Server IIS, or Netscape Server) and as such, provides the connection to the Web browser.

The WGate is an enhancement of the Web server and communicates via the TCP/IP protocol with the AGate, which is responsible for session, user, and service management. Figure 7.4 shows a diagram of the ITS system landscape.

7.3.1　Installation Variants

ITS Release 6.10 is supported by Windows NT 4.0 and Windows 2000, and from Release 6.20 on, it is also supported by Linux. For test and demo installations, you can install the ITS and the related Web server on one host server. This *single host installation* offers the advantage that with very little resources, you can quickly create a link between the browser and the R/3 system for a small number of users.

However, from the point of view of security and scalability, single host installation should only be used for limited productivity, for example, for an information terminal with limited functions. This terminal could, for example, be located in the reception area of a company to execute browser-based registration, show visitors how to get to their contact person, and other similar tasks.

For a more comprehensive use of ITS, we recommend that you set up a *dual host installation*. With this type of installation, the AGate and the WGate are installed on two separate servers. To increase the security of the installation, you can install a firewall between the AGate and WGate. The communications protocols are included in Figure 7.5:

▶ DIAG: Screen-SAP GUI

▶ RFC: Remote Function Call

▶ TCP/IP: Transmission Control Protocol/Internet Protocol

▶ ISAPI: Internet Server API

▶ NSAPI: Netscape API

▶ CGI: Common Gateway Interface

Communications protocols

To further distribute the load, additional AGates can be paralleled. You can also configure additional virtual ITS instances on an ITS, which allows you to address different R/3 systems (to do this, simply repeat the ITS setup, and the additional ITS instances are classified as virtual).

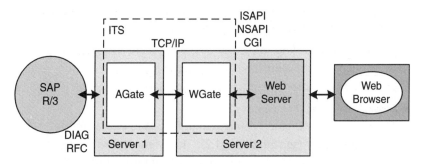

Figure 7.5 Dual Host Installation with the Corresponding Communications Protocols Between the Individual Components

7.3.2 The ITS Files

The ITS allows you to define the services that can be called in the Web browser. They correspond to the familiar transactions from R/3. Each ESS scenario corresponds to an ITS service. For each ITS service, there can be up to five files, depending on the programming model:

1. Service file

2. HTML template files

3. Flow files

4. Language resource file

5. MIME files

There is also a global service file (`global.srvc`) for each ITS instance that contains all the parameters that are valid for all services. The individual files will be explained below.

> ▶ **Service file** `<service>.srvc`
> The *service file* contains parameters to describe the service, to provide a link to the corresponding R/3, to determine timeout-time, to request logon data from users, and so on. The parameters in a particular service file add to or overwrite the parameters in the global service file. What are known as *themes* can also be determined in a service file. In this way, you can call the same service with a different layout. The default theme has the value 99. Themes form practically separate instances of a service.

> ▶ **HTML template files** `<program>_<screennumber>.html` or `<program>_<screennumber>_<language>.html` or for flow applications `<templatename>.html`
> *HTML template files* define the presentation of a page in the browser. These files contain HTML and HTML Business. *HTML Business* is an SAP-specific macro language used to merge SAP data from R/3 dynamically into the template. In addition, control commands (loops, `if`-statements) allow you to display or hide specific areas, or to dynamically build tables. With `include`-statements, you can reuse certain blocks—even those from other services.

> ▶ **Flow files** `<Templatename>.flow`
> *Flow files* are XML-based configuration files used in the *FlowLogic Programming model* (see Section 7.4.2). They define the flow logic of an application on the ITS page (in contrast to Internet Application Component, IACs), where the flow logic is set in R/3 by the flow logic of the R/3 transaction).

> There is one flow file for each HTML template, in which XML statements determine the service flow.

> ▶ **Language resource file** `<service>_<language>.htrc`
> *Language resource files* permit the use of placeholders in HTML templates. At runtime, these placeholders are filled with the appropriate

value from the language resource file for the logon language. As a result, a single HTML template text can be displayed in different languages. The use of language resource files is not mandatory, because you can also create language-dependent HTML templates. The latter, however, is recommended only if you want to use a service in one language, or if you want the templates to appear differently in different languages. For each service, there is a language resource file for each language to be supported.

▶ **MIME files** `*.gif`, `*.jpg`, `*.avi`, `*.wav`
MIME files can contain pictures, graphics, speech, video, Java Applets, and so on. They can also be integrated in templates with the help of dynamic path details. Whereas all of the files mentioned thus far are stored in the AGate, MIME files are stored on the WGate of the ITS.

If these files are not language-dependent, for ESS scenarios, they are stored directly in the folder `/image`. There are subdirectories for language-dependent files, such as `/image/de`, `/image/en`, and so on.

In the ITS set-up program, default paths are suggested for the individual file types. These paths are listed in Table 7.1.

Storage directories

File type	Path
Service	`C:\Program Files\SAP\ITS\2.0\<ITS instance>\services`
Template	`C:\Program Files\SAP\ITS\2.0\<ITS instance>\templates\` `<service>\<theme>`
Flow	In the same folder as the templates.
Language resource	`C:\Program Files\SAP\ITS\2.0\<ITS instance>\templates\` `<service>\<theme>`

MIME	The path for MIME files depends on the Web server installed, because the WGate is installed on the Web server. The default value is usually the root-directory for the ITS instance in question.
	For Microsoft's Internet Information Server (IIS):
	`C:\Inetpub\wwwroot<ITS instance>\SAP\ITS\mimes\`
	`<Service>\<theme>`
	For Netscape's Enterprise Server:
	`C:\Netscape\SuiteSpot\docs\sap\its\mimes\<Service>\`
	`<theme>`
	For Apache's HTTP server:
	`C:\Program Files\Apache Group\Apache\htdocs\sap\its\`
	`mimes\<Service>\<theme>`

Table 7.1 ITS File Types and their Default Storage Directories

With the aid of this information, it should be easy to locate the files for a service so that you can enhance them to meet your needs. It is important to note that only for test purposes should you make changes directly on the ITS. Because the originals of these files (at least for SAP services) are in R/3, they should also be edited there with the help of the Web Application Builder (**Transaction SE80 · Select Internet Service**, see also Figure 7.6) or with the SAP@WebStudio (*WebStudio* for short, see Figure 7.7). In this way, you can also ensure that enhancements can be transported from a test system to a production system.

Figure 7.6 The Web Application Builder in the SAP GUI

More detailed documentation on the Web Application Builder can be found in R/3 Online Help *http://help.sap.com* under **SAP NetWeaver · SAP Web Application Server · <Choose release, e.g., "SAP Web Application Server 6.20 Support Package 19"> · English · mySAP Technology Components · SAP Web Application Server · ABAP Workbench · BC— ABAP Workbench: Tools · Web Application Builder for ITS Services**. The SAP@WebStudio can be downloaded from *http://service.sap.com*.

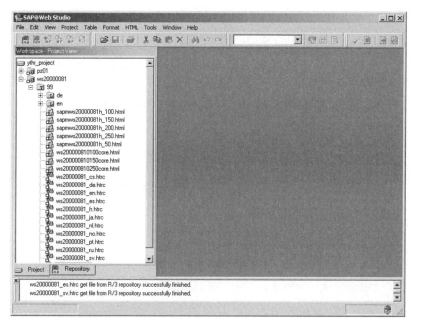

Figure 7.7 Together with the ABAP Workbench, the SAP@WebStudio is the Development Environment for ITS Services

ITS files are R/3 objects with the corresponding TADIR entries—this means that all version management is done by R/3, as is the case for other objects. The R/3 table TADIR contains all objects of the SAP system that can be transported. This transport link means that these files are easy to work with.

SAP@WebStudio

To enhance ITS files, they must be put in an R/3 transport request and then they can be edited in either the Web Application Builder (in the SAP GUI for Windows) or in the SAP@WebStudio. The *WebStudio* is a development environment specifically for ITS services and files. The files to be edited are put in a transport request using Transaction SIAC1; then, they are checked out of R/3, edited locally, published on the ITS for testing, and then checked back into R/3, and transported like any other object.

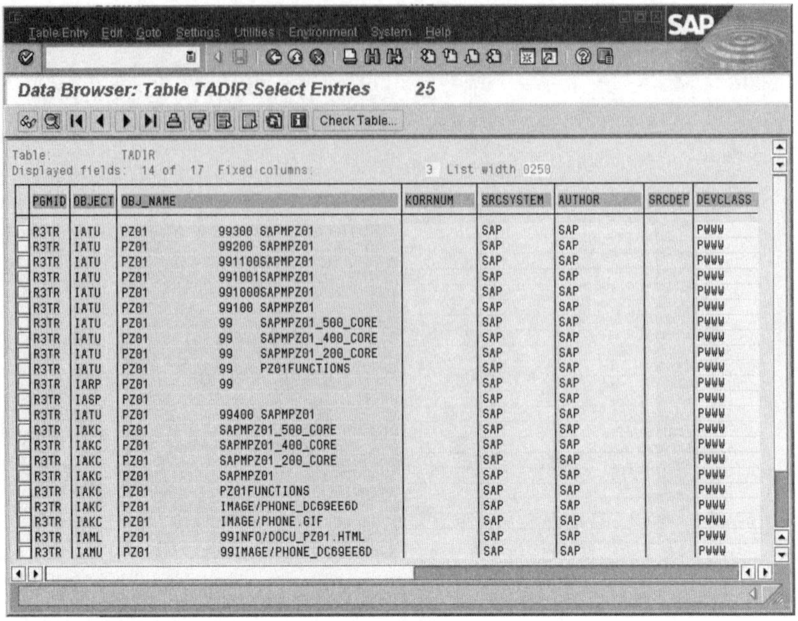

Data Browser: Table TADIR Select Entries 25

Table: TADIR
Displayed fields: 14 of 17 Fixed columns: 3 List width 0250

PGMID	OBJECT	OBJ_NAME	KORRNUM	SRCSYSTEM	AUTHOR	SRCDEP	DEVCLASS
R3TR	IATU	PZ01 99300 SAPMPZ01		SAP	SAP		PWWW
R3TR	IATU	PZ01 99200 SAPMPZ01		SAP	SAP		PWWW
R3TR	IATU	PZ01 991100SAPMPZ01		SAP	SAP		PWWW
R3TR	IATU	PZ01 991001SAPMPZ01		SAP	SAP		PWWW
R3TR	IATU	PZ01 991000SAPMPZ01		SAP	SAP		PWWW
R3TR	IATU	PZ01 99100 SAPMPZ01		SAP	SAP		PWWW
R3TR	IATU	PZ01 99 SAPMPZ01_500_CORE		SAP	SAP		PWWW
R3TR	IATU	PZ01 99 SAPMPZ01_400_CORE		SAP	SAP		PWWW
R3TR	IATU	PZ01 99 SAPMPZ01_200_CORE		SAP	SAP		PWWW
R3TR	IATU	PZ01 99 PZ01FUNCTIONS		SAP	SAP		PWWW
R3TR	IARP	PZ01 99		SAP	SAP		PWWW
R3TR	IASP	PZ01		SAP	SAP		PWWW
R3TR	IATU	PZ01 99400 SAPMPZ01		SAP	SAP		PWWW
R3TR	IAKC	PZ01 SAPMPZ01_500_CORE		SAP	SAP		PWWW
R3TR	IAKC	PZ01 SAPMPZ01_400_CORE		SAP	SAP		PWWW
R3TR	IAKC	PZ01 SAPMPZ01_200_CORE		SAP	SAP		PWWW
R3TR	IAKC	PZ01 SAPMPZ01		SAP	SAP		PWWW
R3TR	IAKC	PZ01 PZ01FUNCTIONS		SAP	SAP		PWWW
R3TR	IAKC	PZ01 IMAGE/PHONE_DC69EE6D		SAP	SAP		PWWW
R3TR	IAKC	PZ01 IMAGE/PHONE.GIF		SAP	SAP		PWWW
R3TR	IAML	PZ01 99INFO/DOCU_PZ01.HTML		SAP	SAP		PWWW
R3TR	IAMU	PZ01 99IMAGE/PHONE_DC69EE6D		SAP	SAP		PWWW

Figure 7.8 R/3 Objects in Table TADIR for the ITS Who's Who Service (PZ01)

7.3.3 Overview of the Most Important ITS Service Parameters

The most important service parameters are explained in Table 7.2. A complete list can be found in the ITS documentation. By default, the parameters `~login`, `~client`, `~password`, and `~language` are not specified in the service file. Therefore, a logon screen appears, in which the user can enter this data. It is also possible to provide values for only some of these parameters, if for example. `~client 001` and `~language en` are entered, when starting a service, the user is then only asked for his or her user name and password (there is no equals sign between a parameter and its value). When a service is called via the portal or if an ITS session is already active, this data is sent with the call and does not need to be entered again.

Parameter	Example	Description
`~client`	001	Client
`~cookies`	0 or 1	The session ID is appended to the URL of a request or stored in a cookie.

Table 7.2 Overview of the Most Important ITS Service Parameters in Alphabetical Order

Parameter	Example	Description
~exiturl	http://www. sap.com	The URL of a static HTML document that is called after a transaction has terminated.
~initialtemplate	page1	Name of any HTML template with which a FlowLogic application is started. The parameter is therefore mandatory for FlowLogic applications. The ending "html" does not form part of this name.
~login	indicator	Logon name
~loginGroup	PUBLIC	Logon group for R/3 load distribution
~language	de	Logon language
~messageServer	MessServName	Name of the message server
~password	des26(123abc)	Password for logging on to the R/3 system (DES encrypted)
~sources	PZLE	Allows all files of another service to be used. This means that apart from the service file, no other ITS files or folders exist for this service.
~systemName	ALN	R/3 system
~theme	99	A variant of a service with subdirectories that have the same names for template and MIME files. The names must be a two-digit number. The default value is 99.
~timeout	10	The timeout of a service, in minutes.
~transaction	pz01	R/3 transaction
~webapplicationtype	miniapp	The type of service. This parameter is mandatory for MiniApps.
~xgateway	SAPXGwfc.dll	The name of the Xgateway DLL for this service. This parameter is mandatory for FlowLogic applications.
~xgateways	SAPXGwfc, SAPXGxxx	All valid Xgateway names must be declared in ~xgateways (separated by commas). Up to ITS release 6.10, only SAPXGwfc is supported.

Table 7.2 Overview of the Most Important ITS Service Parameters in Alphabetical Order (cont.)

The service parameters listed in Table 7.2 can be specified in the service file or attached to the URL when calling a service ("?" is inserted after the first parameter, additional parameters are separated from each other with "&"). A call for an ITS service is closed with an exclamation mark after the name of the service. For example, language and client can be specified directly with the following call: *http://<ITS>/scripts/wgate/<Service>/!?~language=en&~client=001.*

Additional parameters Additional service parameters that are typically only specified with the URL include:

▶ ~command
This enables you to send certain commands to the ITS with the URL. These commands are executed if the registry key "AdminEnabled" in the command interface is set to 1.

Example: `http://<ITS>/scripts/wgate/pz01/!?~command=fielddump` displays numerous ITS variables that are filled when the service pz01 is called and thus allows you to check the ITS settings and to debug the service.

▶ ~okcode
Allows you to set the OK code, which is processed in R/3. Typically, the OK codes in the HTML templates are linked to buttons or links; however, in some cases you may want to send the OK code to the ITS with the URL (for debugging for example). In the ESS menu in Release 4.5, this functionality is used to carry out navigation with service PZM1.

▶ ~secure
Determines whether the ITS runs with an http (~secure = off) or https (~secure = on). This parameter is synonymous to ~http_https.

7.3.4 The ITS Modus Operandi

To illustrate how the ITS works, we will now run through a complete Request-Response cycle (see also Figure 7.9):

1. A request (for example, a form from a browser window) arrives in the Web server. Name/value pairs, referred to as the request context, are transported with it.

2. The Web server calls the appropriate WGate.

3. The WGate forwards the request to the AGate.

4. The AGate loads the corresponding service file, which contains all necessary parameters for the service. These parameters include the name and client of the R/3 system, the R/3 transaction, the service

timeout, and so on. The parameters in the global service file are also considered, but they can be overwritten by parameters of the same name in the service file.

5. The AGate opens an SAP GUI connection to the R/3 system and sends the request. If this is a follow-up request from a known user, the ITS identifies the SAP GUI connection that has already been opened and uses it for the communication. If it is a new request, then a new SAP GUI connection is created. The user session is determined by the session ID, which is either sent from the Web browser to the Web server with the URL, or is saved in a cookie. You can define which of the two possibilities is selected with the service parameter ~cookies.

6. In the R/3 system, the corresponding coding (transaction, report or BAPI) is called or continued. The resultant screen or the corresponding data from a report or BAPI is then sent to the AGate.

7. The AGate finds the appropriate HTML template and if necessary loads the associated language resource file. In FlowLogic, the flow file of the service is also processed, in which, among other things, the template to be displayed is defined. The AGate interprets the HTML template and generates a Web page using the appropriate data from R/3 and the language resource variables.

8. The Web page is sent from the AGate to the WGate.

9. The WGate sends the generated page to the Web server.

10. The Web server sends the HTML page to the browser where it is displayed for the user.

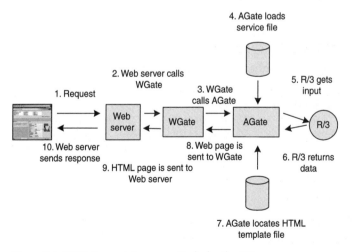

Figure 7.9 HTTP Request-Response Cycle for the ITS

This process can be repeated any number of times.

When the user leaves the service, an exit code (~okcode=/NEX) is sent. This arrives at the AGate via the Web server and the WGate. The AGate then terminates the connection to the R/3 system. In both the R/3 and in the ITS, all memory spaces or contexts are deleted and the resources are available for use elsewhere.

The session is also ended if no request has arrived in the ITS during the time set in the parameter ~timeout. Depending on how long the user should be allowed for entries, this timeout setting can be several minutes long. The lower the value, the faster the ITS resources of unused user connections can be made available again.

Since Release 4.6D, the ITS screens can be converted directly into HTML and displayed in the Web browser—without the need to first create ITS files. The release of ITS corresponds to that of SAP Basis. The ITS can also be downloaded from the SAP Service Marketplace as separate software.

WebGUI— SAP GUI
The advantage of the GUI called *SAP GUI for HTML* is that R/3 transactions can be directly executed in the browser with no additional work. The *SAP GUI for Windows* is called the *SAP GUI* for short, whereas the SAP GUI for HTML is also referred to as the *WebGUI*. The request-response cycle in the SAP GUI for HTML is the same as that described above, but neither a service file nor individual template files are needed on the ITS. The transaction is executed in R/3 and the ITS dynamically generates an HTML page for each screen of a transaction, which is then sent to the Web server. For each screen, there is a check to verify if an appropriate template is available on the ITS. If there is, then it is used. In this way, you can execute transactions in what is known as *mixed mode*. The advantage of using mixed mode is that there are less HTML templates to manage, but you can also make targeted use of the possibilities of HTML in some templates.

7.3.5 HTML Business Functions

Since ITS Release 4.6D, SAP provides HTML Business Functions for ITS. With these functions, you can ensure that the controls for all SAP Internet applications are consistent in their attributes and their presentation, and that they all support the same browser types and versions.

Uniform look and feel
Use of HTML business functions results in a uniform look and feel for Web applications. With the *Style Sheet Designer* (*SSD*—see Section 7.5.2), you can adapt the layout of all Internet services both centrally and to meet your own needs, using HTML style sheets.

You can also write your own functions following the same model as the HTML business functions. These functions can be saved in your own HTML file, or used in any template via an `include` statement.

When generating HTML templates, you can select whether HTML business functions are to be used or not. If they are, the following lines will be generated in the HTML template:

```
`include(~service="system", ~language="", ~theme="dm", ~n
ame="TemplateLibraryDHTML.html")`
```

Thus, you can access all HTML business functions. Further on in the template, you can, for example, use the function `SAP_Button("SEARCH")` to generate a button that is linked with the screen button called **SEARCH**, which means that all screen attributes such as the OK code field, name, and so on are transferred for presentation in the browser.

In the coding of the HTML business function for a button, you can see that business functions can in turn call other business functions, so a high degree of reusability is possible.

```
`function SAP_Button(
          dynproButtonName,
          type="SAP_WEBGUI",
          onmouseover="",
          onclick="",
          buttonWidth="" )
  if( ^dynproButtonName.exists == "X" )
    l_button_label = ^dynproButtonName.label;
    if( buttonWidth != "" )
      l_button_width = buttonWidth;
    else
      l_button_width =
              calc_width( ^dynproButtonName.visSize );
    end;
    write( "<table cellspacing=0 cellpadding=0
        border=0><tr><td nowrap>" );
    makeButton(
      buttonwidth   = l_button_width,
      disabled      = ^dynproButtonName.disabled,
      okcode        = ^dynproButtonName.okcode,
      buttonlabel   = l_button_label,
      iconname      = ^dynproButtonName.iconname,
```

```
quickinfo     = ^dynproButtonName.quickinfo,
onmouseover   = onmouseover,
onclick       = onclick,
with_position = 0 );
  write("</td></tr></table>");
end;
end;
```

Additional HTML functions are available in SAP's *HTML Business Functions Library* for all common HTML elements (tables, fields, groupings, links, buttons, lists, tabs, texts) and for application-related elements (headers, error messages, page start, page end).

7.4 Programming Models

Apart from the "technical" ITS programming models, there is also a "user-oriented" classification of R/3 transactions. Because confusion often exists between these two models, both views will be explained below.

In a classification of transactions or programs, the user group of an application must be specified:

▶ *Easy Web Transactions* (EWTs) are intended for the casual R/3 user, which means that only the most important functions are offered and they are particularly straightforward to use. In addition, the standard Common User Access (CUA) menu is hidden, so as to deliberately limit the many possibilities. These applications are supported by ITS and have been designed for the browser. In some circumstances, they can also be used in SAP GUI for Windows.

The name *Easy Web Transaction* refers to a Web service that, in addition to R/3 transactions, also includes reports and so on (in this regard, the name is a little restricted).

▶ *Power transactions* are intended for R/3 application experts whose main concern is comprehensive functionality. In most cases, these transactions are supported by SAP GUI for Windows, and can sometimes be presented in the WebGUI with the CUA menu.

The addressees of power transactions are the traditional R/3 users who want the most efficient execution of a business process possible. Whether the application runs in the SAP GUI or in the browser is of secondary importance.

GUI support is not linked directly to the programming model, but the standard is that EWTs also run in the browser. This means that they are usually classified as having "SAP GUI for HTML" support. In the area of ESS, all services are classified as EWTs. Transaction classification and GUI support are executed with Transaction SE93 or SE80 (see Figure 7.10). In the gradation between WebGUI and SAP GUI for Windows, there is also the SAP GUI for Java. This is the platform-independent alternative to the SAP GUI for Windows and it supports MacOS, Linux, and diverse UNIX derivatives. The SAP GUI for Java plays no role in ESS.

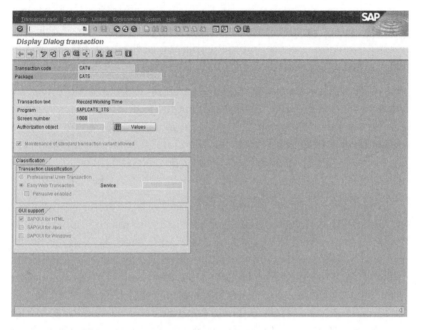

Figure 7.10 Classification of Transaction CATW in SE93

The ITS supports three different programming models, which are also used in the ESS Business Package. The individual models will be presented in the order in which they first appeared:

Programming models

▶ HTML template-based Internet services (IAC)
▶ FlowLogic
▶ SAP GUI for HTML (WebGUI)

In addition to full screen applications, which can be realized with all programming models, there are also applications called *MiniApps*. These applications take up only a small part of the browser interface and can inform the user quickly and easily on certain themes or permit simple processes. Examples of MiniApps are currency converters, news on specific topics, or simple clock-in/clock-out time recording. Typically, a user's ini-

MiniApps

tial page contains a range of MiniApps (according to their user roles). Most MiniApps are programmed with FlowLogic and all applications in this category are only for use with browsers. To present MiniApps in the Enterprise Portal, you can encapsulate them in iViews.

7.4.1 Internet Services Based on HTML Templates (IAC)

From Release 3.11 on, IACs were the only means of implementing an Internet service. For this reason, this programming model was also known as the *Internet Application Component* (IAC). Although FlowLogic and WebGUI services are also Internet applications, the term IAC is—somewhat misleadingly—used only for template-based services.

Internet
Application
Component (IAC)
The oldest ITS programming model is based on R/3 transactions that are visualized in the browser. This means that the logic of a business process can be completely separated from its presentation. The entire service is defined as a transaction in R/3, and therefore, the flow logic follows the transaction logic defined by PBO (*Process Before Output*) and PAI (*Process After Input*). Communication between R/3 and ITS takes place via the DIAG protocol, as you can see in Figure 7.5.

At runtime, the HTML template files are filled with the appropriate values from R/3. Apart from HTML, other scripting languages, such as JavaScript, can also be used to shape the browser pages dynamically. In addition to using HTML Business, since Release 4.6B, it is possible to define and use HTML Business Functions. Since Release 4.6D, the programmer can take advantage of SAP's HTML Business Functions (see Section 7.3.5), which are on the ITS and can be loaded with an include file. You can also use these functions when generating HTML templates (see below) for displaying screen elements and controls on the browser.

Once the R/3 transaction has been completed on the R/3 page, the ITS files can be developed with SAP@WebStudio. Since Release 4.6C, it is also possible to do this directly in the SAP GUI in the ABAP Workbench (Transaction SE80).

In the WebStudio, you first create a project (menu **File · New · Project**) and then enter the path for the ITS files (menu **Project · Site Definition**). You can now use a wizard to generate HTML templates (menu **File · New · File Wizards · Template Wizard**). The various different generation possibilities will be described later in this chapter. All files are stored locally by the WebStudio and must therefore be published on the ITS so that they can be considered for display on the browser (select folders or individual files with your mouse, then use the menu path **Project · Publish Files**).

In the SAP GUI, start by using Transaction SE80: Select **Internet Service**, enter a name, and click on **Display**. If the Internet service already exists, it is displayed in the object tree; otherwise, you can create it. For an IAC, select a **Screen-based application** and enter the transaction code of the application. Select the Internet service and again right-click **Create · Template**, and enter the screen number (see Figure 7.11). As with the Web-Studio, you can select from several generating types. Also, as with the WebStudio, the files must be published on the ITS (right-click on the folder or file and then select **Publish**). The path for the ITS must have been selected previously (menu **Utilities · Settings · Internet Transaction Server**).

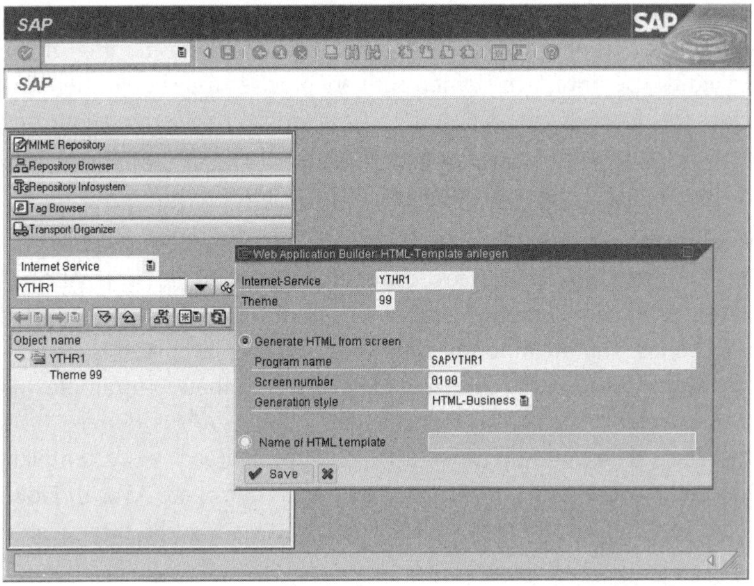

Figure 7.11 Generating an HTML Template in the SAP GUI

Depending on the demands made on the service, the design of the different files requires that you are familiar with HTML, HTML Business, and also with scripting languages and existing HTML Business Functions.

There are various possibilities for template generation, depending on the different objectives.

HTML template generation

1. **Classic**

   For generating pure HTML and HTML Business for displaying screen elements (input and output fields, radio buttons, check boxes, buttons, and so on). In this case, there is no dependence on the HTML Business Functions.

2. **Business**

With "Business" generation, apart from HTML and HTML Business, HTML Business Functions are also generated. After template generation, the positioning of individual elements is realized by using the ⟨p⟩ tag. Therefore, the sequence of the individual screen elements is preserved, but positioning is not pixel-accurate.

We recommend this type of generation if you enhance the templates with particular HTML elements that are not defined by the screen, and if you arrange the individual interface controls differently than they were originally placed on the screen.

3. **WebGUI**

If you use the "WebGUI" style, then HTML and also HTML Business and HTML Business Functions are generated. The positioning of the individual user interface elements is very precise. You should therefore select this form of generation if you are satisfied with the layout of a WebGUI application, but want to enhance the HTML template with additional HTML elements (images, Applets and so on).

WAP service 4. **Mobile Devices**

There is also a "mobile devices" generation style. Instead of HTML templates, WML templates are created to support PDAs and WAP-enabled cell phones. The migration of MiniApps to WML templates is particularly simple, because no changes are necessary in the R/3 (example: the WAP-enabled *Who's Who* (service: *PZ35_MA_WAP*) is derived from the *Who's Who* MiniApp (service: *PZ35_MA*)). For each WML template file, there is a flow file, in which the flow is controlled. As with Flow-Logic applications, the R/3 data is exchanged via the RFC interface.

7.4.2 FlowLogic

Building blocks Customizing and customer modifications for IACs are considered relatively complex. As a result, FlowLogic was developed for the ITS in 1998 and is available with Release 4.6C. The main idea was to create small business units for logging on to the system or filling in an order form. The sequence of these units, known as *building blocks,* could then be modified or they could be exchanged one for the other. This concept is particularly useful in areas such as online stores, where a high degree of flexibility in product configuration is required. FlowLogic was also chosen as the technical basis for MiniApps.

You can use BAPIs or RFC-enabled function modules to separate the user interface (UI) from the business process logic, with the latter being portrayed in R/3; whereas, the flow logic and the UI are defined on the ITS in different files, namely the Flow file and the HTML template file. Communication is done via *Remote Function Calls* (RFC), and can be either *stateless* or *stateful*. In *stateless* communication, no context information is contained in the ITS, whereas in *stateful* communication, data is maintained persistently on the ITS between individual RFCs.

Just like an IAC, each FlowLogic service has one or more HTML templates. The individual HTML template is no longer linked to a screen, however. A flow file is associated with each HTML template. In it, there is a description of how to navigate from one flow file to the next; however, the RFCs/BAPIs to be called are also specified.

In the table in Appendix A, you can see which ESS scenarios are based on FlowLogic.

For FlowLogic applications, as with IACs, there is no specific customer modification concept because it is very easy to copy an existing service and adapt it to meet your needs.

Creating a FlowLogic application consists of the following steps:

Creating an application

1. Describing the process from a business perspective

2. Determining the flow logic

3. Creating or locating the appropriate BAPIs/function modules

4. Defining the service file

5. Creating the HTML template files and the flow files

We will now explain the most important steps in creating a FlowLogic application, using the *Who's Who* MiniApp (service name: *PZ35_MA*) as an example.

Example of a FlowLogic application

Describing the Process

Using different search fields, we want to be able to determine and display data for an employee such as his or her phone number, office, or organizational assignment.

Determining the Flow Logic

In customizing, you can determine which search fields will be displayed in what sequence, and which fields will be displayed in tables, in what sequence and according to what sorting criteria. In customizing, you can also decide which additional information (calendar, organizational chart) will also be provided.

BAPIs/Function Modules

Two function modules are written for the actual problem. They are based on the functions of the ESS standard scenario *Who's Who*:

▶ HR_ESS_WHO_PROG_GET_META (reads the customizing data)

▶ HR_ESS_WHO_PROG_GET_RESULT (carries out the search with the HCM AdHoc Query or the BAPI BAPI_EMPLOYEE_GETDATA).

If existing BAPIs cannot be used directly, it is usually quite easy to enhance them with a new function module.

Defining the Service File

The following steps can be carried out in the SAP GUI using Transaction SE80 or with SAP@WebStudio. In WebStudio, select **File · New**; then, in the pop-up window, select the tab **File Wizards · Service Wizard**. Next, in the wizard, enter the service names, the R/3 system, user logon (you would typically select an individual logon in this case), timeout for the service, and "Use WebRFC" (by doing this, the parameter ~xgateway, which is obligatory for flow applications, will be written in the service file), and click on **Finish**. You have now created the service file. (Individual parameters can now be added or deleted.)

When creating an Internet service, you have to specify whether it is to be "screen-based" or "FlowLogic-based" before the corresponding service file can be created.

Creating the HTML Template Files and the Flow Files

In WebStudio, select **File · New**; then, in the pop-up window, select the tab **File Wizards · HTML Business Template**. Next, select the radio button **R/3 Screen Independent** (see Figure 7.12). Then, you can select the service names and the template names and decide on whether HTML Business Functions should be used.

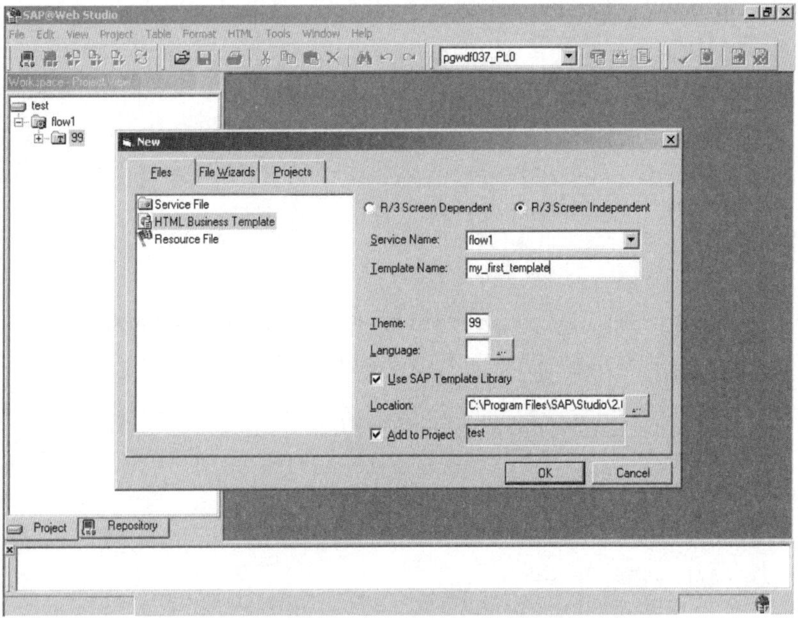

Figure 7.12 Generating Templates for a Flow Application with WebStudio

The result will be the generation of an HTML template similar to the following:

```
`include(~service="system", ~language="",
        ~theme="dm", ~name="TemplateLibraryDHTML.html");`
<html>
<head>
    <title></title>
    `SAP_Stylesheet()`
    `SAP_TemplateJavaScript()`
</head>
<body `SAP_TemplateBodyAttributes()`
        onload=""`SAP_TemplateOnLoadJavaScript()`">
</body>
`SAP_TemplatePostProcess()`
</html>
```

Once the HTML template file has been created, you can select it with a double click. Then, select the menu **Edit · Add Flow File**. A **Flow Source** button is now active under the template and if you click on it, the generated flow file is displayed. The coding below represents a typical flow file.

You can easily get additional documentation on FlowLogic using the Web-Studio Help.

```
<flow>
  <state name="init">
    <module stateful="0"
            name="HR_ESS_WHO_PROG_GET_META"
            type="RFC">
    </module>
    <inputmapping source="~login" target="USERNAME"/>
    <inputmapping source="~language" target="LANGUAGE"/>
...
<persistent name="meta_tab-name"/>
<persistent name="meta_tab-fieldlabel"/>
...
</state>
  <state name="search">
    <module stateful="0"
            name="HR_ESS_WHO_PROG_GET_RESULT"
            type="RFC">
    </module>
  </state>
  <event name="onLoad"    next_state="init"/>
  <event name="onSearch"  next_state="search"/>
</flow>
```

This list shows the typical sections in a flow file. The events triggered by clicking on buttons are listed below. These events bring the flow file to a particular *state* in which a function module or a BAPI is called in R/3. At the same time, the template names that will be displayed when the state changes are also specified. The variables given in the middle of the code list should be maintained as constant in the ITS context between the two R/3 calls.

In Transaction SE80, you can generate the template by selecting the service and then right-click to select **Create**. If you double click on the template name, it will be moved to the large work area for editing. If you select **Edit · Create FlowLogic · Enhancement assignments** in the menu, you will get a flow file in the SAP GUI.

7.4.3 SAP GUI for HTML

Since Release 4.6D, the ITS allows the generation of service files and HTML templates "on the fly." Now, R/3 transactions are called directly in the browser via the ITS, as though it were an IAC. The corresponding screen elements and controls are generated dynamically with the HTML business functions and they show the screens in the browser. Numerous field characteristics and position details are implemented by the screen attributes.

You don't need previous knowledge of HTML, HTML Business, or Web-Studio, in order to write a service based on the SAP GUI for HTML. You can create this type of service with Transaction SE80 and categorize it as being supported by "SAP GUI for HTML". The only prerequisite for displaying transactions on the Web browser is to install the *WEBGUI* service on the ITS.

SAP GUI for HTML

The templates generated only exist in the ITS at runtime. You can also generate individual HTML templates, or the corresponding service file, to enhance them with controls or HTML elements that exceed the features offered by WebGUI (compare also the remarks on mixed mode in Section 7.3.4).

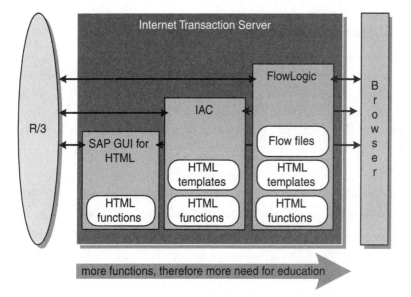

Figure 7.13 Overview of the ITS Programming Model

7.5 Design and Function Enhancements

If you want to change ESS scenarios, you must first verify if you can achieve the functionality that you want, using the extensive customizing possibilities for ESS scenarios. ESS customizing has its own nodes in the IMG. A distinction is made between general ESS settings and service-specific setting possibilities. In some cases, specific ESS customizing is included in individual areas (Benefits, Time Management). Because one of the focal points of this book is enhancements that go beyond what you can do in customizing, we recommend that you review Chapter 7 of the ESS Implementation Guide for a detailed description of the customizing of individual ESS scenarios (see SAP Labs Inc., Employee Self-Service Group: *SAP Employee Self-Service Implementation Guide R/3 Release 4.6C*. SAP Labs Inc., Palo Alto 2000). The following enhancement possibilities for ESS are described in greater detail:

▶ User exits

▶ Design adjustments

▶ Changing fields or flow logic

▶ Generating a new country-dependent service

▶ Generating a new service

7.5.1 The ESS User Exits

Four enhancements

Four user exits are offered in ESS, which enable you to make customer enhancements in the R/3 system. The implementation of a user exit has been already been described in Section 3.6.1. The user exits for ESS can be accessed using **Transaction CMOD · Create project · Assign enhancements** or in customizing (**Personnel management · Employee Self-Service · ESS Customer enhancements**). The following enhancements are possible:

1. Enhancing the search string for *Who's Who.*

2. Checking the start date in "Personal data" (addresses, bank and so on).

3. Changing the proposed value for the start date in "Personal data."

4. Changing the algorithm for creating ESS user names and their initial default passwords.

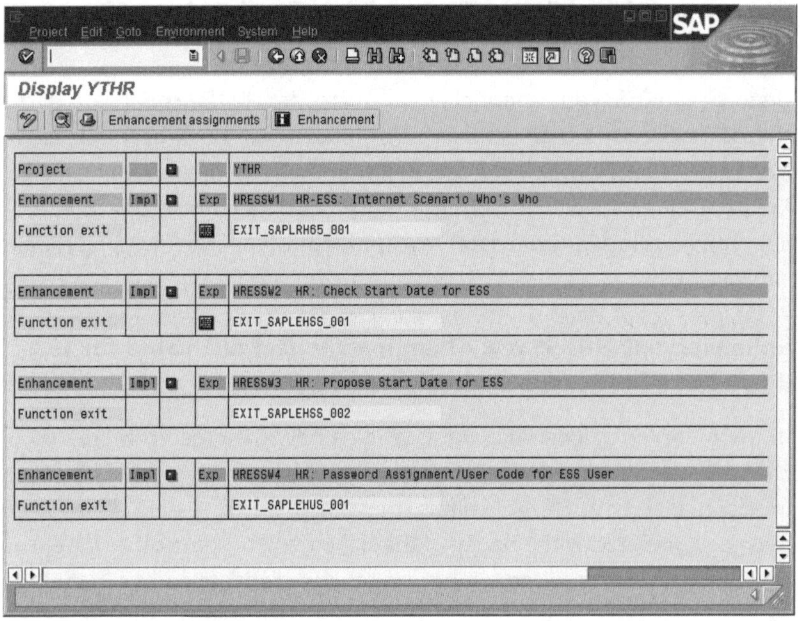

Figure 7.14 The ESS User Exits in Transaction CMOD

Enhancement HRESSW1: Enhancing the Search String for Who's Who

When using *Who's Who,* you can search in the following ways:

▶ For an entire word, such as Murphy

▶ For part of a word, for example, Mur*
(* or % replace multiple characters, + or ? represent just one character)

▶ With just a wildcard character, for example *

Sometimes the use of wildcard characters seems tedious and you may wish that with a search for "Mur," you could find and display all the employees named Murphy, Murray, and so on. But, you can also process the search string in other ways.

Wildcard characters

The user exit for changing the search string logic is EXIT_SAPLRH65_001. In the example, coding the wildcard character * is automatically appended to every search string.

Enhancement HRESSW2: Checking the Start Date in "Personal Data"

Generally, in ESS, you cannot change data records in "Personal data" if the start date is earlier than the last payroll date. With the user exit EXIT_ SAPLEHSS_001, however, you can determine which operations (Change, Create, Delete, ...) will be permitted on what date. This setting affects all infotypes within "Personal data," except for infotype 0023 (*other/previous employers*).

Enhancement HRESSW3: Changing the Default Value for the Start Date in "Personal Data"

In the menu entry **Personal Data**, when a new data record is created or changed, the start date is set to the system date. In some cases however, in accordance with HR guidelines, the start date for a new data record must be correlated with the day of the last payroll or some other date. You can deal with this requirement by using the appropriate coding in the user exit EXIT_SAPLEHSS_002.

Enhancement HRESSW4: Changing the Algorithm for Creating the ESS User Names and Their Initial Standard Passwords

With Transaction HRUSER, administrators can create R/3 users with the corresponding ESS role. You can generate users for all or specific personnel numbers stored in HR. The standard user created is called Pnnnnnnnn, where nnnnnnnn represents an employee's eight-character personnel number. The standard password for all users is "init". This password must be changed immediately when a user logs on to ESS for the first time.

With the user exit EXIT_SAPLEHUS_001, you can implement another algorithm for generating user and passwords. For example, the naming convention of users may have a different structure, or the initial standard password can be derived from the employee's date of birth or social security number.

7.5.2   Design Adjustments

Cascading Style Sheets The design can be adjusted centrally and effectively using Cascading Style Sheets (CSS), which determine the appearance of HTML pages. There are two different tools that can be used to adjust design, depending on the context in which ESS has been started. If ESS is integrated into Workplace 2.11 or if it is running via the menu PZM3 of Release 4.6C, adjustments to the CSS are done using the *Style Sheet Designer*. If the ESS is integrated into Enterprise Portal 5.0, adjustments are made using the *Style Editor*.

Style Sheet Designer

The *Style Sheet Designer* (SSD) allows you to adjust the appearance of Workplace and ESS in the company's *Corporate Identity* browser. Figure 7.15 shows some examples of the design possibilities. Because the design is controlled by the ITS, it must be adjusted for all the Internet Transaction Servers involved, as in some cases there may be several. Changes affect the following:

▶ IACs

▶ WebGUI services

▶ FlowLogic applications

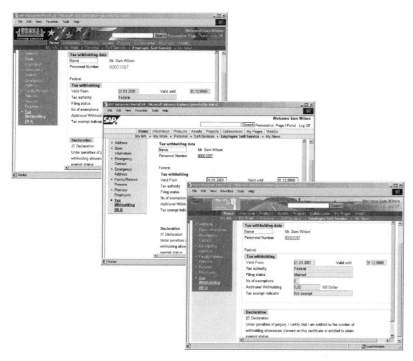

Figure 7.15 Examples of the Design Possibilities with SSD

From a technical point of view, the SSD is also an ITS service that allows you to adjust colors, fonts, and so on. Images, logos, and graphics can also be replaced. If you want to create a new design, you must take the following steps:

1. Install the Style Sheet Designer on the ITS. The SSD can be downloaded from the SAP Service Marketplace. After installing the SSD, you will have the following folder structure on the ITS:

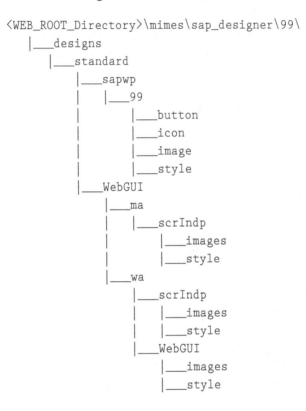

```
<WEB_ROOT_Directory>\mimes\sap_designer\99\
    |___designs
        |___standard
            |___sapwp
            |   |___99
            |       |___button
            |       |___icon
            |       |___image
            |       |___style
            |___WebGUI
                |___ma
                |   |___scrIndp
                |       |___images
                |       |___style
                |___wa
                    |___scrIndp
                    |   |___images
                    |   |___style
                    |___WebGUI
                        |___images
                        |___style
```

2. In the `designs` folder, a copy of the `standard` folder with all the sub-directories will be created. If you want to create several designs, several copies can be created at this point. In the copy of the standard design called `<newdesign1>`, the design will then be changed and saved. The `designs` folder should now look like the following:

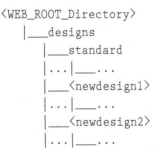

```
<WEB_ROOT_Directory>
    |___designs
        |___standard
        |...|___...
        |___<newdesign1>
        |...|___...
        |___<newdesign2>
        |...|___...
```

3. Start the SDD with the URL
   http://<ITS>/scripts/wgate/sap_designer/!?~design=<newdesign1>

4. You can now select a design element in the left-hand area of the screen. This design element will then be displayed on the right-hand side with its changeable attributes. Set this parameter in accordance with your own design ideas. Once you click on the **Apply button**, the element that you changed will be displayed (see Figure 7.16).

5. To reverse any changes that you made, simply click on the **Undo** button. Then click on **Apply** again.

6. You can also change images by modifying them with a suitable graphics program, or by completely replacing them. Please note that you should not change the image's position in the directory structure or its name.

7. You can save the current record of parameters as a *Design Session* under any name in R/3, so that you can re-edit it at any time.

8. To display the appropriate style sheet, use the menu option **Style Sheets**.

9. Using **Copy** and **Paste,** you can then copy the displayed content of the CSS files in the target files entered above it in the directory ⟨newdesign1⟩.

10. If you want the newly-created design to be used in another ITS, you must now copy the folder ⟨newdesign1⟩ to it (in the designs directory). In some cases, you must first create this directory in the MIME directory.

11. In order to activate the new design, you must enter the following two parameters in the global service file global.srvc:

    ~designBaseURL   http://⟨ITS with new design⟩

    ~design   ⟨newdesign1⟩

12. The next time a service is called *http://<ITS with new design>/scripts/wgate/<service>/!* the new design will be displayed.

Of course, you can also copy the CSS supplied and change it manually, that is to say, without using SSD. To do this, you must create a folder called designs, with a subfolder called ⟨newdesign⟩, in the MIMES folder. Then the folders sapwp, for Workplace, and WebGUI, for all ITS services, are copied to the subfolder ⟨newdesign⟩ and modified there. As in steps 11 and 12, here, too, you must enter the parameters that define the new design into the global service file. The directory structure should look as follows:

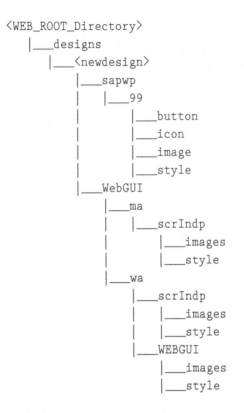

```
<WEB_ROOT_Directory>
  |___designs
      |___<newdesign>
          |___sapwp
          |    |___99
          |        |___button
          |        |___icon
          |        |___image
          |        |___style
          |___WebGUI
              |___ma
              |    |___scrIndp
              |        |___images
              |        |___style
              |___wa
                   |___scrIndp
                   |    |___images
                   |    |___style
                   |___WEBGUI
                        |___images
                        |___style
```

Because the new design is a copy, the standard design stays unchanged. Furthermore, in the event of an SAP update, you are protected against your design being overwritten.

You can also adjust the business functions directly; to change a control (pushbuttons, tab indexes), for example. To implement these changes, you must know HTML, HTML Business, the ITS, and the different browser versions and types.

Kiosk systems If you are considering using ESS with kiosk systems, the concept of different designs also plays an important role. In kiosk systems—together with touch-screen interfaces— readability and usability can also be improved if you make the control elements, fonts, and so on, sufficiently large. At the same time, you do not want to copy services because this increases the maintenance requirements.

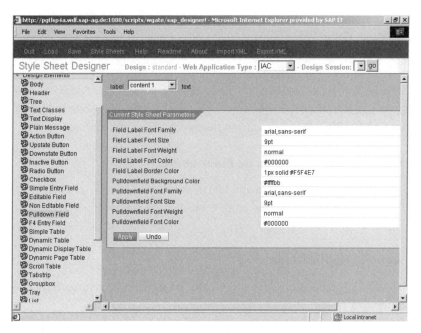

Figure 7.16 Style Sheet Designer with Modified Background Colors (#ffffbb) for a Drop-Down Box

With SSD, the solution is simple. The service file is copied (for example `pz11.srvc` to `pz11_kiosk.srvc`). A new design is prepared—called `kiosk_design` for example. In the service file `pz11_kiosk`, the parameters `~designBaseURL http://<ITS with new design>` and `~design kiosk_design` are entered. In this way, you can ensure that corrections and updates are active in both scenarios simultaneously, and that the design for the browser and the kiosk can be controlled separately—thanks to their different service names—however, both run on the same ITS.

Style Editor for Enterprise Portal 5.0

In Enterprise Portal 5.0, you can access the *Style Editor* using the administrator role by entering **System Configuration Styles**. Just like the SSD, the Style Editor can be used to change colors, fonts, and images. You can adjust the style sheets for the entire Enterprise Portal, all ITS-based services (FlowLogic applications, IAC, and WebGUI from Release 4.6C), and the Business Warehouse (Releases 2.0 and 3.0).

The Style Editor supports both Internet Explorer 5.1 and 5.5 and Netscape Navigator 4.7x. Some ESS scenarios are only supported by Netscape Navigator 6.x and up, and not by Version 4.7x—these are mainly Java Applet-

Browser support

based applications. For more details, see Notes 0380457 and 0378509. The Style Editor offers a somewhat wider range of functions in Internet Explorer; however, it is still fully functional in Netscape Navigator. In addition to having the capability to directly adjust the design of the portal, you can also adjust the design of ITS services using the *ITS Style Editor*. You also have access to the *Style Upgrader*, which is a tool that supports the migration of user-developed designs in the event of a portal upgrade.

7.5.3 Changing Fields or Flow Logic

If you want to add or remove fields in an existing service, or change the flow logic, you must be able to distinguish if the service is a WebGUI service or an IAC service.

WebGUI Applications

In WebGUI applications, you must make the required adjustments directly in the R/3 system in the ABAP Workbench (Transaction SE80).

If you want to remove or simply swap fields, you can generate HTML templates for the screens in question, which you then adjust in the WebStudio or in the ABAP Workbench (see Section 7.4.1). In some cases, it is easier to execute this step than to change the screen. Nevertheless, you must ensure that no inconsistencies are generated in flow logic because of the missing or exchanged fields.

For some services (Salary conversion, Personal data—Japan), you can change the attributes of the screen fields by using table T588M_ESS. This table is of type "C" and is not maintained by SAP, but by the customer. The required entries (client, function module, screen, and so on) are self-explanatory or they have documentation at data element level. Given that this table has only been around since Release 4.6C, it is not considered in scenarios that were in the standard before this time. You can find additional details in Note 542643.

IAC Adjustments

With IACs, you only need a basic understanding of HTML in order to make modifications to the interfaces. In order to prevent your adjustments from being lost, in the event of a release upgrade, you should make a full copy of the service to be modified. Although it isn't mandatory that you make a copy within the customer name range, we do recommend it—in order to avoid conflicts in the SAP standard name range (for example, the original is called PZ02; the copy is ZPZ02). When adjusting or creating new HTML templates, you should use HTML Business Functions where possible, so that the service will still conform to the design of the standard applications.

More far-reaching changes that also affect the flow logic in R/3 must be carried out in the ABAP Workbench. In the event of an upgrade to a new R/3 release, the R/3 modifications must be addressed by using Modification Assistants. The reconciliation of HTML templates is not supported by SAP.

7.5.4 Creating a New Country-Dependent Service

Because there is a high degree of country-dependency in scenarios from the area of "Personal data" (address, bank details, personal details, and so on), and also in tax scenarios, SAP has developed a special framework for these services. This means that you can offer various different country specifications for a service without much effort, or you can quickly add additional country-specific versions of existing scenarios to the ESS menu.

Country specification

The table T77WWW_SC decides therefore, if the international or a country-specific version should be offered, depending on the country code MOLGA (Modifikator Lohn- und Gehaltsart—Modificator for Wage and Salary Type) of an employee. Two screens are provided for each service. The first screen shows an overview of existing data records. There is also a drop-down box that allows you to select a subtype of the appropriate infotype. The buttons **New**, **Change**, **Delete**, and **Display** enable the user to navigate to the second screen. Here, the data is presented in a detailed view and can be edited according to the selected function. After saving or deleting data, the user is automatically returned to the first screen. If the data is changed but not saved, a message will be sent to that user if he or she tries to navigate from the detailed view to the overview page. This SAP framework also supports scenarios that use only one screen. The core element of the country-specific framework is the program SAPMPZ02. It reads table T77WWW_SC, in which two function modules are entered that represent the two screens. These two function modules are in the same function group (see step 3 below).

We can differentiate between two cases:

► Creating a new country-specific version for an existing service
► Creating a new service for a particular country

The first case is described below (also highlighted are the most important steps for the second case scenario):

1. Create a transaction in the customer name range and link it with the framework program SAPMPZ02, screen 1000.

2. ESS scenarios should be classified as EWT, so that the extensive SAP menu is hidden.

3. Copy the relevant function group *EH<x><y>* to the customer name range (<x> stands for the country and <y> for the service). You can use the following tables to determine countries and services, thus, for example, the function group *EHD1* contains functions related to German addresses and *EHU3* deals with American bank details. The more the copied template agrees with the scenario to be created, the less adjustments will generally be needed.

   Country-independent services are located in function group *EH0<y>*.

Country	Code x
Argentina	AR
Australia	A
Belgium	BE
Brazil	B
Canada	C
Denmark	DK
France	F
Germany	D
Great Britain	G
Hong Kong	H
Indonesia	ID
Ireland	L
Italy	I
Japan	J
Korea	K
Malaysia	MY
Mexico	M

Table 7.3 Country and Country Code Used to Identify Country-Specific Function Groups

Country	Code x
The Netherlands	N
New Zealand	NZ
Norway	NO
The Philippines	PH
Portugal	P
Singapore	R
South Africa	W
Spain	E
Sweden	SE
Switzerland	Z
Taiwan	TW
Thailand	T
United States	U
Venezuela	V

Table 7.3 Country and Country Code Used to Identify Country-Specific Function Groups (cont.)

Service	Code y
Absence/attendance	4
Alternative name	18
Bank transfer—Australia	11
Capital formation	16
Education (not yet implemented)	17
Employee address	1
Employee bank detail	3
Employee family member	6
Employee personal data	5
Employment equity	20
Notification of marriage	9
Personal IDs—Singapore	14

Table 7.4 Service and Number Code for Identifying Country-Specific Function Groups

Service	Code y
Previous employers	10
Salary and employment verification	7
Seniority	19
Social insurance	15
Superannuation—Australia	12
Taxes	2
Year-end adjustment	13

Table 7.4 Service and Number Code for Identifying Country-Specific Function Groups (cont.)

4. Adjust and activate the function modules of the new function group of country-specific features.

5. Enter the name of the function modules, MOLGA, and transaction code in table T77WWW_SC (only allocate a new transaction code if it is also a new service, thus, for example a new country version of the address scenario would be assigned the transaction code PZ02).

6. If the screens can be displayed via the WebGUI, you are done. If HTML elements or documents are needed that aren't supported by the Web-GUI, you can generate an HTML template to create an IAC (see Section 7.4.1).

Individual subtypes of an infotype can be excluded from an ESS scenario using table T591A_ESSEX. For the infotypes 2001 (*Absences*) and 2002 (*Attendances*) only, table T554S_ESSEX controls which subtypes cannot be displayed in the context of ESS.

7.5.5 Creating a New Service

Up to now, we have seen the possibilities for enhancing existing scenarios. The main difference between enhancing an existing scenario and implementing a completely new ESS service is in the context of ABAP, therefore, we will close our discussion of ITS and move on to discussing ABAP in the framework of ESS.

Advantages and disadvantages of the ITS programming model

Before writing a new ESS service, you should be clear about the programming model that you want to create (compare Figure 7.13). The advantages and disadvantages can be summarized in the keywords listed below:

▶ **IAC**

Suitable for applications that are strongly transaction- and form-oriented. IACs enable you to achieve a good separation between process logic in R/3 and visualization in HTML templates. There is also ample freedom for configuration, thanks to HTML and HTML Business.

The transaction model in R/3 is not always appropriate for Web-based applications. The performance is not always as good as it is with Flow-Logic applications, because the connection to R/3 is *stateful* and therefore R/3 memory space, session ID, and so on remain persistent throughout all dialog steps.

▶ **WebGUI Applications**

Suitable for applications that are strongly transaction- and form-oriented. WebGUI applications do not require that you know HTML and HTML Business.

The interface can, in parts, be very similar to the conventional SAP GUI for Windows, and the applications don't look like typical Web applications.

▶ **FlowLogic Applications**

Very suitable for *stateless* communication between R/3 and browser (for example, online-shopping), which requires a high degree of flexibility in flow control, or MiniApps.

There is no R/3 support for checking the format, error messages, and so on, because communication takes place via Remote Function Calls (RFCs). Large applications require you to have a thorough understanding of the FlowLogic programming model, in addition to having a sound knowledge of HTML and HTML Business Functions.

▶ **Web Reporting**

A very simple method for presenting R/3 report programs in the browser, widely used in Business Information Warehouse, as well as in ESS (see also Section 7.6).

The reports will not always look particularly Web-like. There is no tool support, very little documentation, and no possibility of adjusting Cascading Style Sheets (CSS), because the HTML is generated in R/3.

Once you have decided on a programming model–IAC, for example, the procedure is as follows:

1. Create an R/3 transaction in the ABAP Workbench, for example, ythr123_trans.

2. Create the corresponding coding and screens.

3. Classify the transaction as EWT, so that no R/3 menu will be displayed in the browser.

4. Create the Internet service *ythr123* and link it with transaction ythr_trans1. If you do not plan to re-use existing transactions, it makes sense to give the Internet service the same name as the transaction, so that the relationship is obvious.

5. Generate HTML templates (see also Section 7.4.1 regarding generation types). Before creating the HTML templates, you should test the functionality thoroughly in R/3; otherwise, any improvements that you make to the generated HTML files will have to be redone in the screen manually, or you may even have to generate the entire file again.

6. Test the service using the URL *http://<ITS>/scripts/wgate/ythr123/!*. The HTML files can be adjusted in the ABAP Workbench or in the Web-Studio.

7. If you want the service to appear in the ESS menu in the Enterprise Portal, you must link it to the portal role.

7.6 Web-enabling Reports

Just as they do in R/3, reports also play an important role in ESS—they serve to make information stored in the system available to the employee in a prepared format.

7.6.1 ESS Report Framework

The ESS report framework allows you to present SAP or customer-defined reports in the browser with the help of the WebGUI.

Reports in ESS   All three report formats—ABAP lists, Smart Forms, and SAPscript—are supported by this framework. ABAP lists are presented directly via the WebGUI, whereas Smart Forms and SAPscript are converted into PDFs before being displayed in the browser. The use of selection screens is supported, but it is not mandatory that you use them. All reports are started as a transaction, which makes it easy to integrate them into a role and to call them up on the browser. They are managed via a central control table that has a special customer name range. Complete encapsulation in this framework means that you don't need to know HTML in order to integrate your reports, because each report is presented in an HTML container.

Depending on the requirements for the report, existing reports may have to be modified for display in the browser. We shall explain this below.

In the simplest case, that is, in the presentation of an ABAP list report, you must adhere to the following four steps:

1. Create or locate a report. Error messages should be of type "S"; otherwise, the flow of the report will be interrupted and the user will have no way of continuing with the execution from the browser (in contrast to using SAP GUI, where you can confirm the error message with the Enter key and continue with the execution of the report).

2. Create the transaction with SE93, enter as program SAPMESSREP, screen 1000, and classify as EWT. The transaction text should be as descriptive as possible, because it will be used as the title for the report and displayed to the user in the browser.

3. Enter the transaction code and report name in Table T77WWW_REP.

4. Call the report using the URL *http://<ITS>/scripts/wgate/<transaction>/!*.

You can also fill the report parameter before calling the report, by defining the parameter or parameters at the event AT SELECTION-SCREEN OUTPUT.

The following is an example in which the start date is set at the last day of the previous month and the end date is set at the system date:

```
AT SELECTION-SCREEN OUTPUT
    START_DATE      = SY-DATUM.
    START_DATE+6(2) = '01'.
    START_DATE      = START_DATE - 1.
    END_DATE        = SY-DATUM.
```

Instead of the start parameter, you may want to display a selection screen in which the user can select the start value. To do this, you must copy the function group HRESSSG_REP, including the function module HR_TAX_IRA_ESS_SG and screen 100. The SAP naming convention is HRESSxy, where xy stands for the ISO code of the country for which the report has been written.

The function module is called before the screen and in it you can define the start parameter, the variables, and so on for the report. When calling the function module from the framework, the personnel number and the employee name are identified by the variables pernr and name if they are defined using the import parameter (pernr like P0001-PERNR and name like P0001-ENAME).

The screen shows the report selection screen and should allow the appropriate selection possibilities for the start parameter of the report, in which PAI and PBO are adjusted accordingly. After the line `FCODE = 'PDF'` at PAI, the line `submit <Reportname>` and `return` must appear. For ABAP lists, the `SUBMIT` must be enhanced with `EXPORTING LIST TO MEMORY`.

The name of the function module and the number of the screen must also be entered in table T77WWW_REP, if they are to be considered in the report framework.

If the report is an SAPscript report, the check box must also be marked accordingly in the table.

Smart Forms and SAPscript reports are converted into PDFs before being displayed. In order for this to happen, the SAPscript reports must be adjusted as follows:

1. In the function module `OPEN_FORM`, you must adjust the variables `options` and `dialog`. If there is no value for `options`, then you must set one; otherwise, when you call the report, a pop-up for the printer settings will appear. Values for this variable can be defined using Transaction SPAD (Spool Administration).

   In addition, the export parameter `dialog` must be initial when called. If you do not want to activate these changes until the report is called in the browser, you can use the hidden parameter `pnpesscf` as it is used in the following example.

   ```
   data: options   type  itcpo,
         dialog(1) type c.
   ...
   if pnpesscf <> space.
     dialog           = ''.
     options-tdgetotf = 'X'.
     options-Tdprinter = 'POSTSCPT'.
   else.
     dialog = 'X'.
   endif.
   ...
   call function 'open_form'
     exporting ...
             dialog  = dialog
             options = options
             ...
   ```

2. The function module `close_form` must also be adjusted to convert the SAPscript form into OTF (*Output Text Format*) data, which can then be represented in the report container. Again you can use parameter `pnpesscf` if the report is to appear in both the SAP GUI and in the browser:

```
if pnpesscf <> space.
   data: otf_table like itcoo occurs 0 with header line.
   call function 'close_form'
     importing result  = result
     tables    otfdata = otf_table.
   perform report_data_convert(SAPLHRESS00_REP)
           tables otf_table[].
endif.
```

The parameter `pnpesscf` can be given in the following form when the report is called:

```
submit <Reportname> with pnpesscf eq 'X'.
```

If the report should also appear in the menu when ESS is called, you must adapt the R/3 role to allocate the corresponding authorizations (see Chapter 4). The role defined in the menu of the Enterprise Portal must also be adjusted. If ESS runs with the start transaction PZM3, then the customizing tables T77WWW_SRVN and T77WWW_SRV must be maintained so that the new report will be included in the menu.

7.6.2 Sample Report in ESS

The previous procedure described will be illustrated in an example using a simple ABAP list report. Suppose that you want to display a report in the browser, listing the names of all employees with personnel numbers between 1000 and 1005.

Employee list

1. Create a report (for example, `ythr_myreport`).

Select Transaction SE80 from the drop-down option **Program**, enter the report name, classify as a report.

```
report  ythr_myreport.
tables pa0002.
data: header1(10) value 'Pernr',
      header2(20) value 'First Name',
      header3(10) value 'Last Name'.
uline.
```

```
write:   'All employees having a personnel number'.
write: /'between 1000 and 1005:'.
uline.
write: /5 header1, 20 header2, 35 header3.
select * from pa0002 where pernr ge 1000
                    and    pernr le 1005.
write: /5 pa0002-pernr,
          20 pa0002-vorna,   "first name"
          35 pa0002-nachn.   "last name"
Endselect.
uline.
write:   '> > > - End of Report - < < <'.
```

2. Create a transaction (for example, ythr_trans1), link with program SAPMESSREP, screen 1000 and classify as an EWT.

   In Transaction SE80, enter program SAPMESSREP, and select **Display**. Right-click on the program name and select **Create,** then select the transaction and create. The customer name range for entries in the table is z*.

3. Enter the transaction code and report name in Table T77WWW_REP.

   In Transaction SM30, enter the table name, and click on the **Maintain** button. Then, select **New entries** and make the appropriate entries.

4. Call the report using the ITS configured for the associated R/3 system and the name of the transaction, therefore, for the above example: *http://<ITS>/scripts/wgate/ythr_trans1/!.*

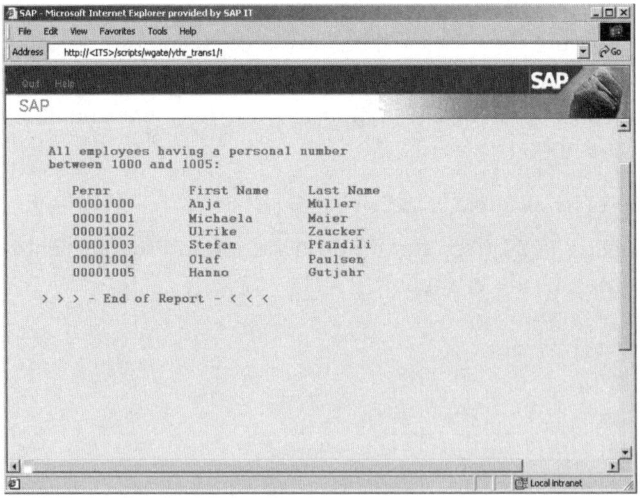

Figure 7.17 Example of an ABAP List Report in the Browser

7.7 Life and Work Events

Certain events in the working or private life of an employee can often be supported by a sequence of information and applications. Such support is provided in the Web browser with Life and Work Events (*L&W Events* for short).

7.7.1 Concept of Life and Work Events

Through a combination of ESS applications and documentation/information pages, employees can be efficiently supported when completing processes. An employee often needs and has to process a lot of forms and information that pertain to an event. One example of a Life and Work Event is "My First Days." At the beginning of a work relationship, the HR department requires an entire range of information such as address, bank details, and so on. They may offer the employee savings plans, a company car, or equity investment savings, while at the same time, provide information about company policies, training programs, and so forth. For decisions regarding taxes or benefits, additional external information—from financial services, for example—may be useful to enable the employee to make an informed choice.

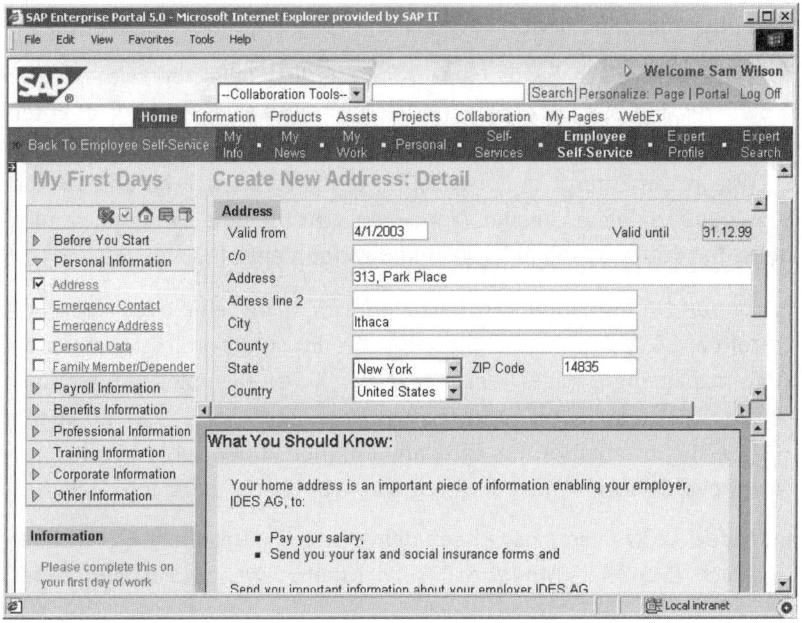

Figure 7.18 Example of a Life and Work Event in the Enterprise Portal

The advantages of these process-oriented user guides are:

▶ The personnel department can explain things to new employees centrally and effectively.

▶ The new employees' superiors will have less administrative work and can therefore focus more on introducing the new person to the content of their work.

▶ All new employees receive the same information, because it is produced and prepared centrally.

▶ New employees create data in the system directly, and therefore, they feel informed and quickly integrated.

▶ There is less print material, and updating and distributing new information is more efficient.

With Life & Work Events, SAP provides a framework that offers browser-based process support. This means that customers cannot only use or copy and adjust the L&W Events provided, they can also define new L&W Events and make them available to their employees in the context of ESS or the portal. Individual process steps can be marked as optional or mandatory, and after editing the L&W Events, the employee can mark them as complete with a check box. In addition, each L&W Event begins with a start page that can provide information explaining the process.

The ITS-based L&W Event framework was first delivered with Release 4.6C Service Pack 8 and can be used in both Workplace 2.11 and in Enterprise Portal. The ESS menu transaction PZM3 does not support L&W Events. In the Enterprise Portal 5.0 SP4, there is a Java-based tool that allows you to define Life and Work Events. At the time this book went to press, this tool was still in its second development phase.

Background information can be helpful for many employee decisions, therefore, L&W Events also allow for the display of professional knowledge management pages (*Knowledge Base*). For example, SAP works in close collaboration with *ProAct Technologies Corporation*, a U.S. provider of HR-specific information for company intranets; however, any other service providers can be linked in the same way via a generic interface.

Individual L&W Events have been delivered since Release 4.6C with Service Packs (SP). The SP and the ITS service names are noted in parentheses.

1. Benefits (PZLE_02, SP 10)

2. A change in employment status (PZLE_06, SP 16)

3. Leaving the company (PZLE_07, SP 16)

4. Creating data when starting work (My First Days) (PZLE_01, SP 8)

5. Divorce (PZLE_03, SP 10)

6. Birth/adoption of a child (PZLE_05, SP 15)

7. Marriage (PZLE_04, SP 15)

The following components can be linked to each other using the L&W Event framework to optimally combine applications with information:

▶ SAP ESS scenarios

▶ The company's own Web pages

▶ Intranet or Internet information from a content- or knowledge-provider

Furthermore, forms can be fed with R/3 data so that, for example, the name and address of an employee can be automatically integrated.

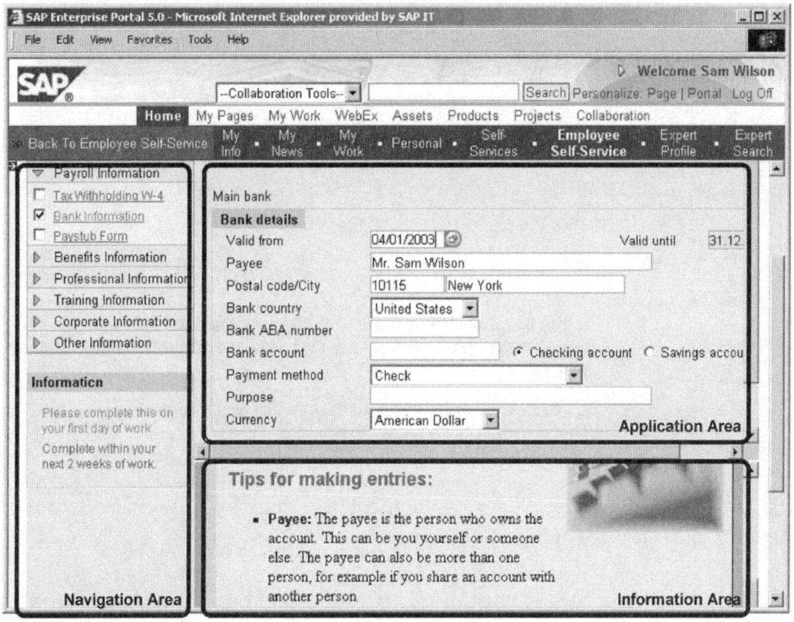

Figure 7.19 The Three Areas of the L&W Framework

7.7.2 Prerequisites and Functionality

The L&W scenarios are all based on FlowLogic, which means that the menu structure is exactly the same as service PZM3, with which ESS can also be used without a portal. The prerequisites for L&W Events are:

- ▶ L&W Event framework

- ▶ mySAP Workplace 2.11 or Enterprise Portal

- ▶ Authoring environment (SAP Knowledge Warehouse, Knowledge Base of the company, *ProAct Technologies Corporation,* or any other knowledge provider)

Characteristics of the framework

You can see the individual aspects of the L&W framework in Figure 7.20:

- ▶ In the navigation area, the individual services are grouped in catalogs. Since the L&W Event framework has its own navigation area, the left-hand side of the Workplace or Portal navigation will be automatically hidden when an L&W-Event is called.

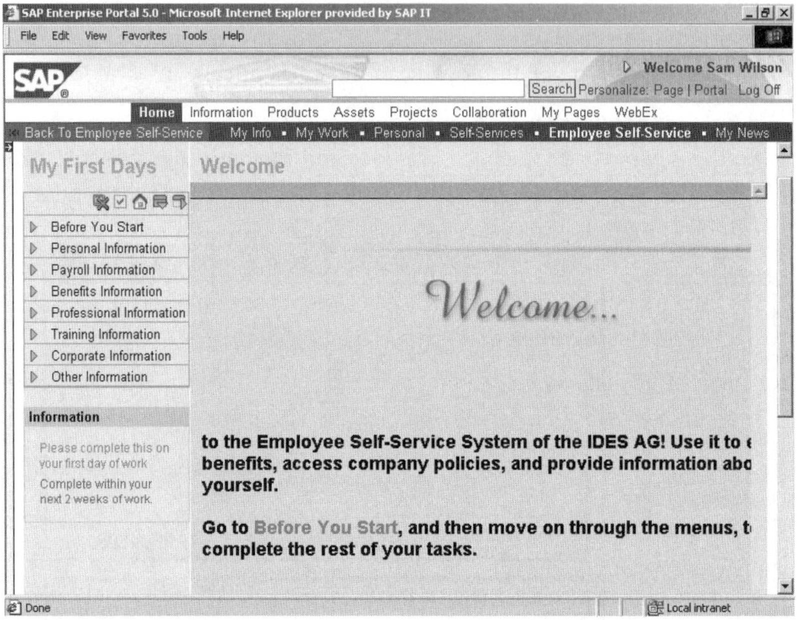

Figure 7.20 Initial Page of the L&W Event—"My First Days"

- ▶ The menu structure is completely variable and can be set according to individual requirements.

- ▶ As in ESS, scenarios can be defined as country-specific and they will then only appear for employees with the appropriate MOLGA.

- ▶ You can integrate any ITS scenarios supplied by SAP or external pages from other sources.

- L&W Events can be activated for a limited or an unlimited period; for example, the "My First Days" scenario need only be offered during the initial period of a new engagement.

- Each scenario can be prioritized in order to represent both optional and mandatory menu options in different colors (colors can be selected in Customizing).

- The user can manage the status of individual scenarios using check boxes (complete/not completed).

- The application and information area are arranged one above the other. If there is no additional information for an application in L&W Events, the information area is automatically hidden. The frame-size of each area can be set for each service individually. The user can change them using the mouse.

- The information pages may contain additional information on forms, help with applications, or other details. These pages must be created by the customer or a service provider and they are also saved outside of the HR system (for example, in the SAP Knowledge Warehouse or external URLs). By pressing a special button, you can print any information page. In the services supplied, there are English placeholders for information pages, into which, for example, the employee's first name and the logon language are transferred (see Figure 7.21).

- The interface allows you to mix data from one or more R/3 systems in the info pages, or you can personalize the info pages by using R/3 data.

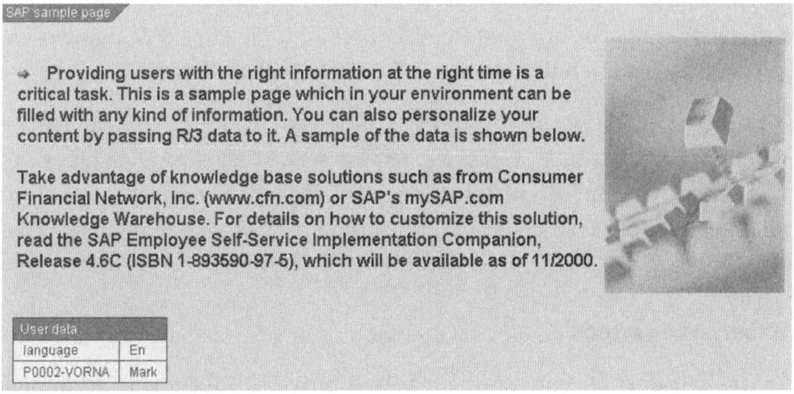

SAP sample page

→ Providing users with the right information at the right time is a critical task. This is a sample page which in your environment can be filled with any kind of information. You can also personalize your content by passing R/3 data to it. A sample of the data is shown below.

Take advantage of knowledge base solutions such as from Consumer Financial Network, Inc. (www.cfn.com) or SAP's mySAP.com Knowledge Warehouse. For details on how to customize this solution, read the SAP Employee Self-Service Implementation Companion, Release 4.6C (ISBN 1-893590-97-5), which will be available as of 11/2000.

User data	
language	En
P0002-VORNA	Mark

Figure 7.21 Placeholder for Info Pages, Displaying R/3 Data from the ITS File if_sap.html

7.7.3 The Framework

FlowLogic
dynamic

Life and Work Events are realized as FlowLogic applications. The individual service files (`pzle_01.srvc` – `pzle_07.srvc`) always refer to the service PZLE, thanks to the ITS parameter `~sources` (see also Section 7.3.3).

L&W Event
vocabulary

The individual terms in the L&W Event framework are explained below:

L&W Event

A L&W Event describes a particular condition of an employee that requires a process of actions and information recording. The different process steps are grouped together, as in a menu, and can be viewed in the browser.

Catalog

Structuring

Within a L&W Event, the services are grouped in catalogs. Some catalogs, such as "Before you start," appear in every event, while other catalogs, such as "Payroll information," only appear where required. Catalogs provide both a certain structure to and an overview of the different steps.

Service Types

In order to manage the scenarios within the framework of ESS and L&W Events, we differentiate between the following service types:

▶ Type S—Typical ITS service

▶ Type U—URL for any address

▶ Type X—URL for any (external) address within the L&W framework, whereby parameters allow for R/3 data to be transferred.

Type X was introduced with Release 4.6C, while the other two service types have been used in ESS since Release 4.5. All three service types can be used in the application area. They can also all be used in the content area, with all possible combinations of different service types supported (see Figure 7.22).

External Services

To make it possible for external content providers to provide additional information in the context of L&W frameworks, their URLs are stored in tables. These URLs can be specified using key fields to ensure access to particular database content. In addition, R/3 data can be supplied via the interface and can then be integrated into the content provider's HTML page.

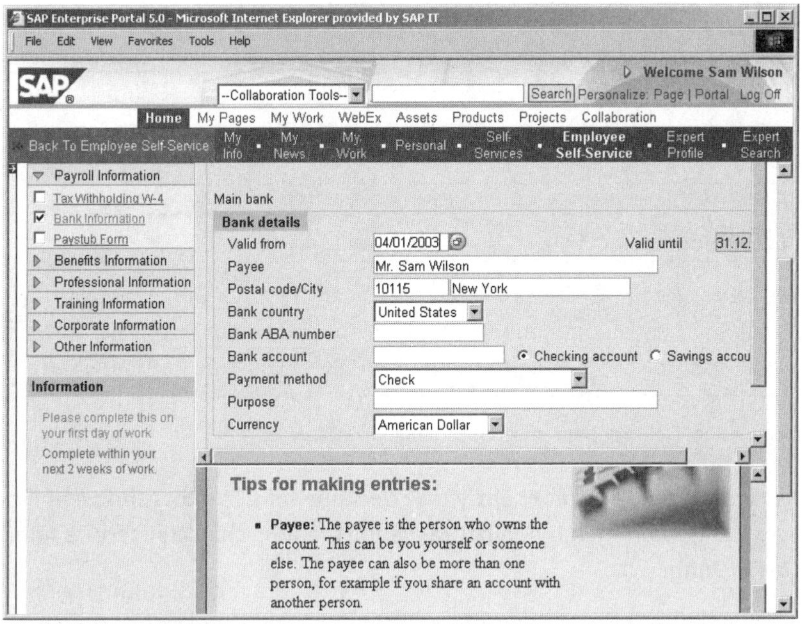

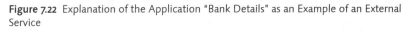

Figure 7.22 Explanation of the Application "Bank Details" as an Example of an External Service

External content providers are stored in the system in table T77WWW_LE_EP. Figure 7.23 shows an extract from table T77WWW_LE_EP. The following entries are required:

▶ **Number**: Unique key for each content provider

▶ **Name**: Name or description of the content provider

▶ **Interface**: Name of the interface that supplies the requested R/3 data to the provider before the latter sends back the HTML page (either with this data or in accordance with this data). SAP supplies two interfaces. You will learn how to create your own interface later in this chapter.

  ▷ *IF_SAP*: This interface shows the SAP sample content page (see Figure 7.21)

  ▷ *IF_DEFAULT*: This is the generic interface for external content providers; it is described later in this chapter.

▶ **BaseURL:** The statistical part of the URL via which the content provider makes information available. The key for the info page in question is stored in the corresponding service in table T77WWW_SRV.

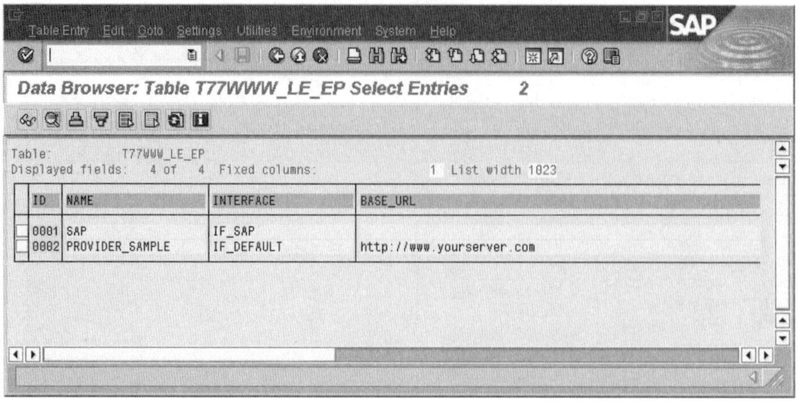

Figure 7.23 Delivery Data for Control Table T77WWW_LE_EP

An appropriate customer entry may be something like that shown in Figure 7.24, whereby the number range for the four-character service number is 9nnn.

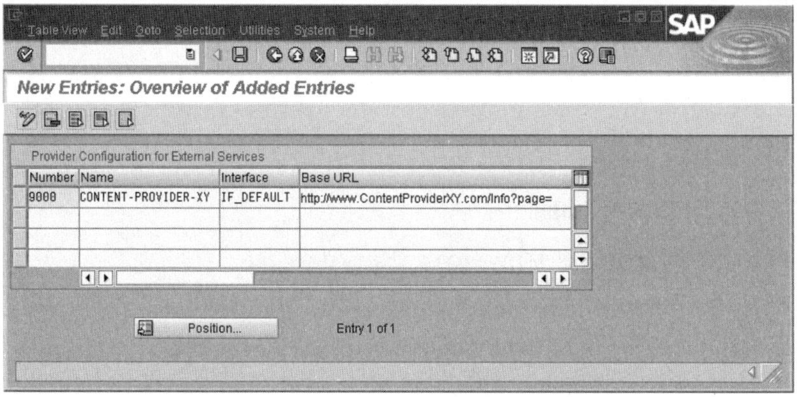

Figure 7.24 Example of an Entry in Table T77WWW_LE_EP

External Services—just like all L&W Event services—are entered in table T77WWW_SRV. The following information is required:

▶ **Service**: unique service number

▶ **ESS name of service:** for example, bank account information

▶ **S. type:** X for external service

▶ **ESS service...:** Content provider number, which has previously been entered in Table T77WWW_LE_EP.

▶ **ESS service parameter:** Here, you enter the key that completes the base URL of the content provider.

To continue with the example above, the entry shown in Figure 7.25 could be added to table T77WWW_SRV.

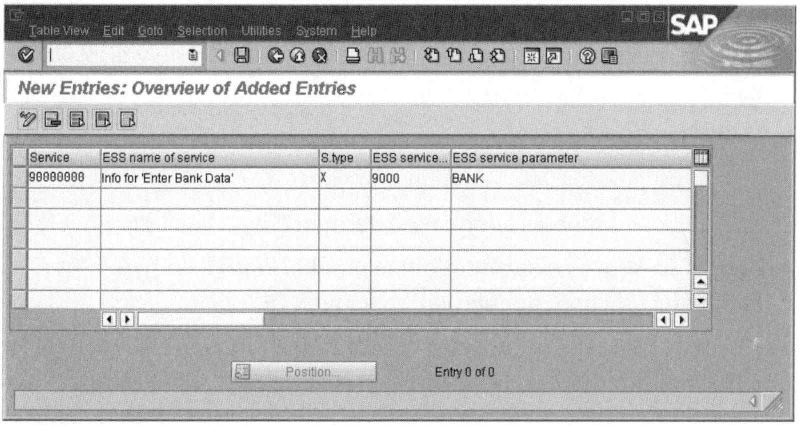

Figure 7.25 Sample Entry in Table T77WWW_SRV

You now have an external service with the number 90000000, which refers to external content provider number 9000 and provides the parameter "BANK". The resulting URL is *http://www.Content-ProviderXY.com/ Info?page=BANK*, which is then loaded in the appropriate L&W Event as an information page.

Blending in R/3 Data

To add R/3 data to the HTML page of a content provider, the infotypes or function modules that provide this data can be specified in table T77WWW_SDATA:

1. **Data from infotypes**
   If the data is stored in an infotype, in table T77WWW_SDATA, you must enter "I" for data type, the infotype number and field name. For example, 0002 NACHNA and 0002 VORNA to retrieve the first and last names of an employee from infotype 0002 (see also Figure 7.26).

2. **Data from a function module**
   If the data is provided by a function module, the data type specified is "F" and the name of the function module is also provided. You can use the function module ESS_DYNAMIC_DATA_READ as a template. This function module fills table SERVICE_DATA, which is then transferred to the external content provider via the ITS file IF_DEFAULT.FLOW.

Integrating R/3 data

Table T77WWW_SDATA is structured as follows:

- **Service:** Key of a service from table T77WWW_SRV
- **Name of Service:** The name of a service (This is not an entry field. The name of the service, from table T77WWW_SRVN, is only displayed in part to give a better overview.)
- **Data Type:**
  - I: Infotype—for data stored in infotypes
  - F: Function module—for data determined by a function module
- **SOURCE:** A four-character infotype number–with data type "I"–or the name of a function module–with data type "F".
- **KEY:** For data type "I," the field name of the infotype is displayed; for data type "F," the field is empty.

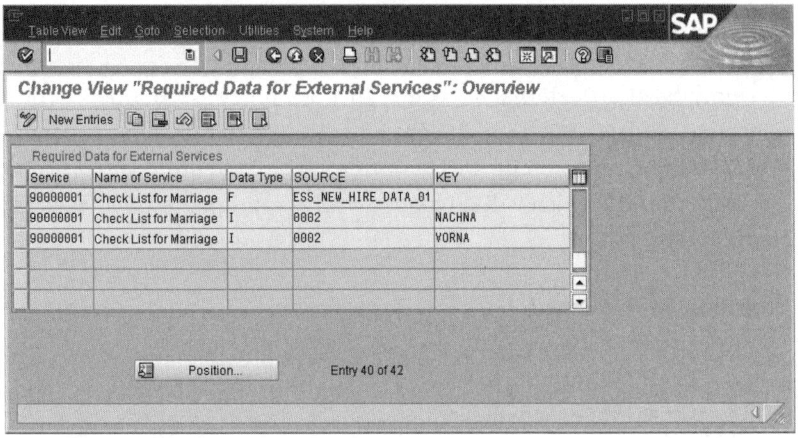

Figure 7.26 Example of Entries in Table T77WWW_SDATA

The interface *IF_DEFAULT* makes it possible to send any R/3 data to the content provider who will then blend this data into their HTML pages, before sending the pages back to be presented in L&W-Events as an HTTP response. SAP provides the ITS files `if_default.html` and `if_default.flow` for this purpose.

The R/3 data from the infotypes or from the function module specified is loaded into function module `ESS_DYNAMIC_DATA_READ` in table SERVICE_DATA. This table is converted by ITS into input fields, of type "hidden" and, as name/value pairs, sent to the content provider in an HTML form. The logon language `~language` is always sent as the first parameter.

The form name is "SAP_data" and the URL (made up of the key and the base URL) is set as `action`. The defined form is sent to the content provider using the command `onload` in the body tag of the HTML page. In keeping with the abovementioned example, the following HTML page was sent:

```
<HTML>
  <HEAD></HEAD>
  <BODY onload="document.SAP_data.submit()">
    <FORM name="SAP_data"
          action="http://www.Content-
                  ProviderXY.com/Info?page=BANK"
          method="post">
      <input type="hidden"
             name="language"    value="DE">
      <input type="hidden"
             name="P0002-VORNA" value="Niels">
      <input type="hidden"
             name="P0002-NACHN" value="Bohr">
    </FORM>
  </BODY>
</HTML>
```

From this HTTP query, the content provider can see that they must send back the information page *http://www.Content-ProviderXY.com/Info?page = BANK* in HTML format. They can also extract the hidden parameters—in this case language, first and last names—and blend them into the HTML page.

Defining a New Interface

The interface *IF_DEFAULT* can be used as a template for creating your own interface in the event that the SAP standard interface is not suitable: if, for example, the external content provider cannot communicate using this interface. The files `if_default.html` and `if_default.flow` are located in the directory PZLE on the ITS. Both files are copied to files of any name, for example `if_new.html` and `if_new.flow`. The HTML file can then be adjusted accordingly, whereas the flow file should not be changed because the connection to R/3 is made in this file. The name of the new interface is entered in table T77WWW_LE_EP, as described above.

Displaying Applications and Information at the Same Time

Combination of
application and
information

If applications need to be shown at the same time as content pages, they can be linked to each other in table T77WWW_SMAP.

Application service	Service that is displayed in the application area
Text	Name of the service that is displayed in the application area
Content service	Service that is displayed in the information area
Text	Name of the service that is displayed in the information area
Height	Height of the information area, as a percentage

Table 7.5 Table T77WWW_SMAP Regarding the Distribution of the Application and Information Areas

You have to enter the key field of the application, the key field of the content service, and the height of the information or content area as a percentage. To provide a better overview, the names of the services are shown, but they cannot be changed. If you do not set the height, the default value is 30%. If you do not create any link in this table, the application or content service in question will occupy 100% of the work area.

Application service	Text	Content service	Text	Height
2	Address	902	Info text on address entry	
3	Bank	903	Info text on bank details	40

Table 7.6 Sample Excerpt from Table T77WWW_SMAP

These entries define a customer-developed info page for both address changes and for maintaining bank details, as can be seen in the example in Figure 7.22. The height of this page is 30% (default value) for the address and 40% for the bank details. If you want to display the information page on address changes in just one but not another L&W Event, the "change address" service is simply entered twice in table T77WWW_SRV. The first "change address" service can then be linked with an info page, but the second is not linked, so it is always displayed alone in the application area.

Priorities

You can set priorities for the individual activities in the L&W Events. The priorities are indicated by the different color fonts used for the service names in the L&W Events menu. A key below the menu explains the colors in a short text. In Customizing, you can decide individually for each L&W Event whether priorities are to be used and if so, how many.

Structure of table T77WWW_LECC for defining priorities:

▶ **Key field:** Unique ID for the color of the menu entry

▶ **Text:** Description of priority, which will be displayed below the L&W Event navigation menu

▶ **Code:** Color coding in hexadecimal representation, for example #FF0000 for red

Definition of priorities

Three entries are supplied and these can be enhanced via a separate customer name range (see Figure 7.27).

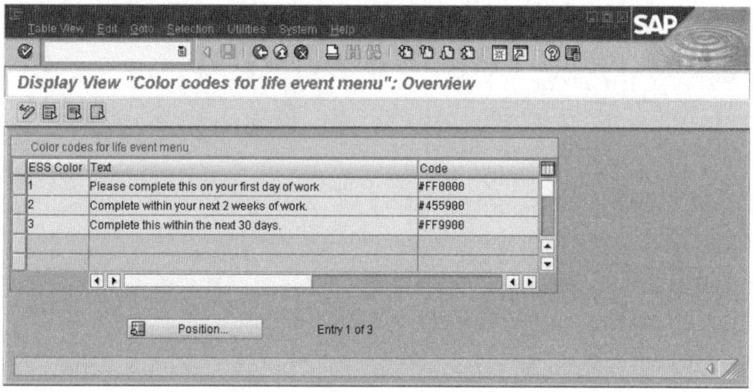

Figure 7.27 Table T77WWW_LECC with the Three Values Supplied

The entries are translated in table T77WWW_LECCT and services are assigned to the defined priorities in table T77WWW_LECCP.

Status Tracking

You can switch status tracking on or off in the service files (`pzle_01.srvc` – `pzle_07.srvc`) using the parameter ~use_status. If ~use_status has the value "X", the status of each service for the user in question is stored in the R/3 system. If the value is " ", there is no status tracking and there are no check boxes in front of the services in the menu either. The individual statuses are stored in table T77WWW_LESTATUS, per user and per L&W Event. The function module ESS_LE_STATUS, for saving the status, is called using the FlowLogic event `onLoad` in the ITS file `set_status.flow`. The status is read using the function module `ESS_LE_STATUS_CHECK`, which also checks if a L&W Event has a time limit and whether this limit has already expired. If this limit has already expired, the return parameter `LE_OPEN` contains the value "0" and the user is sent a message stating that the selected L&W Event is no longer available.

7.7.4 An Overview of L&W Tables

The following tables play a role in the context of L&W Events:

▶ T77WWW_MN (*Menus*): Entry of the event name, such as *My First Days*.

▶ T77WWW_MNT (*menu texts*): Entry of event names in the various different languages that should be available for the user.

▶ T77WWW_LEDATA (*Life & Work Events Data*): Controlling if and what type of start and home page a L&W Event has, whether it is time-dependent and if so, whether you can specify an R/3 function module to check if the permitted time has been exceeded.

▶ T77WWW_CT (*Catalogs*): Entry of all catalogs that link individual services together thematically, for example, *Before you start, Personal data.*

▶ T77WWW_CTT (*Catalog Texts*): Entry of catalog names in the various different languages that should be available for the user.

▶ T77WWW_MNP (*Positions of Catalog in Menu*): The position of the catalog within the menu; you can also de-select catalogs here.

▶ T77WWW_CD (*Country Dependencies*): Contains services that are country-dependent. One or more MOLGA values can be assigned to a table here. Services specified in this way are therefore only available to employees whose MOLGA is the same as one of those specified in the table. For example, the service for the W4 tax form is only relevant to employees in the U.S.

▶ T77WWW_SRV (*Services*): All services of the L&W Events are stored here, for example, change of address.

▶ T77WWW_SRVN (*Service Names*): Entry of service names in the various different languages that should be available for the user.

▶ T77WWW_CTP (*Position of Services in Catalog*): Contains the positions of the individual services in each catalog.

- T77WWW_SMAP (*Split-Screen Mapping*): Allows you to assign application and info pages for simultaneous display in the browser.

- T77WWW_LE_EP (*Life & Work Events External Provider*): Management of information or content pages. Usually external content providers are used, or you may have your own content management system.

- T77WWW_SDATA (*Data Requirements for External Services*): Defines the data sources (infotypes or function modules) for blending R/3 data into the content pages.

- T77WWW_LECC (*Life & Work Events Color Coding*): Contains color coding for the priorities of individual services in L&W Events.

- T77WWW_LECCT (*Life & Work Events Color Coding Texts*): Contains text explaining priorities, which will be displayed under the L&W Events menu in all languages that are to be made available for the user.

- T77WWW_LECCP (*Life & Work Events Color Coding Priorities*): Assigning the priority of services.

- T77WWW_LESTATUS (*Life & Work Events Status*): Stores the status of individual services for all users and for all L&W Events for which this function has been activated in the ITS service file.

7.7.5 Customizing

Extensive customizing is available for L&W Events. The following steps are required:

- First, you must define the individual events (for example, *My First Days*). In the documentation of the IMG, these events are also referred to as *menus*.

- Then, the individual catalogs for each event are defined. For "My First Days," you might include, for example, *Before you start, Personal information, Corporate information, Training,* and so on.

- Services are then defined for each catalog; for the "Personal information" catalog, these include, for example, *Enter address, Enter bank details,* and so on.

- You can then select separate colors to indicate the different priority of services.

Under the menu option **Employee Self-Service**, there is a special entry for customizing L&W Events. The path in the IMG is as follows: **Personnel management · Employee Self-Service · Service-specific settings for ESS · Life & Work Events**.

Customizing was not yet available at Release 4.6C. Therefore, in each of
the following steps, the tables involved are specified so that, with the help
of the description, you can maintain them using Transaction SM30.

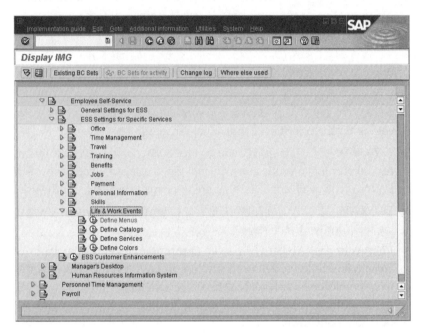

Figure 7.28 Customizing Possibilities for L&W Events

Defining L&W Events

Under the menu option **Define Menus,** there are three activities that can
be carried out.

1. In the first step, you enter the individual Life & Work Events. Each
   event has a unique four-character key. The seven L&W Events delivered by SAP have the key fields *EM01* to *EM07*. Enter these in table
   T77WWW_MN.

2. In the second step, or second activity, the names that are to be displayed for the L&W Events in the browser are set. An entry is made
   here for each language supported. This activity works with table
   T77WWW_MNT, used as a check table for T77WWW_MN. The entry
   in step one is automatically transferred with the logon language; therefore, only additional languages have to be maintained here.

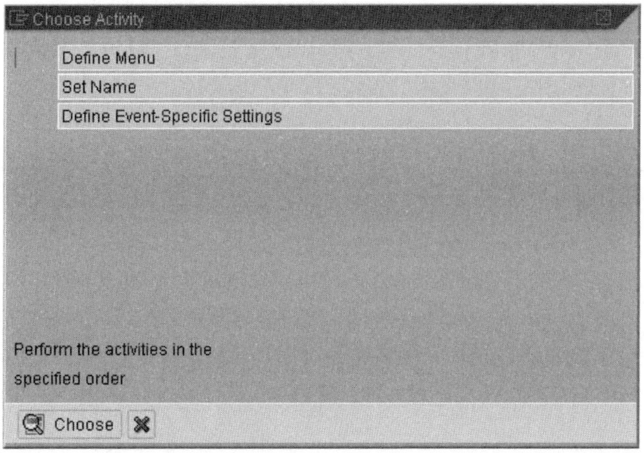

Figure 7.29 Designing L&W Event Menus

3. In the third step, you can set a time limit for the Life and Work Event, which means that it will only be possible to call this event for a specific number of days. You can check the time limit using a function module. To calculate the time between the current date and the start date of a new employee, you can use the function module ESS_NEW_HIRE_ CHECK. If this time is greater than the time specified in Customizing, the function module will give the null value when called and the event will not be displayed.

You can also specify a link to a service as the initial or home page for each event. Table T77WWW_LEDATA is modified in this step.

Defining the Catalog

Under the customizing option **Define Catalog,** the folders or catalogs that group the individual services within a L&W Event are defined.

1. In the first step, the individual catalogs are defined in table T77WWW_ CT, using a four-character key and a name.

2. In the second step, the names of the catalogs are specified in table T77WWW_CTT, in all languages to be supported. Because these names will be displayed in the browser in the logon language, you should make them as descriptive as possible. The entry in step one is automatically transferred with the logon language, therefore, only additional languages have to be maintained here. As with the menus, the check table for catalog names is also table T77WWW_CT.

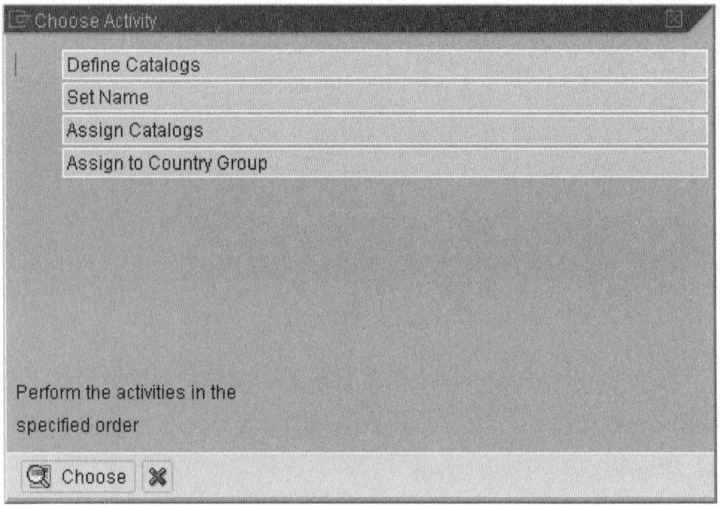

Figure 7.30 L&W Catalogs in Customizing

3. In the third step, the individual catalogs are assigned to the corresponding L&W Event in accordance with the four-character key specified there. The sequence of the individual catalogs is also set. This step maintains table T77WWW_MNP.

4. The fourth and last step in Customizing allows for the country-specific definition of a service. If a service is to be made visible for employees in one or more country groups MOLGA, this service is specified with the appropriate MOLGA in table T77WWW_CD.

Defining Services

You can define a service as follows:

1. In the first step, the services of the individual L&W Events are entered in table T77WWW_SRV. Apart from the key field, the name of the service, the type (ITS service, document, or external service), and the service address or logical address can also be found here.

2. In the second step, the service names are managed in different languages, as are the menus and catalogs. The table involved is called T77WWW_SRVN and the corresponding check table is T77WWW_SRV. The entry in step one is automatically transferred with the logon language, therefore, only additional languages have to be maintained here.

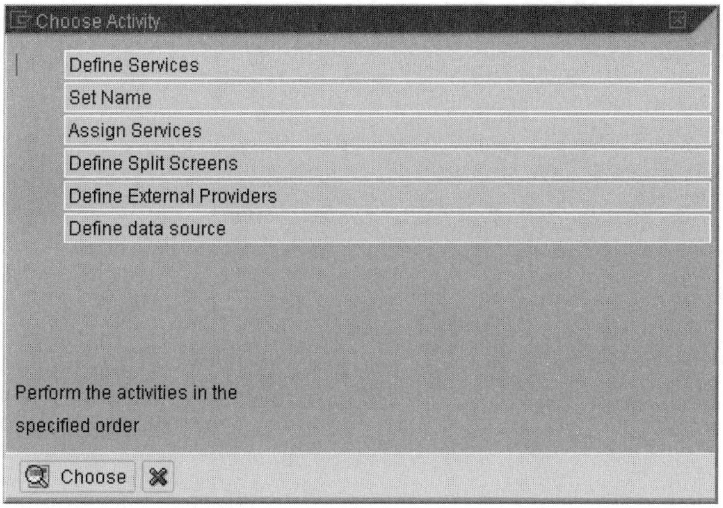

Figure 7.31 Defining L&W Event Services

3. In the third step, you assign individual services to the previously defined catalogs and to define their position within table T77WWW_CTP.

4. In the fourth step, applications are linked with content pages in table T77WWW_SMAP. You must enter the key field of the application, the key field of the content service, and the height of the information or content area as a percentage. The names of the services are shown to improve the overview, but they cannot be changed. If you do not specify the height, the default value is 30% (see also Section 7.7.3)

5. In the fifth step, external content providers can be assigned using table T77WWW_LE_EP. To illustrate the possible entries, two examples have been entered by SAP already: Content Provider: "SAP" with the interface *IF_SAP*, which displays the example page if_sap.html, and a fictitious content provider called *Provider_Sample* with the interface *IF_DEFAULT*.

6. In the sixth and final step of the customizing node **Define Service**, you can define the data sources for filling external content provider forms with SAP data using table T77WWW_SDATA.

Defining Colors

The following three steps are carried out under the customizing node **Define Colors**:

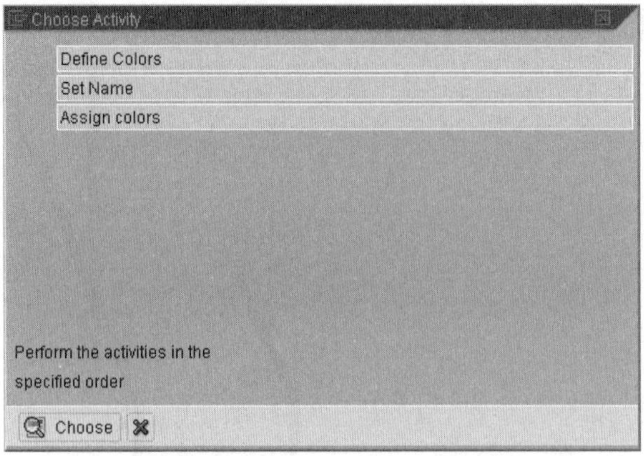

Figure 7.32 Last Customizing Step for the L&W Event

1. In the first step, you can define colors in accordance with the priority of individual activities in a L&W Event. You enter this data in the control table T77WWW_LECC.

   Three entries are supplied, which can be enhanced via a separate customer name range. You can assign as many color codes as you want for each individual L&W service, or none at all (see Step 3).

2. In the second step, as above, the texts are created in the different languages to be offered to the user. The corresponding table is called T77WWW_LECCT:

   ▶ 1 English: Please complete this on your first day of work

   ▶ 1 Spanish: Esto se debe completar el primer día

   ▶ 2 English: Please complete within first working week

   ▶ 2 Spanish: Esto se debe completar durante la primera semana

   and so on

3. In the third and last customizing step, the individual services can be assigned to the priorities created up to now. For this, table T77WWW_LECCP is maintained with the check tables T77WWW_MN, T77WWW_SRV and T77WWW_LECC.

Status management

Status   If you want to enable users to mark individual tasks for a L&W event as complete, you must specify this in the corresponding service files. For this, the parameter ~use_status is assigned the value "X". The service files (pzle_01.srvc – pzle_07.srvc) can be changed using Transaction SE80 in the SAP GUI or in the WebStudio.

7.7.6 Creating a New L&W Event

Because all tables in the L&W Event framework are tables in which cus- L&W example tomers can also make entries, L&W Events can easily be created by the customer.

In the following steps, we shall outline how to create the L&W Event *Ordering a company car*. The process involved will of course be somewhat different in every company; however, the basic elements required will be more or less the same. Some applications, such as *Select taxation type*, require more detailed information in order for the employee to make an informed choice. Other services, such as an *auto configurator*, can only be made available from outside. The following menu is an example of the steps one might take in the L&W Event *Ordering a company car*:

1. Before you start
   - Using the system
   - What's new?
   - Company checklist (driver's license and so on)

2. Information on ordering a company car
   - Company car policy
   - Information and links to car companies/model configurators
   - Simulation of monthly costs
   - Links to authorized dealers for specific questions, test drives, and so on

3. Request & order
   - Request company car
   - Status of approval request
   - Ordering from dealer via form or fax
   - Desired license plate
   - Selecting preferred gas station, ordering gas card

4. Delivery & pickup
   - Delivery date
   - Appointment for car pickup
   - Cost simulation or taxation type
   - Choice of car tax

5. Further information
   - Contacts: Fleet of cars, car companies, Department of Motor Vehicles

To create a new L&W Event, the service file `pzle_01.srvc` is copied to the service `zcc.srvc` (*Company Car*), for example. Then, in the service file, the parameter `~ESS_LIFE_EVENT` is set for the new menu, which means that instead of EM01 it can now be set at ZCCM (*Company Car Menu*), for example.

First, the menu–ZMCC for example–is entered and translated into the relevant languages. Subsequently, the catalog is created in Customizing in accordance with the above grouping; then, the individual services with their translation, and finally the priorities and their corresponding colors are set.

The individual services can be created as IAC, MiniApps, or WebGUI applications, as described in Section 7.5. Figure 7.33 shows the L&W Event *Order Company Car* in the browser.

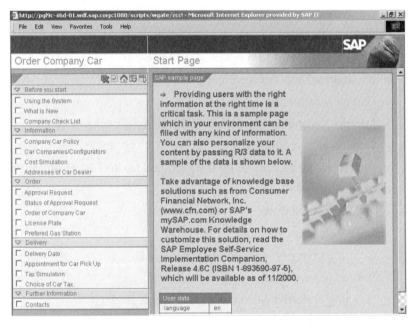

Figure 7.33 Possible Menu Structure for the L&W Event Order Company Car

Additional services such as address of tire dealer, dealer of car telephones, and so on can also be integrated later as needed.

A   ESS Scenarios

This appendix contains an overview of all ESS scenarios, along with their technical names and programming models. The following abbreviations apply:

- ▶ W   – WebGUI (SAP GUI for HTML)
- ▶ F   – FlowLogic
- ▶ F(MA)   – FlowLogic MiniApp
- ▶ T   – HTML-Templates
- ▶ M   – Mixed Mode

Service Catalog	Service	Technical Name	Programming Model
Payroll (Payment)	Semi-retirement: simulation	HRESSDE_ATZ	W
	Paycheck Inquiry	PZ11	W
	Salary Package Modeler: South Africa	P16B	W
	Employment and Salary Verification	WS01000045	W
	Salary Conversion	PZ58	W
	Display Total Compensation Statement	HRCMP0080ESS	W
	Exercising Employee Options	HRCMP0061ESS	T
	Monthly Tax Calculation	P1ET	W
	Net Calculation of Monthly Income	HRESSDE_CNET	W
	Pension Fund Online Simulation	PACG	W
	Tax form 56B: Hong Kong	HRESSHK_IR56B	W
	Tax form 56F: Hong Kong	HRESSHK_IR56F	W
	Tax form 56G: Hong Kong	HRESSHK_IR56G	W

Service Catalog	Service	Technical Name	Programming Model
	Tax form: IR21: Singapore	HRESSSG_IR21	W
	Tax form IR8A: Singapore	HRESSSG_IR8A	W
	Tax form IR8S: Singapore	HRESSSG_IR8S	W
	W-2 Reprint	WS01000090	W
Benefits	Enrollment	PZ14	T
	Retirement Benefits	PZ43	W
	Status of legal right to future pension payments	HRESSDE_AVST	W
	Participation Overview	PZ07	T
	FSA claims	PZ40	T
Personnel Appraisal	My Appraisals	MY_APPRAISALS	M
Office	Inbox (messages and workflow)	BWSP	T
	E-mails and Appointments: Overview	BW03	F(MA)
	Internal Service Request	QISR	T
	Calendar	BWCA	T
	My Documents	ASEM	W
	Microsoft Outlook Tasks	BW06	F(MA)
	Microsoft Outlook Inbox	BW04	F(MA)
	Microsoft Outlook Calendar	BW05	F(MA)
	Who's Who	PZ01	T
	Who's Who: MiniApp	PZ35_MA	F(MA)
	Organizational Chart	PZ26	T, Java Applet

Service Catalog	Service	Technical Name	Programming Model
	SAP Terminology Database	TERM_MINIAPP	F(MA)
	System Messages	SYSMSG	F(MA)
	Telephony	PZSPHW	T
	Appointments	BW00	F(MA)
	Unread E-mails	BW07	F(MA)
	Unread Notifications	BW01	F(MA)
	Workflow Inbox: MiniApp	BCBMTWFM0001	F(MA)
Business Trips	Expense Reports[1]	PRWW	T
	Travel Management	TRIP	W
Life and Work Events[2]	Benefits	PZLE_02	F
	Change of Employment Status	PZLE_06	F
	Terminate Employment	PZLE_07	F
	Data Entry for Hiring (my new job)	PZLE_01	F
	Divorce	PZLE_03	F
	Birth/Adoption	PZLE_05	F
	Marriage	PZLE_04	F
Recruitment (Job Application)	Application Status	PZ22	T
	Employment Opportunities	PZ21	T, Java Applet
Personal Data	Address	PZ02	W
	Bank Information	PZ03	W
	Family Member/Dependents	PZ12	W

1. This service is available only up to Release 4.6B; the *TRIP* service replaces it in later releases.
2. Life and Work Events are available as of HR Support Package 8 (SP8). Enterprise Portal 5.0 SP4 contains a *Life and Work Event Builder* that allows users to define their own events and is completely integrated into EP 5.0.

Service Catalog	Service	Technical Name	Programming Model
	Change own Data	PZ50	T
	Marriage Announcement	TS_WS01200170H	W
	Emergency Address	PZ05	W
	Emergency Contact Person	PZ18	W
	Personal Data	PZ13	W
	Previous Employer	PZ28	W
	Personal IDs	PZ39	W
	Superannuation: Australia	PZ27	W
	Tax Overeiw: Australia	PZ25	W
	Tax Overview: Canada	PZ08	W
	Tax Overview: Thailand	PZ51	W
	Capital Formation	PZ41	W
	W-4 Withholding	PZ10	W
	Alternative Name	PZ42	W
	Direct Deposit: Australia	PZ29	W
	Employment Equity	PZ56	W
Qualifications	Display Requirements Profile	PP_MY_REQUIRE-MENTS	W
	Display Qualifications	PP_MY_QUALIFICA-TIONS	W
	Edit Qualifications	PZ31	T, Java Applet
	Profile Match up with Own Position	MY_PROFILEMATC	W
Training	My Bookings	PV8I	W
	Training Center	PV7I	W
Time Management	Record Working Time	CATW	M
	Leave Request: Overview	WS01000109	T

Service Catalog	Service	Technical Name	Programming Model
	Create Leave Request	WS20000081	T
	Create Leave Request: Japan	WS01000060	W
	Display Work Schedule	PZ17	W
	Time Balances	PZ09	T
	Display Time Statement	PZ04	W

The Authors

Dr. Ewald Brochhausen worked at SAP as HR consultant between 1989 and 1992. Since 1992, he is professor for general business administration, particularly organizational and personnel administration, at the Worms University of Applied Sciences. Within mySAP HR, he focuses on the design, implementation, and customization of HR systems in heterogeneous environments.

Dr. Jürgen Kielisch has worked at SAP since 1991. After many years as a consultant for SAP HR and years of service as an HR account executive, he is in charge of customer development projects in HR development.

Dr. Jürgen Schnerring has worked at SAP since 1989. He was involved in the design and implementation of the HR solution in SAP R/3. Now he is managing development projects in the wider environment of HR master data administration.

Dr. Jens Staeck has worked at SAP since 1997. He has specialized in the design and development of Employee Self-Service (ESS) in HR and in Web-enabling technologies. He now works as a development architect for a project to port ESS to SAP's new Java-based Web technology.

Index

A

ABAP List Viewer 265
Absence type 252
Activity profile 135
additional field 214
AGate 276
Application component 120
Argument, variable 235
Asymmetrical 144
authority_check 127
Authorization check 75, 97
Authorization concept 127
Authorization fields 127
Authorization generation 131
Authorization level 143
Authorization object 127
Authorization profile 128

B

BAdI 122
  call 124
  coding 190
  filter 125
  implementation 125, 189
BAdI Builder 188
BAdI class 123
Basic pay 245
Blocking indicator 144
Blocking logic 105
  function module 105
Buffering 264
Business Add-In 120, 122, 170

C

Cascading Style Sheets 300
CE mode 89
Central person 89
Change of address 144
Check indicator 131
Checks 183
Cluster
  authorization 115
  B1 62
  B2 264

buffering 116
  EXPORT 115
  IMPORT 115
  macro 115
  TX 115
Cluster directory 71, 116
Cluster structure 66
Cluster table 86
Clusters 114
Composite role 129
Concurrent Employment 89
Concurrently employed person 89
Consistency of the data model 57
Content provider 319
Context 154
Context-dependent structural authori-
  zation check 157
Contraction 83
Creation rule 148
Currency conversion 248
Customer exit 120
Customer function 185
Customer objects 120
Customer report categories 80
Customer-defined settings 58
Customer-specific authorization
  object 136, 165
Customer-specific enhancements 37
Customer-specific version of PA30 169
Customizing, L&W Events 331

D

Data retrieval 81
Data selection period 78, 81, 246
Database program 76, 77
Database table PAnnnn 38
Database table PCL2 63, 65
Date specifications 241
DBPNPCOM 99
DBPNPMAC 99
Decentralized time recording 146
Decision tree 28
Default value 183, 211
Definition layer 122

Deleting 145
Depth of display 153
Design adjustments 300
Document evaluation 142
Double verification principle 143
Download 265
Dual host installation 277
Dynamic selection 79, 80

E

Easy Web Transaction 288
Employee Self-Service 271
Enhancement project 185
Enhancement, assign 193
Entry date 107, 244
Error list 260
Error table 259
ESS 271
   kiosk system 304
   MOLGA 307
ESS scenario 144
ESS user exits 298
Evaluation
   sequential 94, 95, 253
   structural 94, 95, 255
Evaluation Path 92
Evaluation path 91, 94, 151, 255
Events 239
EXCEL 265
External object types 43, 54

F

Fast entry 203
Fast entry of actions 208
Feature 108
   attribute 111
   back value 111
   decision tree 112, 199
   maintenance 110
   program operations 112
   structure 111
feature 194, 199
Feature IVWID 40
Features 110
Field attribute 31
Field catalog 268
Fields, customer-defined 191

First of the month 263
Flow of the authorization check 163
FlowLogic 289, 292
   events 296
   example 293
For Period 88
function
   customer-specific 229
Function module 106
   Function Builder 106
   HR 107
Function module exit 183
Function modules
   search 107
Functions 227, 229

G

GDSTR 94, 254
GET PERNR LATE 89
GET_GROUP_ 89
GET_OBJEC_ 95, 96
GET_PAYROLL 86
GET_PAYROLL_ 88
GET_PERAS 89
GET_PERNR 75, 82, 88
GET_PERNR_ 88
GET_PERSON 89
Global organizational level 131

H

HIGH-DATE_ 99
HR report 140
HR_ALV_LIST_DISPLAY 269
HR_ENTRY_DATE_ 244
HR_FEATURE_BACKFIELD_ 110
HR_FEATURE_BACKTABLE_ 110
HR_GET_PAYROLL_RESULTS_ 259
HRUSER 300
HTML business functions 286
HTML templates 290

I

IAC 289
IMG 120
Implementation Guide 21, 45
Implementation layer 122
Import 264

Infotyp
  enhancement 212
Infotype 19, 21, 42
  change 104
  consistency check 58
  control tables 46
  create 217
  data structure 32
  default value 26
  enhancement 183
  external infotypes 55
  feature 28
  header 27
  infotype view 40
  list screen 25
  object identification 23
  organizational management 212
  screen modification 28
  SPA/GPA parameter 26
  structure of a feature 29
  subtype 22
  table infotypes 53
  time management 224, 249
infotype
  subtype 36
Infotypes menus 40
INFOTYPES, statement 81
  AS_PERSON_TABLE 89
  MODE_N 82
Interface FI 240
Interface status 198
Internal object types 43
Internet Transaction Server 276
Interpretation of the assigned
  personnel number 144
Inverse relationship 55
ITS 276
  files 277
  instances 277
  programming model 288
  service parameter 282
iViews 272

J
Job description 253
Join 84
  partial interval 85

K
Key date 105, 238, 254
Kiosk systems 304
Knowledge provider 319

L
L&W Events 272, 317
  creating 337
  customizing 331
Layout 268
Life and Work Events 317
List header 239
Logical database 75
  PCH 91
  PNP 77
  PNPCE 89
Logical structure Pnnnn 51
LOW-DATE 99

M
Macro 98
  PCH 105
Main authorization switch 157
Master data 19
  evaluation 237
Matchcode 78
MiniApps 272
Minimal authorization 172
Mixed mode 286, 297
Modification group 201
Modifications
  without any 170
Module pool 31
Month-end 263

N
Name formatting 100, 240
Naming conventions 229
  report categories 80

O
OBJEC 94
Object ID 91
Object Navigator 181
Object type 42, 91
Operation 227
Org. str. 79

Organizational key 147
Organizational management 91
Organizational management data
   model 41
Organizational plan 150, 151
Overview of L&W tables 330

P

P_ABAP 139
P_APPL 137
P_ORGIN 133
P_ORGINCON 155
P_ORGXX 135
P_ORGXXCON 156
P_PERNR 138
P_TCODE 133
PA70 203
Pair table 59
Payroll 226
Payroll data 258
Payroll program 116
Payroll results 19, 86, 116, 259
  evaluation 88
  reading 116
Payroll status 104
PCL2 86, 264
PDB_PROCESS 75
PE01 227
PE04 231
Period of responsibility 159
Permissible organizational key 148
Person selection period 78, 81
PFCG 274
Plan version 91
PLOG 142
PM01 191
PNP mode 89, 90
pnp-sw-found 98
Power transactions 288
PPCI 212
Primary infotype 40
Profile Generator 129
Projection 83
Proposed value 239
PROVIDE 82
  subtype 83
PSnnnn 36

PSYST 197
PUT_PERNR 75

R

Relationship 42, 44, 54
Reorganizations 150
Repetitive structures 241
Report attribute 75
Report category 78, 86
  SAP default class 78
Report class 237
Report properties 91
Report statistics 261
Report, sample connection of a 315
Reporting period 92
Reports, web-enabling 312
Repository 181
Result data 19
RGDIR 116
RH-GET-TBDAT 106
RH-SEL-KEYDATE 105
RH-SEL-ONE-OBJID 105
Role 129, 273
  composite role 274
  country-specific role 274
  single role 274
Role menu 130
Root object 153
RP_FILL_WAGE_TYPE_TABLE_EXT_
  246
RP_PROVIDE_FROM_FRST 101
rp_provide_from_frst 98
RP_PROVIDE_FROM_LAST 101
rp_provide_from_last 242
RP_READ_ALL_TIME_ITY 103
RP_SET_DATA_INTERVAL 100
RP_UPDATE 104
RP-EDIT-NAME 100
RP-SEL-EIN-AUS-INIT 99
RP-SET-NAME-FORMAT 100
RPUACG00 166
Rules 227

S

SAP enhancement 185
SAP enhancements 120
SAP GUI for HTML 289, 297

SAP* 154
SAPMPZ02 307
Schema 226
Screen 31
Screen control 201
SELECT 96
Selection criteria 79
Selection screen 76, 81, 94
  PCH 91
Selection view 81
Service
  PZLE_01 319
  PZLE_02 318
  PZLE_03 319
  PZLE_04 319
  PZLE_05 319
  PZLE_06 318
  PZLE_07 318
SIAC1 281
Single host installation 276
Sorting 78, 265
Status indicator 119
Status vector 92, 153
STRUC 95
Structural authorization check 127
Structure
  HRIADMIN 50
  HRIKEY 47
  HRIKEYL 49
  HRInnnn 50
  PAKEY 32
  pay99_result 88
  payroll 88
  PERNR 77, 81
  Pnnnn 38
  PSHDR_ 35
structure
  PSHD1 34
Style Editor 305
Style Sheet Designer 301
SU24 131
Subtype 22
Super user 140
Symmetrical 144
Syntax check 233

T
Table
  NT1 61
  T500L 65
  T777D 53, 58
  T777I 47
  T777T 47
  T777Z 47
  T778O 42
  T778T 47
  T778V 45
  T77WWW_CD 330, 334
  T77WWW_CT 330, 333
  T77WWW_CTP 330, 335
  T77WWW_CTT 330, 333
  T77WWW_LE_EP 323, 331, 335
  T77WWW_LECC 329, 331, 336
  T77WWW_LECCP 329, 331, 336
  T77WWW_LECCT 329, 331, 336
  T77WWW_LEDATA 330, 333
  T77WWW_LESTATUS 329, 331
  T77WWW_MN 330, 332
  T77WWW_MNP 330, 334
  T77WWW_MNT 330, 332
  T77WWW_SDATA 325, 331, 335
  T77WWW_SMAP 328, 331, 335
  T77WWW_SRV 323, 330, 334
  T77WWW_SRVN 330, 334
  TEVEN 59, 60
Table infotype 106, 221, 254
Task descriptions 129
Template generation 291
Test date 146
Test procedures 145
Text table 194, 252
Time constraint 82
Time constraint class 24
Time evaluation 226, 263
  results 262
Time event 19, 59
Time logic 161
Time management 103
Time recording devices 59
Tolerance time 157
Transaction
  HRUSER 300
  PFCG 274

SIAC1 281
Transaction data 19
Transparent table HRPnnnn 51
Transparent table PCL1 61
TRMAC 98
TYPE-POOLS 266

U
UPDATE 97
User master records
  different 155

V
Validation check 187

W
Wage type table 262
WAP service 292
Web Application Builder 280
WebGUI 289
WebStudio 280, 294
  publish 291
WGate 276

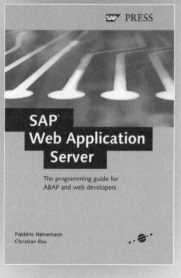

SAP PRESS
550 pages, hardcover
ISBN 1-59229-013-2, May 2003

>>> www.sap-press.com

F. Heinemann, C. Rau

SAP Web Application Server

The complete guide for ABAP and web developers

The SAP Web Application Server (Web AS) is the latest evolutionary stage of the SAP Basis System. The book provides a step-by-step introduction to web development using Web AS. The first section focuses on the key components of Web AS for web development using standards such as XML and HTTP. By using a variety of examples, the second part of the book shows you in detail how to program with Business Server Pages. This must-have resource is written not only for ABAP programmers who need more information on these essential new concepts, but also for web developers interested in Web AS programming with JavaScript.

Recommended Reading
by SAP PRESS

Business

N. Egger
SAP BW Professional

IBM Business
Consulting Services
SAP Authorization System

G. Oswald
**SAP Service
and Support**

Rickayzen, Dart,
Brennecke, Schneider
**Practical Workflow
for SAP**

R. Buck-Emden
mySAP CRM

Technical

A. Goebel, D. Ritthaler
SAP Enterprise Portal

S. Hagemann, L. Will
**SAP R/3 System
Administration**

Brochhausen, Kielisch,
Schnerring, Staeck
**SAP HR Technical Principles
and Programming**

T. Schneider
**SAP Performance
Optimization Guide**

F. Heinemann, C. Rau
**Web Programming with the
SAP Web Application Server**

L. Will
**SAP APO System
Administration**

W.Hertleif, C. Wachter
SAP Smart Forms

H. Keller, J. Jacobitz
**ABAP Objects –
The Official Reference**

H. Stefani (Ed.)
Archiving Your SAP Data

www.sap-press.com

Interested in reading more?

Please visit our Web site for all
new book releases from SAP PRESS.

www.sap-press.com